Urban Revolt in South Africa, 1960-1964

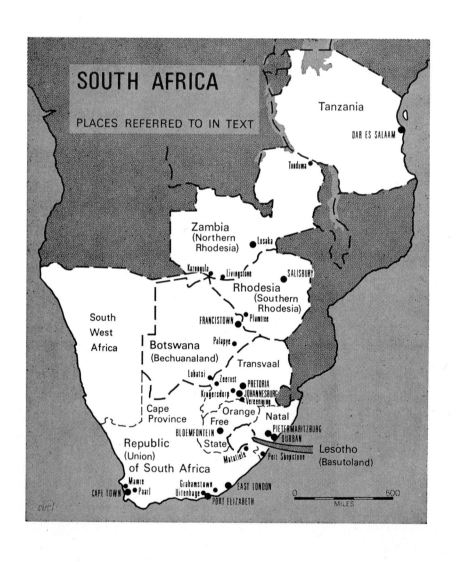

SOUTH AFRICA

PLACES REFERRED TO IN TEXT

Tanzania

DAR ES SALAAM

Tunduma

Zambia
(Northern
Rhodesia)

Lusaka

Kazungula   Livingstone   SALISBURY

Rhodesia
(Southern
Rhodesia)

South
West
Africa

Botswana
(Bechuanaland)

FRANCISTOWN   Plumtree

Palapye

Transvaal

Lobatsi   Zeerust

PRETORIA
Krugersdorp   JOHANNESBURG
Vereeniging

Cape
Province

Orange
Free
State

Natal

PIETERMARITZBURG
BLOEMFONTEIN   DURBAN

Republic
(Union)
of South Africa

Matatiele   Port Shepstone

Lesotho
(Basutoland)

Mamre   Grahamstown   EAST LONDON
CAPE TOWN   Paarl   Uitenhage
PORT ELIZABETH

0   500
MILES

Urban Revolt in South Africa 1960-1964

A Case Study

Edward Feit

Northwestern University Press

1971

968
F 3 / u

Edward Feit is associate professor of government at the
University of Massachusetts, Amherst

MN

Quotation from *In the Fiery Continent,* by Tom Hopkinson, copyright © 1962 by
Tom Hopkinson, reprinted by permission of Doubleday & Company, Inc.

Table of Contents

TABLE OF CONTENTS

Preface

THE PREFACE is the author's last line of defense. Once his book is in the hands of the public, the power to answer back is largely lost. Readers, and more particularly reviewers, have the last word. Although it is rightly thus, for who can judge his own work, certain explanations at the outset can avoid some disappointment and misunderstanding. It is best to say from the start, as I will do here, what the book is *not*— as well as what it hopes to be. By so doing expectations that the work is not intended to fulfill will not be raised, and interpretations that are unintended will not be advanced.

First of all, this book is not intended to be a blow-by-blow account of the South African insurgency of 1960–64. It is in any case too early to attempt such a history, even if this were the purpose. It is not intended as a history of the African National Congress, the South African Communist Party, or their military offshoot, *Umkonto we Sizwe*. What is it then? It is, basically, a case study of attempted urban insurgency. An urban insurgency that took place in South Africa was chosen for study because, as will presently be argued, material from that country allows analysis in depth. The book will seek to explain how the attempt at insurgency was organized; why its initial success was limited; and why, in the end, it failed. It differs from many other studies in two important ways: first, it deals with the early stages of insurgency; second, it concentrates on the foot soldiers of revolution. It cannot concentrate exclusively on these two themes, for they do not happen *in vacuo.* The leaders, therefore, have their entrances and exits, but they play a subordinate role. It is the ordinary man in revolution who is mostly at the center of the stage. It is men such as appear here who fill the ranks of the revolutionary force, who do its work, and who pass from the stage of history largely unsung. As it concentrates on what men *do,* this is in a sense a behavioral study, although it lacks the tables, charts, and diagrams with which behavioral studies usually are replete. Useful as these may be elsewhere, they are of little help here. One such chart is included in Appendix I. As Henry Bienen has pointed out in his new book *Violence and Social Change,* the study of insurgent organizations rarely permits quantification.[1] There is no pretense that the data of this study are complete; no one could be more aware than I am of the gaps that remain to be filled. The significant question is, however, not whether the data are complete, but whether they are sufficient. This they certainly seem to be.

The study has value not only because of the data it brings to light, but also because the lower ranks in a revolution are so often taken for granted. There are exceptional studies, such as Lucian Pye's work on Malaya, but these are rare.[2] Most studies have concentrated on revolutionary leadership and on revolutionary organization as perceived or presented by that leadership. The picture often seems one where the leaders push metaphorical buttons and the metaphorical revolutionary "machine" performs to order. If something is ordered above, something appropriate happens below. This, at least, is the image. The fact that the revolutionary machine may be a myth is seldom ascertained. The idea that such a machine may exist only on paper and in the minds of the leaders is suggested here. This theme will be developed in the body of the book.

The revolution under review did not progress much beyond its initial phases, which is an advantage for the analyst. Materials on this stage of an insurgency are usually scarce and are often left out of account. An insurgency in progress is easier to analyze and makes for more

1. (Chicago, 1968), p. 8.
2. *Guerrilla Communism in Malaya* (Princeton, 1956).

dramatic reading. South Africa is an exceptional case, for here the intended insurgency was nipped in the bud and the would-be insurgents were brought to trial in an open court. Much of what was underground is, in this way, exposed to the light of day. Much remains buried and can never be uncovered. Here as elsewhere, however, the part is often a good guide to the whole. Because of the complexity of the subject, it is insufficient to plunge straight into the story. A great deal of background on African opposition in South Africa is necessary for an understanding of the particular case. The introductory chapter gives some of this background. Knowledgeable readers may wish to ignore it, and can do so, for the rest of the book is self-contained. For a more general background on recent literature about South Africa, the reader could turn to Gwendolen Carter's review article in *Africa Report* of May, 1968.

Being concerned with the formation of an insurgency at its base, and one that took place in South Africa, the book is of necessity somewhat schizoid. The problem of marrying material to theory in an interesting way is particularly difficult. There are no doubt several ways in which this could have been done. The way chosen here is to begin with a chapter outlining the broad theory in rather stark terms and offering an explanation of the social and psychological factors entering into the formation of the insurgency in a general way. The substance of the case follows in succeeding chapters, and theory and material are bound together at the end. The theory is also alluded to in the text where appropriate.

The principal source for this book has been the trials of men who participated in the formation and operation of the insurgency. *Umkonto we Sizwe*, the organization which was to have spearheaded the insurgency, was broken by the police in 1963, although it continued feebly for a short time thereafter. The police had discovered the secret headquarters of the organization, the farm "Lilliesleaf" in the township of Rivonia near Johannesburg. The leaders were caught red-handed and brought to trial. The Rivonia raid was followed by a widespread series of raids in which many of the smaller fry in the principal cities and towns of South Africa were arrested. The so-called Rivonia Trial, which brought the principal officers of *Umkonto* to court, gave international prominence to one of the defendants, Nelson Mandela—known as the

"Black Pimpernel" for his skill in evading police capture—because of his bearing and the impassioned statement of his reasons for participating in *Umkonto*. The lesser men were tried in a series of separate trials and attracted less attention. Some fifteen of these trials, together with the Rivonia Trial, provide the basis for this book. Although the exact length of this material has not been computed, it is in the neighborhood of 10,000 typewritten pages.

Given this weight of material, one might well ask: "How good are such court records as evidence for a scholarly study?" The question is very just and can be easily answered. First of all, the legal aspects of the individual cases are ignored, being of concern more to students of jurisprudence than to students of revolution. The cases are seen less as legal contests than as sources of evidence of how revolution was conducted. Clearly, using court records as evidence has advantages and disadvantages.

An advantage of the use of court records is the independence which the judiciary has still largely maintained in South Africa. Trials are conducted in open courts on the adversary system. They are by no means staged "show" trials. Their general fairness is conceded, even by opponents of the South African system. Verdicts are by no means a foregone conclusion, as the police and prosecution have many times found out to their cost. The court records are public documents, open to the researcher, and from them one can observe not only the fairness of the Bench but also the care with which evidence is sifted. As a research tool, the trial is the work of many hands: it contains some biography of accused and witnesses; its corpus consists of examinations by skilled counsel, with the judge intervening from time to time; and it ends with a summation by the judge, in which the credibility of witnesses and their evidence is scrupulously analyzed. As counsels tend to ask similar questions from one trial to the next, the records have something of the form of an open-ended questionnaire, except that here the truth of the answers is put to some test.

Disadvantages have, however, to be weighed against such obvious advantages. The evidence in court is, to begin with, selective. Men come to court defeated—whether in crime or in revolution. The successful rarely appear. Court evidence, therefore, tends to be biased on the side of failure. Then, in addition, the purposes of the court and the researcher are often at odds. Courts are concerned with facts relating to a particular charge. They are uninterested in anything else. Unhappily, it often happens that what is relevant for the researcher is irrelevant to the court, and a promising line of inquiry is peremptorily shut off by the judge. These things are inevitable and unavoidable.

The difficulties do not end here. Men on trial are in jeopardy: they are hailed before a court to account for acts alleged to have been committed by them, or where they are witnesses to acts to which they may well have been party. Trials often take place months or years after the events, and incidents have to be drawn from fallible human memory, often changed by hindsight or dimmed by time. To this must be added the temptation of men in trouble to lie about what they and others did, either to avoid punishment or to please those who have brought them to court. All that can be done about difficulties of this sort is to take reasonable precautions in the use of men's words. The value of the material buried in court records is sufficient to warrant careful sifting.

To avoid prejudice, evidence both of accused and accusers is largely (but not entirely) ignored. It is used only in the absence of other evidence, and then mainly to establish clear matters of fact. The main body of evidence is from the testimony of witnesses considered generally reliable by the judges in each of the cases cited. Complete reliability cannot be counted on. As one of the judges said, no witness is ever completely reliable. Witnesses are often inexact in evidence of what happened at a particular time and place and are, in addition, not always truthful. This is inevitable, for one cannot expect a witness who turns informer to be wholly truthful and consistent. All that can be asked is satisfaction beyond reasonable doubt that *in its essential details* the story told is true, that it has a hard core of evidence which no questioning or challenge by counsel can chip away.[3] It is evidence of this sort that is used here. It is supplemented by press reports of some of the trials which took place at different times and for which a full court record was unavailable. Comparing these reports with trials that were available to this author in verbatim form leads him to believe that the reports in the press

3. Judgment/*Gcabi*, p. 4.

were, on the whole, accurate. They consisted, more often than not, of "snippets" from the different cases, and a clear picture cannot be obtained from them alone. However, they help round out the picture, especially where descriptive details are needed. In addition to the daily newspapers in the main centers of South Africa, there is the press of the organizations involved, which, as long as it was allowed to function, did contain some useful information. It had, for obvious reasons, to be very circumspect in what it published and, in any case, ceased after 1963. Its usefulness is, therefore, limited. *African Communist*, in its ten years of publication, also had some useful articles, mainly of a theoretical nature. All of these are used to reinforce material derived from the courts. It is hoped in this way to overcome, at least partially, some of the problems indicated.

In spite of all that has been said, no pretense is made that the data are complete and that they have been exhaustively treated. The Communist Party has been illegal in South Africa since 1950; the African National Congress, since 1960; and *Umkonto we Sizwe*, from the time of its formation. It is not in the nature of things for data on organizations such as these to be complete, and the nature of their operations makes description of their activities extremely difficult. It would be foolish, therefore, to imply that this volume contains a full and complete description. Nor can everything be neatly filed and docketed. While an effort has been made to document every fact, facts are subject to varying interpretations. The nature of the interplay among the various organizations which together joined to form *Umkonto* remains shadowy, and much can only be guessed at. Where possible, alternative explanations are included, but not all alternatives are exhausted. Many things could only be suggested, and whether these suggestions are accepted or rejected rests with the reader. This is particularly true where connections with the Communist Party are concerned, which is in many ways central to the book. There are bound to be gaps and guesswork when illegal organizations engaging a powerful state are the subjects of analysis. All that can be promised is that, as far as is possible, the study is solidly bedded on fact, and that opinion is distinguished from fact. This is the firm intention, the goal, and the standard that the author has set himself. The book is written in the firm belief that, however incomplete the facts may be, they are sufficient to provide a clear and accurate picture of the workings of an insurgent organization at its lowest levels.

Writing a book such as this, involving as it does many years of research before anything can be set down, calls for both money and time. I am, therefore, particularly indebted to the Mershon Center at Ohio State University, Columbus, Ohio, for granting me a post-doctoral fellowship that enabled me to have a year away from teaching and other duties in order to concentrate on writing. I am also indebted to its then-director, Professor James A. Robinson, for his encouragement. The initial grant, which enabled me to begin working on this material, came from the American Philosophical Society, and later small grants were made by the Faculty Research Council of the University of Massachusetts. To all of them I owe a debt of gratitude. The work of writing was somewhat lightened by the research assistance I received from Robert Johnson and William Anderson, who patiently punched and entered "Keysort" cards, indexed newspapers, and did other routine things so essential to any project. Work does not stop with research, so I also owe thanks to those who so ably helped in the later stages. Mrs. C. R. Holden typed the final draft, and Mrs. Joy Neuman did a very fine job of editing the manuscript and in seeing it through to the printer. Last but by no means least, I have to thank my wife, whose willingness to let me spend a year in Ohio made the writing possible, and who put up with my bouts of temperament when things were not going well. Needless to say, I alone am responsible for what is written here and for all that is in the book.

Glossary of Organizations

CONGRESS ALLIANCE—the following four racially separated congresses and the South African Congress of Trade Unions:

The *African National Congress* (ANC), founded in 1912, had an all-African membership. It was banned, together with the Pan-Africanist Congress (PAC), in 1960 (see below). It continued illegally and still has offices abroad and elements of an organization underground.

The *South African Indian Congress* (SAIC) was founded in 1906, and joined an alliance (the Dadoo-Xuma Pact) in 1946. Its membership was confined to those of East Indian origin.

The *South African Coloured People's Organization* (SACPO) was founded in 1953, and became the *South African Coloured People's Congress* (SACPC) in 1960. Its early associations with the African National Congress caused it to lose support among the Coloured middle class, and it never attained any significant membership. It was confined to those of mixed descent.

The *South African Congress of Democrats* (SACOD, or COD) was formed to accommodate the white liberals who completely identified themselves with the African cause. Its membership was confined to whites. It was suspected of being a "front" for former Communists after the government banned the Communist Party in 1950. COD was heavily penetrated by former members of the Communist Party, and most of its officeholders had been Party members. Its membership was very small, but the quality of the members gave the COD great influence.

The *South African Congress of Trade Unions* (SACTU), which was multiracial, was formed in 1955 on dissolution of the Trades and Labor Council, as the latter accepted registered (hence largely white) trade unions only. It was characterized by extreme left-wing views, and was joined by a number of African, Indian, and Coloured unions, as well as a handful of white ones. It was largely dominated by a Communist leadership and, with increasing restrictions on its activities, became quite radical.

NATIONAL LIBERATION MOVEMENT (NLM) comprised the combined Congress Alliance and the Communist Party of South Africa.

UMKONTO WE SIZWE (MK)—literally, "Spear of the Nation"—was the military wing of the African National Congress, the rest of the Congress Alliance, and the Communist Party. It was carried on in the name of the NLM.

PAN-AFRICANIST CONGRESS (PAC), a splinter group of the ANC, was founded in 1959 by Potlako Leballo and Robert Sobukwe. The PAC objected to the ANC's adoption of the Freedom Charter; also, the leaders and many of the rank and file of the PAC believed that the other racial congresses had acquired a disproportionate influence over the leaders of the ANC. The PAC was banned, along with the ANC, in 1960.

POQO was the terrorist wing of the Pan-Africanist Congress, though this has been disputed. Its name is the African word for "pure," implying that this was a pure African movement.

Index to Court Cases

Much of the material used for research consisted of court cases, and this presented a problem in preparing footnotes. It seemed futile, for instance, to keep inserting the words "the State vs" in each case. The procedure adopted was, therefore, to cite the last name of the witness or accused referred to, and to follow this with the last name of the first person accused. Thus, Mbanjwa/*Mbolompo*, p. 324, means that Solomon Mbanjwa was a witness in the case of Willie Mbolompo and 44 Others, Rc 240/64, and that the reference is on page 324 of his evidence. There is some confusion in pagination as well, for some trials are numbered for individual witnesses, with each witness's evidence beginning on page 1. Readers wishing to consult the trials, which are available through the Cooperative African Microform Project, CAMP, at the Center for Research Libraries, University of Chicago, will soon learn which is which. A list of some of the trials follows, together with the names of witnesses whose evidence was used. In some cases, only key witnesses were selected, as the evidence of others seemed largely to repeat what the witnesses chosen had said.

INDEX TO COURT CASES

INDEX TO COURT CASES

Urban Revolt in South Africa, 1960-1964

Introduction:

A Short Survey of African Resistance in South Africa

TRADITIONALLY, DECEMBER 16 is a day of rejoicing for white South Africans, commemorating as it does the victory over the Zulu chieftain Dingane at the Battle of Blood River in 1838. But in 1961 this day was marred by a series of explosions in the principal cities of three of the country's four provinces. Newspapers wrote of attacks against electrical installations and government buildings in Durban, Port Elizabeth, and Johannesburg. These attacks, which were made with crude homemade bombs or with dynamite, did slight damage. They were more damaging to at least two of the participants than to the installations against which they were directed, one man being killed and the other seriously injured.[1] But the significance of the attacks exceeded their scope. It was not the damage itself that caused unease; rather, the timing and the methods used seemed to indicate a master plan. Fear was evoked that it was only a matter of time before the saboteurs became more audacious and their

1. One saboteur, Petrus Molefe, was killed and another seriously injured when they tried to set off a crude bomb in Dube, an African township. The attacks were aimed mainly at government buildings associated with administration of Africans and at electric installations. In Johannesburg, for instance, one target was the local pass office (more will be said of passes later) and another was a court which primarily tried Africans. In Port Elizabeth, the Labor Bureau and the Bantu Education Offices were bombed. A complete list of sabotage attempts that resulted in some damage are listed in Appendix I.

3

methods more sophisticated. That the attacks were launched on the day more commemorative than any other of white conquest symbolized their challenge to continued white supremacy. The attacks were soon declared as only the harbingers of coming conflict. A new organization announced them as its work. It said that its name was *Umkonto we Sizwe*, which translates to "Spear of the Nation," and in both English and Zulu its manifesto proclaimed that "the people's patience is not endless. The time comes in the life of any nation when there remain only two choices—submit or fight." *Umkonto* and its members had obviously made their choice and had made it known what this choice was: "Violence," they said, "would no longer be met with nonviolent resistance only."[2]

Thoughts of violence were not confined to *Umkonto* and those recruited to its ranks. Violence was very much in the air. *Umkonto* had both predecessors and successors. First among its rivals was POQO, named for the African word for "pure" to indicate that it was a purely African movement—that it had no allies among other racial groups. The leaders of POQO derided *Umkonto* for diluting African nationalism by admitting members from other racial groups into its ranks. To the men of POQO, *Umkonto* was an organization drawing inspiration from the alien, non-African ideology of communism. POQO thus presented itself as the standard-bearer of a true African nationalism untainted by either an alien membership or a foreign ideology.

The notion of violence was not confined to Africans alone. It seemed a tempting means to others searching for a solution for South Africa's problems. In 1964, one year after *Umkonto* had largely been crushed, an all-white African Resistance Movement was routed in turn, and its members either driven abroad or imprisoned.[3] These were mainly young left-wing intellectuals, some of whom had been members of the South African Liberal Party and some of whom attended the University of Cape Town. They did not last long in the grim business of sabotage.

2. "Bomb Attacks Open New Phase in South Africa," *New Age*, December 21, 1961.

3. For a journalistic account of the African Resistance Movement, see Miles Brokensha and Robert Knowles, *The Fourth of July Raids* (Cape Town, 1965). The story of POQO remains to be written. None of the movements mentioned in this paragraph will be discussed in detail in the present book.

4

Other groups, more shadowy yet, were also espousing violence. A Yu Chi Chan Club, for instance, claiming that it drew its inspiration from the teachings of Mao Tse-tung, flickered briefly across the revolutionary stage. Its membership, according to most accounts, did not exceed its original complement of nine Coloured intellectuals who founded it.⁴ Yet another group which claimed to be a resistance movement was APDUSA (African People's Democratic Union of South Africa), of which little more is known than that it was an offshoot of the violently anti-white, Trotskyite-leaning Non-European Unity Movement.

What, then, gives *Umkonto* its particular significance? There are at least two answers to this question. First of all, *Umkonto* grew out of an association of the two oldest organizations which had most consistently opposed white supremacy—the Communist Party and the African National Congress. Second, because of this association, especially with the Communist Party, *Umkonto* was better financed, better organized, and more ambitious than any of its rivals. In all, *Umkonto* was not large. Its membership, though not exactly known, could not have been more than a few hundred. POQO was believed to be larger. Indeed, POQO was likened to a body without a head, and *Umkonto* to a head without a body. But, as this study will seek to show, there was body to *Umkonto* after all, even if the head was too large. Like POQO, *Umkonto* had roots among the masses, and though the roots may have been thin they ran deep. Because of the quality of its membership, *Umkonto* was able to initiate at least 190 acts of sabotage, according to the evidence of the prosecution at the time of the Rivonia Trial.⁵ Additional evidence led by the state indicated that no less than 300 men had been sent abroad for guerrilla training, to countries as

4. Coloured, spelled in British fashion, is the term that people of mixed descent use to describe themselves and by which they are known to the other racial groups in South Africa. It has no pejorative connotations. Also, Africans are not described as "coloured" despite their skin color. They used to be called "Natives" but are now termed "Bantu" in official South African literature. They themselves prefer the term "African," which will be used here, unless official or other sources that use the other terms are employed.

5. The official name of the trial is *The State vs Nelson Mandela and Others* in the Supreme Court of South Africa (Transvaal Division). It was widely known as the Rivonia Trial because of the name of the township in which the men were arrested. More details of the trial are in the body of the book.

far afield as Algeria, Cuba, Ghana, Ethiopia, Tanzania, and even to Communist China. No other resistance movement could claim to have achieved this much.

Umkonto was also careful to distinguish its methods from those of POQO. POQO attacks were mounted against individual whites, six of whom were killed in a road-builders' camp at the Bashee bridge in the Transkei, and another three in a riot in the Cape town of Paarl. But their claims of great achievements apart, POQO leaders had little to show for their efforts. Umkonto, according to its leaders, disdained attacks such as these. A handbill distributed in the townships set forth their views:

> Poqo is said to have killed five White road builders in the Transkei recently. There are more effective ways of busting the White supremacy state. A few road builders make no difference to the revolution. Instead, smashed railway lines, damaged pylons carrying electricity across the country, bombed-out petrol dumps cut Verwoerd off from his power, and leave him helpless. And these acts are only the beginning—

Not only did POQO mistake the real target, the handbill continued, but it did not know how to conduct the kind of conflict demanded by South African conditions:

> A crowd of unarmed men on a midnight march to town cannot break the police, the army and all the oppression of Verwoerd. That was Paarl—a heroic effort born out of oppression, but badly conceived. It is no good to think of Impis [the traditional African battle units] not of modern guerrilla war. . . . War is not a gesture of defiance. For a sum total of nine Whites killed—only one of them a policeman, and he killed by accident—hundreds of Poqos are in jail serving thousands of years imprisonment. For a wild boast Leballo has caused the round-up of unknown numbers of young fighters. . . . The freedom forces of South Africa must be coordinated —cell with cell, branch with branch, region with region—in revolution. There must be strong discipline—no actions going off halfcock. . . . Freedom fighters must be trained. Ten men, well trained

and organized, can often without fuss, do a job that 200 men, heroic but badly led, would bungle.

Above all, the leadership of *Umkonto* did not downgrade their allies:

Why make enemies of our allies? We say that just as Africans bear the brunt of oppression under the White state, so will the White state be broken by the main force of African people. But this is no reason, we say, to reject comrades of other races whom we know are ready to fight with us, suffer, and if need be, die.

This handbill contains some of the essentials of the *Umkonto* creed. Their leadership was uninterested in killing for the sake of killing. Their aim was to cripple the government by destroying the arteries of power, and to do this, if possible, without loss of life.[6]

Considering the forces arrayed against it, the successes of *Umkonto* can only be described as remarkable. But *Umkonto* could not last against the might of a modern government determined to extirpate it root and branch. Its life span ran roughly from the time it announced its existence, in December, 1961, to July, 1963, when its headquarters were discovered and raided by the police, and the greater part of its national leadership was arrested. Further raids enabled the police to pull in much of what was left of its leaders and followers. Yet those who remained at large would not admit defeat. A circular that they issued was boldly headed: "The ANC Is Alive! *Umkonto we Sizwe* Fights On!" The circular went on to say that, though some of the bravest leaders had been arrested, "the people will never run out of leaders. We have trained deputies, new leaders, a second wave of young militant men. . . . Does Vorster [John Balthazar Vorster, then minister of justice, now prime minister] think the people are barren; does he imagine we have not prepared ourselves?"[7] But these brave words were in vain. Although an attempt was made to carry on after

6. This handbill is repeatedly cited in the Rivonia Trial (see n. 5 above) but can be most conveniently studied in the microfilm series, *South Africa: A Collection of Miscellaneous Documents*, reel 8, published by the Hoover Institution. These films will be referred to as the *Hoover Collection* in subsequent notes.
7. "The ANC Is Alive," August, 1965 [?], mimeographed handbill.

the police raid on *Umkonto*'s headquarters at Rivonia, an outlying white township near Johannesburg, *Umkonto* was well on toward the end of its road. Further arrests netted its remaining leaders, who were given long prison sentences to be served in the maximum security prison on Robben Island off Cape Town. Many are there yet. The rest were, like other leaders of the African opposition and its allies, driven into exile.

From a police viewpoint, the destruction of *Umkonto* was the result of brilliant detective work. It reflected the growing skill of the Special Branch of the South African police and its increasingly imaginative use of counterrevolutionary techniques. It struck a blow at the resistance movement in the country that, according to the *African Communist*, the movement could ill afford.[8] Thus, the wave of arrests in 1963 and 1964 virtually ended active resistance within South Africa. Attempts have been and are still being made to organize Freedom Fighters outside its borders. Some of these men, a recent London *Times* article reports, are being trained in camps in Tanzania and Zambia. They have tried to infiltrate Rhodesia and South Africa and to stage guerrilla attacks on the armed forces of these countries. As far as is known, these raids have been on a small scale and have presented no very serious problems to the governments of Rhodesia or South Africa. Whatever the future may hold, the *Times* correspondents conclude, the black assailants are not a very present threat to the white regimes in their homelands.[9]

II

Umkonto did not spring to life full grown from the heads of its founders. Nor was it the spontaneous creation of men bent from the beginning on violence. On the contrary, *Umkonto* was created by men who, at least on the African side, had long persisted in a nonviolent course only to see it fail. For close to fifty years African leaders had tried all avenues of approach to successive South African governments,

8. No. 18, July–September, 1964. This periodical is published by the South African Communist Party in London.
9. *Times* (London), March 11, 12, 1968.

but to no avail. They discovered that passive resistance only works against an opponent already half-convinced of the resisters' claims. Against a determined and resolute opponent, passive resistance must sooner or later either pass over into active resistance or collapse as the resisters lose confidence in their cause.[10] Because it was so long the form of African resistance and because it provides the background for what follows, some discussion of passive resistance before the turn to violence is necessary. We will follow the fortunes of the African National Congress from its formation in 1912 through to 1962 and continue with the story of *Umkonto*.

Clearly, little more than a superficial summary can be provided in such a brief space. It would take several volumes to do the story full justice. Events which may in themselves be important will have to be left out of the account, while others more directly related to the subject will be stressed. What is true of events is also true of organizations. Some organizations which have played a major role in African opposition will be mentioned cursorily, if at all, because they do not bear directly on *Umkonto* and its activities. The story, as it will be told here, is drawn largely from published sources. Later chapters will rest mainly on primary sources. One thing should, however, be said: throughout the book it is assumed that the reader has some knowledge of political and social conditions in South Africa. Therefore these will not be treated in any systematic way. Anyone with less background in South African affairs may refer to some of the general books cited in the bibliography, or to the many other works with which the bookshelves of libraries and booksellers are so heavily weighted. The plethora of writings on South Africa makes repetition of what has so often been said redundant.

The African National Congress, originally styled the South African Natives National Congress, was founded by a group of African intellectuals in 1912.[11] They formed it out of a number of local African as-

10. Lewis Gann, "Liberal Interpretations of South African History: A Review Article," *Rhodes-Livingstone Journal*, XXV (March, 1959), 55.
11. Probably the best of the straightforward histories of the ANC is to be found in A. P. Walshe, *The African National Congress of South Africa: Aspects of Ideology and Organization between 1912 and 1951* (Los Angeles: University of California Press, forthcoming). This is an uncolored, "blow-by-blow" history.

sociations. The founding fathers were mostly lawyers, teachers, or preachers, many of whom had been educated abroad. The prime mover was Dr. Pixley Ka I. Seme, who is generally conceded to have been most instrumental in its formation. It was he, for instance, who in 1911 called for an African nationalism that would transcend the barriers of tribe:

> The demon of racialism, the aberrations of Xhosa-Fingo feuds, the animosity that exists between Zulus and the Tongas, between Basuto and every other Native, must be buried and forgotten. . . . We are one people. These divisions, these jealousies, are the cause of all our woes and of all our backwardness and ignorance today.[12]

The rise of a more comprehensive nationalism was, perhaps, the product of the color bar inserted into the Constitution of the Union of South Africa at its ratification in 1909. But the main momentum was given by the division of the land in terms of the Natives Land Act of 1913. This act, which apportioned the farmland of South Africa between white and black, gave the African majority only a very small portion of the land available.[13] To Africans, as to all farming peoples, land is of the utmost importance. Often it is seen as the difference between survival and starvation. So, because of the importance of land to them and because of the injustice that the apportionment represented, the act was a persistent source of bitterness to Africans. In addition, it meant that numbers of African squatters on white land would be driven off and rendered destitute. A period of African suffering was clearly about to begin.

Resistance to the Land Act began what was to be a pattern of protest. Petitions to the South African government would be followed by appeals to governments abroad and later to international organizations.

12. Quoted in *The African National Congress of South Africa* (*Excerpts from Policy and Program*), a pamphlet published by the ANC External Mission (Dar es Salaam, n.d.).

13. The Natives Land Act of 1913 had set aside some 10.5 million morgen of land as native areas in which whites could not buy land; the rest of the land was for whites only. The Native Trust and Land Act of 1936 provided for an additional 7¼ million morgen to be added to the reserves. This came to about 13 per cent of the total land area.

The pattern by which African organizations simply reacted to government initiatives, of which Leo Kuper writes, began then: "There were certainly periods of militant action, but it is not easy to point to campaigns in which non-whites dictated the issues and exercised the initiative." [14] This was certainly the case in 1913 when, after vain appeals to the South African government, a mission was sent to Britain to urge the British government to intercede. The First World War interrupted this initiative, and another mission was sent to the Peace Conference at Versailles. All was to no avail. Neither Britain nor the Allied and Associated powers were interested in the pleas of the African organization, the more so as South Africa's General Smuts was a leading light at the conference.

While engaged in these activities, the African National Congress sought to cement its ties with Africans elsewhere, initially by sending representatives to the first Pan-African Congress in Paris in 1919 and later by keeping in touch with African political figures.

The pattern repeated itself once again in 1945 when, as before, the African National Congress sent missions to the United Nations and then to the fifth Pan-African Congress. Again all was to no avail. But in the years following, as one African state after another came into being, complaints sent to the world body began to receive more ready and sympathetic hearings.

Throughout this discussion two things must be borne in mind. First, in the years between the two world wars, African politics were not a primary concern in South Africa. White politicians were concerned with white politics. The main issue was the clash between British rule and a rising Afrikaner nationalism, and intertwined with this was the demand by white workers that their privileged position be inscribed into law. Second, influencing and conditioning the conflict was the clash between the Cape and the frontier. The Cape, more conservative in white politics, was traditionally more liberal in black. The Transvaal, with the mentality of the frontiersmen resisting "savage" onslaughts, was more radical in white politics and more conservative in its racial exclusiveness. Its spirit was embodied in the original constitution of the

14. "The Political Situation of Non-Whites in South Africa," in *Southern Africa and the United States*, ed. William A. Hance et al. (New York, 1968), p. 88.

Transvaal Republic, which enjoined that there should be no equality of white and black "in church or state." [15]

When the ideas of the Cape and the Transvaal came into conflict, generally those of the Transvaal prevailed. It was pressure primarily from the Transvaal that led to the erosion of the few rights reserved to Africans in the Cape. The last of these rights, originally entrenched in the South African Constitution, were removed during the government of General James Barry Munnik Hertzog (1932–39). Having the necessary two-thirds majority in Parliament, General Hertzog was able to amend the Constitution, to delete the entrenched clauses, and to remove Africans from the common electoral rolls of the Cape. Although relatively few Africans had been able to meet the requirements of enrollment, the right was in itself cherished, particularly by the African intellectuals. Separate representation was to be given Africans under Hertzog's new system, and from a separate roll they would elect three white members to Parliament and another two to the Cape Provincial Council. In addition, a Natives' Representative Council, with purely advisory powers, was set up under the chairmanship of the Secretary for Native Affairs, the membership to consist of five nominated white members, four nominated Africans, and twelve elected Africans.[16] However sincere and dedicated the "Natives'" representatives might be, and they were both sincere and dedicated, the separate ballot was obviously a poor substitute for direct representation and was clearly perceived by thinking Africans as just another retrograde step.

Faced with these policies, the African National Congress was a body sorely divided at its annual conference in 1935. One section favored cooperation with the government, not because it approved of government policies but in the hope that, if the Africans showed moderation and a willingness to compromise, their rights would later be broadened and extended. This segment urged giving the Natives' Representative Council a fair trial. The other section favored noncooperation. It wanted

15. Walshe, *The African National Congress: Aspects of Ideology.*

16. For a brief treatment see Muriel Horrell, comp., *Legislation and Race Relations: Revised Edition, 1966* (Johannesburg, 1967), pp. 1–2. A more detailed treatment is contained in Ellen Hellmann and Leah Abrahams, eds., *Handbook on Race Relations in South Africa* (Cape Town, 1949), pp. 511–16.

to boycott this new body and any other established by the government allegedly for the benefit of Africans but actually, in its view, to further restrict them. This latter view did not carry the day. Those favoring compromise won out. Those who opposed cooperation, in what was to become a typical pattern when differences were irreconcilable, broke away to form another organization. African unity in the face of government action seemed always to elude its leadership. As a result, much of the effort of the ANC leadership before World War II was turned to trying to make the Natives' Representative Council work, an effort that, in the event, proved abortive.

Patiently, year after year, the Council, under the chairmanship of the permanent Secretary for Native Affairs heard speeches and passed resolutions calling for necessary reforms in every sphere of native policy and administration. Its discussions reached a level of debate more creditable than that normal in the [South African] house of Assembly, as observers could testify. But all the eloquent words and reasonable proposals were wasted on the deaf ears of the authorities. It is difficult to recall a single important reform introduced as a result of the good advice annually tendered by this "advisory" body.[17]

Frustration with the council grew after the Second World War, and with this frustration came a new spirit. The council's impotence had been underlined in the miners' strike of 1946—a strike of 70,000 African miners for higher wages which the police suppressed only after five days of turmoil—during which the council's pleas were largely ignored. The younger African leaders felt increasingly disillusioned with these "dummy institutions" and "toy telephones"—instruments into which one spoke knowing that there was no one listening at the other end. They began to withdraw cooperation. The older leaders, who derived a certain kudos from membership, wanted to continue in the council. In the belief, perhaps, that the more moderate leaders would soon be isolated and that militancy would spread, the prime

17. Julius Lewin, "The Rise of African Nationalism," in his *Politics and Law in South Africa* (London, 1963), p. 36.

minister of the time, General Jan Christiaan Smuts, offered in 1947 to extend the powers of the council and even to give it some limited authority. But the days of both the Smuts government and the council were numbered. Smuts's United Party was defeated in 1948 and the Nationalist Party, led by Dr. Daniel François Malan, took its place.

Disillusionment with the Natives' Representative Council was not, of course, the only source of the new spirit. It was also fired by the wartime promises of the Allied leaders embodied in such declarations and documents as the Atlantic Charter and the "Four Freedoms." These raised the hopes of African leaders and led them to look for an extension of African rights at the war's end. These hopes, strongly but rationally put, were published by the ANC in 1943 in a booklet entitled "Africans' Claims in South Africa." The claims it contained were endorsed by all African leaders of consequence. A rebirth of militancy also was manifest at this time. A young and fiery African lawyer, Anton Lembede, renewed the call for militancy and noncooperation. These streams of thought, disturbing to Smuts and his government, were to become more strongly focused as the Nationalist government of Dr. Malan began implementing its apartheid policies.

III

The Nationalist Party had won the election of 1948 on its apartheid platform. In its purest form, this plan called for the physical separation of the races in South Africa and the allocation to each race of some "national homeland." Such a policy, the Nationalists claimed, would both assure continued white rule of their territory and reduce racial tension. The whites would, in other words, be unquestionably supreme in their areas, and the Africans would be supreme in the areas allotted to them. The greater and best-developed part of the country would go to the whites, and there they would rule. The policy was, however, ambiguous on many points. The white portion, highly industrialized as it was, depended for its operation on African labor. The white farmers also depended on African labor. Many argued that to apply a thoroughgoing policy of apartheid would mean not only undoing the economy but undoing the entire South African past as well. This argument seemed to make little impact on the Nationalists and their most ardent supporters. Having won the election, they took the first steps to implement their policies.

The status of the African National Congress as an organization representing Africans needs to be clarified. The ANC *claimed* to speak for all Africans, and in principle it undoubtedly spoke for many. But until 1949 it was by no means a mass movement. Writing of the historic conference of 1935, Edward Roux put it this way: "But what did they [the ANC] represent in the way of effective organization? . . . The 400 delegates represented very little but themselves." [18] Things were not greatly changed even in 1947. According to the secretarial reports of the provinces, membership stood at 5,517, with 4,341 divided between the Transvaal and Natal and only 376 in the Cape, the remainder being in the Orange Free State.[19] What is more, the claim to speak for all Africans was continually challenged by other organizations—even by offshoots of the ANC itself. In the twenties it was overshadowed by the massive ICU (Industrial and Commercial Workers' Union) led by Clements Kadalie. The ICU had turned trade unionism to political account and was, for a time, a power in the land.[20] The claim of the ANC was further eroded when R. V. Selope-Thema broke away from the organization to form the racially exclusive Nationalist-Minded Bloc in the 1950s. Despite its age, the respect in which it was held, and the maturity of its leaders, the ANC existed tenuously to the beginning of the Second World War.

The first expansion of the ANC came in 1940 with the election of Alfred Bitini Xuma to the presidency of the organization. It is a measure of the man that he worked his way up from illiterate herd boy

18. Edward Roux, *Time Longer Than Rope: A History of the Black Man's Struggle for Freedom in South Africa*, 2d ed. (Madison, Wis., 1964), p. 289.
19. "Debates at Congress Annual Conference," *Bantu World*, January 3, 1948.
20. The story of the ICU will be found in Roux, *Time Longer Than Rope*. There is also a briefer reference in the ANC pamphlet of n. 12 above. Some aspects of ICU history are in Sheridan W. Johns, "The Birth of Non-White Trade Unionism in South Africa," *Race*, IX (October, 1967), 173–92, and in an unpublished manuscript by Maynard W. Swanson, "Champion of Durban: An African Politician and the ICU," which deals with the riots of 1929 and other matters.

to medical doctor with degrees from leading medical schools in England and on the Continent. Dr. Xuma, on becoming president-general, brought new life to the faltering ANC by drawing in new blood. He sought and won the support of the "hire-purchase" class, the Africans who could afford to buy furniture, clothes, and cars on the installment plan. These were the people whom Anthony Sampson has described as "the lower-middle class of [African] clerks, interpreters, salesmen, and shopkeepers, who were rapidly accumulating in their little box houses around the big cities, and had hitherto been too preoccupied with their furniture and their snobbery to soil their hands with politics." [21] It was Dr. Xuma who formed the first alliance with an organization of another racial group. By signing an agreement in 1946 allying the ANC with the Indian Congress of Drs. Dadoo and Naicker, he laid the foundations for the Congress Alliance of the fifties. The Congress Alliance was later to include, in addition to the ANC and the Indian Congress, the all-white Congress of Democrats, the Coloured People's Organization (later Coloured People's Congress—for those of mixed descent), and the South African Congress of Trade Unions. But this important theme must be reserved for later treatment. In the meantime, an important challenge to Dr. Xuma's authority had developed in the ANC with the formation of the Youth League in 1944.

The Youth League urged less caution, less conservatism, and more militant nationalism. Led by Anton Lembede, already mentioned for his infusion of a new nationalist spirit, it soon gathered an impressive group of "Young Turks." Although Lembede's life was cut short after four years of leadership, his followers, among them Nelson Mandela, Peter Mda, Walter Sisulu, and Oliver Tambo, were to see their names become household words, not only in African politics but also in South African politics. They had two principal aims: the first was to make their *Program of Action* accepted as ANC policy; the second was to make the president-general into little more than a figurehead whom they could manipulate. To this end, they tried to win over Dr. Xuma, who was under fire from his own rank and file, but he refused to take dictation from the Youth Leaguers. When he was approached by

21. *The Treason Cage: The Opposition on Trial in South Africa* (London, 1958), p. 70.

16

Mandela, Sisulu, and Tambo, and asked to accept a three-point program, he described what happened as follows:

> I informed this delegation that I would have been better disposed to discuss their program more calmly if it were placed before me for consideration under normal conditions and not as a condition for my reelection. Under the circumstances, I told them, "I do not want your vote, because I do not want to be dictated to by any clique. I want to remain a leader with freedom of thought and discretion: to deal with situations as dictated by circumstances." [22]

Then, on December 16, 1948, Xuma was visited by Mda, who promised him support for reelection. But the Youth League had no intention of keeping its promise and voted instead for Dr. J. S. Moroka, another distinguished medical doctor.

The Youth League voted for Moroka with misgivings, which, as it happened, proved to be well founded. Under Moroka the *Program of Action* remained a paper program; few of its provisions were even partly implemented. Even the "dummy institutions" were not boycotted. The only action was that militant campaigns, the basis for which had been laid by Xuma, were mounted. The first of these was the Defiance Campaign of 1952, in which members of the ANC and the Indian Congress were to defy unjust laws and to accept prison sentences, refusing fines or bail. The government responded, in part, by arresting all the leaders of the campaign on the charge that they were Communists. Not only did Dr. Moroka insist on a separate trial from that of his codefendants, but he attested his friendship for the Afrikaner people and virtually confirmed the charge against his colleagues. Clearly, such a man was unsuited to lead a militant movement, and the Youth League had no intention of renewing its support when the election came around again at the national conference of the same year. The Youth League was to learn, with this experience, that there are drawbacks to weak leaders.

Disappointed with Moroka, the Youth League began to cast its eyes

---

22. *Guardian* (Johannesburg), March 23, 1950. This newspaper was a predecessor of *New Age*.

over other possible candidates and lighted on Albert John Luthuli; this time it made what was, from its viewpoint at any rate, an excellent choice. Luthuli had been chief of a minor Zulu tribe and had been deposed by the government for refusing to resign from the ANC. Combining a high moral sense, an impressive personality of great strength, and considerable political naivete, he was not the sort of man to cause the Youth League trouble. He was respected; his name was used; but he was taken little into the councils of the men who made ANC decisions. This may require some clarification. Both his own speeches and writings and the evidence of witnesses in other trials bear out that Luthuli was only sketchily informed of what was going on, and then only after crucial decisions were already made. Isolated in the village of Stanger, in Natal—by terms of a law permitting the government, by simple decree, to banish anyone to any part of the country—he was relatively cut off from the movement in 1952. The ban, originally for two years, was continuously renewed until Luthuli's death in 1967. It is hardly surprising, therefore, that his knowledge of what was going on was incomplete. Nonetheless, it is doubtful if he would have been consulted more had he been at liberty. Idealists such as Luthuli, particularly humanistic idealists, do not make good revolutionary organizers—their moral scruples always get in the way of action. So, in November and December of 1961, before and during the time he was awarded the Nobel Peace Prize, he still stressed that the ANC was out to achieve its ends without violence, although the decision to turn to violence had been taken as early as June, 1961, and was already being bruited about the African townships.[23] As a man, Luthuli was not a liar; everything in his character points to the contrary. It can only be assumed, therefore, that he was just not told by his fellows in the ANC leadership of the decision—a decision he may well have resisted.

23. See, for instance, the *Star*, December 12, 1961, which contains an extract of Luthuli's Oslo speech and also a shortened version of the television talk that he gave in London. His views were also reported by the *Rand Daily Mail* of December 12, 1961, headed "Way of Violence Still Rejected"; and in an earlier interview with the African affairs correspondent of that newspaper, Benjamin Pogrund, the same theme had been stated by Luthuli. It would seem, therefore, that, both before and after receiving the prize, Luthuli's views remained unchanged, although they no longer reflected those of the ANC.

IV

The decision to turn to violence had, then, been taken in the middle of 1961. It was taken, as Nelson Mandela said, because the ANC felt that "violence in the country was inevitable; it would be unrealistic and wrong for African leaders to be preaching peace and non-violence." [24] So it would seem that Luthuli, for all his virtues, was the façade behind which leaders more unscrupulous or more desperate, more frustrated or more realistic, sheltered. This estimate will doubtless annoy both admirers and detractors of the late president-general of the ANC. It is difficult, however, to come to any other conclusion, given the facts. Perhaps the judgment can best be softened by saying that it is the mark of a noble nature to err on the side of the humane.

Events had, by 1952, gone beyond the *Program of Action*. But it is to the *Program* itself, in view of its significance, that we must return. It breathed the then-new and militant spirit of the young men who framed it, and this emerges clearly in its introductory paragraphs:

> The fundamental principles of the Program of Action of the African National Congress are inspired by the desire to achieve National Freedom. By National Freedom we mean freedom from white domination, and the attainment of political independence. This implies the rejection of the conception of segregation, apartheid, trusteeship, or white leadership which are all in one way or another motivated by the idea of white domination or domination of Whites over Blacks. Like all other people, the African people claim the right of self-determination.[25]

The *Program* demanded direct representation in all bodies of the state, the creation of a national fund to finance the struggle, the political education of Africans, and the use of the strike and the boycott as

24. See Nelson Mandela, *No Easy Walk to Freedom*, ed. Ruth First (New York, 1965), p. 169. This book must be distinguished from a pamphlet of the same title which Mandela had published earlier. The book, not the pamphlet, is a collection of Mandela's articles, speeches, and trial addresses.

25. The text used here is reproduced in *Pioneer: Official Organ of the ANCYL*, Jabavu (Township), Vol. XI, no. 1, n.d., which seems, however, to have been issued in 1958 or 1959.

weapons in the struggle. The last is of great significance. In the words of a delegate to the 1948 conference: "Unless [the White man] changes his mind about his treatment of the [African] we must use our atomic weapon—withdrawal of labor." [26] Indeed, the power of strikes and boycotts to shape political ends became very much of a mystique among leaders of the ANC.

The *Program* was, perhaps, the most significant of the Youth League's documents. It was not the only one. The members' views were elaborated upon and made known in a variety of mimeographed newsletters, and particularly in one called the *Basic Policy of the Congress Youth League*. In it they tried to make clear where they stood on African nationalism and on the place of the white man in South Africa. Because of its importance to later discussion, passages from this document will be quoted at fair length. Of African nationalism the members wrote:

The African has a primary, inherent and inalienable right to Africa which is his continent and Motherland, and the Africans as a whole have a divine destiny which is to make Africa free among the peoples and nations of the earth. In order to achieve Africa's freedom the Africans must build a powerful National liberation movement, and in order that the National movement should have inner strength and solidarity, it should adopt the National liberatory creed —African nationalism, and *it should be led by the Africans themselves* [italics added]. . . .

. . . The starting point of African nationalism is the historical or even prehistorical position. Africa was and still is the Black-man's continent. The Europeans . . . have carved up and divided among themselves, dispossessed by force of arms, the rightful owners of the land—the children of the soil. . . . Although conquered and subjugated, Africans have not given up, and will never give up their claim and title to Africa. . . . They will suffer White oppression and tolerate European domination only as long as they do not have the material force to overthrow it.[27]

26. *Star*, December 15, 1948.
27. *Basic Policy of the Congress Youth League*, mimeographed, n.d. Available in *Hoover Collection*, reel 8.

And on the status of whites, they said:

> Now it must be noted that there are two streams of African nationalism. One centers around Marcus Garvey's slogan "Africa for the Africans." It is based on the "Quit Africa" slogan and on the cry "Hurl the White man to the sea." This brand of African nationalism is extreme and ultrarevolutionary.
>
> There is another stream of African nationalism (Africanism), which is moderate, and which the Congress Youth League professes. We of the Youth League take account of the concrete situation and realize that the different racial groups have come to stay. But we insist that a condition for interracial peace and progress is the abandonment of White domination and such a change in the basic structure of South African society that those relations which breed exploitation and human misery will disappear. Therefore, our goal is the winning of National Freedom for African people, and the inauguration of a people's free society where racial persecution and oppression will be outlawed.

Clearly, these objectives, while not entirely contradictory, could only be reconciled with difficulty. The interpretation of these ideas and their attempted implementation served as vehicles for feuding factions in the ANC after 1949.

The Defiance Campaign, although earlier spoken of as the first major evidence of militancy, was not the first attempt at joint action with the Indian Congress. On May 1, 1950, an attempt at a nonviolent protest misfired and sparked off a riot in which some eighteen were killed and many more wounded in clashes with the police. The decision to undertake the massive Defiance Campaign was, it seems, made as an aftermath of this tragedy. The campaign was launched with a formal letter to the then prime minister of South Africa, the late Daniel François Malan, demanding the repeal of certain specific laws by February 29, 1952, as otherwise a passive resistance campaign would be mounted. In his reply, Dr. Malan rebuked the writers for addressing him instead of the Minister for Native Affairs and indicated that the government had no intention of repealing the laws differentiating between "European" and "Bantu." Any attempt on the part of the ANC and its allies to compel a change would be met with the full force of the law.[28]

In response to this letter, and indeed no other reaction from Malan had seriously been expected, the congresses launched the Defiance Campaign, in which African and Indian volunteers, reportedly trained in techniques of nonviolence, broke minor apartheid regulations. As part of the plan, they entered facilities set aside for whites in post offices, railway stations, and other government buildings. They entered African townships without the authority required by law. African volunteers went about without the identity documents they are required to carry at all times by law. What mattered was not the nature of the laws broken, but rather that laws were broken. They were broken in the belief that, if courts and prisons were clogged with numberless petty offenders who refused bail or fines, the machinery of repressive legislation would break down through sheer overload. For a time this seemed a promising method. The prisons were filling up and the courts overflowing as some 8,500 volunteers began breaking laws. But the campaign was the victim of its own success. Courts began to apply existing laws more strictly, exacting the maximum penalties. Stiffer sentences and the arrest of the leaders under laws for the suppression of communism took the impetus out of the campaign, which began losing momentum. It had lasted about five months, from the end of June to the beginning of November, 1952, when it finally expired due to lack of support. The campaign was officially called off by the ANC after the passage of the Criminal Laws Amendment Act in 1953, as this act imposed Draconian penalties for attempts to change laws by breaking them.[29]

The Defiance Campaign both enhanced and diminished the stature of the ANC, on the basis of its outcome in various parts of the country. Over most of the land the ANC gained in prestige. Its membership shot up from an estimated 20,000 in 1948 to an estimated 120,000 at

28. *Star*, January 30, 1952.
29. Where offenders were found guilty of resisting laws in order to change them, it was mandatory to impose either a fine of about $840 or three years' imprisonment or ten lashes, or any two of these. If an individual incited anyone else to commit such an offense, this was punishable with a fine of about $2,800 or five years' imprisonment or ten lashes, or any combination of these.

22

the end of the campaign, depending on who made the estimates. In the Eastern Cape, however, violence of a particularly ugly sort broke out, and the brutality of individual actions drove many from the ANC. On the whole, no matter what the losses may have been, the campaign generally enhanced the standing of the ANC among Africans, although it achieved none of its professed objectives.

As a store of unused energy remained from the Defiance Campaign, which would dissipate unless harnessed, the question arose as how best to put it to use. One way was to channel it into a "Congress of the People," which was not a new movement but was to be a vast gathering of delegates drawn from among all the people of South Africa. It would be convened to draw up a new covenant, a "Freedom Charter" incorporating all the changes they wished to see in South Africa. The COP, as it was called, was to be truly national. And to increase the impression of nationalism, organizations of all racial groups and all political complexions were invited to participate. These included, among others, Afrikaner organizations and even the Nationalist Party. Needless to say, few organizations other than those connected in one way or another with the ANC accepted. An exception was the multiracial South African Liberal Party, but its members were soon made aware that, unless they slavishly followed the path that the ANC and its allies had mapped out, they would be frozen out of all decisions. As a result, they left the COP while it was still in the planning stage.

The Congress of the People was duly held, and the Freedom Charter, which had been drawn up in mysterious circumstances before the meeting, was accepted clause by clause by acclamation of the 2,000 to 3,000 delegates attending. Despite their apparently impressive numbers, the delegates did not represent "the people as a whole" but, according to the estimate of Professor Z. K. Matthews, then leader of the Cape ANC and the originator of the idea of the COP, only the 200,000 or so members of the ANC and the organizations allied with it.[30] The delegates did not, as subsequent events showed, even represent

30. "Minutes of the Joint Executives of the ANC, SAIC, SACOD, and SACPO, held 31st July, 1955, in Stanger, Natal," typewritten, unpublished. They form part of the Treason Trial Documents, which are available from the Cooperative African Microform Project (CAMP), Center for Research Libraries, University of Chicago.

the entire ANC, which later split over the very matter of acceptance of the Freedom Charter.

The South African scene had changed in the meantime. The first Nationalist prime minister, D. F. Malan, retired in 1954. He was succeeded by J. G. Strydom, nicknamed "the Lion of the North" because he was considered the fearless spokesman of the Nationalists in the Transvaal. He was the living embodiment of the spirit of the Transvaal, and his nomination as party leader (to the disappointment of Malan, who had hoped that Nicholas Christiaan Havenga would succeed him) made final the dominance of that province. It was Strydom's outspoken objective to maintain *die Baasskap van die Wit man*—"the mastery of the white man"—and to this end he began to tighten and improve the machinery and legislation of apartheid.

Faced with an even sterner opponent than Malan, the ANC and its allies planned a "Resist-Apartheid Campaign." The aim of the new campaign, actually a series of campaigns, was to resist each new apartheid measure as it was promulgated. The effects were disastrous for the ANC. Protests were mounted in rapid succession as the government speeded up the process of apartheid. There was no time for adequate preparation. Promises of alternatives to government services to be boycotted—boycott was still to be the principal weapon—could not be kept. The ANC did not, even at the best of times, have the resources to replace government services, and, with one law following another, was even less in a position to mobilize the means. Thus, for instance, in the "Western Areas Campaign"—mounted to prevent the government from moving the residents from the slums known as the Western Areas, near Johannesburg, to new housing at Meadowlands, farther out of town—alternative accommodations promised to those who refused to move could not be provided. The promise was in itself foolhardy and irresponsible, for there were no other accommodations in the already overcrowded Western Areas, and the government demolished the houses of those who were moved, whether they went to Meadowlands or not. Again, in the "Bantu Education Campaign," alternative education was promised to those who boycotted government schools, although once more it was obvious that no alternative schooling could be provided by the ANC and its allies. The failure of these campaigns did little to add

24

luster to the reputation of the ANC, and pointed up its powerlessness.[31] There is no doubt that there was potential for resistance among Africans. They could and did show courage and determination in opposing measures that directly affected their daily lives. This was demonstrated in such actions as the great Alexandra bus boycott of 1957, in which some 45,000 Africans daily walked the long distance to their work places in Johannesburg rather than pay the higher fares demanded by the bus company that normally carried them to town. This massive refusal to submit was not something that the ANC had organized. It was a spontaneous protest. But sometimes the ANC itself was able to find the sensitive nerve of African resistance. Support for the ANC-sponsored potato boycott is one example. In 1959, as a protest against the miserable conditions under which Africans were being made to live and work on the potato farms, Africans refused to buy potatoes, otherwise a staple of their diet. Despite the hardship this caused them, Africans ate no potatoes, and the crop rotted in the warehouses. But the campaign faded out in the end. The needs of their bodies in the end forced Africans back to buying a food they could not do without. But their refusal for the time of the campaign is a triumph of their spirit. The partially successful "stay-at-home" strike of 1957 is another case in point. About half the African work force heeded the ANC's call not to go to work and to stay in their homes. South African commerce and industry were seriously set back as a result. But these campaigns were exceptional. In most cases the ANC overplayed its hand in a succession of campaigns devoid of thought or responsibility. A call for another "stay-at-home" strike in 1958, for instance, timed to coincide with the General Election, was a fiasco. Africans were not in a financial position to take part in continuous strikes. When all ANC campaigns up to 1960 are accounted for, the debit side of the balance sheet far exceeds the credit side. In no case had the ANC been able to induce the government to change its course by one iota. For all their effect, the campaigns might just as well not have been mounted. They served a function in that they called attention to African protest and the misery of Africans; they drew the eyes of the world to the country and

31. See Edward Feit, *African Opposition in South Africa: The Failure of Passive Resistance* (Stanford, 1968).

to the policies of its government. They awakened the consciousness of some Africans and the conscience of some whites. But as far as the government was concerned, its determination to implement its plans was not one whit diminished.

The realization, painful as it was, that these campaigns were largely abortive and that Africans had to pay the cost, diminished African support for them. For, whatever their effect outside the African community, their effect within was to demoralize and deaden resistance rather than to increase it. The campaigns served the government in an indirect way by pointing up weaknesses in existing laws and enabling these weaknesses to be removed. As Leo Kuper wrote: "New laws and the more efficient mobilization of force control these challenges, which serve, then, on the one hand, to perfect the machinery of domination and, on the other hand to move the struggle for power in a more revolutionary direction." [32] It can be argued that what has been said by Kuper does not accord with what was written above, that if the struggle was moved in a more revolutionary direction, then this was, for the ANC at any rate, a worthwhile result. In a sense this argument is correct. The struggle did act as a catalyst for a group of determined men, ready to take action against the government by violent means. Their story is, indeed, the story to be told in this book. The progression of ideas is evinced in Nelson Mandela's address to the Court at the Rivonia Trial:

> We of the ANC had always stood for a nonracial democracy, and we shrank from any action which might drive the races further apart than they already were. But the hard facts were that fifty years of nonviolence had brought the African people nothing but more and more repressive legislation, and fewer and fewer rights. It may not be easy for this Court to understand, but it is a fact that for a long time the people had been talking of violence—of the day when they would fight the White man and win back their country —and we, the leaders of the ANC, had nevertheless always prevailed upon them to avoid violence and to pursue peaceful methods.

32. Leo Kuper, *An African Bourgeoisie: Race, Class, and Politics in South Africa* (New Haven, 1965), p. 5.

When some of us discussed this in May and June of 1961, it could not be denied that our policy to achieve a nonracial State by nonviolence had achieved nothing, and that our followers were beginning to lose confidence in this policy and were developing disturbing ideas of terrorism.[33]

For some, as Mandela says, violence appeared as an appealing alternative. But for the majority, the failure of one much-heralded campaign after another meant simply that resistance was useless and sullen compliance the only alternative. As Ted Gurr suggests in a recent study in which South African experience is cited, "Inhibition of civil violence by fear of external retribution tends in the short run to increase the strength of anger but in the long run to reduce it." [34] For more than forty years the African National Congress had, by various peaceful means, tried to influence successive South African governments to concede changes favorable to Africans. For forty years it had failed. Its members had little to show for their pains. By 1960 all arrows in the nonviolent quiver had been shot, and the government remained in control more firmly than ever. The ANC and its leaders and their allies only seemed able to offer methods that failed. From this frustration grew an explosive tension within the ANC itself—a tension that grew unbearable. The movement split in two, into the Pan-Africanist Congress and the African National Congress. This in turn, as in a Greek drama, led to the tragedy of the Sharpeville massacre and made the turn to violence inevitable. These themes are treated in the following pages.

The failure of ANC campaigns to achieve "African Freedom," as promised in the original declarations of the Youth League, was seen by a new generation of young Africans as due to the betrayal of African nationalism by their seniors—the radicals of yesterday. Many of this newer generation pressed for stronger policies—above all, for Africans to liberate themselves without outside aid, as called for in the *Program of Action*. They pressed for this at a time when the

33. Record of Rivonia Trial; also Mandela, *No Easy Walk*, p. 168.
34. "Psychological Factors in Civil Violence," *World Politics*, XX (January, 1968), 267.

older leaders—who were not *that* old themselves—were ever more enmeshed in the Congress Alliance and less than ever ready to "go it alone." The younger men, as younger men do, believed that they better understood what was needed. They believed that they had in their hands the key to freedom which the older men had failed to find. They believed that, even if the key were in the hands of the older leaders, they would be too hesitant and lethargic to turn it. Had the younger men known of it, they might have used the term "deradicalized" to describe the older leaders.[35] The leaders seemed to have aged and mellowed, but the movement had not aged and mellowed with them. Deradicalization was, in other words, a phenomenon of the upper layers of leadership. The layers below were increasingly radicalized. A generational gap grew, in which younger leaders came in continuous conflict with their elders. The conflict increased in bitterness as increasing government pressure caused the more moderate and fearful to leave the ANC. The conflict could be resolved in only one way—the breakup of the ANC. This event, which took place in 1958, led to the formation in 1959 of the Pan-Africanist Congress, or PAC, whose members were known as "Africanists," while the majority remained in the ANC, which continued on the path its leaders had charted.

V

The battle raged over the nature of African nationalism and who could claim to be its true interpreter. There was certainly room for confusion and conflict in interpretation. African nationalism was largely an amalgam of imported ideas, notions, and conceptions. Three streams of thought entering into this nationalism are of particular importance, although obviously they are not the only influences that come into play: political liberalism, Bible fundamentalism, and Marxism. Political liberalism was brought by the Christian missionaries,

35. The author owes this idea to an article by Robert C. Tucker, "The Deradicalization of Marxist Movements," *American Political Science Review,* LXI (June, 1967), 343–58.

often the first teachers Africans knew. Its tone was that of the nineteenth century, and its emphasis was on "one man, one vote." It was also from the missionaries that Africans learned their biblical texts, which they took both seriously and literally. Many of the themes that were to recur later were phrased in language redolent of the Bible, and many of the illustrations in speeches came from this source. Marxism, being both "scientific" and "messianic," bridged the other two streams of thought and influenced Communists and non-Communists alike. But Marxism induced a reaction; younger leaders came to believe that the older leaders were too much under its spell and were therefore subject to undue influence of white and Indian Communists. The absorption of their elders with multiracialism and the class struggle blinded them, the younger leaders felt, to the more important matter of African nationalism. The betrayal of African nationalism was, according to this analysis, sealed with the adoption of the Freedom Charter. Adoption of the charter committed the ANC to a multiracial "people's republic" instead of to a South Africa resting on rule by African numbers. Africans, the majority, were going to have to share control with "alien" minorities.

The older leaders hotly denied that there was any betrayal. They denied emphatically that the ANC was under the control of the other congresses or that they (the leaders) were unduly influenced by their allies, as asserted by the Africanists. They denied having fallen into any ideological traps. By entering into alliances with other racial groups, the ANC simply recognized that South Africa was a multiracial country and that it was impossible for Africans to act as if other permanently settled peoples did not exist. In reply to claims that African Communists had infiltrated the ANC, they argued that as an "omnibus organization" the ANC had to admit freely Africans of all political tendencies. Far from the Freedom Charter being a betrayal of the *Program of Action*, it completed what had only been begun in the *Program*, for it defined the places of the different racial groups in the new society.

These arguments left the Africanists unconvinced. As they saw matters, the charter would only ensure that control of the country continued to rest with non-Africans—it was simply the continuance of white rule in a new and more sinister guise, the rule by white Communists. The Africanists, while themselves unsure of the role the other races could assume, insisted on a nonracial democracy which, in the nature of things, would be ruled by an African majority.

The divisions in the ANC ran deep. There were charges and countercharges, the Africanists insisting on their view that the ANC was under the influence of both African and non-African Communists, and the older leaders denying this charge. In an effort to disprove this charge, Duma Nokwe, a lawyer who was also secretary-general of the ANC, set down the names of the principal officeholders from 1949 to 1961 in an article in *Africa South in Exile* to show that not more than three professed Communists were among them.[36] This did not allow for clandestine Communists, and it was known that there were other Communists among the leaders. There was strong evidence, which came out into the open only later, that Nokwe was himself a Communist, although he did not include himself among those he cited as members of the Party. The list, as such, may have convinced a few well-meaning people abroad, but it was little more than a propaganda stunt.

The ANC was increasingly evincing the Marxist trend in African nationalism, while the Africanists were exhibiting the other two trends mentioned above. At the PAC's first conference, for instance, a special correspondent of the same *Africa South*, Peter Rodda, wrote of the "emotional and sometimes eccentric and exclusive Christianity" that characterized the meeting: "Three ministers graced the platform, and in prayers and addresses they referred to the 'hooligans of Europe who killed our God and have never been convicted' and the legend of Christ's education in Africa, while cheers greeted the salute to 'a black man, Simon of Arabia, who carried Jesus from the Cross.' "[37] Religious overtones heightened the anti-Communist line of the Pan-Africanists who, according to Robert Sobukwe, their president-general, believed in political democracy as defined in the West, but with a more equitable distribution of wealth and with a positive neutralism

36. "The Great Smear: Communism and Congress in South Africa," *Africa South in Exile*, VI, no. 1 (October–December, 1961), 6.
37. "The Africanists Cut Loose," *ibid.*, III, no. 4 (July–September, 1959), 23.

in international affairs.[38] So set forth, the Africanist argument seems logical and cohesive, but this was far from the case. In truth, their ideology was muzzy and their perception of goals frequently contradictory. However, one thing emerges clearly: bewildering as were the different Pan-Africanist interpretations of African nationalism, even in any one leader's speech, black racialism was common to much of it. Lip service might be paid to the idea that an "African" was anyone who made Africa his permanent home, but from what the leaders said and wrote it was plain that their nationalism was that of ethnic Africans alone.

Even if the quarrel over values is ignored, and this is difficult to do, another factor of significance remains. Both the ANC and the PAC were competing for essentially the same constituency—the relatively narrow class of politically conscious African activists. Their numbers could not be easily enlarged, given governmental hostility, and new recruits were hard to come by. Each organization gained members more or less at the expense of the other. Competition for this constituency would surely have divided them even in the absence of other factors. As a result, it seemed as if anything the ANC wanted to do would surely be opposed by the PAC, and anything that the PAC wanted to do would similarly be opposed by the ANC. Each did its best to disrupt the other's campaigns. And hostility between the two principal African opposition groups was hardly displeasing to the South African government, which could play off one against the other.

The attempted strike of 1958, which failed signally, illustrates the operation of the mutual animosity between ANC and the Africanists. The strike was called by the ANC. Predictably, its Africanist wing opposed the venture, and the noise made by clashing African politicians served only to assist the Nationalists' fear-mongering among the white electorate. In the event, not only did the "stay-at-home" strike collapse in futility, but the inflation of the affair frightened many whites into supporting the Nationalist Party, which was returned to power with an increased majority in Parliament. To make matters worse, from the African viewpoint, the new prime minister was none other than Hendrik

38. *Ibid.*, pp. 23–24.

Frensch Verwoerd, the architect of the apartheid policy and the man whose influence was most feared by Africans.[39] The year 1959 did not look auspicious for the African opposition.

The ANC spent much of 1959 attempting to heal the breaches in its own ranks. The PAC was faced with a different dilemma. Not only had it to build an organization, but it had to show, and show quickly, that it could do better than the ANC. Failure to act would seal its fate. It would lose impetus, be discredited, and probably fall apart. The problem was to mount a campaign both more effective and more spectacular than those that the ANC had mounted in the past. In order to do this it was necessary to choose an issue on which all Africans felt sufficiently strongly to rally without much organization being needed. This meant choosing an issue on which Africans were sufficiently united to face the forces at the government's command. It had to be something that affected all Africans alike, one that would unite them behind the banners of the PAC. Finding such an issue called for little genius; issues were all too ready at hand. An issue that was ready-made for the PAC leadership was the perennial one of "passes."

The incendiary potential of the pass issue is as old as the laws on which it rests. It can be said that the pass laws were resented above all other discriminatory laws. Since the introduction of passes in 1911, Africans have struggled to rid themselves of this incubus and have sought to prevent their broader application. But once more the interests of the successive South African governments and their African subjects have been at opposite poles. South African governments have generally sought to extend the pass laws, to make them apply to categories of people otherwise exempt. It was a game that the government, in the nature of things, could not lose. Africans might, from time to time, refuse to carry passes. They might even stage large-scale pass-burnings. But in the end the government could always reassert its control, tighten up the laws, and exact penalties for their breach. African frustration and resentment grew accordingly. An understanding of

39. The elections were held on April 14, 1958; Dr. Verwoerd became prime minister on August 24, 1958. The Nationalist Party increased its majority from 94 to 103 seats in a House of 165.

the pass laws and what they implied for Africans is thus clearly a necessity.

The intense and smoldering resentment of passes was due to two things: the limits the pass system put on Africans' mobility, and the harsh manner in which pass laws were administered. The pass itself was a document which the African had to have on his person at all times. It had to be produced every time he left one employment and entered another. In this sense, the pass was primarily a residence and work permit, applicable especially to the towns, and work could not be had without it. It resembled the "internal passport" that had to be carried in Tsarist and later in Communist Russia. Like the Russian document, it had a dual purpose. One was to control influx into the larger towns and cities, both from the countryside and from outside South Africa, ensuring that the supply of black labor balanced the demand. It was also a means of identification and control of individuals. Failure to produce the pass at the request of any policeman or government official would lead to immediate arrest, which made pass offenses the most frequent crimes on the judicial calendar. Nor did matters greatly improve when the government, aware of the confusion caused by the multiplicity of documents an African had to carry (for the pass was only one such document), changed the system in 1952. All documents were consolidated into a new *reference book*, which the government tried hard to distinguish from the old pass, but to no avail. Africans saw the reference book as just another pass; to them the form but not the substance had changed. The new books restricted them just as the older passes had done. The hatred of the old-style pass was simply transferred to the new. Reference books were still called "passes" by Africans.[40]

Indeed, in many ways the new reference book was a retrograde step. It was a particularly bitter blow to African intellectuals. Before the introduction of these books, it had been possible, with much difficulty, for an African to gain exemption from carrying a pass. Now the

---

40. For a discussion of the "pass laws," see Muriel Horrell, comp., "The 'Pass Laws': A Fact Paper" (Johannesburg, 1960), mimeographed.

prized certificates of exemption were withdrawn. The intellectual, like the illiterate, had to carry a reference book, which he more clearly saw as a badge of inferior status. As Lewis Nkosi, an African author, put it, his reference book represented his personality and delineated his character. It defined the extent of his freedom. He felt that he had ceased to be a person and that he had become his reference book.[41] The African laborer, whether literate or illiterate, reacted no less strongly. He felt that the reference book assured his exploitation by preventing him from selling his labor in the best market, that the pass system kept his wages low, and that it kept him out of well-paid jobs in the cities. Government spokesmen and economists have argued that African wages were in fact supported by the pass system, that the unlimited influx of unskilled Africans in excess of a city's needs would force wages below subsistence levels as more and more men competed for the shrinking roster of jobs. A large pool of unemployed and unemployable Africans would collect and provide tinder for incendiary agitators. Social services would become strained and the vast slum clearance projects, completed by the government, would be swamped and new slums would appear. These arguments carried little weight with Africans. African workers were not economists or social scientists. They were absorbed in the lifelong struggle to earn enough to make both ends meet. As C. J. de Ridder wrote, the most obvious trend in the African personality in the towns was the feeling of being discriminated against. The crux of African antagonism to whites, de Ridder suggests, centered on the restrictions that discrimination placed on his desire and outright need to improve his earnings.[42] And the pass was the instrument by which this restriction was imposed.

But that was not all. To restriction must be added police persecution. Such persecution was not official policy. As is so often the case, it was due to individual policemen acting out their own prejudices. There was no lack of fair-minded men on the South African police force—men who, though administering an unfair system, tried to maintain some standard of decent treatment of Africans. Even some

41. Quoted in Kuper, *African Bourgeoisie*, pp. 61–62.
42. *The Personality of the Urban African in South Africa: A Thematic Apperception Test Study* (London, 1961), pp. 91, 93.

who were ill-disposed acted courteously simply because they did not want to make their work more difficult by creating angry and destructive mobs. But the fact remains that in administering the pass laws many policemen were rude and tyrannical, which made the restrictions, already resented, harder to bear. The higher command of the police force tried to reduce this sort of friction. The Commissioner of Police issued a standing order calling for better treatment of "responsible" Africans. They should not be arrested for minor infractions of the law, he urged, but should instead be summoned to appear in court. This order, it must be noted, did not reduce the right of policemen to summarily arrest Africans for pass offenses, but called only for more lenient treatment in cases where individual Africans, obviously employed and law abiding, did not have their reference books with them at the time of asking. The very fact that such an order had to be issued tells its own story. And even after it was issued complaints continued. Police apparently were continuing to arrest even "responsible Africans" for petty offenses.[43]

The effects of the pass laws, their human cost, and the rigor and extent of their application are most clearly seen in the statistics of the arrested: from 365,911 such arrests in 1957, the number climbed to 396,836 in 1958. As the total number of African men, women, and children was estimated to be around three million, it is evident that a significant number of the work force must at all times have been under arrest for offenses against the pass laws. Clearly, the delays and dislocations to commerce and industry must have been considerable, so whites were also discommoded as the pass system was applied.

As whites also lost time and money, why did not more of them press for removal of the pass laws? The most important reason motivating white acceptance of the laws was, perhaps, the control the laws gave them over Africans. Registration is one of the most effective means of

43. Instructions to the police issued in *Circular* 23 of 1954 called on them to use discretion when an offense of a purely technical nature against the pass laws was involved. The attention of police officers was drawn to this circular in January, 1963, and again in March, 1968. Nevertheless, arrests for minor infractions of the pass laws seem to have continued. A ruling by the South African Supreme Court in 1970 lays down that a man must be given an opportunity to produce his pass book if he does not have it on him.

control, and this is particularly true where a minority must control a majority. The use of the pass as an instrument of control was, of course, well understood by many African intellectuals, as this passage from the work of G. M. Pitje makes plain:

> The reference book is an instrument for socioeconomic regimentation, dragooning and control. It creates a pattern with machine-like efficiency, and brings each and every individual throughout life under the direct eye and vigilance of the State machinery. It is an instrument for economic exploitation, social control and regimentation, forced labor and political persecution. It is more than a badge of inferiority. It is a merciless fetter strangling the life of the Black millions of South Africa. Its general effect is to deny or deprive the Blacks of their human heritage—the right of free movement; the right of choice of work; freedom of speech; freedom of thought; freedom of association; freedom of assembly and other basic rights and freedoms such as the inviolability of the human person.[44]

To do away with the pass laws might have meant virtually doing away with white rule. Without the measure of control that the pass laws afforded, administration of the entire system of apartheid laws would soon have become impossible. The pass was the keystone of the arch. The importance of the pass in the administration of discriminatory legislation, in turn, strengthened African leaders in their opposition to these laws.

VI

Opposition to passes had a long history. Indeed, one of the earliest ANC campaigns was precisely on this issue. When the pass laws were introduced in 1911, the leaders of the ANC, not then welded into one organization, led a campaign against the new system. More campaigns were mounted subsequently—one in 1919, and another in 1925, a test case which prevented the extension of passes to women at that time.

---

44. Quoted in Kuper, *African Bourgeoisie*, p. 63.

A new anti-pass movement was initiated by the ANC in 1944, and sporadic protests continued throughout the postwar period.

For these and other reasons, the call by the PAC to resist passes was bound to awaken response. A considerable reservoir of experienced resisters was at hand, and resistance was backed this time by strong emotions. Emotions of the past were kindled anew by the decision of the government to extend the pass laws to women in 1960. Women had earlier resisted the application of pass laws to them and were not subject to their provisions. New laws were now promulgated extending the reference books to women, but it was not mandatory that they be carried at all times. Large demonstrations were now staged, as the women anticipated, with good reason, that it would not be long before the books were made compulsory. The time for mass campaigns against the pass or reference book seemed propitious, as the leaders both of ANC and of PAC knew.

The question of whose decision it was first to launch a campaign against passes in 1960 has been disputed by both the ANC and the PAC. Each has claimed credit for the idea. It seems senseless to argue the point. Of greater importance is the fact that the PAC set the pace and the tone of the campaign, regardless of any prior plans that the ANC may have contemplated. But in terms of time alone, the ANC seems to have devised and disclosed its plans first. At its 47th annual conference in December, 1959, resolutions were adopted for a major campaign against passes in 1960. A few days later the PAC held its annual conference and adopted resolutions for a campaign against passes to be coupled with a campaign for greater courtesy toward and higher wages for Africans.

Both organizations, it seems, came forward with the same idea at much the same time, and each claimed that the other had stolen its thunder. But the planned conduct of each campaign was markedly different. The ANC went about things in its customary cautious and cumbersome way. It looked to a long-drawn-out campaign in three phases. An "Anti-Pass Day" on March 31, 1960, would be followed by an "African Freedom Day" on April 15 to coincide with, and to be directed against, the white celebrations commemorating the foundation of the Union of South Africa. These would be followed on June 26 with both a "National Day of Mourning" and a "stay-at-home" strike, on which day no African was to go to work. According to the overall plan, deputations from the townships would visit administrators and officials in March and urge them to press for abolition of the pass laws. Failure was anticipated, so it was intended to hold numerous protest meetings. All this was typical of the way ANC campaigns were usually conducted, and it was hardly likely to shake the bastions of the government.

The PAC planned something completely different. It decided on a mass campaign in which Africans would simply leave their reference books at home (while not destroying them) and would present themselves at police stations asking to be arrested. The slogan of the campaign was to be: "No bail! No defense! No fine!" By coming in great numbers, demanding arrest, opting for imprisonment, and accepting sentence, Africans could make the entire operation of the pass system unworkable. The leaders of PAC would show the way by subjecting themselves to the same sanctions as their members. They would be among the first to present themselves at police stations. They would be the first to ask to be arrested. They would offer no defense, pay no bail, and accept no fine. They would be among the first to go to prison. All this was reminiscent of the old Defiance Campaign, but this time it was not picked volunteers of all races who were to do the defying, but Africans alone and en masse.

The impact of this campaign could obviously be very great. As was set forth in an article in *Contact*, a news magazine very sympathetic to PAC, this campaign would make or break the movement. Success would catapult PAC to the pinnacle of African leadership, while failure would result in its total eclipse.[45]

The PAC campaign was, in its conception, more in line with the mood of African militants. At the ANC annual conference, the leadership, still calling for caution, was almost overrun by its own supporters. The objections of its president-general, Albert Luthuli, that impetuousness was no substitute for organization, and that poorly

45. *Contact*, March 19, 1960, p. 2.

planned campaigns with unlimited objectives were not only likely to fail but would in addition disillusion Africans both inside and outside the ANC, were simply swept aside. Amidst tumultuous applause, one delegate declared: "Let us force our leaders into a tight corner; if they think in terms of strategy, we think in terms of action." Confidence was in the air. Greater militancy had apparently worked in Natal, and a "Natal spirit" was abroad. African women had, in Natal, seemingly scored a success over the police, and this had heartened ANC sympathizers and had increased enrollment. The enthusiasm of the Natal members infected others at the conference, and the 380 delegates and 5,000 unofficial delegates in attendance demanded "massive demonstrations." The three-phase campaign, outlined earlier, was the upshot.

The ANC did have one advantage over PAC. It could count on some outside support, apart from that of its allies. This support, while not numerically large, came from influential people. For instance, the Anglican bishop of Johannesburg, Ambrose Reeves, long known for his liberal views and sympathy for Africans, sponsored a committee drawn from some fourteen different organizations. These included the Liberal Party and also the "Black Sash"—a movement of white upper-middle-class women who had been demonstrating against the government for years—as well as the white component of the Congress Alliance, the Congress of Democrats. A demonstration supporting the abolition of passes was held on the steps of the Johannesburg City Hall, the usual venue for demonstrations of this sort. In addition, some 5,000 circulars were printed and sent to prominent members of the white community. While the meeting on the City Hall steps was being held, Mrs. Kay Mitchell, a councilwoman, attacked the pass laws in the council chamber, unperturbed by the attempts of Nationalist councillors to heckle her. Support such as this, from obviously respected and respectable sources, heartened the ANC and its allies, leading some to the rather fatuous conclusion that "a direct assault on the [pass] system can secure its abolition." But doubts about the conduct of the campaign remained unresolved even in March when the campaigns were due to begin. There were demands for action in the ANC, but little knowledge of what action to take, who should take it, and what forms the action would assume once it had been initiated. So the initiative to begin the campaign remained with the PAC.

In a press conference, held on March 18, Robert Sobukwe, president-general of PAC, told pressmen what his organization was going to do. The demonstration against passes would begin on March 21, after which Africans would not go to work at all; they would stay away until all demands were met. On the same day Africans would present themselves at police stations for arrest. They would say: "We do not have passes. We will not carry passes again. Millions of our people have been arrested under the pass laws, so you had better arrest us all now." If this plan worked well, Sobukwe said, "this would mean that the people had divorced themselves mentally from passes." It would thus be the first step to freedom. But PAC initiatives were not to end with the pass laws. In addition to "decisive and positive action against passes," PAC would press for a minimum wage of about $100 per month, a demand which exceeded those that the ANC had put forward in the past by some $15 per month, thus stealing a minor march on them.

But beneath a surface *savoir-faire,* the PAC leadership was quite cautious and not as ready to act on its own as it appeared. Faced with the uncertainties of its first major campaign, PAC began casting around for allies. All South Africans, whether ethnically African or not, were now called upon to join in what the PAC leadership called "this noble campaign." Similar caution was shown in the matter of violence. The PAC stressed its opposition to violence, just as the ANC had done. Now, at the dawn of the new campaign, Sobukwe sent a letter to the Commissioner of Police asking him to do nothing that would lead to violence. Sobukwe stressed that the police should not give impossible commands, such as asking a meeting to disperse in insufficient time and then using this as a pretext for a baton charge. If the police would act with restraint, he continued, they would have no difficulty. The PAC would cooperate to make this "a most peaceful and disciplined campaign."

The search for support did not stop with other racial groups or with appeals to the police. The ANC was also approached and asked to participate, but this it would not do. Solemnly admonishing Sobukwe, the ANC urged that no "sensational actions" be entered into, because "it is treacherous to the liberation movement to embark on a campaign that has not been properly prepared for and which has no reasonable prospect for success." Coming from the ANC, whose campaigns were hardly models of political action either in planning, timing, or execution, the advice was laughable. Politics, rather than principles, were doubtless at issue. To have entered into a campaign at the behest of its rivals would have been tantamount to an abdication of the political leadership of Africans which the ANC claimed. The leaders of the ANC expressed disapproval of what the PAC was planning: "While the ANC cannot oppose any people's spontaneous demonstrations," they said, badly prepared campaigns would only harm the struggle and reduce its effectiveness. The ANC itself, they continued, was preparing to conduct a campaign of its own aimed at educating the African masses for "a powerful and united national action which alone could destroy the pass system which was at the root of oppression." It could not "call on or encourage people to participate in the ill-defined PAC campaign" as the ANC was in the midst of preparations for its own action.[46]

Refused cooperation not only by the other major African organization but also by most other opposition groups, except perhaps for a few individuals in the Liberal Party, action on its own was, in the end, the only option for the PAC. The support the campaign gained among urban Africans exceeded what must have been the wildest dreams of its sponsors. Africans participated in the thousands. True to their promise, Sobukwe and his principal officers presented themselves first for arrest. But noble as the conception of leaders sharing the hardships of their followers was as an ideal, it made little political sense. It left the conduct of the actual campaign to young and inexperienced leaders. Yet the very impact of African response gave the campaign a momentum that made up for deficiencies in leadership. The young and untried leaders seized on this initiative, particularly in the Western Cape and in the townships of the industrial complex

46. *New Age*, March 19, 1960.

around Vereeniging in the Transvaal. In both of these areas, in the past, the ANC had been weak. Some men of outstanding promise, such as Philip Kgosana, surfaced, but enthusiasm and energy could not in the long run substitute for political acumen. Lack of leadership led to the Sharpeville tragedy, which, like Léopoldville later, was to symbolize the forcible repression of African unrest.

VII

Tragic as the events of Sharpeville undoubtedly are, they have to be seen in some perspective. Sharpeville, as a township, was no run-down slum. It was a model of its sort, particularly well endowed with amenities. The situation there on that fateful March 21 was tense. The crowd around the police station was large, estimates varying from some 5,000 to some 20,000. The police were few and nervous. Nine police officers had shortly before been murdered in the African township of Cato Manor near Durban, and this had received much press publicity. The event was fresh in all minds. Firing began. When it ended, the area resembled a battlefield. The police, about 50 in number, had fired on the crowd without orders, leaving some 69 Africans dead and 180 wounded. The crowd broke and fled when the firing commenced. Grim as these figures are and tragic as the death of any man or woman is, the statistics do not place Sharpeville among the world's major riots. What gave Sharpeville its percussive impact was as much the year in which it happened as the actual events of the day: 1960 was widely celebrated as the "Year of Africa." It was the year in which most African colonies—British and French—were being granted independence. It was a time of rising hope for and in Africa. The late Dag Hammarskjold, then secretary-general of the United Nations, even spoke of "the African century." This was the high-water mark of anticolonialism. To the international community, South Africa's policies seemed not only unjust but against the historical process. These hopes and beliefs, therefore, magnified the tragedy and enhanced its significance.

Sharpeville was the most spectacular but by no means the only incident of the day. Both in the Transvaal and the Cape other incidents were shaping up.

Crowds collected around the other townships near Vereeniging: some 10,000 in Evaton, some 4,000 in Vanderbijl Park. These, however, were dispersed with minimal injury or loss of life. Other demonstrations took place in Cape Town, the most serious being in the township of Langa, where rioting followed an attempt by the police to break up an apparently peaceful meeting. Some police officers, a few whites who blundered into the area, and about 47 Africans were injured in the resulting fracas. Lesser disturbances took place in other towns in the Western Cape.

Once the trouble had started, the ANC could not long stand aside, much as it might otherwise have wished to do so. At first it did little more than express sympathy for the victims of the riots. But the emotions aroused by the shooting at Sharpeville were clearly too strong for the ANC long to withstand, and with apparent reluctance the ANC entered the lists before the time it had intended. A "National Day of Mourning" was proclaimed for March 28, on which day President-General Luthuli appealed to all Africans not to go to work. Tom Hopkinson, a former editor of the widely read African magazine *Drum*, has described the origin of this event:

In the course of the morning, as we were all talking things over, Nat Nakasa remarked: "You know we can't just leave it like this—two hundred and fifty Africans dead and wounded, and the rest of us do absolutely nothing—as though it were just some kind of a little mistake."

"What do you suggest?"

"Chief Luthuli ought to declare a 'Day of Mourning,' and the whole country should stay away from work as a sign of respect."

Luthuli was at this time in Pretoria, giving evidence almost daily at the Treason Trial, which was still wearily dragging on. I was sure Cecil Eprile would be in contact with him, so went over to his office.

"People on *Drum* are suggesting that 'Chief' ought to declare a national Day of Mourning for the Sharpeville victims. Do you know how to get hold of him?"

"Yes. Dennis Kiley is going out there this evening. He can pass the idea on."

Next morning I asked Cecil what had been decided. "Chief" had told Dennis that he could not make any move without consulting his principal supporters. He would do this as soon as he could, and let Dennis know the result.

However, in Thursday's *Rand Daily Mail* I read that Luthuli had announced the next Monday, March 28th, as a Day of Mourning, when everybody throughout the country should stay away from work.[47]

Luthuli's call received a great deal of press publicity, and a substantial response seemed likely. Even the PAC, now somewhat chastened, decided to throw its weight behind the "Day of Mourning" and, in an unusual move, to support the ANC "stay-at-home" strike.

Even as this was going on, PAC supporters, now in smaller numbers, continued coming to police stations for arrest. Unrest continued in the country. In Sharpeville, the scene of recent tragedy, buses taking workers to their jobs were attacked, and on March 22 they ceased operating altogether. Without transport to bring the workers to their factories, many industries around Vereeniging were compelled to close their doors, while others operated on a half-time schedule.

There were more demonstrations in different parts of the country during March and April. These included the Transvaal, the Western Cape, Natal, and even the Orange Free State where African organizations were not generally strong. The Eastern Cape, though troubled, did not experience as much trouble as the western portion of the province.[48] In all, the ANC's "Day of Mourning" was well supported, and the "stay-at-home" almost complete. Those who had not participated found trouble awaiting them when they came home to the townships. Rioting broke out when the minority who had gone to work were met by irate strikers. In the riots the participants attempted

47. Tom Hopkinson, *In the Fiery Continent* (New York, 1963), pp. 263–64.
48. For a listing of the disturbances, damage, and details of casualties, see Muriel Horrell, comp., *A Survey of Race Relations in South Africa, 1959–60* (Johannesburg, 1960), pp. 55–68.

44

to set fire to government buildings, schools, clinics, and churches. Although serving the African community, these buildings were seen as concrete symbols of racial domination by whites. On March 30 trouble spread from the African townships to Cape Town and Durban. The township of Langa, near Cape Town, had been restive since the disturbances of March 21, when many stayed away from work, but for more than a week after that there was no outward sign of impending violence. This illusory peace was shattered on March 30 when some 30,000 Africans marched into the center of the city. Their numbers were impressive, and their conduct orderly. They were led by a young student, Philip Kgosana, one of the PAC men. They halted in front of the offices of the government, and Kgosana demanded an interview with the Minister of Justice. After a complicated discussion with an official there, Kgosana, it seems, believed that he had been given an appointment with the minister, but the official later said that he had only told him that such an appointment would be considered. Believing his purpose accomplished, Kgosana took his followers away in as orderly a manner as they had come.

The situation was more serious in Durban, where riots occurred in the seething slums of Cato Manor. There a crowd of about 5,000 Africans collected for a march on Durban. On their way they were diverted to a sports ground, where they were addressed by a chief magistrate and by a Bantu affairs commissioner. The meeting ended in uproar. The marchers, their numbers now augmented to about 10,000, resumed their march by a number of different routes. Police and troops were called out, and they met the marching columns. But the columns were not halted. They dispersed into smaller clusters and continued their march on Durban. Eventually some 1,000 of the marchers reached the heart of the city and collected in front of the main prison, demanding release of the prisoners taken earlier. As the mood of the crowd began growing ugly, a young Indian, believed to have been one of the leaders of the Indian Congress, appealed to the crowd to disperse, which they did. Other groups of marchers who had reached the outer suburbs of Durban were met by the police and dispersed.

Confronted with a situation growing hourly more serious, the government reacted with speed and flexibility. First of all, on March 24, it put a stop to all public meetings in twenty-four of the more seriously threatened magisterial districts. The ban was later extended to many more districts, until in the end much of the country was blanketed. In terms of the ban, no meeting, gathering, or procession of twelve or more people could be held in any public place without the permission of the magistrate in that district. Penalties for infringing the regulation were severe, which effectively stopped much of the open agitation among Africans. Taken in conjunction with the earlier relaxation of pass laws, a serious communication problem was created both for the ANC and the PAC. The pass laws had been relaxed as early as March 26, in response to the rising tide of African feeling. This was, of course, even before the riots. The official reason was that the intimidation in the townships (by ANC volunteers) had reached such proportions that Africans were afraid to carry their pass books. So to relieve law-abiding Africans of the burden of fear, Africans without their books would not be arrested but would be asked to appear with their books later at police stations.[49] These measures reduced the possibilities for organized African resistance. Meetings held in the open air were the main means by which African leaders could reach their constituents. These were now prohibited. To call or attend a public meeting would be very risky. In addition, the relaxation of the pass laws started rumors, erroneous in the event, that the laws would not be reimposed—that the battle over passes had been won. Luthuli seemed to give substance to this rumor by personally burning his reference book in public, a gesture intended as defiance but which conveyed a wrong impression. His action also sparked off a number of other pass-burnings in the townships, some of which seem to have been staged for the overseas press. One such incident is reported by Tom Hopkinson:

> We stopped at a house known to our driver, and knocked. Like almost all township houses, it was a tiny dwelling—not much more than a garage divided into rooms. For a moment there was silence,

49. *Star*, March 26, 1960.

then someone from inside recognized the driver through the window, and in a moment a dozen or fifteen men had come pouring out. They told us they had organized a pass-burning which was just about to start. We had hardly begun talking to them before other doors opened all up the street, and in no time there was a crowd of sixty or seventy people.

"Look," I said to a man who was clearly in authority—he proved to be an A.N.C. official. "If the cops turn up suddenly, we shall all be pinched for holding an illegal assembly. Send away all those who have nothing to do with this, and let the others collect on some open ground with a view in all directions."

The official shouted a few words; the women and children, and most of the men, vanished as rapidly as they had appeared. Then he and about ten or a dozen others led the way to a patch of waste ground. They were carrying a quarter-filled sack and what appeared to be a bottle of gin, but which was actually paraffin. When they reached their chosen spot, the leader shook out the contents of the sack, poured the paraffin over, and began burning about seventy of the precious and detested documents. Though there was no kind of ceremony, he managed to give dignity and an air of ritual to the occasion. As the passes—cloth-bound books with a large number of stiff pages—caught fire, men seized one in each hand and began to dance and shout, waving the blazing passes in the air. I was surprised by their readiness to be photographed in this highly illegal activity; when a Fleet Street cameraman who was with us wanted them to pose grinning over the bonfire into his camera, even those who had been doing no burning hitherto rushed to get into the picture.

Ian's quickness and resource astonished me, as they had done before and were to do many times again under more difficult circumstances. I was still wondering how he could get anything usable from the artificial arrangement organized by the Fleet Street man, when I saw he had already darted off ten yards or more to one side. From there no one was looking into the lens, they were all gazing intently away, and the scene as the men pranced and waved their unfolded passes over the little fire looked like some strange tribal ceremony. Next day when we printed up the pictures, he had got three or four vivid shots in which half-burned passes, with the

47

flames curling up from the opening pages, looked like fiery flowers dangling in front of the exultant faces; and he had one close-up of a kneeling man, his face intent and brooding as at an incantation, pressing his charred pass into the flames.[50]

The government had made no secret of its intention of restoring the pass system to full working order at the earliest convenient moment. Thus there was no ground for African optimism. Euphoria over the relaxation of pass laws nevertheless continued until April 4—a mere ten days after the relaxation was announced—when the government declared that the pass system was again to work normally as of April 10. On that date Africans were warned that a country-wide action was planned against those without reference books. This dismayed large numbers of Africans: not only did it mean a return to the hated pass laws, but many found themselves in a worse predicament, for they had voluntarily burned their books. Others had had theirs taken from them forcibly and burned. All now had to replace their books at a cost of about $2.80 each—a large sum to a poor African. Luthuli, who had burned his publicly after the laws had been relaxed, was fined about $280 and given a suspended prison sentence of six months. He was found not guilty of incitement by the court that sentenced him, although pamphlets publicizing his action and urging others to follow his example were found in his room.

The government now took steps to ban the ANC and the PAC. Both organizations, together with all their branches, committees, and local and regional bodies, were declared to be illegal. It was made a crime to seek to carry them on in any form. And although these bans would have to be renewed annually in terms of the Unlawful Organizations Act, few really believed that the bans would soon be lifted. The days of legality were over for both African organizations. An epoch in South African history had come to a close. Legitimate opposition by Africans to the South African governments was to be no more than a memory.

50. Hopkinson, *Fiery Continent*, pp. 265–66.

VIII

When the major unrests had been stilled and the dust had settled to some extent, one disturbing fact emerged: no major center had been completely immune to trouble. What is more, trouble was likely to erupt again. Africans, it appeared, would follow even ineffective leaders who were willing to lead—and especially if they led to action. Radical African movements could, the government feared, always conjure up some sort of support, and this support could come in impressive numbers. The government seems to have believed that there was only one way it could cope with the threat: to physically remove the leaders. A State of Emergency had been declared on March 30 and, in a nationwide sweep, 98 whites, 36 Coloureds, 90 Asians, and 11,279 Africans were taken into detention. The arrested included most of the better-known Congress leaders, the leaders of the various congresses allied with the ANC, as well as militant opponents outside these groups. These arrests served to deprive the ANC and its allies of effective leadership and assured that order was maintained on April 10, when the pass laws were again to be enforced.

This was not, of course, the only measure taken by the government. Others had already been taken and were reinforced once the State of Emergency was declared. The army reserves—the Active Citizen Force and the "Skiet Commandos"—were mobilized and placed on an active footing. From the night of March 31, they surrounded the African townships near Cape Town, letting no one enter or leave, first after 7 A.M. and on succeeding days after 8 A.M. This prevented another march and discouraged further ventures in the direction of Cape Town. At the same time, armed units staged shows of force in various African townships to further discourage anyone who threatened to make trouble. As the government was clearly in control of the situation and the Africans' leaders were imprisoned, the tide of militancy began to recede. What is more, Africans were beginning to feel the pinch. Poor as they were, they did not have the means to fall back on during a prolonged strike. They needed their earnings to remain alive, and many had earned nothing for as long as a week. An irresistible drift back to work began, and this drift swelled to a torrent as the police arrested anyone who tried to agitate for the strike or to intimidate those who wanted to go back to work.

By mid-April order seemed fully restored to the land. The mass demonstrations which the ANC had planned for April 15 had been abandoned. Both the ANC and the PAC began to tentatively organize underground, but, with their leaders detained and with the difficulties described, they elicited little response from the African population. The time for full-scale underground organization had obviously not yet come. Their differences temporarily submerged in the common disaster, the two organizations together called on Africans for another strike in April. This failed dismally. African emotions had cooled, and the people's first priority was their pay packets, not political actions. The arrest of agitators and intimidators, invariable concomitants of all African political campaigns, allowed Africans to ignore the appeal of ANC and PAC in comparative safety. Although they were not completely free from fear of retaliation, the measure of police protection given them made the risk of ignoring the strike call worthwhile. In the same way the "Day of Mourning" planned for June 26 passed without incident, despite exhortations from underground ANC and PAC leaders. Further attempts at mass action were obviously useless. The old ANC techniques could not be employed from underground.

The frustration of the strike calls left the leaders of the African underground with the problem of what step to take next. Clearly, it was unthinkable to give up the struggle. A few halting steps had already been taken toward setting up an underground organization, an attempt made to reorganize and regroup, even before the Emergency ended. But the leaders well knew that underground activity alone was not enough. Contact with the masses, whom an underground organization could not easily reach, would have to be maintained. What is more, even to get the underground working, given the skill and determination of the political police, would take time. In the meantime the ANC would have to keep its image alive in the eyes of its African supporters and the African communities-at-large. It would have to demonstrate that it was still there. What it did would have to be big and important to attract attention not only at home but also abroad. The action would have to involve many people, but at the same time it would have to be something that the government would not be tempted to forbid out of hand.

The ANC was not alone in seeking some way for African political ideas to find expression. African leaders of all political persuasions had begun to seek one another out, to devise a way of carrying on. Invitations had been sent to some forty African leaders at the beginning of December, 1960. In response, radicals, progressives, and liberals all met at Orlando Township, near Johannesburg, on December 17, 1960 —the first time in twenty-five years that men of such mixed beliefs had come together—to discover whether they could sink their differences and make common cause against the government.[51] For a time it seemed that they might succeed. Unity was in the air. It looked as if now the differences that always had debilitated African resistance in the past might finally be resolved.

The government hindered but did not stop the Orlando meeting from taking place. Bans were issued against a number of the leaders, such as Albert Luthuli, the Reverend N. B. Tantsi, and Duma Nokwe, thereby preventing their attendance. Professor Z. K. Matthews, on the other hand, excused himself for personal reasons. Some important leaders, representing significant viewpoints, were thus absent. But enough men of importance were there, and all seemed eager to arrive at unity. In the interests of this unity, important concessions were made to the Africanists present. It was the PAC call for a "nonracial democracy," rather than the ANC call for a "multiracial people's democracy," that was adopted. The Freedom Charter was not invoked, nor were members of other races admitted to the meeting, even though two tried to attend. A white and a Coloured, both members of the Liberal Party, which had African representatives at the meeting, argued that as "Africans" they had a right to be there. They were forced to leave. The ethnic definition of an "African" apparently held. The meeting pleased the PAC leadership, who could, with right, regard it as a victory for their world view.

51. A list of some of the main leaders invited is in the *Rand Daily Mail*, December 8, 1960.

At the same meeting concrete steps were mapped out for an all-out resistance to apartheid. A Continuation Committee was appointed to plan a national conference to unify all African organizations in opposition to government policies.

The government, not unaware of the importance of this conference, had its eyes and ears there. Among the less than welcome visitors were members of the Special Branch—the political division of the police —six of whom observed the conference. They did little to enhance their dubious popularity when they demanded the passes of some of the leaders and then proceeded to arrest twelve of them. All were subsequently released, and those found without passes were given time to produce them. But the government had made its point, if that was what it intended. It had shown how powerless these leaders were in the face of force.

IX

Unity was short-lived. It was soon demolished by quarrels among the leaders of the ANC, the PAC, and the Liberal Party. All subsequently tried to justify their respective stands, each faction producing its own version of what happened. The trouble began when the Africanists left the Continuation Committee, protesting that the agreement reached at the leaders' meeting had been violated. They claimed that the All-In Conference, which the Continuation Committee was calling to unify all African organizations, was being converted to yet another multiracial convention by the ANC, and that such conventions achieved nothing, only serving to again place the African people under the thralldom of foreign elements and foreign ideologies. Shortly after this, the four original sponsors of the leaders' conference also resigned. These men, who had made the first moves to unity, felt that the conference had been subverted by the ANC. Jordan K. Ngubane, a sponsor and a prominent Liberal Party leader, was later to maintain that some delegates had come to the original leadership conference not to unify all Africans but to push their own lines. They had come with a plan already prepared, which they were determined to impose on the other African leaders. When they were voted down, Ngubane says, they did not submit to the majority decision but managed to make the Continuation Committee a "rubber stamp to endorse the actions of an invisible hand that moved events to its own goal." [52]

Money flowed, according to Ngubane, and expensive parties were organized for members of the Continuation Committee. There was, he said, more money than had ever been available in the history of African nationalism. No member of the Continuation Committee would admit to knowing where it came from. But the flow of funds induced friction among the African leaders. Actually, Ngubane asserts, the funds being so liberally spent came by way of Bechuanaland through well-known Communist couriers. They were spent in ways disapproved of by the Continuation Committee, which led to arguments among the members. Quantities of pamphlets, for instance, considered Communist propaganda by some, were printed and distributed in the Continuation Committee's name. Telegrams, asking for messages of support, were sent only to Communist countries, and this again was done in the name of the committee without the members being informed. Indeed, non-Communists on the Continuation Committee were continually being confronted by acts undertaken in their names, of which they had no knowledge and which they did not approve. When they objected, they were soothed with assurances that "mistakes had been made" which would not recur—but the "mistakes" continued to be made.

Although they felt tried beyond endurance, many leaders remained on the Continuation Committee in the hope of salvaging what was left of unity. But they soon saw, according to Ngubane, that unity was not what those in control of the Continuation Committee were after. This became especially clear when the ANC leadership refused to postpone the All-In Conference to allow time for the breach with the Africanists to be healed. Upon this the Liberals left the committee, which meant that the All-In Conference became entirely an ANC affair, although a number of sporting, cultural, and religious organizations also took part.

The version of the divisions in the Continuation Committee put

52. Jordan K. Ngubane, An African Explains Apartheid (New York, 1963), pp. 162–67.

out by the ANC, not surprisingly, differs from that of Ngubane. It argues that the resignation of Ngubane and his fellow Liberals was the outcome of an "unholy alliance" between the Liberals and the PAC people. The PAC leaders, according to the ANC, had for a long time been looking for a way out of the Continuation Committee because powerful PAC leaders in the Cape did not approve of the All-In Conference in principle. The Liberals then took advantage of their failure to postpone the All-In Conference as an excuse to withdraw from it.

Although the All-In Conference now was just a shadow of the unity that had inspired it, the ANC had no intention of giving up something that it had fought so hard to control. Although the government depleted the ANC ranks with arrests and bans, the leaders pressed forward with their plans. Police harassment continued. Five days before the conference was due to begin, the police arrested ten of the original planners, including those who were no longer actively involved. Accused of carrying on an illegal organization, they were released on bail; but those who were involved in the All-In Conference were clearly in no position to play an active part.

Despite these setbacks, the All-In Conference duly met in the Natal town of Pietermaritzburg on March 25 and 26, 1961. The political tone was largely that of the ANC and its allies. Members supporting other political organizations attended in small numbers, but their influence was as sparse as they were. According to *New Age*, some 1,400 delegates came. They not only heard political speeches but also danced, sang, and generally enjoyed themselves. As if to underline the drama of the meeting, the leaders claimed that their meeting hall had been "bugged" by the police and they found a new venue. Singing as they went, the delegates marched to an Indian communal hall two miles away, where the Indian community abandoned a prayer meeting to allow the conference to take place. It is not known whether the original hall indeed was bugged—quite likely it was. But the maneuver gave the ANC an opportunity to display, in an ostentatious way, the advantages of multiracial unity.[53]

53. *New Age*, March 30, 1961.

At the meeting, Nelson Mandela, the effective leader of the illegal ANC, made the keynote speech. It was from this speech that the main resolutions were drawn. The most important of these was one calling on the government to prepare a national convention "of elected representatives of all adult men and women on an equal basis irrespective of race, color, creed, or other limitations" by May 31, 1961. Should the government not comply, massive demonstrations would be mounted from May 29 to May 31, after which Africans would refuse to collaborate in any way with the government. The campaign was to coincide with the celebrations of white South Africans attendant on the proclamation of the Republic of South Africa, a republic in which, the ANC leaders said, legitimacy rested on force alone perpetuating the tyranny of a minority. The planned demonstration was to be another "stay-at-home" strike, in which other racial groups were asked to participate.[54] Thus the stage for the last massive move of the ANC was set.

The success of this strike is, at best, highly debatable. The demonstration, planned to last three days, had to be called off after one day for lack of support. Although Nelson Mandela was later to maintain that the strike had more "solid and substantial support" than was conceded, it was generally considered a failure by those outside the ANC leadership. *Drum*, which conducted its own survey in the townships, concluded that the strike had little real support behind it. It also argued that the strike had failed in its secondary object: poisoning the pleasure of the whites in their republic. The *Drum* reporter wrote that "between breakfast and lunch on Monday, May 29, the Government, the daily press, and the White public had written off the stay-at-home as a failure. By Tuesday, May 30, they had forgotten the threat ever existed. And so R-Day, May 31, was celebrated in triumph."[55]

In his post-mortem on the strike, in an article in *Africa South in Exile*, Mandela tried to explain away its failure.[56] He argued that no

54. *Ibid.*, March 9, 1961.
55. *Drum*, July, 1961.
56. "Out of the Strike," *Africa South in Exile*, VI, no. 1 (October–December, 1961), 15–23.

political organization had ever been faced with conditions as difficult as those that confronted the ANC and its allies. All organizing had to be done in defiance of the laws. The laws permitted suspects to be detained (at that time) for at least twelve days at a stretch. Gatherings and meetings could be prohibited, and high penalties were extracted for advertising or attending such gatherings. The definition of "intimidation" had been broadened, and the burden of proof put on the defendant. These measures struck at the very base of ANC control in the townships.

Legislation was accompanied by large-scale police raids all over the country aimed specifically at the unemployed and footloose young men known and feared as *tsotsis*. It was these *tsotsis* who had been the main intimidators for the ANC. They ensured that workers who might otherwise be reluctant to lose a day's pay by staying at home in an ANC-called strike did indeed stay at home. Huge numbers, estimated at something like 10,000, were arrested, and large numbers of weapons of all sorts were collected by the police. These raids, which broke the back of the ANC strong-arm teams, had been preceded by other raids aimed at bringing in such leaders as had earlier escaped the police net. Again army reserves were activated and put on a combat-ready footing. These steps against the would-be strikers were supplemented by warnings of dismissal issued to Africans in government service and in government-owned industries, such as the railways and the steel mills. Private industry followed the government's lead, warning workers that they would lose their jobs if they took part in the strike. But these were not the only obstacles the ANC had to overcome. The PAC, after a period of hesitation, roundly denounced the demonstration in both speech and print. Added to this defection, a mysterious series of leaflets of unknown origin urged Africans not to take part in the affair. These came out in the name of various African organizations that later denied having issued them.

There is little question, however, that the most effective single means by which the government ensured failure of the strike was by arresting the *tsotsis*. Once these were safely out of the way, workers returned to their jobs. As *Drum* put it: "The 'news' [of the failure of the strike] travelled fast—and many people trickled back to work because they believed that everyone else was at work and they did not want to be the only ones to suffer." [57]

Of course, failure could not be attributed to outside sources alone. Mandela, in the *Africa South* article, pointed to the inexperience of the ANC leadership in underground work. It had been, after all, no more than a scant fourteen months since the ANC had gone underground. This was insufficient time for the leaders to reorganize and retrain their cadres, who were accustomed only to legitimate ways of working. Lack of experience and the reduction of their numbers by the wave of arrests rendered them unable to cope with the barrage of propaganda from the government-controlled Radio South Africa, which continually broadcast messages to the effect that the strike had failed. Their ranks depleted, and deprived of the best leaders, those that remained were unable to attend to problems that arose "as the anti-strike barrage reached its climax during the fourteen days before the strike." [58] The only success that Mandela could claim for the strike was the expense to which the government had been put in frustrating it.

That constant critic, Jordan Ngubane, saw things in a different light. African failure, Ngubane wrote later, could not be seen only in terms of "state power" overcoming "heroic African opposition." Failure was due to other causes as well. The mass of Africans, for instance, looked to Albert Luthuli and not to Nelson Mandela for guidance. But Luthuli was deliberately kept in the background at the All-In Conference (which he was prevented by bans from attending personally), and it was on Mandela's authority, not Luthuli's, that the strike was called. The spending of large sums on propaganda could not overcome deficiencies in organization. The "invisible hand" to which Ngubane always referred, and which was obviously intended to represent the Communist Party, was, he argued, neither efficient nor thorough enough to ensure success. The strike, Ngubane conceded, had a moral effect. The government had to "pour millions down the drain" because a "few thousand Africans had met in Maritzburg and threatened

57. *Drum*, July, 1961.
58. "Out of the Strike," pp. 15–23.

to do certain things." [59] The elements of moral victory were there, but there was no material victory.

A variety of reasons for failure can be advanced which are, in many ways, more straightforward than those given by proponents and opponents of the ANC-inspired strike. The appeal was, in its general conception, too abstract to be attractive to large numbers of Africans. Opposing the establishment of "Verwoerd's Republic" was not an issue that caught their imagination. Most Africans felt that their lot would be little changed under a Republic dominated by Afrikaner Nationalists. They were disillusioned with mass campaigns that never succeeded. Had the leaders been at liberty, they might have overcome this apathy, but they were in prison or in hiding. Only Mandela's name was somewhat familiar. As *Drum* points out, he proved to be the best public relations officer that the ANC had ever had, but to many Africans he remained a shadowy figure, seldom seen, as he evaded the police. With public meetings prohibited, no new leaders could establish themselves, nor could they gather followings. The end result was that Africans were unwilling to sacrifice a day's pay for yet another failed campaign. By going back to work, they voted with their feet.

Even deeper causes for failure can perhaps be found. In asking the government to call a national convention, the ANC in fact conceded the government's legitimacy. It also was being unrealistic; on the one hand, the government was being asked for a concession, and, on the other, were the government to have acceded to the request, it would only have laid itself open to vituperative attack. The concession of this legality, the admission that it was only the government who could call the convention, doubtless also weakened the ANC case.

X

The stay-at-home campaign did teach ANC leaders one thing—that it was unlikely that they could shake the government with the methods of the past. New methods were clearly called for, and the question

59. Ngubane, *African Explains*, pp. 172–73.

now was what these were to be. A tapering-off of old procedures took place in the weeks that followed the establishment of the Republic. An "African Freedom Day," set for June 26, 1961, got virtually no response. But change was in the wind. As Mandela hinted to the press in a statement on the May strike, there was a rethinking among the African leadership: "Will the stay-at-home type of campaign be abandoned?" he asked. "The African people will understand that there is no sense in announcing our next tactics now. Let us just say that new ways will be found." [60] At long last, it seemed, the failure of passive resistance had convinced men like Mandela that there was nothing further to be gained by it. A resort to violence was all that remained. The die was cast. In partnership with the Communist Party, the planning of *Umkonto we Sizwe* began. Acts of sabotage were undertaken in the hope that these would lead to the downfall of the South African government. Should these fail, plans for *Operation Mayebuye* were devised.

It is difficult to know when these plans were put together in the form of a document. Clearly, the document formalized many ideas already current and extended the scope of actions already under way. Much of what the leadership of *Umkonto we Sizwe*, the organization that was to carry the plans into effect, had in mind was made clear when, in the police raid of July 11, 1963, masses of documents, along with their authors, were captured. A few words about the place where the plans were made and about the men who made them might facilitate understanding of what was involved.

The farm "Lilliesleaf" in Rivonia, near Johannesburg, was purchased as the headquarters for *Umkonto* and as a refuge for men on the run from the police. The purchase had been secretly arranged, through a white sympathizer, and every step possible was taken to ensure concealment. Lilliesleaf was a fairly large property, standing in some twenty-eight acres of farmland. *Umkonto* also came into possession of two other properties. A house named "Travallyn," on seven and one-half acres, was purchased in the Krugersdorp district of the Transvaal, seemingly to serve as an arms factory. A third house, a cottage in

60. *Drum*, July, 1961.

the Johannesburg suburb of Mountain View, was rented apparently as another hideout. The purchase of these properties involved money, more money than the ANC had had at the height of its legality. The Rivonia farm, for instance, was bought for about $44,000, and Travallyn for another $12,500. Although in neither case was the full purchase price paid, the money involved is an indication of the funds flowing to the ANC once it had firmly allied itself with the Communists. These funds came from a variety of sources. Some came from what were ostensibly charities abroad and were passed on to the ANC and *Umkonto* through the London offices of the former organization, and from there to its contact in Bechuanaland. Some funds came from African states, particularly after Nelson Mandela had paid them a visit. Other monies came from more mysterious sources. The known total, which came to *Umkonto* through a trust fund in the law firm in which one of the alleged conspirators was a partner, amounted to about $70,000. The Rivonia site, of greatest interest here, was fully set up to conduct underground activity, having such things as typing and duplicating equipment, radio transmitting and receiving apparatus, and a secret road by which it could be reached and left. Strict secrecy was applied even to ANC members, who could only secure contact with the national headquarters of the underground ANC at Rivonia by a complex system of contacts.

Secrecy was further fostered by an elaborate system of pseudonyms and disguises adopted by the ANC and Communist leaders at Rivonia. Ahmed Kathrada, an Indian, was disguised as a Portuguese and named "Pedro"; Walter Sisulu was "Allah," and Govan Mbeki was "Dhlamini." One of the whites, Dennis Goldberg, did even better; he had two pseudonyms, "Williams" and "Barnard." Lilliesleaf had been selected for its remoteness and, to add to the disguise, some genuine farming was carried on there. Care was taken to sell the produce, some of which even went to the local police station.

But farming was not of course the intended purpose of the Rivonia farm, for it was from here that *Operation Mayebuye* was to be conducted. The plan itself was a nine-page typewritten document. It called for the extension of sabotage and guerrilla warfare and the invasion of South Africa by foreign forces. The purpose of the plan was clearly set forth in its preamble: "[The state] has presented the people with only one choice, and that is its overthrow by force and violence." This overthrow was to be accomplished by sabotage and guerrilla operations, and the people in the rural areas (the "people" referred to in such documents are Africans only) would have to be trained to support the guerrillas. For this reason, great stress was laid on political work among Africans in the countryside. The plan itself followed the somewhat standardized procedure that has become a commonplace among advocates of guerrilla war. Initially, a "massive onslaught on selected targets" was to take place, and this would create "maximum havoc and confusion." Four areas were singled out for attack: Port Elizabeth, Port Shepstone, the northwestern Transvaal, and the northwestern Cape. In each of these "main areas," some 2,000 men would be deployed, except in the Cape, where 1,000 were deemed sufficient. Once the plan was in operation, it was estimated that the ranks of the insurgents would soon swell to some 7,000 men in each of the main areas.

The growing success of the guerrilla operation would open the way for the invasion of foreign troops, who would be aided by the guerrillas already operating in the main areas. Together, they would accomplish the overthrow of the South African regime.

Building even the initial force called for a core of "freedom fighters" who would be landed by submarine after having received training abroad. Four groups of about thirty men each would, thus, be landed in each of the main areas, and they would supply arms to the population and recruit the initial 1,000 or 2,000 with the aid of the population. Base areas would quickly be established, and the government, taken by surprise, would be unable to react, given the popular support of the insurgents. In due course, with the operation in progress, a political authority would be erected, and this would be transformed into a provisional revolutionary government. Support was, at the same time, to be expanded abroad. The international trade union movement was to be urged to press boycotts of trade, and a "noise" was to be made at the United Nations. These actions were to be combined with intensive propaganda inside the country, while acts of sabotage were stepped up further.

61

Clearly, *Operation Mayebuye* was an ambitious plan which, for its successful working, required that the government be both foolish and uninformed, neither of which could be said of the South African government.

The first steps to initiate action under *Mayebuye* had been taken. A number of committees, some of which will be discussed in more detail later, had been set up to handle such matters as intelligence, external planning, logistics, and transport. Reports from these were to be ready by May 30, 1963. Indeed, the year 1963 was to be the year of liberation.

There was, however, a vast and unbridgeable gap between plan and execution. The Technical Committee, for instance, called for the manufacture of some 210,000 hand grenades and 48,000 antiperson-nel mines. One of the committee drew the plans for a furnace in which parts of the grenades could be cast, and quotations were sought for wood of the size and thickness to make the mine housings. All this came to naught. It seemed unlikely that the raw material would be obtainable, let alone the feasibility of manufacturing and storing such a quantity of explosive devices. And even if these problems were to be overcome, the manufacture of such a quantity of arma-ments at Travallyn would have been bound to draw police attention.

In all, *Operation Mayebuye* was the stuff that dreams are made of. It had that element of fantasy that enters into all the plans and con-ceptions both of South African Communists and of the African organi-zations. The arrest of the leaders and the discovery of Rivonia de-stroyed the plan.

Resistance did not, of course, come to a close with the capture of the *Umkonto* leadership. Sabotage, it is true, declined almost to the vanishing point, and training for guerrillas in South Africa became virtually impossible. Training now had to be given abroad, and the trainees infiltrated into the country. How successful this has been re-mains an enigma. Information is hard to come by, and the informa-tion to be had is, naturally, biased and impressionistic. A report in the *Times* of London, based on a visit to Tanzania and Zambia by a team of its reporters, tells of arms and training being supplied by Communist China. A guerrilla training course takes six months, according to their information, and they have spoken to Africans who were trained there. Guerrilla bases have been set up in Zambia and Tanzania, and small-scale incursions against Rhodesia and South Africa have been mounted. The success of such attacks is, once again, hard to assess, but according to the *Times* team, little damage has been done. This seems borne out by the report of the Rhodesian chief of general staff, Major-General K. R. Koster, who spoke of a lull in guerrilla activity in 1968, due, he said, to the effectiveness of South African and Rhodesian countermeasures.[61] That the activity continues is attested to by the award of a medal for bravery to Constable F. J. Slabber for his part in repelling an attack on a police post at Chisuma (?) in which a number of police were wounded. The guerrillas, in this engagement, were described as having fought with "great determination." They were believed to be members of the (Rhodesian) Zimbabwe African Peoples Union.[62] Another source of news of continued resistance is the sentencing of men arrested for having undergone training abroad and returned to South Africa. These, again, are not many in number. It is clear, however, that such actions are continuing. What the ultimate outcome of the struggle is going to be is hard to foretell. It remains an open question.

Evidence that the ANC is perhaps still attempting to organize in South Africa is indicated by the arrest of the "22" on May 12, 1969. Brought to court on December 1, all pleaded "not guilty" to a variety of charges connected with ANC activity. The case continued for more than two months, with a number of state witnesses giving evidence of alleged physical and mental assault on them during police interrogations. The state did not challenge the truth of their evidence. The proceedings were stopped on February 16, 1970, when the Attorney-General advised the judge that he was stopping proceedings. He withdrew prosecution, and the "22" were found not guilty and acquitted. The court was then cleared, and the accused were rearrested under the Terrorism Act. Despite nationwide protest, as well as appeals

61. *Star*, July 7, 1970.
62. *Ibid.*, July 9, 1970; *Daily News*, July 9, 1970.

from relatives, the "22" were held in detention, and a decision was taken to bring some twenty of them to trial on August 3. The case was still proceeding as this book was written.[63]

With this the story comes full circle. It does not pretend to be a complete story. Many men, movements, and events have had to be omitted for lack of space. What has been said is, it is hoped, sufficient to provide a framework for the more detailed examination of revolution at the "grass roots" that follows.

63. For a summary, see *Cape Times,* June 17, 1970. The date of the trial is in the *Star,* June 19, 1970. The events and the protests were extensively reported in the South African press from the date of the trial to the time that the manuscript of this book went to press.

I

A Theoretical Framework of Protest

THIS BOOK is concerned with the organization of revolt in cities and towns, and in particular with the formative stage of that revolt, when cadres are being assembled, recruits are still few and largely untrained, and terrorists are hesitant and inexperienced. It is a theme on which little has been written. In order to make the theme comprehensible, and for its own intrinsic interest, the case of an attempted insurgency in South Africa is made central. The use of this case is not intended to exhaustively present what happened but to illustrate an aspect of and to illumine theory about revolutionary organization. The theoretical constructions and the conclusions are largely the author's own, supplemented with other ideas where necessary. But the very paucity of writing on the theme has made theoretical supports difficult to find in other works. Should readers wish to go beyond the perspectives of this study, should they want a larger picture of revolution, there is an excellent essay by Lawrence Stone that surveys the field.[1] As those who look to Stone will discover, most books on insurgency or revolution concentrate primarily on leaderships and on broad causes. In addition, there are "cookbook" studies of insurgency which are mainly concerned with providing governments, or sometimes insurgents, with

1. "Theories of Revolution," World Politics, XVIII (January, 1966), 159–77.

formulas for waging successful campaigns. If the formative phase of the insurgency is treated at all, it is covered in a few pages with a handful of generalities. Authors of such books are concerned with insurgency as a going concern, rather than with a revolt taking its first faltering steps.[2]

The theme of this book, then, is the initiation and early organization of urban revolt.

II

There are several ways in which the author's outlook differs from the more customary view of revolutionary organization, which owes much to Lenin, to his hagiographers, and to his imitators, and which can be called the bureaucratic and ideological view of revolution. In its pure form, this envisages a revolutionary organization as a cadre of professional revolutionaries, hierarchically organized, bound by ideology, acting in a planned fashion to bring about a revolution. It will be argued here that the ideological revolutionary bureaucracy is a myth, and that the theories based on this view are guilty of "bureaucratic" and "ideological" fallacies.

The "bureaucratic fallacy" is that which ascribes bureaucratic structure to revolutionary organization. It analyzes revolutionary organization in terms of hierarchies of command and in terms of flow charts and boxes. Instructions come from above; information flows up from below. The "ideological fallacy" is more subtle and insidious. It ascribes to the revolutionaries a structured set of values and norms, a shared ideology, which gives them their primary motivation. The view

2. The following works are typical in that they confine their discussion of the formation of insurgencies to a few generalizations in one or two chapters: Otto Heilbrunn, *Partisan Warfare* (New York, 1964), chap. 1; John J. McCuen, *The Art of Counter-revolutionary War* (London, 1966), pp. 30–35; John J. Pustay, *Counterinsurgency Warfare* (New York, 1965), chap. 4; David Galula, *Counterinsurgency Warfare* (New York, 1964), chap. 2; Roger Trinquier, *Modern Warfare: A French View of Counterinsurgency* (New York, 1964), chaps. 2 and 3.

to be urged here is that revolutionary organization is characterized largely by its absence, that it is loose and informal, and that there is little of a common ideology, unless a set of slogans, often only half-understood, can be so dignified.

What is the reason for these fallacies? This question can be answered only partially. It may seem strange that scholars and soldiers, given their differing aims and perspectives, should both begin with the same assumptions about revolution. The success of the Russian revolution and the persuasiveness of Lenin's doctrines doubtless have much to do with this. So, too, has the availability of material on the leadership of revolutions and insurgencies. This means, in turn, that revolutions are seen largely through the eyes of revolutionary leaders, whose descriptions often make them both advocates and judges in their own cases. Many of these men, speaking from hindsight, saw their organizations as bureaucratic and so described them in their writings. It is hardly surprising that those relying on these works mirror this perception. Then, again, by the time an insurgency is in full flower, the structure may well have hardened. The analyst, therefore, who arrives on the scene late, tends to describe the organization as if it had been there all along.

It is plain that neither the bureaucratic nor the ideological fallacy is confined to outsiders. For various reasons revolutionary leaders tend to foster either one or both of these fallacies among their own followers and to promote them to the world. The African National Congress, for instance, after it was declared illegal, sought to convince outsiders and insiders that it consisted of a tight net of cells, branches, district and regional councils, and a secretariat—all under a National Executive. Were anyone to read the M-Plan, which will be fully described later, the impression of hierarchic organization would be overwhelming. The real workings of the organization, which were quite different, would not be apparent.

Just as leaderships try to paint a convincing picture of an organization marching in lock step, so they try to convince everyone that their actions are governed by an articulated set of shared beliefs and practices. It can, indeed, be argued that the logic of the situation

67

compels leaders of an insurgent organization to do this. It is surely in their interest to convey the impression not only that those in the organization share a common set of beliefs bound in a program but also that this is shared by a great number still outside the organization. Yet this picture holds neither for leaders nor for followers. Leaders wage bitter struggles among themselves over the interpretation of the ideology—conflicts often more intense than those between the leaders and their outside opponents. Followers are often almost completely ignorant of the ideology and act for reasons little related to it. The impression of ideological unity is nonetheless fostered: first of all, because it gives the insurgent leadership a fighting edge over its opponents, themselves usually divided, by conveying to them that they are fighting a united force; and, second, it is more likely to elicit favorable response from other countries with a similar ideology. To the lower ranks it conveys the impression that their leaders are educated men who have a program, and who, therefore, can predict what is going to happen—and that what is going to happen is revolutionary victory, no matter how impressive the opponent's forces may seem. It also provides the basis for the shared set of slogans on which a perception of reality different from that of a nonrevolutionary majority is posited. This, however, is different from the rigorous mesh of values and norms customarily perceived as an "ideology."

If the notions of bureaucratic organization and ideological unity are rejected, what is to be put in their places? Here a theory of a general sort is proposed, one which deals not with factional conflict within groups, notably the government and the insurgents, but with conflict between them. Now to theorize one must abstract; and abstraction involves oversimplification. This is not a disadvantage, though it is sometimes interpreted as one. A simple theory with few variables, which is manageable, often has the virtue of providing both insights and a starting point for research, where a more complex theory merely leads to confusion. The fear of monistic explanations has, however, led many to confuse complication with quality and to assume that any theory that can readily be comprehended is necessarily bad. It has led to what Paul Roazen has called "a kind of pluralism; often the upshot is an unimaginative college-examination mentality." [3] No apology is therefore made for the relative simplicity of the theory to be forwarded here.

Understanding insurgency involves understanding a system theoretically free of insurgency—a system which, as an abstract construct, has no real counterpart. Although it will be called an "ideal" or "perfect" system, this is meant in a purely mechanical sense. No moral judgment is intended in this use of terms—rather the reverse, for most people would find such a system intolerable. It is posited as a point of departure rather than as something to be emulated.

A political system will be said to be functioning "perfectly" when everything that happens within it can be predicted with certainty. In the language of communication theory, it would be in a constant state of zero entropy. Although everything would be predictable, this would not mean that there were no changes but rather that changes would be known before they happened. [4] There would be no room for spontaneity in a system of this sort; every act would follow every other act in a certain fashion.

Although completely unreal in itself, a system such as this is the direction toward which all human organization tends. It is the apotheosis of bureaucracy. In crude form it is what all theories of bureaucracy can be reduced to. It is not confined to large formal groupings alone. Even small informal social groups, if Erving Goffman is right, have their own rules and ways of punishing transgressors. [5] The dream of mankind is to know the future. Organization, which orders relationships, procedures, and structures, makes for ease of prediction. Organization allows us to expect regular patterned behavior from others. The greater the extent to which behavior is made predictable, the greater the social order; and, in turn, the greater the order, the better the efficiency of prediction. Although a sterile and perfect order

3. See Paul Roazen, Freud: Political and Social Thought (New York, 1968), p. 89.

4. Ira G. Wilson and Marthann Wilson, Information, Computers and System Design (New York, 1965), chaps. 3 and 4.

5. See, for instance, his Behavior in Public Places: Notes on the Social Organization of Gatherings (New York, 1963); Encounters: Two Studies in the Sociology of Interaction (Indianapolis, Ind., 1961); and Interaction Ritual: Essays on Face-to-Face Behavior (Chicago, 1967).

would satisfy only robotlike homunculi, the craving for order among men is hardly to be denied. It is this craving that gives the work of theorists, such as Thomas Hobbes, its force and which is to be found even in the writings of modern sociologists of the consensual school. Talcott Parsons, for instance, points to the effort men make to remove "ambiguities" in the social system, either through government or in interaction with others.[6] So it can be said that the major function of government is to create and to maintain order. A government that cannot maintain order may continue as a government in law or in name but has ceased to govern in fact.

If it is agreed that governments exist to maintain order, then the purpose of insurgents is clear: It is to prevent the government from maintaining order. The aim of insurgents is to create and maintain an unbearable level of *dis*order. If they can do this for a long enough time, they will succeed; otherwise they will fail. Putting the point in slightly different form, the aim of insurgents is to prevent the political system from approaching "perfection" in the sense defined above. To decrease the level of predictability is to lower the level of perfection in functional terms. The function of the insurgent is to maximize the level of "imperfection." The "ideal" insurgent would completely achieve his aim if nothing in the attacked system could be predicted. Then disorder would reach an absolute limit. This, too, is an abstract construct. Any real system would break down long before this point.

Needless to say, neither insurgent nor government states its aims so crassly. Both set out symbolic aims such as "liberty," "equality," "popular rule," "expropriation of the expropriators," and so on. This is not to impute insincerity to either party in any conflict. They may believe in their own goals or use them to gain other ends. What matters here is not so much whether the goals are genuine, but rather that they are associated with order, on the one hand, and disorder, on the other. Order and disorder are not final ends but instrumental ends; for the government, order must be maintained to preserve certain value po-

6. William C. Mitchell, *Sociological Analysis and Politics: The Theories of Talcott Parsons* (New York, 1967), p. 29.

sitions, and for the insurgent, disorder is used to attain certain value positions, whatever these may be.

The ends of disorder cannot, however, be dismissed completely. In some groups disorder may have a ritual function; it may be part of a psychodrama demonstrating to polyarchies that a rising group is not powerless, that its politically relevant sectors wish to enter the political process. Disorder is fomented, certainly, by such groups, but they cannot be classed with insurgents. How then can groups engaging in ritual revolts be distinguished from those that aim at disorder and overthrow? The distinction is to be found in the purpose for which disorder is created. If the aim is to change the existing system, to create new patterns of prediction within it, then there is no insurgency. If the aim is to break the system apart so that an entirely new system can be substituted for the old, then there is an insurgency. An insurgent organization aims at the *complete restructuring of society by means of disorder.* This can be considered the complete definition of an insurgent organization. Thus, one can argue that before 1960 the African National Congress was not an insurgent organization and, indeed, dissociated itself from anything that could be construed as insurgency. After 1960 it associated itself with *Umkonto we Sizwe,* a sabotage organization it was instrumental in creating, and became part of an insurgency. In any case, it is only a small step from fomenting disorder for the redress of grievances to fomenting it for the purpose of restructuring the system. Nonetheless, as long as an organization aims at reform, it will not be defined as insurgent.

The definition of insurgency needs further elaboration. Implicit in it, for example, is the idea that the means by which disorder is achieved is less important than the creation of disorder itself. Insurgents have to be concerned less with individual acts than with the creation of a climate of uneasiness. Such uneasiness is the result of fear induced by terrorism. Because the terrorist strikes at random, his actions seem more threatening to individuals than the concrete result of any single action. Dramatic acts such as assassinations, bombs in supermarkets, and random attacks on individuals are less important for the numbers killed or wounded than for the shock waves they can set in motion. Indeed, given the right conditions, a climate of disorder greater than the disorder itself can be created. A grisly law of conservation of terror may enable an insurgent group to seem more powerful than its actions warrant, as rumor and misperception magnify their effectiveness. The law of conservation of terror also is reinforced if two similar terrorist attacks follow each other. The climate of civic violence in America was increased when the tragic assassination of President John F. Kennedy was followed by the assassination of Dr. Martin Luther King and later of Robert Kennedy. These acts seemed to symbolize a period of rising crime, unrest among the poor, and disaffection among intellectuals—a malheur which made "law and order" so appealing a slogan in the 1968 presidential election.

Isolated terrorist acts are not enough. Insurgents have to maintain the tempo of terror—to increase the rate of incidents until opposing formations are overloaded to the point of breakdown. As the frequency of incidents increases, the government's options shrink to the point where only surrender remains.

It is implicit in thinking of this sort that the government will be unable to mount effective resistance. Two reasons are given for this: first of all, the nature of the government's forces makes them unsuitable for unconventional warfare; and, second, history is on the side of the insurgent.[7] On the one hand, the forces of the government are assumed incapable of learning; on the other, moral corruption and infirmity of purpose will make the defeat of the government no more than a matter of time. In terms of the much-overworked "fish in water" theory, the people themselves will help the insurgents and hinder the government until, in the end, the government and the social system sustaining it are overthrown.[8]

As in all arguments, there is an element of truth in that of the insurgents. It may apply to corrupt polities, what David Rapoport has

7. For an extreme statement of the efficiency and power of insurgent organization, see Robert Taber, *The War of the Flea: A Study of Guerrilla Warfare in Theory and Practice* (New York, 1965), chap. 1.

8. This analogy—that the insurgent should be to the people as a fish is to water, swimming among them, separate but in a natural habitat, so to speak—is attributed to Mao Tse-tung and has been used again and again in books on insurgency.

called "praetorian societies."⁹ In such states government is emptied of purpose, becoming no more than a formless pursuit of individual gain on the part of rulers without popular roots. Governments in societies of this sort may well succumb to insurgency, as was the case with Batista's Cuba. The argument does not seem to hold where governments have the will and moral fiber to resist. Rapoport himself draws attention to this distinction, arguing that where "population" and "public" differ, conflicts between the two are almost like foreign wars in their effects. The threat from the "population" unites the "public" and the government; and if the armed forces are drawn from the "public," they will think no more of firing on the "population" than they would on a foreign foe. In South Africa, where the "public" is white and the "population" black, the army, drawn from the whites, would be fully ready to support the authorities in almost any circumstances.¹⁰

The insurgent myth is, however, based on an even more fundamental fallacy: that order is easy to shake. This illusion is not confined to revolutionaries but is shared by their opponents. David Galula, for instance, in a book on counterinsurgency, speaks of disorder as "the normal state of nature" and as "cheap to create and very costly to prevent."¹¹ Here the opposite argument will be put: that order is the normal state of things and that disorder is very difficult to sustain. This becomes evident where a revolutionary leader writes a candid account of his experiences, as did Che Guevara. Guevara pointed out that, though the Cuban peasants had little reason to love Batista, they continually deserted or betrayed Fidel Castro's forces.¹² The problem was even more acute in Bolivia and led to Guevara's death and the defeat of his forces. Guevara's principal lieutenant, on being granted

9. "A Comparative Theory of Military and Political Types," in *Changing Patterns of Military Politics*, ed. Samuel P. Huntington (New York, 1962). For a better exposition, see Huntington's *Political Order in Changing Societies* (New Haven, Conn., 1968), chap. 4.
10. David Rapoport, "The Political Dimensions of Military Usurpation," *Political Science Quarterly*, LXXXIII (December, 1968), 560–61.
11. Galula, *Counterinsurgency Warfare*, p. 11.
12. *Reminiscences of the Cuban Revolutionary War* (New York, 1968).

asylum in Chile, said that they could not win peasant support because "peasants are always with the forces of power and strength." [13]

It is not only peasants who will side with "forces of power and strength." Townsmen will do this also. The reasons are simple: Most "little" people are not much concerned with "big" issues—the cosmic concerns of political idealists are not for them. People, by and large, would rather be left alone to eke out their daily lives as best they can, to win their bread and whatever else is available for the winning. Mundane concerns such as these constitute an obstacle for both government and insurgents. The people, like the jungle, are neutral. They will side with whoever can best protect them. Protection means order. Disorder makes life difficult. Order is, therefore, the crucial issue.

The "minds of the people," it is therefore suggested, are "won" by the side that can maintain order. Rhetoric is not without effect for a time, but in the long run it is bread and butter that counts. If there are doubts on this score, one need look no further than Hadley Cantril's study of human concerns, which shows that economic welfare heads the list of personal and national concerns of his respondents, who represent some 863 million people in twelve nations.[14] The study showed that material concerns were uppermost among them, at least 60 per cent voicing personal economic hopes or fears. Similarly, the most common "power" value was security. The South African case might also serve as an example. The government of that country has been able to maintain stability in the face of a hostile world, to spark an economic boom of vast proportions, and to resist an incipient insurgency—all at the same time. It has been able to do these things without any hope of "winning the minds" of the majority—the blacks—who are denied most political and many economic rights. These achievements have been attained not only by repression but also by the maintenance of order and by economic improvement, some of which, at least, spills over to the black people.

The first point has now been made: to succeed, the African insurgents in South Africa would have had to maintain an increasing rate

13. "Guevara's Band Admits Failure," *New York Times*, February 24, 1968, p. 12.
14. *The Pattern of Human Concerns* (New Brunswick, N. J., 1965), pp. 69–70.

of disorder, beyond a level which the government could control. Their efforts to do this and the conclusions that can be drawn from such efforts will constitute a major part of the book. Disorder is not an end in itself, however, but only a means to an end. To produce disorder in an instrumental way calls for organization, and the nature of such an organization is an equally important part of this book.

III

Before describing the workings of an insurgent organization in its early stages, it may be well to reconsider its counterimage—the insurgent organization as it is popularly presented. The organization is shown as a tiered structure manned by a disciplined force under orders from a central directorate. It is described as a dedicated body of men and women ready to put orders into immediate effect—a band of ideologues able to wield pen or gun in their cause. This picture, which has been generally subsumed here under the heading of the bureaucratic fallacy, is misleading. Nonetheless, this is the image projected both by the insurgents and by their opponents. It may well be asked why this image is so persistent if it is grossly unreal. The perception of the insurgent organization as disciplined and ideological persists, it is suggested, because it serves the purpose of both sides. The counterinsurgents can better claim funds and measures of support from a government if the organization they are opposing is powerful. Should they suffer setbacks, these can better be explained away if the opponents are deadly and dedicated than if they are seen as an ill-organized band of ragamuffins. Defeating an armed rabble brings little glory; losing to them is worse. The existence of a powerful and organized opponent encourages cohesion and the sinking of factional differences among the government's supporters. The counterinsurgents thus have every reason to enhance the dangers their opponents present. The insurgents, on the other hand, need to gain support both at home and abroad. The willing or unwilling support of people in the country is easiest won if threats and promises appear to be made by a powerful body. For these and other reasons, therefore, both sides have everything to gain and little to lose by propagating the bureaucratic fallacy.

The matter goes deeper than mere image-building. Leaders of insurgent organizations seem genuinely fascinated by bureaucratic forms. They continually try to force their organizations into a bureaucratic mold, often with far from happy results. One reason for this effort is their need to maintain control of the forces they have brought into being. Such control obviously calls for a chain of command. The effort to create such a structure tends to break down fairly early, although it remains an ideal always in the minds of the leaders. The breakdown is due to the simple fact that it is almost impossible to carry out a revolution with a bureaucratic organization, the structure of which calls for order. To act at random seriously threatens the integrity of such a structure. Bureaucratic organization soon tends to lose revolutionary zeal and to establish an orderly relationship with outsiders, often the powers that be. The story of the German Social Democratic Party in the years before the First World War illustrates this theme. What began as a revolutionary workers' party ended as a bureaucracy loyal to the established order. Even if these factors were not to operate, however, technical considerations make bureaucratic forms dysfunctional for revolutionaries. The flow of information and directives essential to bureaucratic survival is easily disrupted. Bureaucracies are easily penetrated by hostile forces. Action on the part of bureaucracies is slow and tends to caution, whereas immediate decisions and bold action are absolute requirements in revolutions. The substance of revolutionary organization is, thus, very different from its perceived forms.

An insurgent organization can be said to pass through three stages from its conception. In the first phase a schema of organization is drawn up; in the second, attempts are made to put it into effect; and in the third, the organization emerges in its largely unstructured form, defying all attempts to restructure it. In the third phase, the structures imposed on the organization erode and condense into a variety of simpler, largely autonomous groupings. The tendency is for the intermediate levels to disappear, merging partly with the leadership and partly with the cadres. Leaders and cadres are, in turn, tenuously bound by some form of contact or mail-drop. Their functions are also differentiated: the leaders concentrate on the manufacture of slogans;

their followers concentrate on the construction of bombs. The slogans represent a broad indication of desired directions; and these are implemented, if at all, in the ways the autonomous activist groups interpret them. The leadership provides broad guidelines but can neither supervise effectively nor enforce policy. Yet, and this is of utmost importance, the preeminence of the leaders is not seriously questioned. The leaders are leaders and are so recognized. This is not at issue. What happens is that the organization is destructured and then regrouped in dual form; there is a leadership with one set of functions, and activists with other functions, the two being only loosely tied together.

So far we have been discussing leaders and cadres, and "the people" have been mentioned only incidentally. Yet the role of "the people" is perceived in most important ways by the insurgents. If we think of the insurgent organization as consisting of leadership and cadre, or "struggle group," the masses can be thought of as a "support group." These three levels make up the loosely articulated insurgent organization. The support group consists of "ordinary people" who often are not formally a part of the insurgent organization at all. They are, however, perceived to be broadly sympathetic to many of its ends, inasmuch as they understand them and can be relied on to appear in numbers at critical times. They come to parades and demonstrations, shelter men on the run, supply information, and pay "taxes." Their reasons for support may be mixed, varying from fear of retribution, to belief in the goals, to confidence of gain should the insurgents finally win. The aim of insurgents is to extend the boundaries of this group until it includes most of the population. Once this is accomplished, the "mass uprising" of which most insurgents dream will take place.

The idea of a mass uprising seems to dominate the thinking of insurgent leaderships in most parts of the world. It is based on the idea of disorder brought to the point where the masses will see that the government is corrupt and cannot protect them and, on discovering this, will overthrow it, and with it the social system. A mass uprising involves more than disorder; it also involves the people making the necessary connections between disorder, the sufferings imposed on them by the government in its efforts to suppress disorder, and the social system as a whole. Political education would have to be directed to this end, as the insurgent leaders well realize. The belief, nonetheless, has many qualities of a mystique. "Essentially it consist[s] of the belief that the [insurgents] could develop the revolutionary consciousness of [the masses] to such a pitch that at some golden moment there would come a spontaneous uprising, and the people would seize political power, led of course by the [insurgents]." [15]

The fact that the insurgent organization is not a mass movement, that the people are not, on the whole, part and parcel of it, means that substitutes for organization have to be found through which the support group can be extended and mobilized. To this end a political cadre organized into a series of "fronts" is employed. These "fronts," although more ideological in outlook than the insurgent group, tend to follow a similar pattern of organization. As Douglas Pike has pointed out, the National Liberation Front in South Vietnam began with a paper network of nationwide village associations and then proceeded to turn this paper structure into reality.[16] The front organizations are intended to reach groups not otherwise accessible and to win their cooperation. Trade unions, political clubs, and associations furthering a specific purpose are among the vehicles by which the insurgents hope to reach larger numbers. Many indeed have no overt political purpose. The target populations, such as students, women, peasants, workers, and so forth, may not even know that they are serving the insurgents' cause. Indeed, the success of many fronts is measured by how effectively they can conceal their political connections. They can, in this way, serve as a source for ideas without making the origin of the ideas known.

Ideally, the actions of the cadre, or struggle group, should evoke responses from the support group. The struggle group engages in persistent provocation of the authorities, courting reprisal as a lever to raise support among the uncommitted. Such interaction has been well described in a book by Patrick Seale and Maureen McConville on the French student-worker uprising of 1968:

15. Douglas Pike, *Vietcong: The Organization and Techniques of the National Liberation Front of South Vietnam* (Cambridge, Mass., 1966), pp. 76–77.
16. *Ibid.*, p. 110.

A tiny revolutionary avant-garde detonated a large scale spontaneous movement of student protest. This mass, generating its own
dynamic, could be only loosely manipulated and controlled by the
revolutionary core. It clashed with the police, threw up barricades,
bred a legend of heroism, occupied the universities. The students'
fighting example then fired the workers to strike and occupy in
turn. This was the next and vital stage, longed for by the revolutionaries, but only indirectly brought about by them. It was as if the
French industrial working class, lulled by the prizes of a consumer
society, had suddenly relearned from the students forgotten tradi-
tions of militancy.[17]

This description encapsulates the entire aim of the insurgents and describes the workings of the various groups. It is extended in an interview, described by the same authors, which a leader of the students,
Daniel Cohn-Bendit, gave to Jean-Paul Sartre. In this interview
Cohn-Bendit admitted that there was no question of overthrowing
"bourgeois society" in one fell swoop. The tactic was to stage a series
of revolutionary shocks, each of which was intended to set off an
irreversible process of change. These were to be the work of an activist
minority who were to be strongly grounded in revolutionary theory.
They were to act as "detonators" without attempting to control the
explosion they had touched off. The strength of their movement rested
on an element of uncontrollable spontaneity, Cohn-Bendit said, and
the aim was not to reform "capitalist society" but to break with it.[18]
Again, this conception of revolution accords well with that proposed
earlier in this chapter and reflects reality more closely than do many
more "sophisticated" arguments.

There would, thus, seem to be a discernible similarity of pattern in
insurgent organizations, particularly in the formative phase. Action
follows the establishment of the leadership group and the formation of
the first cells. Then either the leadership group and the cells work in
loose alliance, or an attempt is made to introduce bureaucratic forms.
Stratified organizations, when erected, either break down into a

17. *Red Flag, Black Flag: French Revolution 1968* (New York, 1968), pp.
16–17.
18. *Ibid.*, p. 17.

different form or cease to be revolutionary. Strangely enough, governments may mirror insurgents, or perhaps each mirrors the other. The government is, of course, formally structured as the conflict is joined. But in the course of conflict it too may break down. The central leadership might then act as a source of slogans, while administrators in the field, increasingly cut off from the center, are compelled by circumstances to act autonomously. It might then be suggested that development is asymmetric. As the insurgency succeeds, the insurgent organization becomes increasingly structured, while the government loses structure, becoming more like the insurgent organization at its outset. This, however, is an altogether different question; and although it is posed for the sake of interest, it will not be examined here.

IV

"The mere existence of privations is not enough to cause an insurrection," wrote Leon Trotsky; "if it were, the masses would be always in revolt." [19] Be that as it may, it would seem that a concentration of a potential revolutionary clientele is essential if an urban revolt is to take place. It is for this reason that what has popularly come to be known as the "ghetto" is a ready-made hotbed for insurgency. The complex geography of its alleys and byways, its streets and buildings, provides a better jungle than nature has provided in Vietnam.[20] It is in the ghetto that the revolution has to be forged; it is there that it draws its strength; and it is there that it has to be fought.

Ghettos have particular significance in the South African setting, for there is no city or town without one or more of them. There they are known as "locations"—actually, townships that are virtually separate (but by no means equal) black cities. The only contact between dwellers in the black city and those in the white city is an economic tie; blacks come to the white city or town to work or to buy, and these few contacts are being further restricted by government fiat. Each of

19. As quoted in Ted Gurr, *Why Men Rebel* (Princeton, N. J., 1970), p. 104.
20. Colonel Robert C. Rigg, "A Military Appraisal of the Threat to U. S. Cities," *U. S. News and World Report*, January 15, 1968, pp. 68–71.

the locations has unique features, and yet all have much in common. Those illustrated here were chosen not because they are the worst or the best but because they are featured elsewhere in this study or because material on them is available.

Since the events that are described in this book there have been vast changes, begun in the fifties and continued into the sixties, which have transformed the townships. An extensive program of slum clearance and rehousing has removed many of the excrescences that will be described, without, however, altering the basic pattern of segregation. Many of the conditions which existed at the time when *Umkonto we Sizwe* was operating have changed greatly for the better. The slums of East London, where much of the action to be described took place, have been almost entirely eradicated. Mdantsane, a new township, begun in 1963, where families are housed in unimaginatively but solidly built dwellings, each with its own plot of ground, has replaced the wood-and-iron shacks of the old townships. African housing, before that time, had consisted in small part of municipal houses and mainly of wood-and-iron shacks, unhygienic and unresistant to weather.

Wood-and-iron sections were to be found in all townships, though their extent varied. A description of such a section was published in the *Eastern Province Herald* of August 8, 1966, for its largely white readership. This description is reproduced below. The report describes the so-called Red Location—a name given it not because of its political coloration but because of the red blankets worn by Xhosa countrymen. It was, as the paper's correspondent wrote, "a mass of decaying wood-and-iron shacks and squalor":

Over the long rows of red shacks, built at the turn of the century, hangs a pervasive smell which lingers in the visitor's nostrils long after he has left the place. It is the smell of smoke from open fires and the stench of overflowing latrines.

This is the place which the Medical Officer of Health has said could be "the explosive force behind an outbreak of disease," and which a former mayor has called a "blot on the landscape."

Behind the long rows of shacks, most of which have crumbling doors, floors, and windows, there are smaller shacks. They are built of old barrels, paraffin tins, wood, scrap iron, rope, and string.

These crude homes, many of which house families of between eight and ten, stand barely five foot high. In some cases people have to crawl into them on their hands and knees.

Between each row of houses is a communal toilet and nearby a solitary tap, both of which serve hundreds of the location's residents. Water for washing or for other purposes often has to be carried hundreds of yards in buckets, barrels, and tins.

The toilets can be smelt from about 30 yards away as I learnt in a morning visit to the location. On several occasions I had to jump over the overflow that streamed from the latrines.

One woman said that there were days when the taps failed to work. She said that the bucket toilets were not emptied at the most important times—when the men spend the weekend at home.

In spite of the toilets the children urinate freely in the most convenient places.

Between the shacks of the overcrowded location wander donkeys, fowls, and other livestock. Mangy dogs grovel in the dust for scraps.

Children, scantily clad, and many with bloated stomachs, play in the stagnant water while their mothers wash clothes. The clothes are hung on fences, draped over roofs, and in places wash lines have been strung across the roads.

The gravel roads throughout the location are strewn with old tin cans, broken bottles, and other refuse. Large stones make them almost unnegotiable with a small car.

Between the rows of shacks women sat at tables selling raw uncooked meat. Flies buzzed from one bowl of meat to another.

Yet in spite of the location's conditions the people are always cheerful and friendly. They talk to visitors and wave as you drive past their homes.

It is hardly to be wondered that the townships serving Port Elizabeth for so long constituted a stronghold of the African National Congress. Conditions were equally bad in other townships without generating this solidarity. Solidarity was greater in the townships near Port Elizabeth because of their tribal homogeneity and early contact with Western ideas brought by missionaries.

The crux of the problem was the continual influx of country people.

Lawfully or unlawfully, they came to the towns in droves; and the wood-and-iron shacks were often erected by Africans to be rented to the new settlers. Every available bit of space was put to use. Houses were built two to three feet from the curbside, with only a maze of narrow alleys, running in all directions, separating them. Once built, the houses were let and sublet, with the object of getting as many people into a room as it could hold. The residents were mostly men— migrant workers—and the more that could be squeezed into a shack, the more the revenue that could be derived. Tenants, in their turn, sublet their bit of space to spread the burden. The results were obvious: dangerous crowding and the deterioration of health.[21]

Even before the government entered the field with major slum-clearing schemes, a little had been done by the white municipalities, though four-fifths of the township dwellers lived in wood-and-iron shacks. As one report put it:

African townships have two faces. There are new rows of cinder-block family houses . . . [and] despite determined efforts at construction the flimsy [wood-and-iron] shacks also remain, forming a sleazy satellite town to the neat cinder-block locations.[22]

Such was the physical environment in which the organizations we will be dealing with flourished. Much of what took place originated in the wood-and-iron sections of the locations, such as the Tsolo section in East London. The poorest parts of the locations were seedbeds not only of crime but also of revolt.

What were the effects of these surroundings on the way Africans saw political possibilities? It is difficult to generalize on the political attitudes of Africans. There is, of course, much spontaneous resentment of government policies and of the way in which they are enforced. The picture is complicated by two other factors. The first is that political opinions are often expressed in clichés culled from the press and from political leaders—both white and black. The second is

---

21. Much of the material on East London townships in the preceding paragraphs was from B. A. Pauw, *The Second Generation: A Study of the Family among Urbanized Bantu in East London* (London, 1963), chap. 2.
22. S. Nolutchungu, "Time to Remember," *Sunday Times*, August 7, 1967.

that Africans are subject to certain pressures from among their own ranks, the nature and extent of which are difficult to define. There is much sympathy for nationalist movements, but often this is not backed by a desire to participate personally.[23] Both B. A. Pauw and Philip Mayer, for instance, agree that the membership of the ANC did not comprise more than 10 per cent of the township dwellers at the best of times and that activists were even fewer.[24] Even so, it is worth noting that this is a higher proportion than held true for the country as a whole, where membership was nearer one-half of one per cent.

It can, of course, be argued that radical organizations generally have small memberships. Without going into a detailed comparison, the findings in American cases are interesting. For instance, in a survey of ghetto violence, T. M. Tomlinson found that 62 per cent of his respondents saw the riots as a Negro protest. Only 38 per cent described them in terms of revolutionary rhetoric. To 64 per cent the riots were justified and the victims deserving of attack. The significant fact is that few of those asked feared white retaliation; those fearing unfavorable consequences totaled only 18 per cent, while another 24 per cent were uncertain of the outcome. Nevertheless, the actual number participating was only some 15 per cent. The clue to this difference in affect may lie in the respondents' fear of harm to themselves or to their property, for 71 per cent expressed dismay at the killing, burning, and destruction.[25] Were a similar poll taken in South Africa—in itself unlikely—many of the answers might be similar, with perhaps greater fear of retaliation. Although there are no survey findings, the response of Africans in East London to the riots at the time of the Defiance Campaign of 1952 does provide some clues.

The riots that broke out in 1952 alienated much of the support of the ANC in that area. Though sparked by an incident in the Defiance Campaign, the riots were also an outcome of the internecine strife in the ANC in East London. Quarrels and splits among the ANC leaders

23. Pauw, *Second Generation*, pp. 184–85.
24. *Ibid.*, p. 184; and Philip Mayer, *Townsmen or Tribesmen: Urbanization in a Divided Society* (London, 1961), pp. 52–53.
25. "Negro Reaction to the Los Angeles Riot and the Development of a Riot Ideology," unpublished manuscript, 1968.

had delayed the start of the campaign by one month; and, as a result, it seems, the campaign was pursued with more than ordinary intensity. Not only were Africans called on to defy laws, as called for by the leadership, but also inflammatory speeches were made in the poorest parts of the townships. These were not without effect. Anger and resentment grew in the wood-and-iron sections. Concerned at the growing signs of unrest, the government banned all public meetings in November of 1952. In spite of the ban, a large crowd collected in one of the squares of the township for what had been advertised as a "religious service," although everyone knew it was to be a political meeting. No sooner had the meeting opened than a detachment of police arrived and ordered the crowd to disperse in five minutes. The crowd disregarded the order. The police then hurled themselves forward in a baton charge. The Africans threw rocks. The police opened fire with small arms. The crowd then dispersed and the police returned to their station. On returning they heard that the mob had turned on the few whites in the township at that time and were killing them. The dead were chiefly business people, but one case seemed particularly shocking. Sister Aidan, a medical nun who had devoted her life to care of the sick, was killed, her mutilated body being found beside the wreckage of her car. Pieces of flesh had been cut from her body and eaten by African women who had hoped thus to absorb her (to them) magical powers of healing.

Writing of these events, D. H. Reader, whose account is largely used here, has this to say: the riots occurred mainly in the shack areas of the location, and the main brutality was the work of young boys and girls. The riots broke out spontaneously, after provocation, at the end of a long period of incitement. Finally, many of the shack dwellers stayed away during the riots; only a minority took part. The riots were a response to the overcrowding, indecency, vice, and lack of privacy, accompanied by the measures of control to which the inmates were every day subjected. Sullen apathy was replaced by malignant rage when the wailing of those hurt at the meeting was taken up by antisocial unemployed youths known as *tsotsis*. The riot remained largely a shack riot, for few from the nearby municipal houses joined in; they had too much at stake to commit themselves actively. They had their homes and gardens to consider, for such accommodation was scarce. "Bolted doors and silent streets were the order of the day in municipal housing during the disturbances, and many of the residents sought safety in flight or at the police station."

It was hardly surprising that the main violence should have come from the *tsotsis*.

Offspring of temporary and shiftless liaisons, involuntary by-products of one of the few leisure-time activities available to the shack-dweller, they had come into the world unwelcomed and un-loved, an additional burden on already overtaxed resources. . . . Often, by a hideous process of natural selection, these gangs were the more alert, the more crafty, the more vicious of an unoriented and dispossessed class. . . . Rejected alike by the society which spawned them and by the economy in which they had no place, these children distilled in their moment of frenzy all the bitterness felt by their community at large against those who appeared to crush and exploit them.[26]

At that time any white person, no matter how well known and well loved, would have been struck down. Humanistic or individual as-sociations cannot be pleaded in this context, according to Reader. Yet, after the events, genuine horror seems to have been felt by the older and more respectable residents, especially at the murder of Sister Aidan, whom many had known. The waves of shock spread even to the shack area, and it is estimated that some 5,000 left in the next three months. The African National Congress lost face and had not re-covered by 1958, six years after the events described.[27]

The riots have been treated at some length not only because of the comparison they afford with those in the United States but also because of their effect on the ANC. These incidents must be borne in mind when the actions of the ANC in East London are considered later, for they reflect on the options open to that organization and to the sabotage group. The immediate effect seems to have been to show how limited the appeal of violence is. It is estimated, for instance,

26. D. H. Reader, *The Black Man's Portion* (London, 1961), p. 28.
27. *Ibid.*, pp. 25–30.

that no more than 2,000 of the 50,000-odd inhabitants of the townships took part. The difference in levels of participation—15 per cent in America and 4 per cent in South Africa—may be taken to reflect something of the difference in fear of retaliation between people in the two countries. This does not mean, of course, that those who did not participate abstained because they loved whites and were satisfied with their lot. The reactions of those who did not participate were probably similar in both countries. In South Africa, and apparently in America as well, there was a sense of racial separateness, an inclusive African nationalism, a consciousness of racial distinctiveness and identity, even when cooperating with whites. The South African situation was made more complex by the legal disabilities of Africans and by tribalism, for, even when nationalistic in outlook, Africans retained their sense of the tribe to which they belonged and were determined to uphold its identity.[28]

A variety of sources can provide us with information on African attitudes. For the urban African generally, the study of C. J. de Ridder is still standard. There is also a major study by Leo Kuper, and a number of individual surveys. One of the most interesting studies, however, appeared in the *Rand Daily Mail*, a Johannesburg newspaper, of November 1, 1965. The writer of the article, who visited a number of shack dwellers, says that the walls were hung with pictures of the household's political heroes, Robert Sobukwe, Nelson Mandela, or Albert Luthuli. The article says:

The cheap printed portraits are getting tattered now, most of them were distributed before the demonstrations of 1960. But the words "People's Hero" are still printed beneath them. And the residents of the shacks tell the visitor that Sobukwe, Mandela, or Luthuli are still their heroes, although they shake their heads vaguely when you ask them when they might come to power.[29]

Middle-class Africans seem to be more politically conscious and more articulate. Surveys among them show some expected and some

28. Pauw, *Second Generation*, p. 186.
29. The author of the article did not say whether the interviewer was white or African; this might have affected the answers.

unexpected results. A survey by E. A. Brett, conducted for the South African Institute of Race Relations, shows that a sense of non-white racial solidarity hardly exists. Africans tend to prefer white South Africans of English descent to either Indians or Coloureds. Whites of Dutch descent (Afrikaners) are strongly resented and seem to serve as a target for much of the hostility to whites as a group. More significant, for what is discussed later in this book, is that the survey shows that in 1963 the Pan-Africanist Congress was more popular than the African National Congress. Where existing political parties were concerned, the Liberal Party, which accepted racial equality, was naturally the most popular. This was closely followed by the Progressive Party. The parliamentary opposition to the Nationalist Party, the United Party, was rejected as little different from its opponents. So strong was the preference for the Liberal Party that, as a body, it was preferred to the Congress of Democrats, with which the African National Congress was allied. Kuper has written:

> Race consciousness is canalized in a sharply antagonistic form by both the concept and the reality of races in competition for power and wealth, while discrimination is invited, since self-preservation [for whites] is assumed to depend on withholding from the subordinate races, as far as possible, any opportunity which might contribute to their power as competing groups.[30]

The African middle class, aware of racial competition, resents the denial of access to power and wealth and realizes that there is little to choose between English- and Afrikaans-speaking whites in this respect, it being merely a choice of harder or softer discrimination.[31]

The preference for the PAC, which was most evident among younger men, was due to a belief that it had a better answer to the African's problems than had the older ANC. They believed that its brand of militancy would be most effective in shaking and perhaps even in overthrowing the government. Looking into means, Brett and

30. Leo Kuper, *An African Bourgeoisie: Race, Class, and Politics in South Africa* (New Haven, Conn., 1965), p. 36.
31. Pierre L. van den Berghe, "Race Attitudes in Durban, South Africa," in *Africa: Social Problems of Change and Conflict*, ed. Pierre van den Berghe (San Francisco, 1965), p. 254.

his colleagues found that most of those questioned were willing to accept a great deal of aggression, nearly half holding that the use of force was inevitable, since all peaceful means of protest had failed (by 1963). The degree of violence that respondents would accept tended to correlate with support for PAC and rejection of ANC, the former tending to attract the more violent and aggressive members of the middle class. These constituted a majority, for of those sampled less than a fifth held that consultation and airing of grievances would be the best way of influencing the government.

Despite these findings, it would possibly be an error to see the middle class as a whole as militant. The *Rand Daily Mail* report, cited earlier, makes this point. Pictures of African leaders are rarer in the cinder-block homes of the middle class and are less prominently displayed.

Though far from palatial, the cinder block homes have more furniture showpieces and it is almost as if the first stirrings of middle-class affluence have downgraded the "People's Heroes." The new homes also contain a fair sprinkling of men who say that they have given up on the dreams of the ANC and the PAC [that was, after all, 1965] and grasped those of Dr. Verwoerd's separate development. This shift comes not from the heart but from political realism . . . nearly all those who support separate development have told they would prefer integration. "But let us be realistic," one said, "the Whites won't let us in." They believe that this ap-plies to nearly all Whites—United Party supporters who may be more subtle about it as well as Nationalists.

Some individuals to whom the reporter spoke said that they preferred the Nationalists in power. They believed that if power were in the hands of the United Party separate development would be neglected without any compensating increase in integration.[32]

A marked shift in perception of political realities can be traced if the two reports are taken together. The tracing can also be extended

32. The "Bantustans" are the separate autonomous areas which the government is developing and in which Africans will have the vote and a number of ministerial and administrative positions. See also p. 92 below.

back to the fifties and early sixties. These shifts can, of course, be set out in only the most general terms. Prior to 1960 there was a strong belief among those politically relevant and their supporters that militant nonviolence could induce a change of heart among certain classes of whites. The idea was abandoned after 1960, to be replaced by a belief that a more violent militancy would induce desirable changes. The new mood seems to have lasted until 1963, when the police began breaking up the secret organizations of both ANC and PAC. So, by 1966 many intelligent Africans had apparently resigned themselves to the inevitable. They were willing to try the government's separate development plans as a second-best alternative.

Resignation to political realities involved psychological costs difficult to estimate. Many Africans, condemned to a vegetable existence in the townships, lost their self-respect. The African bourgeois was, in any case, in an anomalous situation. The professional man, in particular, suffered from status incongruities of a special sort. As Kuper describes it, the exaggerated adulation which he received from his own people contrasted with a "contemptuous denigration of his ascribed racial status by Whites." [33] It is inevitable that members of the African bourgeoisie should have reacted with deep resentment against this degradation of their status and should have sought to set aside a system which imposed on them such humiliating conditions of living.[34] The failure to do this and subsequent resignation to the inevitable were damaging. The plight of these people is set out almost poetically by Sam Nolutshungu: "I saw men of stature, sensitive and intelligent, crumble one after the other. The acid of their lives had consumed them." [35]

The bourgeoisie is only a small proportion of the African population, although its numbers have slowly been increasing. The great majority of urban Africans are laborers, unskilled or semiskilled, many of whom are recent arrivals from the countryside with their roots still in the soil. The town dwellers, according to Nolutshungu, live in an ambiguous world—a world that remains partly traditional but has become

33. Kuper, *African Bourgeoisie*, p. 398.
34. *Ibid.*, p. 401.
35. "Time to Remember."

partly modern. There is a weird intermingling of values, of traditional social morality and "half-understood, half-accepted standards of White civilization." [36] This description accords closely with the more scientific findings of de Ridder. Africans, he found, are still rooted in the beliefs of their ancestors. They still hold to witchcraft and magic, accompanied by religious bewilderment when these clash with the relatively "new" ideas of Christianity.[37] Fact and fantasy conflict, producing a confusion of imagery. This confusion, in turn, seems to contribute to the deep-seated feelings of anxiety and insecurity induced by the attacking environment in which they live their lives. Africans have to fear not only their own people but also the power of the police, who are unable to protect the individual from thugs and also contribute to anxiety by arresting people for minor contraventions of the law. To the fear of assault and attack are added fears of curses, spells, and the "evil eye." The absence of protection anywhere adds to a sense of helplessness and frustration.[38]

The effect of this frustration is a strong latent aggressiveness which is not balanced by sufficient moderation or control.[39] This is expressed in violence toward others, African or white. If an African attacks, the argument runs, he can only attack with violence. Clearly, the conditions that have been described are not conducive to gentleness. Illegitimacy, lack of parental love and guidance, a high rate of unemployment, fear of aggression by others (physical or supernatural), and police restrictions, together with low wages, are not likely to breed a saintly outlook. It is not to be wondered at if African townsmen, in a hostile environment, view the world with hostility.

Another finding of interest is the African's obsession with money. The quest for more money, de Ridder states, has become the African's basic motivation. Limited by law in the range of occupations he can choose from, the African moves from job to job in search of higher wages. When this search is thwarted in any way, hostility to whites as

---

36. *Ibid.*
37. C. J. de Ridder, *The Personality of the Urban African in South Africa: A Thematic Apperception Test Study* (London, 1961), p. 104.
38. *Ibid.*, p. 82.
39. *Ibid.*, pp. 86, 158–59.

a group grows greater. The main crux of black-white hostility, according to these findings, is the sense that the white man is, for his own gain, preventing the African from increasing his earnings. He feels exploited and underpaid. Exploitation is not a figment of the urban African's imagination. Although wages and conditions are slowly improving, the vast majority of Africans still live from hand to mouth, unable to maintain a proper diet or a decent way of living.[40]

In an insecure world the known gives comfort; and it is for this reason, perhaps, that the cities and townships are not the solvent of tribalism. "Africanism" is a political concept and is used in the "unity is strength" kind of argument. For the vast majority of Africans, however, tribal affiliation is still the fundamental association.

> Detribalization . . . is exemplified rather by the neglect and disuse of many traditional tribal folkways rather than by an absolute rejection of the mores of [white] society. The completely tribally emancipated African is a psychological rarity.[41]

The extended family provides the urban African with some measure of security, and his fellow tribesmen will help in his encounters with "strangers." They will also assist in the search for a better job and provide food and shelter while it is sought, often at the cost of some unsuspecting white employer. An additional and by no means minor factor reinforcing tribalism is the government's promotion of tribalism as part of its separate development policies. These policies, although restated in different forms at different times, are in general aimed at preventing black solidarity through establishment of tribal "nations" within tribal "homelands." To this end, education in African languages is encouraged, tribes are often residentially segregated, and feelings of tribal exclusiveness are generally promoted. These actions reinforce the other factors referred to above.

This is not to deny the existence of the African nationalists who, even if they are not entirely free of tribal ties, are more politically motivated than many of their fellows. The African nationalist, according to de Ridder's findings, is among the more intelligent and

40. *Ibid.*, pp. 92–94, 164–65.
41. *Ibid.*, pp. 160–64.

ambitious of his people. He is more conscious of discrimination and more outspoken about it. Indeed, it is his extreme consciousness of discrimination that distinguishes the African nationalist from others. Other Africans also feel the lash of discrimination, but with the nationalist it becomes an all-consuming passion. The nationalist, like most Africans, seldom voices hostility to individual whites; it is the police—the various bodies administering the laws that control him—and the government that are the main objects of enmity. The weapons used by African nationalists, de Ridder wrote in 1961, were boycotts and strikes. Rioting was more associated with police raids on African beer halls than with political action. The weight given strikes and boycotts came from the realization of the importance of African labor to the economy. Withdrawal of labor was seen as a means of prying concessions from the government. The terms "strike" and "boycott" had become militant catchwords, though boycotts were considered to be better as they reduced risk of involvement with the police.

Despite his greater awareness and militance, the African nationalist seemed a strange amalgam of revolt and dependency. Although he perceived the government and its agents as "the enemy," he also perceived it as amenable to reason. The aim of political pressure was to get the government to "give" freedom, to which end the government was to be induced to "call" national conventions which would grant the African what he wanted. When these things did not happen, the African nationalist felt angry and frustrated, not understanding why his reasonable requests had failed to meet with a readier response. Thus, the apparently unreasonable nature of the authorities, and of the whites as a group, added to other frustrations. Restricted on all sides, the African nationalist envied all the more the "wonderful glow of the white race"—the glow of money, opportunity, and power.[42] The most fitting close to this chapter is, perhaps, the words of Nolut-shungu: "For kindness the African has learnt to accept charity; for legality, the liberties of a pampered gendarmerie—avid of wrongful power and taught by years of precedent and error to mete out un-evenhanded justice."[43]

42. *Ibid.*, pp. 118–28.
43. "Time to Remember."

II

The Reconstruction of the ANC

AN ORGANIZATION must obviously change drastically if, after a period of toleration, it is to exist in defiance of the law. How great the changes must be and how easily they can be made vary from one organization to another but depend on how it was structured before being banned. The final form it will assume, once it is illegal, will depend partly on this, partly on the wishes of its members, and partly on the pressures exerted by those ranged against it. A small, tightly knit band, conspiratorial in character, could probably adapt to underground operation quite easily. It is a different matter when the organization is as sprawling and ill-disciplined as the African National Congress was in 1960. The members of the ANC were among the most independent-minded of Africans, volatile and talkative. The organization, largely urban, was concentrated first in two and later in three major cities. The traditional strongholds were Johannesburg (along with the Witwatersrand) and Port Elizabeth, which were some 800 miles apart. Durban, which was 400 miles from Johannesburg, had always had an active ANC, but the membership expanded greatly in the late fifties. Coordination and communication were difficult, a difficulty compounded by tribal differences in the three centers. As a result, each area functioned more or less independently, having loose connections with the national headquarters and marginal connections with the others. This had not been intentional. The aim was to have a multi-tiered, closely knit organization, with all parts acting together in response to instructions and directives from above. If the annual reports of the ANC Secretariat are taken seriously, and there is no reason why they should not be, the organization was continuously plagued by problems of discipline and unity in action.

A brief discussion of the structure of the ANC in its palmy days of legality may assist an understanding of the changes that followed when it went underground. As planned on paper, the ANC had a series of hierarchies—national, provincial, and local. In theory the highest body was the National Conference of the ANC, which met once a year. This was a large and unwieldy body, with members from all over the country; and the organization would have been hamstrung had it been dependent on policy matters being proposed and decided there. A National Executive Committee, often referred to as the NEC, was therefore empowered to decide policy matters between meetings of the National Conference. But, as with the conference, the members of the NEC were scattered and could only be brought together with difficulty. As a result, policy matters were in effect decided by the Working Committee of the NEC, whose members had to live within a radius of fifty miles of Johannesburg, the national headquarters of the ANC. This arrangement gave a dominant place to the ANC leaders in the Transvaal, which was resented in the Eastern Cape and contributed to the lack of harmony.

The provinces, in their turn, had Provincial Conferences, similar in intent to those of the national body, and Provincial Executives. They had no Working Committees, for it was assumed that, as the provincial headquarters corresponded with the main provincial centers, there would be no difficulty about meetings. In addition, there were branches and regional committees. The regional committees are something of a mystery, and it is difficult to know precisely how many there were or what they did. Some of those involved in the cases speak of the Cape being divided into an eastern and a western region; others speak of further divisions elsewhere. The question of how many regions actually existed is only of academic interest. However, the ways by which the regions attempted to achieve the purposes intended for them is interesting and will be discussed below.

The branches are in general more important from our viewpoint, and are treated in more detail later. A few comments may nevertheless be appropriate now. The branches operated openly when the ANC was still legal. The minimum membership for a branch was ten members, but branches varied in size from no more than ten to one or two thousand. Since membership fluctuated and no records were kept, their size is a matter of estimate. There were a number of reasons for this fluctuation, one being that members became valuable only at two times in the year: when dues were to be collected, and before a National Conference, when representation depended on the number of members enrolled. Another cause of rising and falling enrollment was the success or failure of one or another ANC campaign. The inflow and outflow of members, largely uncontrolled, made the ANC a poor vehicle for covert activity.

Although the ANC operated openly before 1960, secret groups nevertheless formed within the organization. Some of these were devised to serve the individual interests of a leader, such as the "Bafabegiya," which was intended to keep MacDonald Maseko, a branch leader, in power. Others were shadowy and seem to have worked outside the branches. An example was a group which, according to rumor, was known as the "Silent Sixteen" and was believed to have burned down the offices of the (white) superintendent of their township near Cradock in the Eastern Cape. According to the same source, this group was active from 1955 to 1957, but little solid evidence of its activities emerges.[1] It may have been a part of the "Freedom Volunteers" which the ANC recruited at this time to help in their campaigns, or it may have been part of a *tsotsi* gang. *Tsotsis* were known to form gangs with colorful names, such as the "Spoilers" or the "Msomi."[2] The "Silent Sixteen" may have been such a gang, or it may have been a gang operating within the ANC although not necessarily with the

1. Sikaka/*Buka*, p. 5.
2. De Ridder, pp. 82–83, 150; see also *Star*, November 28, 1962, and January 7, 1963.

knowledge and consent of its leaders. One thing seems clear: the frustration which the ANC policy of nonviolence, then in practice, must have generated may have induced some of the younger men to take matters into their own hands. They are mentioned not for their historic importance, which is slight, but rather to indicate some of the undercurrents flowing through the still legal ANC.

The driving force for militancy in the late forties had been the ANC Youth League, also known by its initials, ANCYL. Although viewing the ANC as its "mother body," the Youth League was independently organized. The arrangement was, however, that one could not be a member of the ANCYL without at the same time being a member of the ANC. Even where these bodies had separate leaderships (with some overlapping) one was part of the other. The ANCYL leadership was, however, the more radical of the two. The ANCYL thus acted as a pressure group, attempting to change the mother body's policies when these did not seem sufficiently militant. The Youth League had a ceiling age of thirty years and was a small body, reportedly having only some 120 members in 1949. As its members played increasingly important roles in the ANC, and as they grew older, they became less willing to accommodate those who took their places in the ANCYL. They now urged the younger men not to engage in criticism of the mother body but, instead, to concentrate on drawing the "masses of the youth" into the ANCYL and thus also into the ANC.[3] The ANC, in addition to the Youth League, had a Women's League; however, it is not very significant for our purposes.

This brief description might convey the false impression that the ANC was far more structured than it was in fact. The autonomy of the different components has been mentioned and must again be stressed. The branches, in particular, not only acted on their own, putting whatever interpretation they chose on directives from national or provincial bodies, but also seldom informed higher bodies of their activities. Branches were formed and vanished without anyone higher up knowing much about it. Worse still, the branches were tardy in remitting funds, although the ANC Constitution required them to do

3. Mbanjwa/Mbolompo, p. 744.

so. Consequently, the ANC treasury was often empty and important work was stalled. The flow charts, in short, bore little relation to reality, for the ANC had no more than a rudimentary structure.

II

If a "political struggle" is distinguished from an "armed struggle," as it is in the context of Vietnam, then by 1960 it would seem that the political struggle in South Africa was lost. By the middle of 1961 the ANC leadership realized that their years of nonviolent protest had yielded little return. The idea of continuing with some form of armed struggle was now pressing. The prosecution of such a struggle meant organization, and the question of form now had to be decided: Was the ANC to be a body of professional revolutionaries in Leninist style, or was it to continue to cultivate a mass base? If the mass base was to be retained, how could this be done by an illegal organization? These questions obviously needed to be answered.

The idea of underground organization of the ANC was not new in 1960. There had, for some years, been fears that the organization might be banned, and a plan had been drawn up by Nelson Mandela (for whom it was named the M-Plan) which was intended to make it possible for the ANC to continue in spite of the law. In the mid-fifties, when the plan was first put forward, there was little serious effort to apply it; since it departed sharply from earlier practices, it met considerable opposition. As a plan it was not particularly original, following in its outlines the traditional pattern of secret organization. The basic unit was the small *cell*, a number of which were linked to the next highest unit, the *zone*, by *contacts*. The zone was to be similarly tied to a *branch*; the branch, to the *region*; and the region, to the National Executive Committee. The key men were obviously the contacts, for theirs was the task of ensuring the downward flow of directives and the upward flow of information. They were the links in the chain of command. If all went smoothly, the National Executive Committee would be in control of the organization. It would know what was happening at the grass roots, and the branches and cells would know what was wanted by their leaders.

The seven members of each regional committee were to be appointed by the National Executive Committee and were intended to replace the old provincial committees, which were unpopular among the more militant members of the ANC. Each province was to be divided into one or more regions, with Natal, for instance, being divided into seven.

The task of the regional committee was to ensure that the ANC retained a broad base for the coming conflict. Although the main burden of the armed struggle would fall elsewhere, the ANC was to continue its political work among the African masses. To this end, the seven members of each regional committee were to divide their region into branches, appoint branch committees, and then help them in zoning their branches and subdividing the zones by streets and blocks. They were to supervise the branches, once formed, and see to it that the work of the ANC was done. The ANC had been a democratic body, with the election of officials at all levels. This practice had to be abandoned once the organization went underground, as it was practically impossible to carry out.[4] The regional committee appointed the branch committee; this in turn appointed a zone leader, termed a *chief steward*; and he together with the branch secretary appointed individual cell leaders, known as *cell stewards*, one for each street or block.[5] Care had to be exercised that cell stewards did not duplicate cell memberships; this was done by permitting recruitment only from the area under each cell steward's jurisdiction. An overlapping membership was dangerous because it meant that a man might know more than the members of his own cell. As the ANC was always plagued with informers and probably with provocateurs, this was a necessary precaution.

4. Mbanjwa/*Mbolompo*, p. 755; Njikelane/*Rvtr*, pp. 23–24; Kunene/*Ngakane*, pp. 125–26.
5. Petros/*Makinane*, p. 49.

III

The purpose of the M-Plan was to replace public meetings, the main way in which the ANC's diverse bodies had worked, with face-to-face contacts among small groups. A major problem in applying the plan was the general looseness of the ANC as a body. No one really knew how large the organization was, who was and who was not a member, and who was in which branch. Estimates of its size varied greatly and depended on who was making the estimate. The police put its membership at 60,000; ANC leaders claimed anywhere from 100,000 to 200,000. The most reliable estimate would appear to be that of Walter Sisulu, who put it at 120,000, basing this on orders for membership cards placed with the printer.[6] The estimate was incomplete, claimed Sisulu, because the printer could not keep up with orders and the branches printed their own cards. The ANC had contracted for 96,000 cards from January to December (1959?); and if the branch orders are taken into account, the total might be close to the figure Sisulu named. It is clear that the membership of the ANC was substantial and that the task of arranging face-to-face contact would take some doing. The magnitude of the task was somewhat diminished by what otherwise was a drawback for the ANC: its fluctuating membership. Many members of the ANC were "fair-weather friends," willing to remain when membership was legal but unwilling to take risks once it was not. The ANC, as do all political organizations, had its share of passengers. And if it is difficult to judge the overall size of the organization, it is even harder to estimate its activist core. A guess can be hazarded that this was not more than, say, somewhere between 1,000 and 3,000 persons.

The M-Plan was never fully applied in practice. The Port Elizabeth region came closest to realizing it—which is not really surprising. Africans there had had longer contact with whites, were highly Christianized, and were, on the whole, better educated than Africans else-

6. Sisulu/Rvtr, pp. 263–64.

where in the country. It was this area, after all, that had produced leaders of the caliber of professors Jabavu and Matthews, Dr. Xuma, Sisulu, and Mandela.[7] The ANC flourished in Port Elizabeth, legal or illegal, and in the end proved harder to eradicate there than elsewhere. According to one of the investigating police officers, Sergeant Jonathan du Preez, some twenty-one cells had been established in New Brighton Township and another thirty-three in Kwazekele Township.[8] This was a remarkable feat, especially when the difficulties facing the organizers are taken into account. The network of cells, created in the teeth of skilled and unrelenting police work, soon became a thorn in the side of the police. Sergeant du Preez speaks of petrol drums, large rocks, and even nails being thrown in the streets to impede police vehicles and buses. Things were "absolutely abnormal" in the townships from 1960 and reached a climax in 1962. It was not until 1963 that police action began to take effect, for in that year many of the ANC cells were uncovered. A measure of the strength of the ANC underground in Port Elizabeth is that more than 900 people were arrested, of whom 800 were tried. Some 452 had been sentenced by 1965 to a total of 2,339 years' imprisonment.[9] This was the result of one of the greatest security crackdowns in South African history, a crackdown that reduced the ANC organization in Port Elizabeth to little more than a shadow of what it had been. Even now, however, news of ANC revivals continues to come from the Eastern Cape. There are a number of reasons why the plan worked less well in other parts of the country. Some centers were just too small to allow for cells and zones. In Cradock, for instance, after an attempt to apply the M-Plan, the effort was abandoned and the branch was run as before.[10] The M-Plan was, on the whole, oriented to big cities.

Another obstacle to its application was the resistance of incumbents in existing ANC formations who, having built up a power base, were reluctant to relinquish it. The M-Plan, if it was to be applied, meant dissolving the old branches and committees. While the extent of re-

---

7. Editorial, *Rand Daily Mail*, July 24, 1965.
8. Du Preez/Rvtr, pp. 12–13.
9. Du Preez/Magwayi, p. 146; see also *Daily Dispatch*, February 27, 1964.
10. Sikaka/Gcabi, p. 9.

sistance is hard to divine, there is one case that might be illustrative of others, for it is hard to credit that this was the only one of its kind.

The ANC Youth League in Port Elizabeth was given instructions to dissolve itself in February, 1961. The ANCYL was to be merged with the ANC and reorganized along the lines of the M-Plan. Under the circumstances, the leadership of the Youth League might have looked to its own members for support; but the leaders were no longer trusted, as they were suspected of misappropriating funds. The members of the ANCYL had, indeed, already pressed for the dissolution of the league and its absorption into the ANC. The Executive of the Youth League, before the order for dissolution came, had treated the complaints of its members with disdain. When pressed on the matter of funds, the leaders had parried with the answer that they acted only on instructions from Johannesburg and that no instructions to disband had been received from there.[11] Once the directive was in their hands, a crisis developed among the leaders. The visit of Vuysile Mini brought matters to a head. Mini, in his role of contact between the NEC and the region, demanded compliance with the M-Plan. The Youth League leaders tried to sidestep the issue (in the same way as they had with their own members) by arguing that they could not accept his authority. There was no proof, they said, that he was empowered to make this demand for the NEC. There was no satisfactory proof that the order came from anyone other than Mini himself. Mini, in his turn, insisted that the Youth League branch in Grahamstown had agreed to adopt the plan. The Port Elizabeth YL leadership hurried there in a vain effort to dissuade their colleagues. In a series of meetings they were told that the plan had already been adopted, the new fees had been collected, and the initial steps had been taken. The old Youth League was already being dissolved; and a branch committee of seven, as laid down in the plan, had been appointed. There was no turning back. Although the Grahamstown leadership had needed persuasion to adopt the plan, they were now satisfied with it. Dissatisfied with this outcome, the Port Elizabeth Youth League leaders took the last step open to them: they sent one of their number to Jo-

11. Njikelane/*Siwundla*, pp. 8–23.

hannesburg to check on Mini's orders with the National Executive. Once the orders were confirmed, the ANCYL leaders could do nothing but comply, however reluctantly.[12]

These were largely transitional problems. More serious was the rigid view of the M-Plan taken by the NEC itself. The plan had to be uniformly applied everywhere. If there was any difficulty in applying it, due, say, to local conditions, the matter was to be referred to the NEC, which would either send a report or an NEC member to visit personally and assist in finding a solution.[13] In practice this remained a pious hope. Branches simply adapted the M-Plan to their conceptions and needs. It is difficult to see how they could have avoided doing so. Nonetheless, the bureaucratic fallacy persisted among ANC leaders, to whom the idea of uniform application of the M-Plan continued as an article of faith.

IV

A three-stage patterning of events was envisaged by the ANC and its allies in achieving their goals: the first step would be the creation of an efficient underground organization; the second, an intensification of the struggle by means of a sabotage campaign and the training of men abroad; and the third, guerrilla war. The pattern could be changed by events. A mass uprising of Africans was one contingency; a change of heart among the whites, another. Changes had been anticipated, and plans were added later as the sabotage campaign expanded. But the efficacy of paper exercises depended, in the long haul, on the men who were to perform the necessary actions in the field. It is they who now come on stage.

After the State of Emergency was declared on March 30, 1960, the ANC was left leaderless. It flickered on feebly in the months that followed, but those who remained at large were determined that its flame should not be extinguished. Because of these activists, steps would be taken to put the M-Plan into effect almost as soon as the

12. Njikelane/*Siwundla*, pp. 3–6; Hewana/*Mtalana*, pp. 42–49, 53, 62.
13. Mbanjwa/*Mbolompo*, p. 774.

Emergency ended on August 31, 1960. Secrecy was the aim, but secrets were hard to keep. It soon became generally known that the ANC was being reformed, with reports appearing even in the white press. The reports told of cells being formed in the townships and of a "caretaker committee" to implement the plan. "It is claimed," the report went on, "that nobody outside the caretaker committee, not even the cell leaders, know who the members of the committee are. Everything will be done in 'underground fashion'—if anything is done at all." [14]

Despite the story in the press, the truth was somewhat less romantic. The hard core of activists who were determined to revitalize the ANC were themselves uncertain as to how it could be done. A variety of organizations had formed almost spontaneously. "Residents' Associations" were formed in the townships of Natal with the dual objectives of holding the ANC membership together and of keeping open the lines of communication by which African grievances could be aired to the authorities. The first objective was the more important. "Our object then was to organize, to raise the different branches of the African National Congress so as to keep the organization alive, that it should not die, so that we could carry on the objects of the organization, which we did before it was banned." [15]

For all that, the members were left pretty much on their own for the rest of 1960. Their devotion kept the ANC going in a rudimentary way, while they awaited instructions from the National Executive. They were convinced that, with the ending of the Emergency, the government would lower its guard and their organization would revive. The existence of these groups enabled the NEC, emerging from the post-Sharpeville ruins, to call the movement back to life in 1961. A directive was issued telling members to form branches despite the ban; and in July or August, 1961, the branches began re-forming. It was at this time, too, that the committees that had remained functioning seem to have become the regional committees of the ANC.

14. *Star*, September 13, 1960; see also Kunene/*Ngakane*, p. 129.
15. Quoted in Kunene/*Ngakane*, p. 128; see also Mtloko/*Magwayi*, p. 63; *Star*, June 27, 1960, and September 13, 1960.

Here again, the emergence of these committees cannot be satisfactorily documented.[16]

The best way of making things clear is, perhaps, to look briefly at specific cases. In Durban, authority to form branches was conferred on the regional committee there by no less a personage than Walter Sisulu, who came soon after the Emergency ended to urge the committee to extend the organization. Later another ANC leader, Milner Ntsangane, was sent by the NEC to assist in implementing the M-Plan. Under pressure from Ntsangane, the regional committee began contacting both former ANC stalwarts and other likely men who might be interested in joining the underground ANC. The drive for recruits was limited by the simple fact that the organization was illegal and that to continue it involved risk of imprisonment. Many who were approached were reluctant to return; and the recruiters had, in any case, to be circumspect. Recruits could not, as a result, be drawn into the ANC in large numbers.[17]

The pattern was similar in the Eastern Cape. The groundwork had been laid by those who had remained with the movement in the silent days of the Emergency, thus enabling Raymond Mhlaba, an emissary of the NEC, to reconstitute it on the basis of the M-Plan. Put in charge of organization for the entire Eastern Cape, Mhlaba had in fact anticipated instructions. Realizing that the days of legality were numbered, he had already begun implementing the M-Plan early in 1960. Port Elizabeth had been zoned, and a committee was functioning in each zone when the Emergency was proclaimed. The choice of Mhlaba as full-time organizer was, thus, an obvious one. Summoned to National Headquarters in 1961 by Duma Nokwe, then national secretary of the movement, he was duly appointed and given instructions. But, as Mhlaba later said, he already knew of the decision to appoint him organizer, for he had been told of it by Govan Mbeki, then contact between the NEC and the region. Upon confirmation of his appointment on October 26, 1961, Mhlaba abruptly left the firm of

16. Kunene/Ngakane, pp. 17–18.
17. Kunene/Ngakane, p. 21.

lawyers with which he had worked for eight years, visited Nokwe in Johannesburg, and told him that he accepted the decision of the National Executive. Mhlaba remained as organizer, on a full-time basis, for some fourteen months, reporting the conclusion of his mission at "Lilliesleaf"—the farm that served as Umkonto and ANC headquarters—in December, 1962. After two weeks under cover, he returned to the Eastern Cape to check organization in centers other than Port Elizabeth and to make sure that there was no falling off in zeal.[18]

Port Elizabeth, for reasons mentioned earlier, was one of the easier centers to reorganize. East London was a different proposition. The ANC had not recovered from the 1952 riots, and the measure of support for the organization, even when it was still legal, had remained small. Now illegal, the organization would be still harder to resuscitate. Nonetheless, East London was too important a center to ignore, so one of the most able of the ANC organizers was put in charge of reorganization. The man was Vuysile Mini (later executed for instigating the murder of a state witness), whose first task was to organize a regional committee. Mini first visited East London for this purpose in October, 1960, found such of the old ANC leaders as were available, and called a meeting. A small room, not more than nine feet square, served as the meeting place. The meeting itself had both a semipublic and a secret part. In the semipublic meeting, which took place first, Mini told those present that, as the ANC was now an illegal movement, it would disband. This, he said, was the directive of the NEC. All ANC literature was to be destroyed, together with any membership cards that were still retained, as possession of such a card could lead to instant arrest. On this note the first part of the meeting ended. It was doubtless designed to put any police informers off the track and to provide a cover for Mini's presence in East London. The secret meeting, which followed immediately, apparently took a different tack and the true reason for Mini's visit was revealed.

That small group of men held back for a "private talk" when the semipublic meeting dispersed were, by and large, the members of the old Executive. The meeting was short, lasting from about 4:30 to 4:45

18. Mhlaba/Rvtr, pp. 6–8.

in the afternoon. It was kept short because of the risks involved. Those attending could harbor few illusions. They had been chosen for the business of reestablishing the ANC.[19] As Mini told his auditors, "Even now, while we are at this meeting, this is an offense." [20] The actual working of the underground organization, as it was proposed, does not emerge clearly from the evidence. The reason is, at least in part, that the protagonists did not seem to fully comprehend its complexities themselves. As far as can be made out, however, it would seem that the pattern was to be the following. The men present at the meeting were told to put the M-Plan into effect, with a number of alterations. They were to organize branch committees in all East London townships and were to appoint one contact for all these townships. The branch committees were to consist of the zone leaders. After appointment, the names of members of the branch committees were to be reported to Port Elizabeth, from where they would receive further instructions. Nothing more was to be done until those instructions were received.[21]

The divisions proposed followed the procedure that was laid down in the M-Plan. The West Bank location, for instance, was to be divided into two zones named, respectively, A and B, and each was to have a zone leader who would sit on the committee of the West Bank branch. Port Elizabeth would know who the branch committee members, or zone leaders, were, but not the names of members in each zone.[22] To aid the regional committees in setting up branches and zones and in supervising the working of the M-Plan, a number of subcommittees were set up and given specific functions. A propaganda subcommittee was to prepare leaflets for distribution in the townships and to see to the political education both of its members and of Africans generally. As this would cost money, a finance subcommittee was to collect dues from the branches and contributions from sympathizers. Contributions were also extorted by threats, but this was not official policy. To reach the majority of urban Africans, trade union activity

19. Kumani/*Bongco*, p. 196.
20. Kumani/*Bongco*, p. 214.
21. Kumani/*Bongco*, p. 214.
22. Mashinyana/*Bongco*, p. 226.

was urged. A subcommittee was appointed to maintain contact with such African unions as existed and to assist in the organizing of others. Trade unions were also to be looked to for recruits. In the past the ANC had been weak in the countryside, so another subcommittee was to work there. The regional committees made their own assignments to subcommittees and appointed their own chairmen and secretaries. They were to meet weekly from 5:30 to 6:30 P.M., as the members had full-time jobs. The weekly hour should, it was believed, give them enough time to transact all necessary business.[23]

A system such as the above was put into operation, but the NEC soon found that it worked badly. It was successful neither in Natal nor in the Eastern Cape. The regional committees, in particular, failed to function to much effect. The attrition in authority of the middle levels had begun with the organization of the regional committee itself.

V

The regional committee was impressive on paper, but reality was different. Little worked as planned. The need for change became evident soon after the first regional committees had been appointed, for they did virtually nothing. In Durban, for instance, the members of the committee attended meetings irregularly and generally neglected the branches. In a sense, this neglect was understandable. Here was a group of intelligent men, among the most militant of the Durban ANC, bent on gaining their freedom but with no avenue open for action. They led a political organization whose scope was limited, particularly for political action of the kind to which they were accustomed. Though there was much talk of revolution and of freedom, there was little that could actually be done. Heady talk may have been inspiring to the lower echelons; but to the men on the regional committee, whose minds were attuned to legal protest, inactivity must have been both frustrating and disheartening. One group failed at first to succumb to the feeling of defeat. It strongly believed in the ANC

23. Kunene/Ngakane, pp. 30–32, 130.

as a means of liberation and attracted others of like mind. It organized a new body which it called the *secretariat*; this was not part of the regional committee but operated independently. Many on this body were allegedly members of the Communist Party, which was said to inspire their activism, but this point will be discussed later. The secretariat began performing the functions that supposedly were to be performed by the regional committee. It supervised branches, advised on the M-Plan, and initiated the serious revitalization of the organization. Formed at some time between September and November, 1962, the secretariat functioned in Natal until February, 1963, when the National Executive dissolved both the old regional committee and the secretariat and set up a new regional committee.[24]

With the change, a fresh scheme was mooted. The reconstituted regional committee in Durban was now peopled solely by those who had participated actively in the old committee and in the secretariat; the others were dropped. At the same time an ad hoc committee was set up. The idea was apparently for the ad hoc committee to supervise the regional committee. It would, in other words, be a revamped provincial committee.[25] Little that has emerged in evidence makes clear the working of either the new Durban regional committee or the ad hoc committee. The outlines alone are discernible. Like the regional committee, the ad hoc was to be organized on functional lines. Five (or seven) members were each to have a particular role. One was to be in charge of propaganda; another, finance; a third, trade unions; the fourth, to organize the countryside; and the fifth was to be secretary. It was a body that would keep in close touch with and could act in lieu of the National Executive. It would, as a permanent body, do what individual members of the National Executive had done during their periodic visits: it would supervise the implementation of the plan in each region and would advise on necessary changes to the plan itself. The appointment of the ad hoc committee was necessary because police surveillance made travel risky for members of the NEC and because many had been deported or exiled to remote parts of the country. Personal contact had to be kept to a mini-

24. Kunene/*Ngakane*, pp. 22–25, 123–27.
25. Kunene/*Ngakane*, pp. 25–27.

mum. It was easier for members of the lower echelons to be brought from Durban to Johannesburg than for the leaders to visit the region. The ad hoc could be peopled with the most active and energetic members in the region, those who maintained links with the NEC through contacts and so could act in its place. This was the scheme proposed for Natal, to be carried out by the ANC in Durban. It created more problems than solutions.

The relationship of the ad hoc committees to the regional committees has not been satisfactorily explained in the accounts of those involved either in Durban or elsewhere. It is not clear, for instance, whether the ad hoc committees appointed the members of the regional committees. True, it was one of their duties to establish regional committees where none yet existed, but what of those already established? Did the NEC make the appointments, or was this done by the ad hoc committee? This question cannot be answered with any finality, for practice seems to have varied. Indeed, for all the ANC efforts to lay down lines and structures, there seems to have been little standardization in the actual working of the group. Another strange thing is the relationship of the ad hoc committee to *Umkonto*. Although it may be anticipating later discussion, it can be said that the interpretation of the role of this committee differed between the prosecution and the defense in the Rivonia Trial. The prosecution maintained that one of the principal functions of the ad hoc committee was to act as liaison between the ANC and *Umkonto*. The leaders of both organizations denied this. The state's case seems the more convincing in this instance, but the question remains open. There was so much overlapping of function between individuals and organizations that the question of who was a member of what is often more a matter of definition than of difference. Often what could not be done in the name of one body could be done in the name of another by a person who held some sort of rank in both.

There were, however, important differences between the committees. Greater care seems to have been taken in selecting people for the ad hoc committee than was exercised in the case of the regional committee. One reason may have been the enlarged experience of the NEC with underground work and its having gathered a cadre of tested men; another may have been a growing disenchantment with the regional committee as a means of mobilization and organization. In Durban, the city we have been describing, Govan Mbeki, a man of education and ability, supervised the appointments to both the ad hoc committee and the regional committee when he visited in February, 1963. The more important of these tasks seems to have been the ad hoc committee, and it is significant that a man of Mbeki's personal stature and importance in the ANC was selected for the task. Soon after arriving in Durban Mbeki called together the old regional committee and told the members that the committee was dissolved. A new regional committee of the more active members was appointed. Accepting the NEC's powers of dissolution, the regional committee complied, no doubt with relief. A number of the members of the old regional committee had, in any case, become disenchanted with underground work and were quite willing to surrender their shadowy authority. Many who had been lukewarm thus fell away, leaving what were presumably activists on the new regional committee. Appointments to the new regional committee, like those of the more important ad hoc committee, were made with great secrecy, and the membership of one was not supposed to know the membership of the other. The veil of secrecy was not impenetrable, and soon the members of each committee knew the identity of members of the other one.

The appointees to the new regional committee did present some problems to the leadership. Asked what they knew of the much-vaunted M-Plan, many of the new members admitted that they did not know of it. One of those present either was asked or had offered to explain it, but it was evident that he did not understand it. Others then tried, and eventually the outlines of the plan emerged.[26] But the course of the discussion is significant in itself. Here was a plan that had been circulating in the ANC since the mid-fifties. Each succeeding secretarial report had stressed the need for implementing it. It had been made official ANC policy in 1959. Yet a group of the most devoted ANC men knew little of it. There is surely not much more to be said about the bureaucratic fallacy than this.

26. Kunene/*Ngakane*, pp. 33–34.

The creation of the ad hoc committee and the newly reconstituted regional committee apparently did not solve the problems afflicting the underground organization in Durban. The duplication of functions created rivalries and frictions. In an effort to reduce these and to ensure better working relations, a liaison was appointed to sit on both committees. In addition, joint meetings were to be held on specific issues. The first of the joint meetings was held in Durban two weeks after the old regional committee had been dissolved; that is, at some time in March, 1963. Despite the importance of this meeting, the members of the new regional committee were as remiss in attendance as the members of the old committee had been. Although the new committee supposedly contained the "activists," there was considerable absenteeism.[27]

It was at this poorly attended meeting that the old committee handed over to the new such monies and properties as the ANC had in Durban. These included a typewriter and a duplicating machine, the favorite tools of the underground, and a panel van so ramshackle that it had to be scrapped. Some funds had been placed by the former treasurer with an Indian attorney, who had secretly kept them with his trust funds, and other amounts had been concealed in an ordinary savings bank under the name of "African Savings Club." The amounts so hidden were small. In all, they did not amount to more than $280, for the ANC was not particularly affluent at this point. Such monies as did come to hand had to be used to pay for the various secret headquarters and hideouts *Umkonto* had bought and also for the transportation of men for military training abroad. There was little left for the ANC proper.[28]

Reports were given on the state of the branches, and it seemed that four branches were working according to the M-Plan; the others had not yet been organized. There were other serious deficiencies. The rural areas' subcommittee, for instance, was not ready with its report. This was worrisome to a movement which had made "work among the peasantry" a primary goal. It was the more worrisome because it

27. Kunene/*Ngakane*, pp. 62–66.
28. Kunene/*Ngakane*, pp. 47–51, 134–35.

seemed that there was not much that could be reported anyway. A report was, however, promised for the next meeting. As no proper minutes were kept (which is hardly surprising), all that remain are notes made by the secretary. This was done for the sake of secrecy and may have helped toward that end, but it does make reconstruction of what transpired very difficult. It cannot, therefore, be said whether or not the report was eventually delivered and what was in it if it was read.

Another significant matter which came up at these joint meetings was the question of how much should be made known to the ANC president-general, Luthuli. The government had exiled Luthuli to his old home in Stanger, Natal, and he was eager to know what was taking place. The matter was drawn to the attention of a meeting by a prominent ANC leader, M. B. Yengwa, who was present although he was not a committee member. Yengwa asked permission to explain his presence and then told the meeting that he was there as liaison to Luthuli, to whom he owed the appointment. His instructions were to attend meetings that dealt with issues relating to the ANC as a whole. He did not elaborate on the nature of the appointment or how it had been made, but merely said he would sit as a nonvoting member.[29]

The reason Luthuli needed an observer is puzzling, for, after all, he was the president-general and should have been privy to all deliberations. This was not, however, the case. Luthuli probably knew less about the deliberations of the organization of which he was titular leader than did the South African police. Indeed, this was made painfully clear when Yengwa told the regional committee that Luthuli was dissatisfied with the reports he was receiving. What particularly worried the president-general was the news of *Umkonto*, which was being described as the military wing of the ANC. Luthuli had told Yengwa that he was opposed to violence and would resign from the ANC, severing all connection with it, should it resort to violence. In view of Luthuli's public prestige and the reputation he enjoyed in

29. Kunene/*Ngakane*, pp. 33–34.

South Africa and abroad, his repudiation of the ANC would have been a moral blow of the first magnitude. Luthuli had asked Yengwa for advice and had also asked him to put the matter to the regional committee. All those there admitted that they knew little of *Umkonto,* and all agreed that, from the little they knew, it would be advisable to dissociate it from the ANC. By and large, they believed that their members did not favor violence. If violence were to become ANC policy, it would only put the organization in a bad light. After the short meeting at which this was thrashed out, Yengwa said that he would tell Luthuli what had been agreed. Later, as he drove home with another member of the regional committee, Yengwa returned to the subject, saying that Luthuli was thinking of resigning from the ANC because he personally opposed violence but did not want to stand in the way of a majority if they insisted on it.

The visit of Milner Ntsangane to Durban (see p. 105) apparently deepened the concern of the members of the regional committee. This visit, which took place shortly after Yengwa's initiative in the regional committee, was planned to investigate the difficulties Mbeki had reported on instituting the M-Plan in Natal, and to press for more energy in reorganization. The tensions generated by this visit led to a further round of consultations. Ntsangane consulted with Kunene, a member of the regional committee, and both agreed to consult with Luthuli at his place of exile, Stanger. Luthuli was then told of Mbeki's report. At the same time another issue was raised—that of the Zulu paramount chief, Cyprian Dinizulu, who had called a meeting of chiefs and indunas (that is, all males old enough to have a voice in tribal councils) and had urged them to support the government's policies on Bantu Authorities. As Dinizulu had much authority among the Zulus, this was obviously a troublesome development. Zulus were the preponderant tribe in Natal, and loss of their support would be a severe setback for the ANC. A decision was made to issue leaflets pointing out that, though Dinizulu was paramount chief by law of the land, he had no more authority than any other chief by tribal custom and that he could not force the other chiefs to agree to the system of Bantu Authorities if they were opposed to it. Luthuli also urged the appointment of a full-time ANC organizer for Zululand, offering to pay him out of his own pocket for two months if the ad hoc committee did not have the money.[30]

This meeting and its outcome seem to confirm what was indicated earlier. There is no doubt that Luthuli had a considerable personal following among the older men in the ANC. His stature, both in South Africa and abroad, made it impossible to drop him or even to allow him to resign. He provided a respectable façade that would be difficult to duplicate. But his influence on the ANC and on decisions taken at the highest levels was marginal. He was apparently little consulted or informed and was taken seriously only when he forced a showdown or when members of his following chose to go to him for arbitration. In general, he was confronted with decisions already taken. It is significant that he had to learn of Mbeki's report from Milner Ntsangane, and then only because the latter had come to Natal on other ANC business. Like the moderate political sector of which he was the most prominent representative, Luthuli's role seems to have declined with the taking up of the armed struggle.

In a sense, the argument regarding violence had become academic, for the regional committee was losing its importance—if, indeed, it ever was important. To the men of *Umkonto*, the regional committee simply consisted of frightened men, unready to take any serious steps toward freedom. The political struggle with the South African government was losing its importance to the radicals, and the armed struggle was about to begin. The ad hoc committee increasingly bore the banners of revolt in Natal. Its belief in its mission was strengthened by its reputedly large Communist membership, and, as a leaflet put it, "A branch with Communist members does not fade away. Its members know what they have joined for." [31] Increasingly, the Communists (who were often at the same time ANC militants) devoted themselves to *Umkonto*, while the non-Communist "soft-liners" tended to remain in the ANC.

For these reasons, and no doubt others, the reformed regional committee did not prove much more effective than its predecessor.

30. Kunene/*Ngakane*, pp. 54–61.
31. This quotation from a Communist pamphlet appeared in *Cape Times*, May 22, 1964.

Attendance again was irregular, and meetings often could not be held for lack of a quorum. Branches were seldom and cursorily visited. Taken to task, the members of the regional committee would simply state that they did not have the time. Between April and June of 1963, the regional committee virtually ceased to function. Apparently the members felt that they were being undercut by the *Umkonto* command, and that by meeting they were running risks and accomplishing nothing.[32] Where the regional committees had tried to intervene, their intervention had not proved particularly helpful or useful.

Kunene, who was active on the regional committee at this time, speaks of a meeting of all branch committees held sometime in February of 1963. Some fifty people, among them many women, crowded into the small home of the Reverend Mtlabata, a cleric very active in the ANC. They came to discuss the proposed extension of the hated pass system to women. The laws had been on the statute books for some time but had not been enforced. The government now planned to make it compulsory for African women to carry reference books. The regional committee had made the government's intentions known and had proposed steps to combat them. The municipal beer halls were to be boycotted, and this boycott was to be followed by a strike, which was by now almost a ritual of protest. By hitting at the Durban municipality's beer hall profits, the regional committee hoped to make African dissatisfaction plain to the authorities. The reasoning ran something like this: beer revenues would fall; the City Council would become afraid; it would inform the government that Africans did not want their women to carry passes; the government would then relent under pressure from the municipality. These plans were the subject of sharp debate between the Durban African women and the committee.

The women objected, not to the principles of the plans, but to the fact that, as they said, the regional committee had taken so long to decide on the campaign that insufficient time was left to organize it effectively. Four members of the regional committee now came to the house of Mtlabata to convince the women that the time was still

32. Kunene/*Ngakane*, pp. 70–73.

ripe. To prevent disorder, and in the hope that the women would "not make so much noise" in front of a man so respected, Dr. Pascal Ngakane, Luthuli's son-in-law, was put in the chair. At the end of the meeting, the women reluctantly agreed to issue leaflets calling for the boycott and telling how it was to be conducted. Once the boycott was under way, the regional committee would meet again and consider reports from the branches telling of the progress of the campaign. Rather self-importantly, the spokesman for the regional committee told the women that they should realize that the regional committee had a big job on its hands and, because the boycott was difficult to organize in time, should accept the regional plan without any fuss.

Having won its way, the regional committee began the job of mimeographing leaflets and arranging for their distribution. But the inevitable happened: with the campaign set off prematurely, the beer-hall boycott proved an utter failure. African men, much as they treasured their women, prized their beer more. They continued to flock to the beer halls despite the ANC's ban. Members of the regional committee, passing the beer halls, noted that they were as full as ever. There had, it is true, been some fisticuffs on the first day, and a bomb had been set in one hall, but most of the men drank undeterred.[33]

Much of the same pattern is evident in East London, though Port Elizabeth showed more resolution from the beginning. There were a number of reasons for this. First of all, the ANC in East London had split before the riots of 1952, the split indeed being a contributory factor. Its loss of members, added to the dominance of Port Elizabeth, must have had an effect on the outlook and morale of the East London leadership, who seem to have been prepared to sit back and let Port Elizabeth bear the brunt of the underground campaign. Once Mini had left East London, after his organizing efforts there, only half-hearted attempts were made to revive the branches.[34] Since Port Elizabeth was the fount of activity, this will be treated first, and then more will be said of East London.

33. Kunene/Ngakane, pp. 39–45.
34. Njikelane/Rvtr, pp. 22–24.

Taking up the story involves briefly going over some already traveled ground. In 1960, the regional committee had held a meeting in Port Elizabeth at which it was decided to form a *caretaker committee* should the ANC be banned. The ANC was, shortly thereafter, banned; and the committees, working in secret, did their best to hold the organization together, maintain the morale of members, collect fees, and pay some of the expenses of detained members and the support of their families. After the State of Emergency ended, and the detained leaders were released, the members of the caretaker committee were invited to a meeting where the M-Plan was explained to them by Govan Mbeki and Raymond Mhlaba. If Mbeki and Mhlaba had hoped for eager acceptance, these hopes were quickly dashed. Most of the members of the caretaker committee were against it, some even threatening to resign if it were implemented. Mhlaba pleaded that the decision to implement the M-Plan had been taken by the NEC and urged them at least to put it to the test. Mbeki, he told them, would be contact between the Port Elizabeth regional committee and the National Executive, but even this otherwise popular step failed to satisfy them. Disappointed, Mbeki and Mhlaba left.[35]

The conflict remained unresolved, and Nelson Mandela came from Johannesburg in April, 1961, to end it. As one of the most prominent members of the NEC and as author of the M-Plan, he hoped to convince the reluctant members of the wisdom of adopting it. Mandela explained his plan at a meeting called at the home of an Indian physician, Dr. Pather, in Korsten, a Port Elizabeth township long an ANC stronghold. Despite his prestige in the country, Mandela was not known to some of those present. He had to be introduced, and only after that could he ask why his plan was not adopted. Objections were paraded before him. Among the most important was the reluctance to dissolve the old ANC formations, which was required if the plan was to be put into effect. Matters had, what is more, descended to the physical level with pro- and anti-plan people threatening each other. Those who opposed the plan insisted that it had not been

35. Njikelane/*Rvtr*, pp. 24–26.

recommended by the NEC but had been designed by hotheads who were trying to push its acceptance in the hope of a *fait accompli.* Mandela did his best to quiet and reassure both the warring factions. He assured the doubters of the authenticity of the NEC resolution. And because it was an ANC resolution, he said, it was incumbent on all there to try it for at least a short time. They had to see if it would work. It was wrong, he stressed, for members for or against the plan to assault each other. Once its practicability had been demonstrated, all would adopt it for they would see that it could work for them. Mandela also spoke of the stay-at-home strike that was to coincide with the white proclamation of the Republic on May 29–31, and urged everyone to work for that campaign, also.[36]

This, it would seem, should have set all doubts at rest. Some committee members remained dissatisfied, however, even after the meeting with Mandela. They argued that, during his visit, Mandela had mainly concerned himself with those favoring his plan and had not really met its opponents or heard their views. Opponents of the M-Plan felt that they had been inadequately represented and, as a result, were in no hurry to put the plan into effect in their branches. If the obstacles to reorganization were not overcome, one thing at least was accomplished: the name of the new organizational unit was corrected. Before Mandela's visit, the regional committee (or caretaker committee) had begun to style itself the "Port Elizabeth High Command." Mandela had advised against this, saying that only the National Executive should have the right to call itself a High Command; and the term was later adopted for the leadership of *Umkonto.* Although much had remained unsettled when Mandela left for home, the outcome of his visit was that the remaining (and still stubborn) resistance to the M-Plan was overcome in Port Elizabeth. East London remained a problem.[37]

Vuysile Mini's visit to East London has already been mentioned. He had come to spread the gospel of the M-Plan but had achieved only

---

36. Njikelane/*Rvtr*, pp. 26–30.
37. Mashinyana/*Bongco*, p. 226; Njikelane/*Rvtr*, p. 30.

meager results. Further effort had to be expended to realize the M-Plan. After the abortive Mini visit, another man was sent as an official organizer, Tamsanqua Tshume, who came to East London from Port Elizabeth around April 13, having visited several smaller towns on the way. He was to see to the establishment of a functioning underground apparatus, running to pattern, in East London. His methods, like his role, resembled those of other ANC organizers. He was to set up a number of branch committees, each consisting of seven men, in the West Bank and Epiphunzana townships. As East London had a regional committee and this was really its job, why was Tshume's visit necessary? The reason was, as doubtless is apparent from what was said of Durban, that the regional committee had done little. Tshume hoped to remedy this state of affairs. He intended to call the members of the regional committee together but found that they were not easily contacted. The meeting he had planned for Thursday had to be postponed to Friday, which increased the danger of detection. The source of Tshume's difficulties is not far to seek. Coming to organize an illegal revolutionary organization, he could hardly advertise his visit. Were he to have done so, the news would surely have leaked out and come to the attention of the police, whose eyes and ears were everywhere. Tshume had to arrive unheralded. As a result, the first the contact knew of the visit was, literally, Tshume's appearance on his doorstep.

As things turned out—and again this is a consequence of attempting to force the organization, or what existed of it, into a bureaucratic mold—Tshume's visit did more to add to the confusion than to clear it up. While it is difficult to trace in detail what happened, it seems that he contacted the branch executive of the ANC in Tsolo Township and solicited its aid in selecting the West Bank branch executive. The Tsolo people then were to appoint those so selected. This was done, and Tshume met with the future West Bank branch executive—all of whom had been in the ANC branch there during the days of legality. Other committees were difficult to put together and would not meet with him for a variety of procedural reasons. Tshume's evidence is not clear on these points, but it seems that committees were reluctant to meet, and those that were appointed remained generally inactive. Not much happened after Tshume left, at least on the regional and branch levels. The question increasingly became one of linking branches and the NEC, rather than branches with the regional organizations, though this continued to bedevil the ANC leadership.[38]

38. Tshume/*Bongco*, pp. 177–92; Kumani/*Bongco*, pp. 199–220.

III

The Struggle Group and Its Linkages

IN ALL ASPECTS of ANC organization, the number seven seems to recur repeatedly. Indeed, this was the number of members not only of the various committees at different levels but also of the cells and other units. The need to limit membership of the different groups was self-evident. The integrity of the organization could not otherwise have been preserved. If each group of seven knew no one else, their ability to implicate others was limited to their own number. As Tshume, whom we met in the previous chapter, later put it: "Seeing that the organization was underground, members should not be too many wherever they are meeting in an underground movement." [1] The idea was sound. The way it worked out in practice was another matter. Security was never very good, and members of different cells often learned the identity of others who were involved. Nonetheless, the broad scheme remained and was implemented to various degrees by different individuals.[2]

The effectiveness of the cells depended not on the national leadership but on the lowest-ranking members of the underground ANC. It depended on the courage and initiative of zone leaders, cell stewards,

1. Tshume/*Bongco*, p. 176.
2. Tshume/*Bongco*, p. 176; Mashinyana/*Rvtr*, pp. 4–7.

and volunteers. These were the real activists, the "struggle group."
What they did and how they did it is, therefore, particularly interesting.

II

In discussing the organization of the ANC, it is always necessary
to go back to that year of decision, 1960, which divided the legal
from the illegal ANC. The exact way in which branches were organized before 1960 is difficult to determine. The organization of the
ANC, flow charts to the contrary, was largely a matter of local leaders
adapting to local conditions. The confusion of forms is worse confounded by halfhearted applications of the M-Plan. Even in Port
Elizabeth, where the plan worked well after the ANC had been driven
underground, it was not fully applied in the time of legality before
1960. Elsewhere the plan hardly took on at all before the ban. One
thing is clear: the branch remained the fundament of the ANC. Although branches varied in size and importance, functioned in various
ways, and were often torn apart by feuds, in the last analysis they
were the ANC. The curtain fell in 1960, and the State of Emergency
and its consequences changed everything. The existing organization
was disrupted; its leaders were arrested and put in jail, or remained in
hiding. Nothing could be done openly, and yet the branches were untrained in secret work. It is not surprising that much of the membership remained quiescent and that even New Brighton, normally a
hotbed of ANC activity, held no meetings until February, 1961. As
one of the members put it, "Most of the leaders had been arrested,
and all members just decided to remain quiet." [3]

Those with associations with the ANC knew that the loyalty of its
stalwarts had not been affected. To bring the organization back to life,
they had only to be called together, given tasks to perform, and instructed to change the way in which they worked with the public.
This was the task assigned to the branch committees, each of which

3. Qumpula/Hlekani, p. 18.

was established by a member of the regional committee. They were to reorganize the branches along the lines of the M-Plan, which set out how this was to be done. The members of the branch committee, with the aid of the regional committee, were to nominate former members of the now (officially) dissolved ANC to act as zone leaders in the new underground. Others could, in addition, be nominated by the contact. As the regional committees hardly were bustling centers of activity, it can be assumed that the contact was probably the most effective originator of nominations. The idea was that the zone leaders (renamed *chief stewards*), however they were selected, would be men familiar with their zones and would know of reliable ANC people (whose loyalties had remained intact) whom they could appoint as cell stewards. The cell stewards, in their turn, would know their smaller locales and whom to recruit as cell members. The organization could, thus, be re-created from the ground up.[4]

III

Given the spread of small units in the organization, two officers became increasingly important: One was the *contact*; the other was the *volunteer-in-chief*.[5]

The importance of the contact rested on his being the channel by which orders from the higher bodies were conveyed to the lower bodies. Originally, there was supposed to be a chain of contacts, linking each tier with the others. According to this scheme, the regional committee would be linked by contacts both to the NEC and the branches; the branches would be linked to the cells, and so forth. In effect, linkage was increasingly between the NEC and the cells through a limited number of contacts.

The contact and the regional committee were not appointed together; rather, they were appointed separately. They did not know each other at the outset, and had to be brought together. Thus,

4. Mashinyana/*Bongco*, pp. 225–30; Ngoza/*Magwayi*, p. 48; Gulwa/*Mapolisa*, p. 2.
   5. Mashinyana/*Bongco*, p. 231.

Tamsanqua Tshume told the East London regional committee that it would be receiving orders from a contact presently unknown to it and to him. The contact, when he appeared, was to be simply the conduit through which orders would be brought down and reports carried back. The contact and those he contacted were to be no more than the willing instruments of a command unknown to either of them by name.

The contacts, then, were the men who were to bind everything together. They were to keep open the lines of communication between the different centers. They would keep cells, branches, and regions tied to the National Headquarters. But because of the nature of his work, the contact operated between units. Locally, the volunteer-in-chief seems to have played a much larger role.

IV

The volunteer-in-chief's rank, but not his functions, was a carry-over from the days of the Congress of the People. The volunteers-in-chief had led the "Freedom Volunteers"—an organization originally called into being to assist in ANC campaigns. This group, which has not been referred to before, was intended to consist of a corps of 50,000 young men who would help organize the Congress of the People, and who would later assist in other organizational work.[6] In fact, the number 50,000 was far too ambitious, and only a few thousand actually volunteered. Great care was taken to emphasize that the Freedom Volunteers were not the same as the volunteers that had been called for in the Defiance Campaign, and that they would not be asked to actually break any laws. This promise was broken when the Freedom Volunteers were asked to assist in the Western Areas Campaign (see p. 24) and to do all in their power to prevent the government from moving people to new townships from the Western Areas.[7]

6. Mashinyana/Rvtr, pp. 37–38; see also Edward Feit, *South Africa: Dynamics of the African National Congress* (London, 1962).
7. Edward Feit, *African Opposition in South Africa: The Failure of Passive Resistance* (Stanford, 1968), chap. 4.

The character of the Freedom Volunteers had changed even when the ANC was legal; now it was to change even more.

With the ANC banned, the volunteer-in-chief was to be the man in charge of violence, but his acts could not be carried out without the sanction of the NEC.[8] The key role of the contact is again evident. There was at least one difficulty for those who would control violence through a chain of command: there was no way those above could know what had been done unless informed in advance, and there was no way for those below to know whether their orders were genuine. Everything depended on the good faith of those involved, and experience soon showed good faith to be a broken reed. Contacts and volunteers-in-chief often acted independently—either singly or together—without official NEC sanction.

Given the importance of the violent struggle, the relationship of the volunteer-in-chief to the regional committee is of interest. The regional committee, according to the evidence, was completely divorced from the violent struggle. The committee was confined in its activities to the political, to propaganda and organization—though it was itself no model of the latter. The volunteers seem to have thought that the less the regional committee knew of their plans, the better. Acts of violence required neither its approval nor its assent. The regional committee was to be a bystander, or supporter, and not a participant.[9]

The exclusion of the regional committee resulted more from the need for secrecy than from any organizational factor. The members of the regional committee were often talkative and boastful, though they were not alone in this.[10] The volunteers also talked and boasted. Both were unable to repress that exhibitionism which people of low status sometimes display, emanating from the desire to enlarge oneself and to appear important. Boasting, as a form of compensation, would have been harmless were secrecy not involved. The tendency of the regional committee members to be indiscrete was understood by

8. Mbanjwa/*Mbolompo*, pp. 751–52.
9. Mdube/*Bongco*, pp. 361, 369, 379.
10. Ngoza/*Magwayi*, p. 44; Mdube/*Rvtr*, p. 12; see also *Congress Voice* (April, 1961), mimeographed, unnumbered.

the NEC and the contact, and they feared that anything said in front of the committee would soon be the common talk of the townships. Excluding the members was, therefore, not only a matter of keeping their consciences inviolate but also of keeping their mouths shut. The regional committee was only told of acts of violence after they had happened and when they were the work of people unknown to the members.[11] The committee was agreeable. If ignorance was bliss, it was clearly folly to be wise. Protection from the loose tongues of volunteers was more difficult to achieve, and it remained a continuing problem.

There was a clear distinction from the beginning between the ordinary members of the ANC, who belonged to cells, and the volunteers. Volunteers were, as one of them put it, the most "hotheaded" people in the movement; they had agreed to do whatever was ordered by their leaders, even to committing murder if need be. Once having become a volunteer, a man could not refuse an assignment; if he were to do so, his own comrades would kill him. Refusal of an assignment was automatically to be labeled a traitor and to become a legitimate object for execution by former companions.[12] The volunteers, apart from participating in individual acts of violence, also served to control the "support group"—those who could be called on to come out for the organization, while not actually belonging to it. The support group would act to support the struggle group when mobilized for various purposes and at different times. The turnout of marchers for the PAC in Cape Town in 1960 (described in the Introduction) is an example. The volunteers would see to it that a turnout was provided when needed or that a boycott call was answered. As one volunteer put it:

A cell steward and a volunteer one would class as a policeman of the African National Congress. . . . There are ordinary members who believe in the African National Congress. All we had to do was to collect money from them. They did not attend meetings. . . .

11. Mdube/*Bongco*, p. 363.
12. Kulele/*Mgalunkulu*, p. 82; Mdube/*Bongco*, p. 385.

127

They are supporters of the African National Congress. They approved of what we are doing.[13]

The volunteer was, thus, a man with special status in the ANC, and this special status was frequently emphasized in ANC propaganda. A member had to formally become a volunteer; it was not something that just happened. Again, those who seemed likely to join were sounded out, and if they indicated willingness were invited to a special secret meeting where they would be enrolled. There, in something like an induction into an army (which in a sense this was), they were asked first to fill out questionnaires and then to stand with balled fists upraised and to repeat the words, "Amandla Ngawethu" ("Strength Is Ours") and to sing the hymn of the African National Congress, "Mayebuye i Afrika." The questionnaires were deliberately made very detailed, and those who needed it were given help in filling them out. They were asked about all the details of their lives. They had to give their names, ages, education, training, employment, and other details of a more intimate nature. The completed forms were carefully checked with the recruits, who then had to sign them. The purpose of all this was not only to make the occasion solemn but also to have a hold on the volunteer. The organization now "knew everything about him, and had written evidence which could be used against him should he decide to leave," which made a double grip. Clearly, it was more advantageous for the organization to deal with a possible traitor, but, in the event that this was impossible, the records could be put where the police would be sure to find them. Handing a man over to the police was dangerous because he might betray others. And as it was difficult for Africans to move around, the pass laws being what they were, there were few avenues of escape open to the man who betrayed his organization.[14]

Everything possible was done to impress on the volunteer the importance of his act and to ensure that his loyalty remained unimpaired. His commitment was stressed from the outset by having the oath taken individually rather than en masse. The tie with the ANC was

13. Sizani/*Khayingo*, p. 33.
14. Tanana/*Bongco*, pp. 333, 349; Mdube/*Rvtr*, pp. 5–6, 22–26.

emphasized at all times. Once the individual had volunteered, it was impressed on him that he had to carry out instructions.

V

The chief steward was the main link with the grass roots of the organization. The contact kept in touch with him and gave him instructions, receiving information from him in return. To prevent chief stewards from learning too much about the organization, the contact would meet no more than three of them at a time and would include a *prime steward* or two as well. The latter, who has not been mentioned before, seems to have had varying functions and an undefined jurisdiction. Few of the witnesses who spoke of him could describe his exact functions. The consensus seems to be that he was the volunteer-in-chief of the zone and, presumably, under the volunteer-in-chief of the region. Calling him the *prime steward* may have been intended to prevent confusion.[15] The tasks of the prime steward were obviously different both from those of the cell stewards and those of the chief steward. He had, therefore, to be given some other rank. The prime steward was clearly an important man. In many ways he ranked above the chief steward of the zone, but in others he accepted the latter's direction. The way things worked out was roughly that the prime steward accepted the leadership of the chief steward in all political matters but was supreme where violence was involved. When it was a matter of "political struggle," such as raising funds, circulating leaflets, or organizing tea parties or concerts at which ANC propaganda could be disseminated, he followed the lead of the chief steward. But in the "violent struggle" he and not the chief steward had the last word and acted on instructions of the regional volunteer-in-chief.[16]

One of the chief steward's main functions was to select cell stewards,

15. Mashinyana/R*vtr*, pp. 6–7; Mdube/R*vtr*, pp. 21–22.
16. Dondashe/M*galunkulu*, pp. 30–33; Petros/M*akinane*, pp. 46–49; Gulwa/M*apolisa*, pp. 3–4; Mdube/B*ongco*, p. 362.

and the importance of this task must be stressed. A word in the wrong place could, clearly, do incommensurable harm to the organization and could lead to the discovery and arrest of the chief steward and those of the cell stewards already appointed. The chief stewards were compelled to select carefully by force of circumstances and, as a rule, they so well knew whom to select that invitations to join the illegal organization were seldom refused. A man who was likely to refuse was also a man likely to inform, so he was simply not approached. This preselection process also ensured that those appointed would be pleased with their rank of cell steward, as seems always to have been the case.[17] With care, a number of people could be pulled together and organized.

A prospective member first was engaged in conversation and sounded out. If he seemed to be reluctant, the matter was dropped. Once offered a position in the underground movement, however, some pressure was exerted to ensure that he joined. Having revealed themselves to the prospective recruit, the recruiters put themselves in jeopardy. At this stage, if a man did not join willingly, he was dangerous and had to some extent to be intimidated into joining.[18] Fear of punishment for refusing the proffered membership must have played some part in motivating acceptance. There is objective evidence of the fear Africans have of personal assault, predicated upon their generally dangerous lives in the townships. As de Ridder states, "The fear of attack and its resulting anxieties have become ingrained aspects of the urban dweller's personality."[19] The fear of attack is not, of course, a uniquely African phenomenon. City dwellers everywhere know and understand fear of this sort. The urban African, however, lives in a particularly dangerous environment, and his fears are sharpened, not unjustifiably, by the reality surrounding him.[20] So, whether through conviction, fear, or a combination of the two, men entered the ANC.

17. Dondashe/Mgalunkulu, pp. 25–26; Petros/Makinane, pp. 49–50.
18. Petros/Makinane, pp. 32–36; Mbanjwa/Mbolompo, p. 758; Dondashe/Mgalunkulu, p. 17; Kulele/Mgalunkulu, p. 81.
19. C. J. de Ridder, The Personality of the Urban African in South Africa: A Thematic Apperception Test Study (London, 1961), p. 82.
20. Ibid.

VI

The cell stewards were largely concerned with recruitment and with what can be termed "agitation and propaganda." The nature of the cell steward's role had changed. The idea had originally been for each cell steward to organize a cell of seven members around himself. These recruits were, in turn, to find others, build new cells, and themselves become cell stewards. An almost organic growth of the movement was envisaged, as each cell member created a cell and these, in turn, did the same. Through such growth, the ANC would in time become a decentralized mass movement, in a position to carry on an intensive struggle against the government. The cell stewards whose members formed cells of their own would be rewarded in their turn by being made chief stewards. This, however, proved illusory. The movement failed to grow to any great extent. The cell stewards who were originally recruited only rarely recruited any others. They did not build any cells. Cells, in the end, were largely made up of cell stewards and led by a chief steward. The cell stewards were thus, in effect, the lowest-ranking members of the underground ANC.[21]

The scarcity of recruits, given the South African situation, was, as suggested earlier, one of the enigmas of African politics. It is the more remarkable because the numbers the ANC intended to recruit initially were so small. No one thought at the outset of thousands but only of tens and hundreds. However, even these numbers were hard to come by. The cells seem to have drawn few fresh recruits, their size remaining more or less constant to the end. New members were recruited infrequently, in ones and twos. There was, of course, the ever present hope that the organization would grow. What inhibited it? First of all, there was the fear of arrest. This prevented all but the most fervent from joining. It also inhibited those seeking recruits. Unwilling recruits were a danger to the whole cell. It was better to leave it at its existing size than to put pressure on others to join. Although every

21. Dondashe/*Mgalunkulu*, pp. 33, 49; Kulele/*Mgalunkulu*, pp. 64–65; Petros/*Makinane*, p. 49; Gulwa/*Mapolisa*, pp. 4–5.

African was a potential recruit, this potential could only be tapped at great risk.[22]

The underground ANC, as a result, consisted largely of those who had joined it in the first months of illegality. Those who came later remained a minority. If a profile were to be drawn of the typical underground worker, one could say that he was a man with an elementary-school education or at least some elementary schooling, who had been either in the ANC or the ANCYL while it was still legal, and who had, at that time, participated actively in its campaigns. The members were those whose allegiance to the ANC had never been shaken. So the pool from which underground workers could be drawn was limited. It consisted of the most ardent of the former ANC people, usually those who had played some active part. Once re-cruited, they could be accepted without any serious checking of credentials. Checking of credentials was not, in any case, the long suit of the ANC. Generally, when a new member was recruited to the cell, he was simply brought in and introduced to the others by the man who had brought him. The recruiter might simply say, "Com-rades, here is a new member I have obtained," and the question of his suitability was not raised.[23] This, it need hardly be added, made penetration of the underground ANC easier for the police.

The police were aware of this situation and acted both to train people to penetrate the underground ANC and to spread propaganda favorable to the government. African and Coloured detectives were taught in special classes to work not only as agents but also as "educa-tional missionaries." They were hand-picked men, and their special syllabuses were designed to teach them to explain the dangers of subversion to Africans and the future role of the African in the country. The prospects for Africans in the new autonomous areas, or *bantu-stans*, were to be painted in the brightest hues. These men were well trained and often worked in a center away from their homes, thus making it difficult for ANC organizers to detect them. As later inci-

22. Mali/*Magwayi*, pp. 117–19; Mtloko/*Magwayi*, p. 92; Dondashe/*Mgalunkulu*, pp. 19–21; Ncingane/*Makinane*, p. 112; Mbanjwa/*Mbolompo*, p. 769.
23. Ncingane/*Makinane*, pp. 175–76; Zepe/*Mtalana*, p. 37; Kulele/*Mgalunkulu*, p. 67.

dents will indicate, they frequently were able to penetrate the ANC and to secure the arrest of important personages.[24] Secrecy in ANC work, as a result, remained an unresolved problem.

It is difficult to get away from the question of secrecy in any discussion of an underground organization. Faced with the dangers of defection and penetration, the leaders of the cells tried to devise ways of countering these problems. Defection was, in most ways, the easiest to deal with. Penetration was much more difficult to overcome. One way was to ensure that the different cell stewards knew no one in the organization other than their own chief steward. They did not know the contact or the members of the regional committee, who might sit as ordinary members of a cell and be unknown in their roles as members of the higher body. Apart from trying to prevent the members of cells from finding out who members of other cells were, an effort was made to restrict the information given any cell; the members were told only enough to enable them to carry out their orders. The cell stewards were not told all the decisions that had been taken, even those that involved their own activities, unless informing them served a specific purpose. In this way, it was thought, not only could members of the cells disclose no more than their fellow members' names if caught by the police, but they could not even inform on what actions were planned. Similarly, should a police informer penetrate the cell, all he would learn would be the information given in this one unit, which would be incomplete. He could not learn what was being planned for the movement as a whole. The organization in the larger sense would be protected from the dangers of betrayal and penetration.

Apart from recruiting, the cell stewards were to carry out a variety of tasks. They were to be the main agitators and to accomplish their tasks by means of leaflets and by face-to-face contacts. The work of converting Africans to the cause of the ANC, once a matter of public meetings, now had to be carried out in this personal manner. One way of pursuing such associations was through tea parties and concerts, which were difficult for the authorities to prohibit. These were

24. *Evening Post*, February 18, 1956.

open and could be attended by anyone. The tea parties were also a source of funds. It may sound strange to the reader, particularly to those reared in the British tradition, to find tea parties a means of subversion. The thought is almost comical. But in the South African setting, ways had to be found to conceal the character of meetings. At concerts, for instance, ANC songs could be sung and people could talk among themselves. These functions provided an escape from the political aridity to which Africans had been reduced by the laws confining them. The organization of tea parties was the duty of the zone, and all cells were expected to make an effort to get people to attend them. Attendance was taken as a matter of course. What is more, the members of the cells were expected to set a good example by contributing to the collections. These affairs thus provided not only a source of money but also a platform and a recruiting ground.[25]

Tea parties were held quite frequently, each zone being encouraged to hold at least one a week, generally on Saturday morning, a time when most people were not working. Anyone who wished to pay an admission fee, whether he was a member of the ANC or not, was welcomed. As entertainment in the townships was limited, both tea parties and concerts seem to have been well attended. Many who came were, obviously, in the know. Others came for the fun of it and did not care who eventually received the money that was raised. People simply came in off the streets for what promised to be an entertaining time. The beverages sold at these tea parties varied. Some witnesses claimed that drinks stronger than tea were offered for sale and that the name "tea party" was just a euphemism for a drinking bout. At such parties, witnesses later said, the women home brewers, known as "shebeen queens," officiated and it was this that made the parties particularly memorable. African women often supplemented their meager incomes by brewing various kinds of "kaffir beer" at home, and they were celebrated according to the potency of their brews. It is certain, therefore, that the presence of "shebeen queens" at the parties would have been neither surprising nor unwelcome. Whether beer was sold, as some have claimed, or whether it

25. Ngoza/*Magwayi*, p. 2.

134

was not sold does not really make much difference. It may, however, have contributed to the humor of the occasion for some to think of the pleasant way in which they were contributing to the downfall of the system they hated.

Both food and drink were sold at the tea parties, and the profits were sent to the ANC National Executive, after those who had organized the parties had been repaid their expenses. There is, of course, no way of knowing what these were, but it obviously paid to give tea parties or the practice would not have been continued.

The role of women at the tea parties has been touched upon, and their role in the ANC itself is of some interest. Only one witness said that no distinction was made in his zone between men and women members. Others stated a contrary view. African society is, indeed, a very masculine one. The dominance of men was reflected in the organization of the ANC. There is some question, if all the evidence is sifted, as to whether women were allowed to attend the meetings of the cells at all and, if they were allowed to do so, in what capacity. They were not, it would seem, allowed to take part in discussions of violence, sabotage, or such policy matters as could be discussed at cell level. Their role was primarily that of fund raisers and caterers. Where meetings were held in the homes of cell stewards, as most of them were, the women and children were expected to leave the room in which the men would meet. As one man put it, "If a woman were to have come, we would have chased her away. We did not want any women concerned with the affairs of Zone F." [26] African men are, as Laura Longmore has shown in her study of African women, greatly opposed to the idea of equality of the sexes.[27] Even the Communists described women as "very troublesome." With something of masculine optimism, however, they argue that, once women are taught the ideas of Karl Marx, their troublesomeness comes to an end.

26. Dondashe/Mgalunkulu, p. 50; Gulwa/Mapolisa, p. 18; Qumpula/Hlekani, p. 14; Mbelwana/Tsishela, p. 35.
27. Laura Longmore, The Dispossessed: A Study of the Sex Life of Bantu Women in and around Johannesburg (London, 1959), pp. 112–23.

VII

Finance and recruitment were the topics discussed most frequently and most seriously. Without more recruits, the organization was bound to become moribund, the more so as there was constant depletion by arrest. The matter of funds was always pressing also, for the ANC was an organization of poor people. Indeed, until *Umkonto* got under way and the Communists began to bring in funds from abroad, the ANC was always in a parlous plight. It had to rely mainly on membership dues and on funds that could be obtained from genuine or reluctant sympathizers. ANC volunteers, for example, were not averse to extorting money from unwilling African shopkeepers. These funds were needed not only to keep the organization going as such but also to provide support for those who had been imprisoned and their families. Then there was the additional problem of paying people who were trying to build up the movement in the countryside.

The former ANC dues, about 35 cents per annum, were obviously no longer enough. More was needed. A new fee of 28 cents per month was instituted. Changes were made in the way receipts were issued. It was necessary for receipts to be issued, for there no longer were membership cards, and in any case a check had to be kept on those who did and those who did not pay. The receipt, a simple statement of a house number and an amount, was to substitute for the old membership card, and, to distinguish it, the receipt had a picture of a bird imprinted on it. Otherwise, the receipt was blank. To ensure that all the members of the cell paid their dues, the payment was levied in public; that is, at cell meetings. The chief steward sat at a table and the members placed their fees on the table before him. When payments were made with particular promptness, the chief steward might be inspired to praise the members of the cell for their diligence and sense of duty. Any money collected from those outside the organization—from the shopkeepers, for example—was paid to the chief steward at the same time. When members did not have enough money with them, they would borrow from one of the

136

others in order to turn it in at the meeting. Thus the members paid their dues, and the sum collected was passed by the chief steward to the contact, who, in turn, sent it to the National Executive.[28]

The "freedom struggle" could obviously not be financed by such small contributions alone. More was needed than could be raised in this fashion. Apart from funds needed for detainees and dependents, even the most primitive arms and explosives cost money, particularly when they had to be procured by illegal means. The organization did not get enough from members to provide these things. There frequently was insufficient money to pay the maintenance of supporters, making things very hard for various individuals. Special committees to look after the victims of government action were sometimes formed in the hope of providing additional assistance. These needs—money for arms and for men—were to be a constant prod to the activities of the political branch of the underground.

28. Ngoza/*Magwayi*, pp. 2, 6, 49–50; Mbanjwa/*Mbolompo*, p. 751; Mashinyana/*Bongco*, p. 234; Tanana/*Bongco*, p. 332; Qumpula/*Hlekani*, p. 4; Joxo/*Mtalana*, p. 45; Dondashe/*Mgalunkulu*, p. 13; Zepe/*Mtalana*, pp. 15–16; Gulwa/*Mapolisa*, p. 3; Petros/*Makinane*, pp. 32–36; Mashinyana/*Rvtr*, p. 7.

IV

The Struggle among the People

THE STORY SO FAR has been of the organization of the struggle group
and how it was related to the other elements of organization. What
is sometimes termed, in revolutionary jargon, "the struggle among
the people," has hardly been touched upon. Clearly, neither the national leadership nor the struggle group could hope to succeed by its
own efforts alone. To succeed they needed the active support of the
"masses" in their campaigns. Indeed, the need for organizing mass
support at the appropriate times was, like secret organization and the
need for funds, repeatedly stressed in ANC literature. An example of
this is to be found in the mimeographed newssheet *Congress Voice*,
which appeared irregularly from the underground:

> [The aim of the ANC was] to organize Congress on the basis
> of the M-Plan.
> To make all members aware of the immense task facing
> them and the grave responsibilities resting upon them.
> To start a house to house propaganda campaign for the purpose
> of raising the political consciousness of the masses, and to stir up
> hatred and indignation amongst them against oppression.
> To keep the people in a state of permanent readiness so that we
> can always act swiftly to forestall the enemy.

138

To impress on the people the importance of messages conveyed by word of mouth.

To see to it that every member is disciplined, punctual, and always alert.[1]

II

At the same time, new rules for enforcing secrecy were set forth. Although these have been touched on earlier, a brief recapitulation may help toward an understanding of the difficulties in carrying out the broader struggle. The rules were as follows:

1. Organize in small groups instead of large branches.
2. Don't ask questions and don't answer questions.
3. Use leaflets instead of public meetings.
4. Utilize centralized leadership instead of general meetings and conferences.

The need to organize in small groups was, of course, inherent in the M-Plan. But it is difficult to see how, without asking or answering questions, popular support could be obtained. Leaflets also had their limitations. Centralized leadership, again, was more in line with the M-Plan than with the rallying of popular support. It was, *Congress Voice* declared, "the purpose of [the ANC] to give leadership, and if [it] did not do that [it] might as well do nothing at all. Being underground [meant] that [it had to] give leadership in a different way from before." This leadership was attempted with patchy success.

The network of cells has already been called a remarkable achievement, which indeed it was, but the workings of the entire chain of committees and cells were not as good as its sponsors had anticipated. There were many reasons for this. Much of the difficulty was, of course, due to the dangerous conditions in which the organization had to function. The effects of enforced secrecy on what was formerly

1. *Congress Voice*, Vol. II, no. 2 (May, 1960), mimeographed.

a mass movement and which still looked to the masses for support cannot be overestimated. Some of these difficulties are made plain in another issue of *Congress Voice*, which complains that, for all the stress on discipline and sacrifice, the ANC was still not functioning efficiently. This applied not only to the cells but also to the higher echelons. Slackness could not be excused on the grounds of secrecy, the *Voice* continued.[2] It chided the "slackers," stating:

> When we say that security rules must be observed strictly, we do not mean that less work or no work should be done. Some people hide their laziness by saying that they are observing security rules precisely because we have to do so much work under dangerous conditions. Those who do nothing need observe no security at all. It is those who work hardest who must be security conscious.

A further exhortation rounded out the appeal and is worth repeating:

> Friends, let us work hard—much harder than we did before we became an underground organization. Because if we do not, on the one hand, we run the risk of being arrested and sentenced to long terms of imprisonment, for a weak organization—this would be criminal. On the other hand, other elements who do not have the experience nor the sincerity of our organization might step in and sow confusion among the people because of our inactivity. This too would be criminal. If we have to take great risks let us do so for a powerful organization which has the confidence of the people.

In the creation of an insurgent organization of large proportions, the risks were obviously great. The authorities would use every wile to penetrate and to observe it.

Information came to the police not only through their carefully built network of informers but also through the astonishing casualness with which recruiting was often carried out. People frequently were recruited without sufficient care, and members of the underground boasted of their activities. Those arrested, either through indiscretion or through mischance, showed great readiness to betray their erst-

2. *Congress Voice*, (April, 1961), mimeographed, unnumbered.

while associates and thus further threatened the existence of the underground. Some resisted pressures to inform better than did others, but all too often confessions flowed readily. Information was thus forced out, given out, or leaked out. As the May, 1960 issue of *Congress Voice* stated:

> The police have long ears. . . . We know that most of our people are brave and loyal, that they will refuse to become informers on their fellow Congressmen—the worst crime a Congressman can commit. But some people are too fond of talking. They may give away a secret to a friend not meaning any harm . . . and then it is passed from one mouth to another until the Special Branch picks it up.[3]

On the question of secrecy, which clearly is a key one in illegal opposition, the matter of temperament must be taken into account. If de Ridder's interpretation of the character and personality of the urban African is accurate, Africans in South Africa would find it psychologically difficult to function in silence and in secrecy. The combination of anxiety, latent aggressiveness, insufficient moderation and control, exhibitionism, and other components of which he speaks are hardly conducive to the patient and painstaking task of building a secret organization. They are, in fact, more the qualities of men who tend to act on impulse and who think that their bravery would be demonstrated by open admission of their connection with the secret ANC. In 1961 *Congress Voice* found it necessary once more to caution members:

> Observance of security rules is important because it is treacherous to be careless about our organization, as it might expose loyal and hardworking activists to unnecessary arrest and imprisonment. Some of our members confronted by our new methods of work have tended to be impatient with the emphasis on security and they have regarded this as a sign of timidity and cowardice. This is wrong.[4]

3. *Congress Voice*, (May, 1960).
4. *Congress Voice* (April, 1961).

There can be little question, therefore, that there was conflict between working for the ANC underground and not letting this be known. There was also conflict between securing broader support and maintaining secrecy. Those who entered the ranks of the illegal ANC knew well that they were taking risks. They must have had strong motives for shouldering these burdens. Yet they were often indiscreet and, as we have seen, willing to turn state's evidence. A few words on this topic may, therefore, not be out of place before attention is turned to what was actually done to elicit and maintain the support of the larger African constituency.

Police methods of obtaining confessions differed from one group of officers to another. They ranged from coarse and arrogant brutality to quite refined techniques of interrogation. The cruel methods police interrogators used were often brought to the attention of the courts, and in many cases the police officers concerned were punished. Other cases, it must be assumed, passed unnoticed. Brutality was, however, only one aspect of interrogation. Indeed, brutality tended to be self-defeating. Judges in South Africa, as in all civilized countries, found extorted evidence unacceptable. Where evidence had been extorted, the fact often came out in cross-examination, to the embarrassment of the prosecution. The accused, in such cases, were often acquitted and the police censured—a situation hardly to the latter's liking. There was, therefore, greater emphasis on psychological methods of interrogation, which could obtain the same results without throwing evidence into disrepute. Such methods, it seems, came into more general use and replaced the "third degree" methods so rightly condemned by criminologists everywhere. Where more subtle methods are employed, the aim is, as Sir Robert Thompson has said, to defeat the insurgency rather than the individual insurgent.[5] Individuals who prove obdurate might have to be punished, but the man who collaborates with the police need not fear that his past crimes will be held against him. Roger Trinquier makes the same point, saying that

5. Robert Thompson, *Defeating Communist Insurgency: The Lessons of Malaya and Vietnam* (New York, 1966), pp. 55–56.

the best agents are those supplied by the enemy and that, where there is sufficient flexibility in interrogation, individuals might even be persuaded to change sides. Such persons, if offered protection and immunity, can be made the most faithful of tools.[6] Bruno Mtolo, a man of whom we will hear much more, is a case in point. Mtolo not only gave evidence at a number of trials, revealing a great deal of what went on inside the ANC and *Umkonto*, both of which he had formerly served, but he even wrote a book excoriating the organizations and their leaders.

There is no doubt that the South African police took to heart the lessons learned in counterinsurgency. They were assisted in applying the rules by laws which gave them almost unlimited powers of detention. Not only could they hold people as long as they wished (within certain sketchy limits), but also they could offer immunity from all punishment to those willing to tell everything. Evidence obtained from a few individuals could be made the basis for obtaining more evidence from others, until nothing remained hidden. Again and again, when former underground workers were cross-examined as to why they had betrayed the ANC, they said that it was obvious that the police knew everything and that nothing was to be gained by concealing what they themselves knew. The police seemed to know the smallest details of what had been planned and done, a witness said, and it was apparent to him that others had bought their freedom by talking. It would be foolish, therefore, to remain silent and be punished while others who had done even more got away scot-free. It was best, another said, to tell the police the truth, for they knew it all anyway, and he wanted to see his wife and family again. Some, on hearing what the police knew, felt that they had been betrayed by their fellows. Many had been promised safe passage to the (former) Protectorates once they fell under police suspicion, but it had not been provided. They were angry and, as a result, willing to talk. Then there were those who felt that if they did not confess they might be

6. Roger Trinquier, *Modern Warfare: A French View of Counterinsurgency* (New York, 1964), p. 37.

accused of crimes they had not committed as well as those they had; it was best, therefore, to admit what had been done to escape a worse fate.[7]

Two themes recur constantly: the police knew everything about the supposedly secret organization, even to the parts played by individuals; and the highest leaders, such as Nelson Mandela and Walter Sisulu, had admitted the actions of the underground in open court. The words of one witness sum up the feelings of many:

The activities of the African National Congress as well as that of *Umkonto we Sizwe* were secret. I was, shall I say, dumbfounded when I was confronted by the police with activities in which I had partaken. As a matter of fact . . . after my release from custody I went to [another member is named], as a matter of fact, he had not at that stage been arrested yet, and told him that all the activities in which we had partaken were known to the police. I then told him also that I had in fact spoken and advised him to do likewise.[8]

Many felt as this man did, that the police knew all about them, down to their street and zone numbers, and that they knew who had been at meetings, who had distributed pamphlets, as well as other things that had been said and done. "Who was I then to deny such things?" another cried. "What could I hide?" [9] One man had a reason for confessing that was at the same time comic and tragic. The ANC had told him that he would land in trouble if he divulged anything about his work in the movement. But having been arrested he was already in trouble. Therefore, there was no longer any sense in concealing anything.[10] This is completely understandable. Less comprehensible is the reasoning of another man, who said that he told the police everything *because* he had not achieved freedom. When the astonished counsel

7. Mtloko/*Magwayi*, pp. 71–72; Ngoza/*Magwayi*, pp. 11–12; Joxo/*Mtalana*, pp. 59, 65–67.
8. Ngoza/*Magwayi*, p. 13.
9. Mali/*Magwayi*, p. 112.
10. Ntsongana/*Mbolompo*, p. 799.

questioned him on this, he said that he had decided to work with the government because Matanzima had achieved freedom through working with the government (that is, Chief Kaiser Matanzima, the present prime minister of the Transkei, one of the government's Bantustans). He felt that the Africans could never achieve freedom any other way, because the government kept arresting the members of the ANC.[11]

There were, of course, other reasons which led men to denounce the ANC. One was the conduct of leaders in leaving the country. Logically, there was sense in the leaders going abroad to continue the fight, but many in the ranks did not see it this way. If the leaders could run away and save their skins, the reasoning ran, then why should I not save myself with a confession. Others resented the style in which the leaders lived, while ordinary members endured hardships.[12] A passage in Bruno Mtolo's book brings this out, though the rationalization of betrayal must be treated with suspicion. There is enough supporting evidence, however, to make the argument at least theoretically acceptable:

Seloro had shown me Sisulu's house after the party. He had made no bones of his hatred for some of the A.N.C. leaders who were living on the fat of the land. He told me that when Sisulu was sentenced to six years imprisonment he had appealed and was granted R6,000 bail. While out on bail he had bought himself a brand new motorcar, which was later involved in some accident. I don't know much about the quality of furniture but even I could see that Sisulu's furniture was of the best. I am sure that very few Europeans had such furniture. His house looked like one of the showrooms in West Street, Durban. The carpet only showed the turn-ups of your trousers and it felt as if you were walking on cottonwool.[13]

Yet, even when they confessed, few witnesses went as far as Mtolo and renounced their loyalty to the ANC and their commitment to its goals.

11. Kulele/*Mgalunkulu*, pp. 62–63.
12. Zepe/*Mtalana*, p. 31; Mali/*Magwayi*, pp. 113, 127.
13. Bruno Mtolo, *Umkonto we Sizwe: The Road to the Left* (Durban, 1966), p. 73.

III

The ANC, then, was to do what it could to generate the support it needed from among the "people." The planning of this is to be found essentially in three sets of meetings in which important policy matters were made known. These were held in 1961 and 1962 to make clear to the cell memberships what was intended for the organization as a whole. At these meetings the phases of the armed struggle were disclosed to the by no means reluctant members of the ANC. The dates of the meetings are difficult to fix. The memories of those participating differ, and not all the meetings were held at the same time. The meetings were, however, called by the NEC to initiate the implementation of the M-Plan. Little need be said of the initial meetings, which have been discussed in the previous chapters. It is the second set that is of more immediate concern. This set of meetings was held, as closely as can be determined, between May and June of 1961.[14] They marked the turning point in the ANC, for it was at these meetings that members were told of the abandonment of nonviolence as the principal plank of ANC policy, and of the limited violence which was to be allowed members of the organization.

Although specific wordings differ, there is a common pattern to what was said at each of these meetings, so it can be assumed that a set of instructions was given all chief stewards. Where necessary, individual cells will be described; otherwise, what is said of one applies to all.

The meetings began with an attack on the intransigence of the government and then outlined the steps to be taken, ending with a call to resist the police should they attempt to interfere with ANC meetings or activities. At one meeting, for instance, the following statement was made:

We have often spoken to the Government but they won't listen, we've done all sorts of things including boycotts, distribution of

14. Nongubo/*Ngcumane*, p. 15; Gulwa/*Mapolisa*, p. 5; Petros/*Makinane*, p. 33; Kulele/*Mgalunkulu*, pp. 56, 82–83; Dondashe/*Mgalunkulu*, p. 7; Ngoza/*Magwayi*, p. 3; Qumpula/*Hlekani*, p. 18.

leaflets, strikes—the object being to get the Government to pay heed, to listen to us. In spite of this the Government has not listened. The time has now come when violence would be resorted to . . . members must now arm themselves when they go to meetings so that if a policeman should enter and disturb us we shall kill him then and there. Even when distributing leaflets if we should come across a policeman who wants to arrest us or disturb us, we must kill him.[15]

Another speaker, at another meeting, added that "the ANC was now tired . . . [it] had tried to address the Government but the Government just would not listen." This theme was constantly repeated. The government was deaf to entreaty. It had remained unmoved when the ANC tried to induce it to change its course by nonviolent campaigns. Violence might make it take notice.[16]

Yet the violence advocated at this point was defensive in intent. It was just an extension of the nonviolent struggle. The initiative in violent encounters remained with the government. If such a relatively peaceful activity as distribution of leaflets was allowed to take place unhindered, there would be no violence. The ANC would only react to police action. Violence was not to be carried to the opponent. Meetings were to be defended, as were the distribution of leaflets and the collection of money, but that was all. If the police turned a blind eye and left well enough alone, there would be no serious consequences for anyone.

Where violence was to be used, however, the means at the disposal of the ANC remained crude and primitive. One chief steward, saying much the same as all the others, put it this way:

I told them of this policy of violence and informed them that they had to arm themselves with whatever arms they had available, even if this was only an old axe or spear. Even if he had a revolver he was no longer to keep this in hiding but to bring it with him should he come to meetings.[17]

15. Ngoza/Magwayi, p. 52.
16. Dondashe/Mgalunkulu, pp. 7–8; Zepe/Mtalana, pp. 12–13; Ngoza/Magwayi, pp. 3–4.
17. Joxo/Mtalana, p. 42.

147

Leaders had viewed the change from a policy of nonviolence to one of violence with some trepidation. The ANC had so long preached nonviolence that it was feared members might be alienated by the change.[18] To some extent this was based on precedent; East London's reaction to the 1952 riots was not forgotten. Times, however, were different. Some of the leaders, particularly Luthuli and the men close to him, might deplore the new turn, but to those who had joined the cells the decision was by no means an unwelcome one. The general reaction was satisfaction, for the members felt that now they would get their freedom.[19]

The determination to defend ANC activities against the police soon bore fruit. When the district commandant of police in Port Elizabeth, Major O. Kjelvie, tried to stop a group of Africans on the march, he was stabbed to death. The men were all volunteers, according to later testimony, and were distributing leaflets announcing a bus boycott, or stay-at-home strike, for the following day, June 26, 1961.[20] This day had been nominated a National Day of Mourning by the ANC, and Africans were ordered not to use any of the municipal services as a sign of their solidarity with the African National Congress. The police did not accept this version. According to police evidence, the men who killed Major Kjelvie were a gang terrorizing the township's residents. Terror was being employed to compel all Africans there to participate in the boycott. While it is impossible to say whether either version is entirely true, it would seem that there was substance in both stories. There can be little question, given what did happen on June 26, a day on which buses were stoned and passengers attacked, that terror was part of the plan. Be that as it may, the attack on a high-ranking police officer brought an immediate response. Some 100 known volunteers were arrested, and the police staged a show of force in the townships, driving some 10 armored troop carriers around the streets while another 50 to 100 police patrolled on foot. The boycott did take place despite these actions, but the presence of the police

18. Bernstein/*Rvtr*, p. 30; Nelson Mandela, *No Easy Walk to Freedom*, ed. Ruth First (New York, 1965), pp. 169–70; Sisulu/*Rvtr*, p. 151.
19. Zepe/*Mtalana*, p. 13; Magidwana/*Tsehla*, p. 47; Joxo/*Mtalana*, p. 43.
20. Du Preez/*Magwayi*, p. 143.

ensured that it remained small.[21] There were violent incidents, but these were fewer than were to take place the next year, 1962, when attacks on buses, drivers, and passengers assumed far greater proportions.[22] At any rate, the incident illumines one way of politicizing the public.

IV

As the idea of a mass uprising tends to dominate the thinking of an insurgent opposition, political action is given pride of place. So the distribution of leaflets was seen as one of the most important of the tasks of ANC members. The cell stewards, really the lowest-ranking members of the ANC, were in charge of this. They went out at the dead of night to distribute their leaflets, which were the only means of publicizing ANC attitudes and activities and so of holding the support of the Africans.

As distributing leaflets of a banned organization was illegal, the means of doing so had to be carefully arranged; the methods evolved with local variations, although a general pattern does emerge.[23] By and large, the procedure followed these lines: the cell stewards were summoned to the home of the chief steward at night, usually between 10:00 and 11:00 P.M., when most people were asleep in their homes. African workers, as a whole, were too tired at night to keep late hours; mostly they went to bed from 8:30 P.M. onward, some even retiring on returning home from work. As a man of forty-five put it, "This keeps me off the streets and prevents my getting drunk and being assaulted." [24] So, by 10:00 P.M. the cell stewards could be reasonably certain that the streets would be clear and that they could go about unseen. Unlike the meetings of the cells, the nights for the distri-

21. Du Preez/*Magwayi*, pp. 141–43.
22. Ngoza/*Magwayi*, pp. 15–16.
23. Qumpula/*Hlekani*, pp. 15–17; Lucingo/*Makinane*, pp. 88–89; Petros/*Makinane*, pp. 66–68; Gulwa/*Mapolisa*, pp. 12–15; Joxo/*Mtalana*, pp. 48–49, 60; Zepe/*Mtalana*, p. 63.
24. B. A. Pauw, *The Second Generation: A Study of the Family among Urbanized Bantu in East London* (London, 1963), p. 24.

bution of leaflets were not fixed, and members could be called on to distribute them at any time.

The leaflets would be given to the cell stewards at the home of the chief steward. Since some of them were illiterate, they did not know what was in the leaflets unless the chief steward told them. He might, for instance, tell them that the pamphlets concerned some campaign, such as the Day of Mourning, and outline the instructions given in the pamphlets concerning it. But this was not always the case. At some times the chief stewards simply handed out the leaflets without comment, telling the members nothing of what was in them. Whether this was done in accordance with instructions from the NEC or not is unknown. It may have been a matter of individual whim, and this indeed seems the most likely explanation. All that can be said with certainty is that there was no standard procedure.

The means of avoiding suspicion were more standardized. To avoid attracting the unwelcome attentions of the police, the individuals who were to distribute leaflets would sometimes time their arrivals at the chief steward's house so that they would not all appear together. They would trickle in, in twos and threes, rather than coming in a body. On arriving they might find that some had already departed and others had not yet come. But this policy of arriving and leaving separately was subject to change. There were times when the cell stewards all came together and then went out together in a group of five or six, working their way down their route, street by street. They would carefully place the leaflets under doors or, if a house had a locked gate, under a stone near the gate. Though there was no rule, they sometimes split up into two groups, each working a different side of the same street. It was rare, in any case, for the group to split completely and, as single individuals, to each work a street alone. At least a few would stay together for moral support and for protection.

Just as the chief steward was apparently at liberty to explain the contents of the leaflets or not, so he might or might not accompany the cell stewards on their rounds. It was customary for the chief steward to take the place of any absent member or in some cases to act as lookout, going ahead of the team. These activities, it appears, were a matter of choice on his part.

The cell stewards, by all accounts, enjoyed distributing leaflets. There was, doubtless, a certain sense of community and shared danger in going out at night, and a sense of responsibility was kindled in the more experienced members who guided those less experienced and, therefore, ignorant of the dangers. With the distribution taking as long as an hour, the danger of arrest was quite real. If the distribution began at, say, 11:00 P.M., it was usually completed by midnight, at which time the cell stewards reported back to the chief steward. At first they had all come in a body, but this was later considered too dangerous and they came and made their reports one by one. It is interesting that seldom was one man appointed to represent all, though this might have been the most logical and least dangerous way of doing things. There is no explanation of why this method was not adopted.

To describe the mode of distribution tells little of the impact of the leaflets. There seems no question that the leaflets were effective, particularly when backed by intimidation. The effectiveness of the leaflets was assured because those who could read passed on their contents by word of mouth. How many were reached in this manner is a matter of conjecture. But the results were evident. The leaflets usually called for a boycott in one form or another, which often required Africans to refuse municipal services such as electricity or transport. In addition, Africans were urged not to read certain newspapers critical of the ANC, such as *Elethu, Imvo, Mirror,* and *Zonk.* They were also told not to listen to the rediffusion service of the South African Broadcasting Corporation (a government-owned company that had a monopoly on broadcasting), which was seen as a means of indoctrinating Africans to accept government policies. Those who did not heed the instructions set out in the leaflets were often savagely and at times fatally assaulted. Fights were particularly prevalent on and just before the National Day of Mourning, which, since 1960, had taken place every June 26, when volunteers would often attack workers and be attacked in return. The fights were not over support of government policies, for few Africans would have defended those. The fights broke out because many African workers did not want to have to walk to work or to lose a day's pay by staying at home. Others, however, did as they were told. They walked to work and, as June is midwinter in South Africa, froze in the cold and ate uncooked food rather than use electricity. They also displayed their solidarity with the ANC by lighting small fires outside their homes, as the ANC had insisted they do.[25]

Although it was hazardous for the ordinary African to refuse to follow the lead of the ANC, for those in the organization danger was a constant presence. It was dangerous to distribute leaflets and it was dangerous to hold cell meetings. Steps were taken to reduce the dangers, such as rotating the meeting places. Each meeting would be held in the house of a different member in turn. One week it might be in the house of the chief steward; another, in the house of one of the cell stewards. But no matter where the members were to meet, the night of the week was always the same. A cell might meet on Tuesday nights. In this case they might meet at the house of any one of the members, but it would always be on a Tuesday night. From the first meeting of the cell to the last, the night of the meeting would be unchanged.[26] As one member put it, "Meetings were held in the houses of all the members in turn, the reason being to try and confuse the police."[27] Another said, "The object was that we did not want to be caught at it. The object of having these meetings on a rotatory basis was that we did not want it known. Because then we would be arrested."[28] Security may have been better fostered had the meetings been held at different hours and on different nights, but this would probably have involved insuperable problems of administration even for so small a unit as a cell. Once the night was fixed, all that the members needed to be told was in whose house the next meeting was to be held. When a member was absent from the meeting, at which time the place of the next one was given, it was his business to find this out from one of the others.[29]

25. Ncingane/Makinane, p. 112; Joxo/Mtalana, p. 49; Mtloko/Magwayi, p. 66; du Preez/Magwayi, p. 142.
26. Magidwana/Tsehla, pp. 43–44; Kulele/Mgalunkulu, p. 68; Dondashe/Mgalunkulu, p. 13; Qumpula/Hlekani, p. 4; Lucingo/Makinane, pp. 27–32, 87–88; Petros/Makinane, pp. 82–83; Gulwa/Mapolisa, p. 8; Zepe/Mtalana, pp. 20, 34; Joxo/Mtalana, pp. 54–55; Ngoza/Magwayi, p. 2; Mtloko/Magwayi, p. 63.
27. Gungulu/Khayingo, p. 7.
28. Zepe/Mtalana, p. 21.
29. Gulwa/Mapolisa, p. 34.

The atmosphere of such meetings can only be partially recaptured. A participant speaks of one meeting as follows:

There is no electric light in the section where the meeting was held, but there was a central lighting fixture. The curtains were closed but one could see clearly in the room. When one enters these houses, in this section, [one enters] the front room and there is a room on the right and a room on the left, and these meetings were always held in the room on the right.

The room was small, the witness said, and crammed with furniture. The men sat wherever there was space, or stood around the walls. The only illumination was from an oil lamp hanging from the ceiling.[30] It is easy to picture them there in the poor light, discussing the hardships of their people and the steps they intend taking against the government. It was in rooms such as this that the struggle group took decisions to act according to their interpretation of what the leaders had demanded.

The need for unity was a constant theme at meetings of the cells. People had to unite to gain their freedom, and many suggestions were made as to the expansion and continuation of the freedom struggle. Newspapers, particularly *New Age*, were read with rapt attention. Articles on how other peoples had gained their freedom were studied with particular care. There were often discussions on specific points, such as the demand for equal wages with whites and the right to unrestricted travel through abolition of the pass laws. The chief steward generally selected the themes that were discussed. Once the discussion was over the chief steward asked whether the members supported him in opposing these measures. Not surprisingly, the answer was always affirmative.[31] Another matter that came up from time to time was that of traitors and informers, whose names were passed out at these meetings. A general anathema was pronounced against those who left the ANC. They would be severely dealt with, it was said, because if anyone left "one could not know which side he was on." [32] Violence was a theme that recurred in the cells. A cell was told of the "achieve-

---

30. Qumpula/*Hlekani*, p. 17.
31. Mbelwana/*Tsishela*, p. 30; Gulwa/*Mapolisa*, p. 8; Joxo/*Mtalana*, p. 51.
32. Mhlawuli/*Mapolisa*, p. 23.

ment" of other "comrades," such as those who had killed Major Kjelvie, and were admonished because they had not done likewise.[33]

Not all meetings consisted of friendly discussions of issues and tactics. As a participant at one meeting recalled: "We merely went there to listen to what is being told to us." What they were told was to be at a certain house at a given time, say 7:00 P.M., and when they came the meeting would begin. Members (who had been instructed on whether to come singly or in pairs) would assemble and then would be given the latest instructions from the NEC by the chief steward. There usually were no questions at meetings of this sort, and the group broke up quickly after the chief steward had spoken. Such meetings lasted no more than four or five minutes so that the participants could vanish before the police got wind of the gathering.[34]

The first pattern was doubtless prevalent early in the period of secret operation; the second, after the police net had been tightened.

Members were also cautioned about carelessness in observing security rules and were told of another cell which had been arrested while a meeting was in progress.[35] Yet for all the brave talk about resisting the police, fear of arrest remained strongly implanted. Resistance to the police was rare. The general reaction, when confronted by a police contingent, was to run away and hide. Fear of arrest and of indefinite detention haunted the underground and colored much of their thought. The functioning of an entire cell might stop, for instance, on the arrest of a single member, particularly if that member was the chief steward. Frightened, the others would not want to call meetings in case they were, in turn, arrested.[36] An arrested man was suspect when he was released. "We were afraid of people who had been released," one witness said, "because we did not know whether they had informed the police about us."[37] Arresting and releasing ANC members, whether they confessed or not, thus was another arrow in the police quiver. The cell structure of the ANC could often be disrupted

33. Joxo/Mtalana, pp. 43–44.
34. Zepe/Mtalana, p. 21.
35. Mbelwana/Tsishela, p. 28; Gulwa/Mapolisa, p. 7.
36. Qumpula/Hlekani, p. 15.
37. Kulele/Mgalunkulu, pp. 75–77.

154

even when a suspect was not held or there was no concrete evidence that would stand up in court.

Cell meetings were attended regularly because attendance was compulsory. Members did, of course, miss the occasional meeting; but "it was the rule that, anybody unable to attend the meeting was to report the fact and give the reason why. . . . The person unable to attend, was to report to the nearest member, and would ask his nearest member to report to the Chief Steward why he was unable to attend the meeting." [38] The cells seem to have been less permissive of slack attendance than were the higher committees; this may have been because they felt themselves functional rather than appendages without power or influence.

Control over attendance was assured the chief steward because of the smallness of the cell. It was obvious at any meeting who was present and who was absent; elaborate membership rolls were not needed. Such lists would have been invaluable at the time when the ANC operated openly, but they were not kept. Later, they would have been dangerous and pointless. Suspicions, always near the surface in the underground ANC, were aroused against a member who attended irregularly or was often absent without reason. Absence for more than two successive meetings would, for instance, be held as defection tantamount to treason. Such a member, if found, might be beaten up or even killed. He was now an object of fear, for he had taken part in the work of the cell and he knew what the others had done. These things would be useful coin to buy immunity from prosecution. The idea was, therefore, to apply deterrent sanctions before the hostile act was consummated.[39]

Fear of sanctions from their fellows thus served to bind the members to the cell as much as did belief. People who may have wished either to leave the ANC or to inform on it had to remain on whether they liked it or not. While this policy served to cement the cell, it was also self-defeating in many ways. Often, members who had informed, or who out of fear had given information when arrested, continued to attend

38. Gulwa/*Mapolisa*, pp. 10–11.
39. Ncingane/*Makinane*, p. 118; Tanana/*Bongco*, p. 351.

meetings if they believed that their actions were not known to the others. There was at least one case of a member who had made a statement to the police when he was arrested, and who continued to go to meetings because of fear of other cell members. The police allowed the cell to function one month more, it seems, to assemble the evidence for a cast-iron case.[40]

VI

The all-pervasive anxiety among urban Africans has been commented on in the work of de Ridder. Joining the underground ANC was bound to increase anxiety. Why then did men join as chief stewards or cell stewards? This question is, in the nature of things, difficult to answer. It can only be answered in part from such evidence as is available.

Witnesses in the courtroom who gave their reasons for joining the ANC were obviously influenced by the circumstances in which they found themselves. Nonetheless, the nature of their evidence enables us to place some reliance on it. Few, for instance, repudiated the ANC, although some said that the turn to violence had been a bad thing. The deportment of the witnesses may have run the gamut from defiance to unctuousness, but by and large they remained true to the objectives of the ANC. The wish, expressed in the Constitution of the ANC, to unite the African people in "a powerful and effective instrument to secure their complete liberation from all forms of discrimination and national oppression" remained their wish. So too was the aim of striving "for the attainment of universal adult suffrage and the creation of a united democratic South Africa." [41] They may not, as the Constitution did, have endorsed the Freedom Charter, the terms of which few knew, but the general idea was there. The ordinary member may not have expressed his ideas in such elevated language and may

40. Mali/*Magwayi*, pp. 114–17.
41. *Constitution of the African National Congress* (n.p., n.d.), mimeographed, p. 11.

not have known what particular phrases meant, but he knew that he wanted what he named his "freedom." This was the one point on which no doubt seemed to exist. It was expressed in a more earthy way but was in tune with ANC aims. One man, for example, said that he approved of the ANC because it sought freedom for Africans and sought to achieve this without bloodshed. Through strikes, boycotts, and other demonstrations, it would "force the Government to pay attention to the ANC." [42] A leader in East London, who had been a member of the legal organization from its first days and then a member of the underground, confirmed that the ANC had sought its ends without violence. They had tried to "secure the entire liberation for the African people from pass laws and to extend the franchise." [43] The view that the franchise was the end of all ills was not held by everyone. Pressed on this, one of the witnesses admitted that the question of "one man, one vote" was vast and that it was "quite fundamental in this that it would still have to take us time when if we were to achieve our object, to start educating the remaining percentage of the community, and the 'one man, one vote,' how would one explain to the masses what that meant?" [44]

Hatred of the pass laws emerges, as one might expect, as a prime motivator. It was the pass laws, an African said, that constituted the Africans' greatest grievance. Hatred for these laws was of long standing and has been discussed. It only remains to note how often the question arose.

Men joined the underground ANC, then, because they wanted their freedom and hated the pass laws. There were, of course, other reasons also. Some seem dubious, such as that of a man who claimed to have joined because a prominent African leader in Cape Town told him to. The story runs that he was asked to join the organization and, when he asked what it was, was told that he could not learn this until he joined, as the organization was secret. He thereupon joined and was told that the aims were to fight the pass laws and to collect

42. Gungulu/*Khayingo*, p. 17.
43. Mashinyana/*Bongco*, p. 246.
44. *Ibid.*

money for the support of imprisoned leaders. There was more to it than that, he was also told, but these other things he would learn later.[45] If this is true, then the readiness with which he entered an obviously illegal organization may seem suspicious. On the other hand, many of those who came to town from the countryside were naive and trusting, particularly toward their kinsmen, and could thus be recruited directly into the underground or into the support group. They were likely recruits because they too opposed the pass laws.

As the ANC grew more militant, the motives for joining became more purposive. One witness, speaking for many of the others, said that he joined because he wanted to engage in acts of sabotage against the government. He saw in sabotage the only way of gaining the vote. With the franchise, he said, Africans could always outvote the white man.[46] Another young man confessed to being one of a group called together to fight the white man. They were initially told nothing of how this was to be done but had later learned that this was to be through guerrilla war, for which they were to be trained overseas.[47] Not all members favored violence for its own sake. A man changed his political allegiance from POQO to the ANC, for instance, because he preferred ANC policy, which saw "all races were brothers and sisters and would stay in South Africa, whereas POQO wanted to drive the Whites into the sea." Whites should only be driven into the sea, he contended, if they persisted in refusing the African his freedom.[48]

VII

Gaining a support group is less a matter of "winning men's minds" than it is a matter of securing their compliance. Minds may be won, of course, but their numbers at any time are likely to be small. It is *haltung* rather than *stimmung*—conformity rather than agreement—

---

45. Sigwilli/*Mbolompo*, p. 872.
46. Tollie/*Fazili*, p. 94.
47. Makeke/*Bongco*, p. 414.
48. Mgemtu/*Mbolompo*, p. 705.

that is necessary.[49] This is true both for government and for insurgents in a revolutionary time. Winning the belief of sufficient numbers is slow and often impossible. Imposing the will of the organization is easier and quicker. Indeed, as Roland Gaucher rightly points out, the mere fact that a population is in ferment by no means assures the revolutionaries of a fighting force.

> However favorably disposed the population may be, its fighting capacity is uncertain, its will is weak and its capacity to resist is subject to the pressure of state power. In order for [revolution] to be victorious it must first impose its law not on the enemy but rather on the population that it wishes to lead into battle. It must subject the people to a power that is a permanent challenge to the established power. . . . Any armed movement that is rooted in the masses is more or less forced to apply the same violence that it directs at the enemy to the masses themselves, whether in major or minor form.[50]

The purpose of the insurgents is to maximize disorder, but this demands discipline in their own ranks. The revolutionaries can accomplish their goals only if they can continually increase the force they are able to exert on their opponents and, at the same time, are able to protect their adherents. Once force is called for, violence and the threat of violence are the indispensable adjuncts to revolt. Indeed, displays of force from time to time are essential. Force is a weapon that gains greater efficacy as it is employed. There is surely no more ineffective weapon in the revolutionists' arsenal than the exploded threat. Threat without capacity is not only valueless against an opponent, but it is also destructive of revolutionary morale. The only positive result of sterile threats is preemptive counterviolence on the part of the opponent, a result distinctly unfavorable to the insurgents. Power, in this sense, is measured by the capacity to make threatened actions real. It depends not only on sanctions against those who do not comply but

49. Jacques Ellul, *Propaganda: The Formation of Men's Attitudes* (New York, 1965), p. 25 n.
50. *The Terrorists: From Tsarist Russia to the OAS* (London, 1965), p. 30.

also protection for those who do. The ANC planned to use the M-Plan to this end. The plan was aimed at controlling not only the ANC but also Africans outside its ranks.

One purpose of this control was to create a pool of potential members and also, later on, of potential recruits for military training. To this end a number of organizations were set in motion, which, though not so labeled, were widely understood to be continuations of the banned ANC. Only two of these will be discussed at this point: the *Olutja* Youth League (also known as the Youth League and by other names) and the General Workers' Union. These bodies, which had little of the corporate structure so dear to the hearts of African leaders, are difficult to describe for that reason. They were shadowy, and indeed could be little else given the laws. The best description is that they were something between a movement and a mob. Their existence and intended role make them interesting.

There is evidence to indicate that some effort had been made to organize young African men even before direct instructions had been sent by the NEC. In its directive calling for the establishment of *Olutja*, probably sometime in 1961, the NEC urged that thought and attention be given the matter, as it was of first importance for the future to have young people organized. The members knew that to conduct an active opposition an inflow of young men would have to be assured. Men would be arrested and others would be sent overseas; replacements had to be on hand. In particular, once *Umkonto* had been established, its manpower must necessarily be drawn from the ANC, so future recruits had to be readied. Therefore the NEC, it seems, directed the branches to form *Olutja*. The form the organization was to take and the means of recruitment were left to the local bodies —a rare example of escape from bureaucratism.

Given these facts, recruitment for *Olutja* did not greatly differ from that used for the ANC, except that less care was needed. The aim in drawing in the young men was to entice them to join without making an overtly political appeal. The inducements were to be sport and recreation, and also parties, concerts, and other meetings with popular appeal for young people. Those who attended regularly were to be engaged in political discussions to determine where they stood on the issues. Once this was known, and if the aspirant favored the aims and methods of the underground ANC, he was asked to join. Anyone else would be left out. The purpose of employing this method was to avoid wastage of potentially useful men and to keep out those who might betray the organization.[51] At the risk of anticipating later argument, it may be added that *Olutja* was seen as a funnel by which men could be directed to *Umkonto*. There is something of the pattern Trinquier describes for Algeria in all this. The FLN in Algeria aimed at bringing people into the insurgency by degrees; slowly they would be drawn in until they were too deeply enmeshed for escape. Often it began with demands for money. Once a man was established as a contributor, he might be coerced or persuaded into becoming a collector. Then step by step he would be driven more deeply into illegality until he was completely absorbed in the revolutionary organization.[52]

The first of these steps was put into practice in the youth movement. Extortion of contributions was nothing new to the ANC and was admitted even by the press sympathetic to the organization. Although the press admitted this, it made clear that such extortion, where it took place, was not sanctioned by the leadership of the ANC. The NEC, it was argued, was against extortion, but once *Olutja* was set up, extortion began. The leadership issued a strong denunciation of the extortions uncovered in the bachelors' quarters at Langa, a township near Cape Town. Gangs using names by which *Olutja* was known, such as *Oo vuk 'ayibambe*, were threatening residents with knives, clubs, and similar weapons. They forced men to join *Olutja* and extracted a "joining fee" from them. The ANC argued that the *Olutja* men involved were not from the same *Olutja* it had sponsored but were members of PAC, which, it was claimed, had in the past forced people to join.[53]

Whoever they were, their techniques were simple and direct, as the two examples quoted will show. The first is the case of Ngangunze Ndude, who told this story to the newspaper:

51. Mbanjwa/*Mbolompo*, pp. 758, 761; Gqosha/*Mbolompo*, p. 834; Mtloko/*Mbolompo*, pp. 868–69; Ntlenzi/*Mbolompo*, p. 849; Bomvana/*Mbolompo*, p. 860; Mgemtu/*Mbolompo*, p. 704.
52. Trinquier, *Modern Warfare*, pp. 14–15.
53. *New Age*, May 3, 1962.

161

There was a bang at the door and a big group of heavily armed men dashed in. They told us to come into the main hall of the block and ordered, "Those who are with us this side, and those who support Verwoerd—the other," but no one moved.

They then demanded that the residents produce their Reference Books and took down names. These were assumed to be new recruits and had to pay 25 cents [i.e., U. S. 35¢] "joining fee." [54]

Ndude was indignant when his name was taken down, and he protested: "Withdraw my name, because I do not want to join and no good purpose will be served by your forcing me against my will." The men from *Olutja* were angry and advised Ndude to reconsider. Another resident of the bachelors' quarters, a Mr. Mdlikiva, whose place was also invaded by these men, told of their claim to be organizing people to "unite and fight for freedom." When Mdlikiva asked them what the policy of their organization was, he was told that it was contrary to their instructions to discuss this. On this Mdlikiva chased his potential recruiters out of his home. Whether these men were authorized or not, the ANC was scathing in its comments:

This criminal handling of the people, the extortion of their money, and the bedevilling of the struggle which we who are concerned with the liberation of our people must view with great seriousness must be exposed and condemned with the contempt it deserves. It imposes a responsibility on us and all those who are opposed to gangsterism to fight it with all the determination we can muster.[55]

In spite of these strong words, the ANC either would not or could not constrain these "organizers." In the end the residents took matters into their own hands. They formed a Vigilance Committee, set out in search of the extortionists, and, on finding them, attacked them. A fight broke out which ended only with the appearance of the police, who arrested anyone on whom they could lay hands. The fight was, in due course, followed by another police sweep in which, according to

54. *Ibid.*, May 10, 1962.
55. *Ibid.*, May 3, 1962.

New Age, they were assisted by an informer who pointed out the individuals involved to them.[56]

The formation of the General Workers' Union has some points of similarity with *Olutja*. The idea of a trade union as a "transmission belt" by which the "party motor" could drive the "working classes" is quite a common simile among Communists. This is discussed later; all that need be pointed out now is that the Communist Party was already working in close association with the ANC. The South African Congress of Trade Unions, one of its "fronts," was a member of the Congress Alliance (see Glossary of Organizations). As a trade union coordinating body, SACTU could encourage the formation of independent unions, and General Workers' Unions were created in different centers from 1955 on. Their purpose seems to have been less to perform the traditional functions of trade unions, i.e., to secure better wages and working conditions for their members, than to act as an organizational substitute for the ANC.

During the State of Emergency, the starting point for much of the clandestine organization, ANC activity fell to a low ebb. Some of the most devoted members carried on in various ways, but for the majority continued activity was not feasible. A rumor soon spread that the ANC was to be continued in a different guise. The General Workers' Union, it was bruited about, was actually the ANC. Indeed, there seems to have been little attempt to disguise this. A member of the audience at a union meeting later recalled that this was hinted at in quite an obvious way. Symbols associated with the ANC were adopted by the union, the salute to be used resembled that of the ANC, and a new cry, "Amandla Ngawethu," replaced "Mayebuye i Afrika." These were, of course, the same symbols as those adopted by the ANC volunteers. To maintain the masquerade as a trade union, questions of working conditions were brought up at meetings, but apparently no grievance raised at a meeting was ever brought to the attention of an employer. In addition to salutes and the trappings of unionism, symbols redolent of the ANC were sold to raise funds. Neckties in the union's colors, which coincided with the colors of the ANC (green and black), were

56. *Ibid.*

offered to members.[57] In one rather amusing exchange, a witness recalled refusing to buy the tie because it was homemade and he wanted one "made in a store." In any event, Africans saw the symbols and drew the obvious conclusions.[58]

As was earlier suggested, the General Workers' Union was affiliated with the South African Congress of Trade Unions (SACTU), which was not a banned organization, although its officers were continually harassed. In at least one case, an officer who was an alien was deported. There were continual police raids on SACTU offices, with the accompanying confiscation of documents.[59] Inasmuch as the organization could still operate openly, however, its meetings provided one of the few platforms available to the ANC. A meeting called under SACTU auspices would, for instance, be addressed by a man delegated by the ANC who, although known as such, would not openly identify his connection with the underground movement. To have made his associations known openly would simply have invited arrest. The tenor of the speech presented would, however, make his role abundantly clear.[60] There were many meetings of this nature, and it would serve little purpose to run through them all. A few are, however, worth special attention. In 1961, for instance, Vuysile Mini, then underground organizer for the ANC, spoke. He called for the bus boycott, or stay-at-home strike, on June 26, which turned out to be violent.[61] At another meeting, in Durban, G. Mbhele, described as a "former organizing secretary of the banned ANC," read a speech of Luthuli's. Among the things called for by Mbhele was to "smash and render unworkable Bantu Authorities both in rural and in urban areas." [62] The speech clearly referred to the violence in Pondoland at that time and to the violence that was to be brought to the cities.

57. Ntsongana/*Mbolompo*, pp. 792–97; Mcelu/*Mbolompo*, p. 817; Mcebi/*Mbolompo*, p. 826.

58. Ntsongana/*Mbolompo*, p. 797.

59. There are many reports of this in *New Age;* two typical ones are those of March 24, 1960, and in the renamed paper *Spark* of January 10, 1963. There was also correspondence with the International Confederation of Free Trade Unions on the deportation of Edward Davoren, a SACTU official, in 1964.

60. Mbanjwa/*Mbolompo*, pp. 754–66; Dirker/*Mbolompo*, p. 1121.

61. *New Age*, February 2, 1961.

62. *Ibid.*, October 26, 1961.

The use of SACTU as a mouthpiece is hardly surprising. One would expect the ANC to use every one of the few loopholes remaining to circumvent the ban on its activities. As a result, a list of speakers at SACTU meetings reads like a list of ANC leaders not yet silenced. The list, however, grew smaller and smaller.

On their side, the SACTU leaders, many of them reputedly active Communists, were well satisfied. The use of SACTU as a channel increased their hold on the ANC. Since their platforms were being used, they had a voice as to the speakers. This did not constitute the only hold they had through SACTU. If organizers were to give much time to their tasks, they would be unable to hold regular jobs and thus had to be paid some sort of salary. ANC organizers could be employed by SACTU, ostensibly as trade union organizers, and paid as such. This would, at least in theory, give them access to African industrial workers, who were considered particularly ripe for entry into the ANC. As union organizers they could address groups of African workers.[63] The meetings could also be used as a device to turn Africans against their fellows who were not in favor of the objectives of the ANC. One case in Port Elizabeth, for instance, concerned a factory personnel officer (an African), who had had a man dismissed as an agitator. The dismissed man held a meeting at the factory in which he apparently called for a strike and said, at the same time, that 1963 was to be the year of the black man. The whites were to be massacred or booted out, and black traitors—like the personnel officer—were to be killed.[64]

The result of the use of unions was that memberships of the ANC, *Umkonto*, and SACTU overlapped. The case of Solomon Mbanjwa—one of the most useful of the witnesses—clearly indicates this. Mbanjwa was, according to his admission, at the same time an ANC branch secretary, a volunteer-in-chief, a member of the Natal Provincial Executive of the ANCYL, and a fulltime SACTU organizer. Later he became active in *Umkonto* as well.[65] The close relationships of ANC, SACTU, and *Umkonto* can also be read between the lines of the crypto-Communist press. ANC leaders, now defined as "former" leaders,

---

63. Mbanjwa/*Mbolompo*, pp. 754–55, 758.
64. *Eastern Province Herald*, December 5, 1964.
65. Mbanjwa/*Mbolompo*, pp. 748–49.

praised the close support they obtained from SACTU. Walter Sisulu said that the "struggle for liberation" depended largely "on the organization of the workers into the trade union movement," whose function it was to "educate and lead the workers so that their position can finally be improved by their full participation in the struggle for political rights." The title of this *New Age* article is in itself indicative: "The Trade Unions and the Fight for Freedom." [66]

66. *New Age*, March 8, 1962.

V

The Move to Umkonto

THE FUEL FOR REVOLT was certainly at hand in the South Africa of the sixties. The belief that change could only be achieved through violence was growing among Africans. The hard facts were, as Nelson Mandela said at his trial, that fifty years of nonviolence had only brought fewer rights and more repressive legislation. The ANC had, in the past, tried to moderate the growing trend to violence and had urged nonviolence, but "when some of us discussed this in May and June of 1961, it could not be denied that our policy to achieve a non-racial state by non-violence had achieved nothing, and that our followers were beginning to lose confidence in this policy and were developing disturbing ideas of terrorism." [1] Discontent was growing in the noisome wood-and-iron slums, as was testified by the mounting support for PAC and its terrorist wing, POQO. The question, thus, was not of violence or nonviolence but of an acceptable level of violence. It was no longer a matter of whether or not to fight, Mandela said, but of how to fight.

Although some of the ANC leaders were active Communists, and some others traveled the party line, they were not rash or imprudent men. On the contrary, when they erred, it was usually on the side of

1. Nelson Mandela, No Easy Walk to Freedom, ed. Ruth First (New York, 1965), p. 168.

caution. *Umkonto we Sizwe,* formed in partnership with the Communist Party, was shaped slowly and was only made known to the branches some months after its foundation.[2] The leaders were somewhat reluctant, it seems, to make known to the members the decision for violence and the organization through which it was to be employed. It is difficult to divine the reasons for the delay. It is equally difficult to determine the exact dates when the members were told. The acts of sabotage of December, 1961, had received broad press coverage, and *Umkonto* had put up stickers on walls and telegraph poles declaring itself author of the deeds. Then why the reticence? Why did the ANC leadership wait till sometime in mid-1962 before telling its members? The reason may have been twofold: first of all, the turn to violence may have sparked opposition from those leaders still committed to the political struggle; and second, all the leaders may have agreed that some preparation was needed before the decision could be made known.[3] The degree of acceptable violence would have to be stepped up from the defense of meetings to attacks on government property, and some members may have been unready for the change.

II

Umkonto did not achieve its final form all at once but passed through a series of developmental stages. Its founding seems to have been empirical. Those who came together at the beginning, in mid-June, 1961, joined a nameless organization. Groups of Africans, whites, and Indians, most of whom were members either of one of the Congress Alliance organizations or of the Communist Party, were assembled in different centers. Their only qualification, at that stage, was the willingness to undertake acts of sabotage.

The founding of such a group in Durban is perhaps typical of the way it was done elsewhere. According to Bruno Mtolo, this still name-

2. Qumpula/*Hlekani,* p. 18; Gungulu/*Khayingo,* p. 1; Kulele/*Mgalunkulu,* p. 57; Dondashe/*Mgalunkulu,* pp. 8–9; Zepe/*Mtalana,* p. 14; Gulwa/*Mapolisa,* pp. 5–7; Petros/*Makinane,* pp. 33–34; Ngoza/*Magwayi,* p. 54.
3. See, for instance, Lucingo/*Makinane,* p. 94; Mthembu/*Rvtr,* pp. 3–4.

less group was brought together during the visit of one Lionel Bernstein, who, it is alleged, was a member of the Communist Party. His mission was to tell them of the decision for violence and to ask them to form a regional command. This command, Mtolo said, was to receive its orders from a National High Command in Johannesburg.[4]

The Regional High Command was then formed, and its members instructed at least partially in the arts of sabotage. Then, early in December, they were visited by another white, who Mtolo says was Harold Strachan. Strachan, according to Mtolo, told those there that the decision to undertake violent acts had been taken, that acts of sabotage should be begun, but in no case were these to involve risk of human life. The attacks were to be aimed only at buildings—particularly government buildings—and were not to be launched before December 16, 1961. In the event, the Durban people decided to choose their own time, and, impatient to begin, with their bombs ready, they launched their attacks one night early, on December 15. This premature attack, which might have given the game away to the police, was to be typical of the sort of thing that happened in the face of demands for discipline.[5]

Six months later Nelson Mandela, as deputy national president of the illegal ANC, visited the regional high command in Durban and told the members that the organization was named *Umkonto we Sizwe.* The group born half a year earlier now had a name. Its purposes had still to be made known to the ANC in the various regions.[6]

The way this was done differed with the regional committees and with the branches. In 1961 a man from Johannesburg (probably Nelson Mandela) visited Port Elizabeth and told the regional committee, together with its contact, Govan Mbeki, that from December 16 of that year a new wing of the ANC would embark on sabotage at all the major centers of South Africa. The targets, they were told, were to be symbols of apartheid—particularly offices from which the government's policies were executed. In addition, power lines and

4. Mtolo/*Rvtr*, p. 23.
5. Bruno Mtolo, *Umkonto we Sizwe: The Road to the Left* (Durban, 1966), p. 15.
6. Mtolo/*Rvtr*, p. 24.

transport were to be attacked. The intention was to shock the white electorate into a realization of African needs, as perceived by the ANC leadership, and at the same time to hearten Africans, encouraging them to resist the government.[7]

The ANC had entered upon a campaign of violence with great reluctance; violence was adopted only as a last resort. This being so, the leaders were concerned with its effects on their followers. As Nelson Mandela said from the dock at the Rivonia Trial:

> It was only when all else had failed, when all channels of peaceful protest had been barred to us that the decision was made to embark on violent forms of political struggle, and to form *Umkonto we Sizwe*. We did so not because we desired such a course, but solely because the Government had left us with no other choice.[8]

It was not only at the higher levels that there was concern over the question of violence; those at the lower levels were also worried about the effects of the new policy on their followings. They debated whether the rank and file should be told of *Umkonto* or not. One man described such a debate:

> Should the [Branch Executive Committees] be told that the Spear of the Nation is the baby of the African National Congress? That matter was discussed very fully at the meeting. Some of the members said it would be nice if the members of the Branch Executive Committees were told that the Spear of the Nation was the baby of the African National Congress. Some said no, that this must not be done. After a lot had been spoken about this matter [one] said that it is not for this meeting to decide about this matter or to discuss this matter. . . . He said there was a Regional High Command of the Spear of the Nation. It was them who should say whether they should let the others know that the Spear of the Nation is the African National Congress. In the end it was then decided that the Branch Executive Committees should not be told.[9]

7. Mashinyana/*Rvtr*, p. 11.
8. Mandela, *No Easy Walk*, p. 169.
9. Kunene/*Ngakane*, pp. 265–66.

It was felt that members of the cells would have to be told for a number of reasons, although this practice may have been dropped later because of the threat to security it posed. They had to be told because otherwise they might mistake members who had joined *Umkonto* for informers or "sellouts." This might not only endanger the individuals, but in addition disrupt the cells, as members feared that defectors might have informed the police. Procedures by which the cells were informed seem to have been devised.

Once the decision to tell the members of the cells had been taken, the actual briefing was left to the chief stewards, who seem to have been given a common line. The context of one was much like another, and one can do for all: "Comrades," they began, "I have got good tidings for you about the ANC. The ANC has a new branch, termed *Umkonto we Sizwe.*" All speakers said, more or less, that *Umkonto* was the new "fighting branch" of the ANC, and they appealed for funds for its support. A member present at one of the meetings told of it in this way: "He [the chief steward] said we should collect money and recruit new members because the head office in Johannesburg wanted or needed the money. That money would buy arms from other countries for this branch [*Umkonto*]." [10] Another speaker said: "Men and money will be required. People will be required." The money collected, he went on to say, "would go to this new branch for the purpose of purchasing weapons." [11] The weapons to be bought were to consist initially of dynamite, gasoline for bombs, wire-cutters to cut telephone cables, and other small tools of sabotage.

The way in which the turn to violence was received showed the fears of the leaders to have been groundless. Violence did not alienate their followers. "They [the members] were joyful," a witness said later; "they said: 'Well, at last we are on the road to our freedom.'" The speeches of the chief stewards reflected the same elation. As one put it, "They all seemed in a hurry and eager for this awaited freedom."

The eagerness to attain freedom and the acceptance of violence distorted the policies of the ANC, which often were not well under-

10. Kulele/*Mgalunkulu*, p. 57.
11. *Ibid.*

stood by the rank and file, who interpreted them as they wished. An example of this follows, in which terrorism was coupled with a call for volunteers, although the former was not in line with the decision of the ANC and *Umkonto* executives. The speaker was quoted thus:

> He said the African National Congress is not the same organization any more, like the one that did not believe in the shedding of blood. He said that even if it does not believe any more in not shedding blood he said *it doesn't mean that the outside world must get to know of that* [italics added]. He said the African National Congress, as it was then, did not, was not like the old one, that didn't believe in shedding blood any more, but it shouldn't be told to the outside world. . . . He said the Government is using force to crush the people who were fighting for their freedom. He said that is why, for that reason, the African National Congress wanted volunteers.[12]

The volunteers, he went on to say, would do the dirty work of the ANC.

The spreading of violence, while broadly approved of in the ANC cells, did worry others, especially some of the older members. A woman, giving evidence at a trial, spoke of approaches made to her to rejoin the ANC. She had left it in 1952 because of her repugnance to the killing of Sister Aidan, a medical nun, in the East London riots. She first excused herself by saying that the organization was illegal and that she could not join. Although the chief steward persisted, she stuck to her decision because, as she said, she knew of the plans for violence.[13] A member of a regional committee of the ANC, Elias Kunene, recalled his rejection of leaflets inciting to violence and wrote to the NEC in Johannesburg to this effect. It seemed, however, that there was nothing that could be done, precisely because the branches were enthusiastic about the new organization and were prepared to help raise both men and money for it.[14]

12. Kunene/N*gakane*, p. 238.
13. *Daily Dispatch*, February 19, 1964.
14. Kunene/N*gakane*, pp. 275–76.

III

Although *Umkonto* began in seemingly unplanned fashion, attempts to mold it in the format of a modified M-Plan were soon made. Like the ANC, it was seen as a web of commands linked by contacts. Departures from the M-Plan, which it was otherwise to emulate, were to be for functional reasons.[15] Thus the organization of *Umkonto* followed the general lines of the M-Plan, with the National High Command corresponding to the National Executive Committee and, like the latter, appointing the members of the regional bodies, which likewise had their counterparts in the ANC. The organizations also resembled each other in their emphasis on face-to-face contact. A major difference between the ANC and *Umkonto* was that the latter accepted people of all races, while the ANC restricted its membership to Africans.

From what can be learned, the nuclear unit was already in existence. The volunteer-in-chief and his followers in each locality could form an instant cadre. Thus the volunteer-in-chief was a key figure, as was also the contact. The contact, at each level, was charged with maintaining liaison. He passed instructions to the volunteer-in-chief, who now as before was obligated to obey. Below the volunteer-in-chief were the ordinary volunteers, whose business it was, to borrow Mussolini's slogan, to "believe, obey, fight." They swore this oath: "I am a soldier of *Umkonto*, I promise to obey without question. As a soldier I promise to serve our people and my country with my life, to uphold the policies of the National Liberation Movement led by the African National Congress, and to safeguard the rights and dignity of the people from all attacks." [16] The volunteers understood the discipline that this oath imposed on them, that they had to obey those placed above them. "He cannot challenge [a] directive," said one former member; "if the Volunteer-in-Chief called you, woke you up, whatever the time of day or night might be, you have to get up immediately

15. Mbeki/*Rvtr*, pp. 66–67, 173.
16. *Rand Daily Mail*, May 7, 1964.

and go with him. You have to carry out his instructions, you can't challenge them. You can't challenge the Volunteer-in-Chief." [17]

Apart from publishing the Manifesto and the First Anniversary Message, everything in *Umkonto* was done through its chain of contacts. The importance of this chain is evident not only in the links of contact and volunteer-in-chief at the different levels, but also in the way in which targets were selected. The regional high command was to choose the general class of target and to advise the lower echelons of its choice. Members of the lower echelons would then find appropriate sites to be attacked and would, in turn, advise the regional command. Permission would then be given or withheld. This, at any rate, was *supposed* to happen. It did not work out so neatly in practice. By and large, the local groups did pretty much as they pleased, acting on their own interpretations of national objectives and settling a few local grudges as well. This emerges in the evidence of Walter Sisulu, who said that "the proper approach [of the local groups] would [have been] that people should do what they [were] told." He continued, "It does happen in life that people do the opposite. But that is not our instruction and that is not our understanding. We tried to the best of our ability to say how it should be done, and what should be done." [18] If "it"—that is, violence—was not carried out in the limited sense the ANC prescribed, there was little the ANC could do to ensure that its prescriptions were adhered to.

Perhaps prescriptions for limited violence were not filled because there were no clear and specific instructions in the first place. The leadership slogans confined themselves largely to rhetoric; and as the expansion of *Umkonto* was limited, the saboteurs were mostly drawn from the regional command itself. This, at least, emerges from what Bruno Mtolo wrote. Acts of sabotage, as he describes them, were carried out by members of the ad hoc committee and regional command. As nearly as can be determined, it worked along the following lines: the highest officers at the regional level were the *corporals*, whose seconds-in-command were named, not inappropriately, *second-corporals*. This

17. Mashinyana/*Rvtr*, p. 10.
18. Sisulu/*Rvtr*, p. 103.

was at least an original table of rank. The "soldiers" were organized into sections of three men each, under a section-leader, four such sections making a platoon.[19] The targets to be attacked were chosen by the section-leaders, who, if they acted according to the schema, would report this to their platoon leader. This man would, in his turn, tell the contact of what was chosen, and the contact would take matters up with the regional command.[20] If the action was approved by the regional command, again in theory, the action was undertaken.

The fact that this was *theoretically* how things were to happen has to be continually stressed. For, as Walter Sisulu's remarks above indicate, the complex procedure by which the leaders could control violence was often short-circuited. It is in any case difficult to see, given the need for secrecy and the difficulties of communications between the major centers, how this chain of command could have been kept operating. Approval, when sought, was usually sought for something already done; where this was not the case and the channels were used, permission sometimes came after it was no longer possible to perform the act. The desire to impose bureaucratic controls was there. It was harder to make them work. The structure of *Umkonto*, as of the ANC, remained far looser, and its units far more autonomous, than the flow chart of authority would indicate.

IV

The different purposes of the ANC and *Umkonto* meant that some formations not needed by the former were essential to the latter. Among these was a body to train saboteurs, and another to take recruits for military training out of the country. These jobs were assigned to specialized committees.

19. Mbanjwa/*Mbolompo*, p. 751; du Preez/*Rvtr*, p. 13. It is unclear how this arrangement fitted in with that of the volunteer-in-chief mentioned previously. The only conclusion is that ranks were chosen largely by the men themselves, and had little official sanction. They are cited as indicative of the way in which the organization was viewed, rather than as a formal statement of organization (see also p. 226 below).
20. Mbanjwa/*Mbolompo*, p. 751.

The first of these committees to have been set up, which was done before *Umkonto* was even formally named, was the Technical Committee. It was charged with the training of saboteurs.[21] In the early phases white Communists, some of whom had had war experience, came to the various centers to show selected recruits how to forge the tools of the saboteur's trade. The training given ranged all the way from sabotage to the rudiments of guerrilla war. In particular, the recruits were shown how to make and master all kinds of simple bombs and explosives. A favorite was the gasoline bottle bomb, or "Molotov Cocktail." [22] The ambitions of the Technical Committee seem not to have stopped with such simple devices; they seem to have had visions of manufacturing large quantities of more formal weapons—some 210,000 hand grenades, 48,000 anti-personnel mines, and 15 tons of gunpowder, among other things. It was soon evident that this would be impossible, although initial steps to test the feasibility of such a plan had been taken.[23] Nonetheless, the general importance of the committee cannot be underestimated.

In addition to the Technical Committee, which was concerned mainly with the ongoing struggle in South Africa, there was a Transport Committee, which smuggled men out of the country for training abroad and also helped those fleeing the government to cross into the then Protectorates. In addition, it had to bring those who had been trained back across the frontiers.[24] It also tried to import weapons from abroad. Other committees were concerned with intelligence and logistics. The Intelligence Committee was to obtain information on police plans and on military and police installations. The Logistics Committee was to arrange for the supply of explosives and equipment. The importance of the committees will become clearer when *Operation Mayebuye* is discussed later. In the meantime it must be admitted that the functions of logistics and intelligence committees were performed largely by the local groups for their own benefit.

One brief point may be worth passing attention, and that is the in-

21. Sisulu/*Rvtr*, p. 363; Mbeki/*Rvtr*, pp. 374–75.
22. Nyombo/*Mbolompo*, pp. 651–54; Ngoza/*Magwayi*, pp. 39–40.
23. Goldberg/*Rvtr*, pp. 128–49.
24. Sisulu/*Rvtr*, pp. 324–25.

creasing militarization of *Umkonto*. Arthur Goldreich, who participated both in the Technical Committee and in the training program
for *Umkonto*, styled himself "Comrade Commandant." Curnick
Ndhlovu, who was prominent in Durban, gave himself the rank "Comrade Captain." Others began using the ranks "Comrade Lieutenant"
and "Comrade Sergeant." [25] These styles seem to have been used
simultaneously with the less pretentious first- and second-corporal and
section-leader titles.

V

Although the members of *Umkonto* were recruited from the ANC,
they were also drawn from the Communist Party and from the various
congresses that made up the Alliance. But where did one body end
and the other begin? This question remains unanswered and perhaps
unanswerable. Singly or as groups the *Umkonto* volunteers were largely
Africans. They number by far the greatest of those arrested and tried
for sabotage. Indians undertook some sabotage in Natal and the Transvaal, but they numbered few and their acts were limited. Some whites
participated in sabotage, but in the main white Communists seem to
have been planners and instructors rather than executants. As in South
African society at large, the hard manual labor, in this case the perpe-
tration of sabotage, fell to Africans. An illustration of this is to be
found in Mbeki's evidence. On being questioned, Mbeki could not
think of a single *Umkonto* member in the Eastern Cape, the main
area of revolt, who was not an African. Much the same could have
been said of the rest of the country.[26]

The method by which volunteers were drawn from the ANC into
Umkonto is not entirely clear. According to Milner Ntsangane, who
organized *Umkonto* in Natal, the volunteers would sign a card at their
branches and subsequently be given training. He (Ntsangane) spent
his time visiting branches and calling for volunteers. "This organization
requires volunteers, volunteers like it had at the time of the Defiance

25. Davids/Rvtr, B2–B3; Mtolo, *Umkonto we Sizwe*, p. 23.
26. Mbeki/Rvtr, p. 173.

Campaign." [27] The difference, of course, is that the Defiance Campaign was conceived as nonviolent and *Umkonto* as violent. The volunteers seem to have been viewed ambiguously by the leadership, at least in the beginning. Nelson Mandela, for instance, said that the volunteers were *not* "soldiers of a Black army pledged to fight a civil war against the Whites" [28] but were simply dedicated workers ready to lead campaigns initiated by the ANC. Their job was to distribute leaflets, organize strikes, and to do whatever a particular ANC campaign called for. This argument may have been true in the fifties, but it did not hold for the sixties. The foundation of *Umkonto* changed the character of the volunteer groups. From strong-arm men and propagandists, they became the violent arm of the ANC.

The transition from one organization to the other was facilitated for the volunteers by the very loose structure of the ANC and its allies. The overlapping memberships made it difficult to draw any hard and fast line on which organization was responsible for any one action.

The volunteers were known as *Amadelakufe*, which means "those who do not fear death," and was abbreviated to MK, by which initials *Umkonto* was also known. (When MK is used here, it is as an alternative style for the organization.) The term *Amadelakufe* was not a new one, having been known as far back as 1952, but it now acquired a new significance. The *Amadelakufe* were to be not nonviolent but violent resisters. As the struggle was to be violent, a new breed of men would have to be found and brought into the organization to strengthen the volunteers already there. The recruitment of these men was the business of the *Umkonto* regional command, who could draw on the ANC and the Communist Party where necessary. In practice, however, the rank and file were drawn from the former and the leaders from the latter, unless memberships overlapped.

A variety of problems arose in recruiting from the ANC for *Umkonto*. For one thing, secrecy was as important as in the underground ANC, but some disclosure seemed unavoidable. People were recruited in somewhat the following fashion. A prospective "soldier" would be

27. Kunene/*Ngakane*, p. 241.
28. Mandela, *No Easy Walk*, p. 166.

approached and, when his approval had been obtained, the matter would be referred to his ANC branch executive; it is questionable whether anybody else was informed, for it was later argued that even the ANC leaders at the regional level did not know who was and who was not in *Umkonto*.[29]

Apart from reasons of secrecy, it would have been impossible to simply convert the ANC into *Umkonto*. The ANC included not only young men of military age but also the elderly, the unfit, and women. Such members could hardly have been incorporated into a "liberation army." Membership of *Umkonto* was, therefore, based on recommendation by an existing member who knew the prospective recruit.[30] A man need not have been in the ANC to be recruited for *Umkonto*, but it was customary to join the ANC first. Once in the cell the man could be watched and his suitability for *Umkonto* assessed. The weakwilled and cowardly could be kept out.

Initially, men were to be transferred from the cells to *Umkonto*. This was done in a variety of ways, some of which have been recalled by witnesses. One man, with the imposing name of Oceanic Ngoza, remembered that the chief steward had told the cell that two members would be going over to the new branch; his name and that of another man, Meglory Magwayi, were then given. Ngoza had not volunteered to go to *Umkonto*, although he was quite happy at the prospect of doing so. He stressed that neither he nor Magwayi had been consulted beforehand; the chief steward had merely announced their names to the cell. Both, though willing, were apparently surprised, for they had been told at other meetings that only volunteers would be enrolled, and now they found themselves drafted.[31]

The fact that recruits were not necessarily sought from the ANC cells alone has already been mentioned. In one case a man who had joined told of his recruitment. He and another man were walking in Duncan Village, one of the townships of East London. They heard singing coming from a house which happened to be that of Malcolmess Kondoti, the chief steward of that area. They recognized the songs as

29. *Rand Daily Mail,* December 7, 1963.
30. Mbanjwa/Mbolompo, p. 753.
31. Ngoza/Magwayi, p. 54.

179

ANC songs, which were repeated again and again, songs such as "Mayebuye i Afrika," and "Mandela Must Lead Us." The songs seem to have struck a chord other than musical, for after paying a small entrance fee they joined in the singing. The group sang till dusk, when Kondoti asked the women to leave. Once the women had duly gone, the men were told that the party had been in aid of the ANC, which aimed at freeing the nation by fighting the whites. Though the aim was to fight, Kondoti continued, they would have to await his instructions before beginning. On hearing Kondoti's speech, the witness at once joined the ANC, together with his companion, but was not assigned to a cell. One week later he attended another meeting, this time in the bushes near the cemetery, a favorite ANC meeting place. There he and the others present were given leaflets for distribution, in much the same manner as the cells performed this task. This was the next stage in his induction. The third was when he attended a meeting at Welsh High School, where he was told to come armed to future meetings. An added note was the instruction that those who left the ANC were to be "done away with" as traitors. The more mundane matter of fees—a hardy perennial—also came up. The importance of payment was stressed, as the struggle was impossible without money; unemployed members were told that they needed to pay only half the fees. At a later meeting the men were told that they were volunteers, and the system of discipline was explained to them. As a volunteer, the witness was actually a member of *Umkonto* and later was involved in acts of sabotage and attempts to dispose of traitors. Here, as in other instances, the organizational affiliation is not always clear. Men in the lowest reaches often failed to distinguish between *Umkonto* and the ANC, a fact which the police frequently used against the leadership of the ANC.[32]

Some were drawn into *Umkonto* slowly and others more quickly, the recruiters using a variety of methods. They would even quote Scripture for their purposes, as David Mataung testified. He was at first reluctant to join *Umkonto*, but the recruiter showed him a passage in the Bible—the Epistle to the Ephesians—which justified revolt against

32. *Daily Dispatch*, February 26, 1964.

an oppressive government. It was pointed out that, if this was approved by the Bible, then surely Mataung could not object. Mataung agreed and went with the recruiter to a meeting at Eastwood, near Pretoria, heard a speaker justify sabotage, and then joined Umkonto because, as he put it, the teachings of the Bible should be followed.[33]

Despite the overlapping of memberships, an effort was made to keep the two organizations, ANC and Umkonto, separate. Officially, at least, the ANC did no more than "permit" its members to join Umkonto, which enabled the ANC to maintain its "nonviolent" façade.[34] In other words, it would not disallow its members from joining another organization fomenting violence, but it would not countenance violence in its own name. Before this decision, members joining a violent organization had to leave the ANC. No such obligation was now binding on them.

Another reason for keeping the ANC apart from Umkonto was to ensure that only trustworthy people entered the latter. As Communists felt that their members were the most advanced politically as well as the best disciplined, it was logical to bring them in and to keep out others. Seeing themselves as endowed with both the determination and the appropriate philosophy, they viewed those who were not Party members with detachment or scorn.[35] The Communist Party leadership was no less cautious than that of the ANC. It was opposed to terrorism, according to Piet Beyleveld, a former member of its Central Committee, who argued that his view was supported by all available documents. The aim was to guide Umkonto toward strategic sabotage, and in this the Party was at one with the ANC leadership. Where they differed was in long-term aims. In the short term, the Party was prepared to work with the ANC and the Congress Alliance to "extend a share of the Government to the non-White people, and in the long term it stood to establish a Socialist State."[36] The distinction is somewhat unreal in fact, and more will be said of it later. It is, nevertheless, indicative of the attitude of the Communist leadership.

33. *Rand Daily Mail*, August 25, 1964.
34. Mbeki/*Rvtr*, pp. 31–32, 180; Sisulu/*Rvtr*, p. 157; Mandela, *No Easy Walk*, p. 170.
35. Rahamadi/*Fazili*, pp. 31–32; Sisulu/*Rvtr*, p. 157; Mbeki/*Rvtr*, pp. 33–34.
36. *Star*, March 30, 1966.

There is clearly substance to Nelson Mandela's assertion that the ANC and *Umkonto* were separate entities.

There has, of course, been overlapping of functions internally as well, because there is a difference between a resolution adopted in the atmosphere of a committee room and the concrete difficulties that arise in the field of practical activity. At a later stage the position was further affected by bannings and house arrests, and by persons leaving the country to take up political work abroad. This led to individuals having to do work in different capacities. But though this may have blurred the distinction between Umkonto and the ANC, it by no means abolished that distinction. Great care was taken to keep the activities of the two organizations in South Africa distinct. The ANC remained a mass political body of Africans only carrying on the type of political work they had conducted prior to 1961. Umkonto remained a small organization recruiting its members from different races and organizations and trying to achieve its own particular object.[37]

Memberships may have overlapped and those in one organization may have functioned in the other, but by and large each remained a separate body. The ANC members who were not drawn into *Umkonto* seem not to have participated in sabotage. Indeed, by all accounts, there were those in the ANC who had not even heard of *Umkonto*.[38] ANC members who suspected one of their number of being in *Umkonto* were not, according to Bruno Mtolo, supposed to ask about it.[39] Govan Mbeki went even further: he tells the somewhat touching if incredible story of husbands and wives, both in the ANC, but only one of whom was in *Umkonto*. In such cases, he said, the wife might have to go out at night and be unable to tell her husband where she was going. Marriages broke up on account of the need for secrecy, Mbeki went on, "but in the course of time they get to understand, where the husband also gets to understand that well if my wife is going out on this sort

37. Mandela, *No Easy Walk*, p. 176.
38. Mbanjwa/*Mbolompo*, p. 218; Mtloko/*Magwayi*, p. 75; Mashinyana/*Bongco*, p. 240.
39. Mtolo/*Rvtr*, p. 23.

182

of work, I mustn't ask too many questions." [40] This may sound strange at first, for women had not been particularly welcomed in the cells of the ANC, although they had not been barred entirely. In the field, rules were made to suit individual leaders, chief stewards, rather than in response to some table of ranks. In the case of the volunteers, women do seem to have been asked to become members (see p. 183). There is no evidence, however, that women were actually employed in sabotage by *Umkonto*.

All in all, it is not perhaps unreasonable to suppose that those who were neither contacts nor in commanding positions in *Umkonto* were unaware of who other members were, unless these members gave the show away by revealing themselves.

VI

The Pretoria organization is more difficult to describe than the others, for no trial record is available. The story had to be pieced together out of the fragments reported in the daily press. Confusion was more confounded by the vagueness of the different witnesses, and perhaps also because of errors in the reports. This seems more important where organization was concerned, and less on the matter of action, where all reports seem in close agreement. The exact number of sections or cells (the names are used indiscriminately) does not emerge with any clarity. The relationships of sections or cells to each other, the way they cooperated, remains obscure. There are, unfortunately, many gaps. But the richness of the story itself, and the insights it affords, makes its inclusion essential. The Pretoria group is important not only from a human angle but also because of the range of its activities and because of the damage it did. [41] In 1962 and 1963 its members attacked the office of the Minister of Lands, gutting it and an adjoining office. They attacked the "Old Synagogue" now used as a courthouse, in which many ANC leaders had been tried. They also made an abortive

40. Mbeki/*Rvtr*, pp. 369–70.
41. *Cape Times*, May 12, 1964. The record of this trial was unavailable; therefore, press reports were used.

attack against a post office at Innesdale, near Pretoria (see numbers 84, 148, and 159 in Appendix I). These incidents by no means exhaust their actions or even their plans.

The Pretoria organization seems to have followed the general pattern of sections and platoons, which members sometimes seem to have referred to as "cells." In order to avoid more confusion than need be, the term "cells" will be retained. *Umkonto* cells (or sections) seem to have been smaller than those of the ANC, and to have consisted of from three to seven men. There seems, in addition, at least in Pretoria, to have been close cooperation among the cells.

Although the Pretoria case involved some 22 men who were either accused or co-conspirators, these seem to have been made up of a mixture of leaders and smaller fry. The main leader in Pretoria was, it would seem, Andrew Mashaba. Others were Peter Mogano and Levy Moses Molefe, with Tseleng John Mosupye and Pieter Mampane also playing a part in the story.[42] What part each man played, and particularly his rank in MK, is difficult to determine from the reports. Andrew Mashaba was, for instance, contact between National Headquarters in Johannesburg and the Pretoria cells. He also did some instructing in the use of explosives and had obtained a pistol for the group. He was in charge of explosives, distributing them through Peter Mogano, in the latter's role of transport officer. Mashaba had drawn Mogano into the organization. Mogano, indeed, was an old ANC hand, having been a member as long ago as 1952. He now became local volunteer-in-chief, and recruited cell leaders, among whom was Tseleng John Mosupye. In addition, as volunteer-in-chief, Mogano had to approve all targets selected by the cells, whose members "spied them out." The cells generally acted independently of each other, though there was some cooperation, not recorded here. Mosupye, in his turn, recruited Levy Molefe and another accused, Nelson Diale, and together with them formed a cell. Molefe later became one of the chief ex-

42. The accused were Andrew Mashaba, Peter Mogano, Levy Moses Molefe, Nelson Diale, Jackson Ntsoane, Andries Seoma, Alpheus Bokaba, Enoch Matibela, Petrus Nchabaleng. The co-conspirators were Elias Motsoaledi, Johannes Letboko, Judas Legware, Klaas Mashidi, Darius Lephago, Pieter Mampane, Tseleng John Mosupye, Frans Mosupye, Frans Mashilo, John Moepye, Alfred Nkadimeng, Petrus Segwarithle, and Morris Matsimolo. All accused were found guilty.

ecutants of MK policy in his role of cell member, being one of the most active saboteurs. Mosupye, who was also leader of the Catering Workers' Union, a division of SACTU, found this post of assistance in his task. Most of those active in the group were waiters, cooks, or in some way connected with the catering trade. Pieter Mampane, again, was leader of a cell in Mamelodi Township, and only enters the story later.

Once the cell was formed, the cell members began looking around for possible targets. A number were suggested. One was the home of the Minister of Justice, who was then planning the ninety-day law which could land all the conspirators in jail.[43] The aim, as Mosupye made clear at the trial, was "to make [the minister] open his head and listen to what we asked him for." In order to do the bombing, Mosupye and another of the *Umkonto* men went out to shop for ingredients to make "black powder." They had no difficulty in buying saltpeter and sulphur but could not get charcoal, even when they told the pharmacists that they needed it to bake cakes. Eventually they obtained the charcoal in lumps and retired to the home of another member to make the gunpowder. It is difficult to determine whether the attempt was made on the minister's house. Frans Mashilo, who was accused as one of the group, said that they had taken a bomb to the house of a "highly placed person" but had failed to plant it because there was a white workman there and also because the lights in the adjacent house were on. As attacks on several ministers' houses had been planned, it is hard to say which one this was.

There were talks of other targets. One of those considered was a church in Brooklyn, a Pretoria suburb, although churches were not on the list of *Umkonto* targets. The idea of bombing the church was quickly abandoned as impracticable. One of his aims, Mogano said at his trial, was not to bomb buildings when they were in use, a double check being made at this point. Mogano also maintained that he had instructed the sabotage teams to go unarmed and just to run away if

---

43. The ninety-day law allowed the Minister of Justice to have any person held for ninety days without a formal charge being leveled against him. On completion of the ninety-day period, the person could be rearrested for another ninety days, and so on *ad infinitum*. The period was later extended to 180 days.

the police appeared. Anyone caught was not to be assisted, as this might lead to a fight and to loss of life.

The prosecution called Mogano a "mealymouthed hypocrite" at his trial, but it seems that his evidence was substantially true on these points. There does not seem to have been any serious effort on the part of the MK men to resist arrest, and their sabotage efforts seem to have been staged so as to minimize the risk of injury. An example may illustrate the point. Mosupye mentioned that, while giving evidence at the trial of nine Africans, he had examined the possibility of an attack on the Pretoria Magistrate's Court, where the trial was being held. He believed that an attack was feasible and planned it for December 16, 1963, to mark the anniversary of the formation of *Umkonto*. Mosupye, Levy Moses Molefe, and Mashaba then made a bomb with dynamite and black powder in a shoe box. Molefe went out to inspect the Magistrate's Court, which he saw was not only in a busy part of the town but had the additional disadvantage of being near a police station. He therefore returned to his confreres and reported unfavorably on the court as an object for attack. Mosupye was nonetheless determined to go ahead, and Molefe and another man were given the bomb and told to place it in the courthouse. Instead of doing so, however, Molefe and his associate broke a window of the Brooklyn telephone exchange and put their bomb in there. This was December 18, 1963, and the next day, Mosupye, who read of the event in the paper, shook Molefe's hand according to the custom of *Umkonto* and said to him: "You are a man and have done a man's job. My heart is white [i.e., I am very happy]."

The members did not, however, know that the police had penetrated their cell. Constable Bernard Mochisane had been sent to Pretoria from Kimberley, and had managed to meet Pieter Mampane, who was leader of an MK cell in Mamelodi Township, near Pretoria. Operating under an assumed name and being personally unknown in Pretoria, he was able to win Mampane's confidence by lavishly praising the ANC. Mampane made him a member of the group, and through it he met Molefe, who had been instructed to blow up a rest house for visiting chiefs at Mamelodi. This, it should be added, was only one of the projects then being considered, as this was a very active group. A further attack on the Old Synagogue was planned, as well as the killing of two African detectives who were thought to have discovered the cell and to be watching it. There was debate as to which project should be tackled first. The cell, as a whole, favored first shooting the detectives with the gun Mashaba had provided, whereas Mosupye insisted on the bomb attacks first. It was on the night of the intended attack on the rest house that the police struck, doubtless primed by Mochisane. Mosupye was walking down a Pretoria street when a police car drew up and he was arrested. On entering the police car he saw Molefe there in handcuffs.

Although Mochisane had been planted in the cell, the police later insisted that the arrest of Mosupye had been "fortuitous." The chain of events began with the arrest of Molefe, who was found with a tin containing gunpowder, as well as a variety of chemicals. He had, in addition, a number of lapel badges with Nelson Mandela's picture and the coat of arms of SACTU. Molefe, on his arrest, offered to tell the police what he knew. On being taken back to Pretoria in the police car, he pointed out Mosupye. At the police headquarters, Mosupye urged Molefe to tell everything to the police. "We must tell the truth," he allegedly said. "Go and show them where the pistol is and where the others live." Molefe complied. Mosupye, in turn, showed the police the secret cache in the hills near Lady Selborne where Umkonto's supply of explosives—dynamite, gunpowder, timing devices, and "bombs"— had been buried.

Actually, the incident belongs in low comedy, were it not for the sad overtones. In order to make the attack on the Mamelodi guest house, gasoline was needed. None of the others had money to buy it, and Mochisane said that he knew where he could borrow some. He slipped off and went straight to the police station, told them of the plan, was given money, and bought the gasoline. The police were waiting; Molefe was arrested, while Mochisane "escaped" with Mampane. The chain of events described earlier was thus set in motion. In all, Mochisane had a difficult role to play, for to maintain his "cover" he had to plot attacks against other African policemen. There was a plan to bomb the house of an African police sergeant, for instance, and Mochisane could not warn the sergeant for fear that, if he did so, suspicion might be aroused. This particular attack was called off for lack of materials, but Mochisane indicated that he would have participated in it had it come off as planned.

The Pretoria group, like many others, was handicapped by inexperience in the use of explosives. An instance is the attack on the Innesdale Post Office on February 12, 1963. The senior inspector of explosives, called to the scene, said the place was thick with dynamite dust, for only the timing device had blown up, pulverizing the sticks of dynamite without exploding them. This was either because the dynamite was damp or because the timing device had been poorly packed. The Pretoria saboteurs were more determined than efficient.

The penetration of MK by Constable Mochisane was not an isolated instance and, while few police penetrations are reported, at least one other instance can be mentioned. A policeman from the Eastern Cape was transferred to Cape Town. He was told first to take work as a common laborer and then to penetrate the ANC. He did this and was so successful that he was elected a delegate to the ANC annual conferences in 1958 and 1959. He was deliberately arrested and held for one month in the Emergency of 1960. After the ANC became illegal he remained as a member and helped organize the ANC cells in the township of Nyanga East near Cape Town. As a cell steward he collected membership fees, keeping in touch with his police superiors all the while, informing of all that went on till the cells were destroyed in 1962.[44]

The functioning and betrayal of the Pretoria *Umkonto* cell sheds light on the problems of the organization as a whole. It shows the difficulties and dangers involved in recruitment and in attacking any preselected target, as well as the limited extent of damage that could be done. All in all, one must keep in mind that ANC and *Umkonto* were not neatly structured bodies following prescribed lines. Lines were blurred even for members; often they were not really certain which organization they had joined or been transferred to. This vagueness, together with the tendency for members of *Umkonto* to say that

44. Covering the entire Pretoria case, see *Rand Daily Mail*, August 17-22, 25, 1964; *Golden City Post*, August 23, 1964.

they were ANC, was used by the police in nailing ANC leaders. The same vagueness was evident in the methods used. Despite restrictions laid down by the leadership, the M-Plan often was a point of departure rather than a constraint on the form organization took. Even had organizational improvement of *Umkonto* been attempted, and such efforts were sometimes mooted, there was the ever present danger of police penetration. It was almost impossible to firm up an organization which was illegal, aimed at sabotage, and known to the police—especially its Special Branch. It is to these problems, and others, that we must now turn.

VI

Information, Action, and Violence

INFORMATION IS THE LIFEBLOOD of counterinsurgency, and the South African police made no secret of their interest in its collection. Infiltration of *Umkonto* itself was one method of collection, as has been mentioned. But the possibilities of such infiltration were necessarily limited, for it meant finding police officers who not only had the intelligence to pose, perhaps for a long time, as revolutionaries but also who would not, from the police viewpoint, be corrupted by contact with others whose views must have evoked some sympathy, some fellow feeling. Both courage and cunning, coupled with intelligence and loyalty, were called for; and there are seldom enough men with these qualities.

Informers, who would turn in bits and pieces of information which could be collated by the police, were thus another important source. The police made it clear that they would pay, and pay well, for information given. They would, in addition, protect those who informed from avengers among their own people. An efficiently functioning net of informers is not expensive, as Roger Trinquier pointed out in his work on modern war, and while an entire people will seldom play the part of informer, individuals frequently will. The relatively low living standards of Africans, as compared with whites, and their consequent concern with money made informers willing and their services cheap.

Informers were encouraged to derive their main income from regular employment, while what Trinquier has called "premiums for production" were paid them to sustain their enthusiasm for continuing to inform. These premiums, which seemed lavish to Africans, made little dent in the budgets of the police. The District Officer of the Criminal Investigation Department of Wynberg (near Johannesburg) said, in a statement to the African newspaper World, on August 6, 1963:

Any reliable informer can be assured of making a comfortable living by giving information. A man with attentive ears can easily net something in the neighborhood of R250 [about $350] per month as an informer. . . . We treat all information confidentially and protect the identity of our informants. It is essential for the men who volunteer information to deal only with the White staff.

One day later, in a report to the same newspaper, the deputy chief of police, Major-General van den Bergh, said: "We pay an average of R50 [about $70] for every information we receive from members of the public." [1] He is also reported as saying that those who supplied "scoop" information, leading to the arrest and conviction of "enemies of the state" and those with "subversive ideas," got bonuses, there being a maximum fee for information of this sort. The temptation that these payments represented can best be understood by comparing the earnings of an informer (on the basis of the figures above) with the wages of an ordinary African. In 1959 the average wage of an African worker was between R24 (about $34) and R42 (about $60) monthly; although the wage had risen by 1963, when the police statements were published, the former figures are indicative of scale. They show that an African could earn as much with a single piece of information as with a month's toil, and sometimes even twice as much. Clearly, informing paid, and informants, if they could live with their consciences, could live well.

The price paid for information was a worthwhile investment for the police, and doubtless still is. Penetrating an underground organization and obtaining information on what is planned, who is doing the

1. World, August 7, 1963.

planning, and then arresting the executants red-handed enhances police prestige and debilitates the morale, as well as the numbers, of the would-be insurgents. Indeed, as Sir Robert Thompson has lucidly demonstrated, terms such as "subversion" and "insurgency" tend to obscure the identity of those performing subversion and insurgency. People tend to think of these as vague and ill-defined threats, whereas they arise entirely out of the actions and intentions of individuals. Threats to internal security are the work of individuals acting in concert. It is, therefore, the aim of intelligence work to identify individuals and, having identified them, either to remove or eliminate them, or at the very least to render them neutral. The key is to know the names of persons and then to prevent these known persons from carrying out illegal acts against the government.[2] Ingenuity is clearly involved in piercing the veil of secrecy with which subversive organizations seek to enshroud themselves.

Some of the ways of piercing the veil are quite old, though they always seem to work. New Age, for instance, warned against "beautiful women" who were being hired by the police "to inform on the leaders of the people." The same report spoke of raids on the houses of known leaders of opposition movements and of police being placed in fields where crowds were known to collect. Men in plain clothes would prowl around the townships at night, the article reported, "and in the many lanes of New Brighton [near Port Elizabeth] . . . these snoopers are trying to find out houses where illegal meetings are held." [3]

The police did not, of course, have everything their own way. Informers were often unmasked. In a letter to New Age, Dr. Lethele, the ANC contact in Bechuanaland, warned of a police spy who had served in the police force for thirteen years and who was now seeking to discover the secrets of the ANC. His discharge from the police force had apparently been engineered in June, 1959; the reason given was that he had carried on business as a photographer without permission of his superiors while on the force. Work of such sort was against regulations and provided a convenient pretext. Soon after his discharge he joined

2. Robert Thompson, *Defeating Communist Insurgency: The Lessons of Malaya and Vietnam* (New York, 1966), chap. 7.
3. *New Age*, March 29, 1962.

the ANC at a public meeting in Kimberley, the ANC still being legal at that time. As a member, he attended meetings regularly and lost no opportunity for taking pictures of ANC leaders. Once established in the organization, he tried to get elected as an ANC delegate to the annual conference in Durban. Somehow—the means are not established—he had aroused the suspicion of the ANC Executive in Kimberley, who decided to take matters into its own hands. The members invited the man in for a visit, during which time his quarters were searched by other ANC people. As the newspaper *New Age* wryly put it, the ANC searching a policeman's quarters was something of a change, things usually being the other way around. On the premises conflicting documents were found, together with expensive photographic equipment. One document certified his discharge from the police force, but his reference book showed that he was still working for the police. The book contained no record of any discharge from the service. Upon this discovery he was expelled from the ANC, and soon afterward the Special Branch sent a van around and took the man and his equipment away. He was reported to be back on active duty after his brief stay in the ranks of the ANC.[4]

II

Just as the police sought to attack the ANC from within, so the ANC sought to bar entry to them. In addition, attacks on informers and on African policemen were frequently mounted. There are seventeen such attempts on the dwellings of Africans (excluding hostels) listed in Appendix I, as well as six attacks on the properties of policemen. This does not include at least two attacks on African stores. The attacks were designed to intimidate those who were in any way collaborating with the government—not only informers and policemen but also representatives of chiefs or members of Advisory Boards (Africans in the townships elected to advise the administration). Those who were suspected of collaboration were identified, often in ANC leaflets or in

4. *Ibid.*, February 4, 1960.

graffiti scrawled or painted on the walls of washrooms and other public buildings. A quotation from an ANC leaflet may give something of the flavor:

> Africans, what do you think, this is happening to Africans. Leaders of the former organization are being accused by fellow Africans with indefinite and unusual accusations. . . . It has been discovered that there are men now who still give evidence. . . . These men are [a list follows]. Now these men have disappointed the people very much. It hurts to be let down by someone who you had every confidence in, especially a person like Diza, whom you all know and whom we have been protecting. . . . Now this deceitful Judas Iscariot has shown his true colors by now joining the Transkeian Regional Authority. . . . Therefore people of East London it would be wise to know and be careful of these miserable specimens because there are now innocent men facing sentences because of traitors like Diza Ntonjeni and Ndjaba Matoti. . . . The freedom struggle is ours and will succeed. They are the sell-outs of the people. These are the traitors who may die tomorrow, leaving their sons, us, nothing but to die from oppression.[5]

Some of the biblical fervor of African propaganda is apparent in this brief quotation.

There would be little point in recounting each attack on informers or policemen by the ANC or by *Umkonto*. It is unlikely that all are known, even were it worthwhile to set them all down. However, certain actions that were taken are of particular interest for the light they throw on how both the ANC and MK worked, and these will be briefly discussed.

Attempts to silence informers permanently tell much of the workings of an insurgent organization and give insight into the minds of the killers. Killing, after all, is a drastic step. This is particularly true when the victims are former friends or actual neighbors. Study of their methods may serve to dispel the notion, sometimes given currency, that insurgents are dedicated men, ideologically inspired, working with single-minded efficiency. This may be an image of what is desired by

5. Quoted in Judge's summation/*Bongco*, p. 667.

leaders and feared by governments, but reality is far different. The insurgent is often a frightened man, muddled and ill-trained, aware only dimly if at all of his place in the revolutionary movement. He is often one who, having become involved in insurgency, has no choice but to carry on, sometimes without knowing what he stands to gain. However, the fact that such men are confused does not necessarily diminish the danger they represent. A man with a gun or gasoline bomb may not be well up on Marx or Mao, but he remains a menace. In fact, his very confusion may make him more, rather than less, dangerous.

The system of selecting and punishing informers was planned similarly to the selection of objectives for sabotage. The target was chosen by the volunteer-in-chief, who told the contact, the latter then obtaining permission from the higher command. In East London, for instance, the local volunteer-in-chief would decide, on the basis of reports from his men, who the traitors were and would tell the contact, who passed this on to regional headquarters in Port Elizabeth. The next step was for the Port Elizabeth contact with Johannesburg to be advised and then for him to get permission from Johannesburg. Permission being obtained, the news of this would be passed back.[6] It surely need not be stressed how cumbrous a process all this was, and it is not at all surprising that theory and practice diverged sharply.

Attacks were made on individual Africans. Why were these men selected as victims? Reasons differed, and the differences have already been hinted at. Joseph Matoti, for instance, had left the ANC in September, 1953, and his resignation was particularly resented as he had been chief organizer for East London. Because of this there was a permanent grudge against him among those who remained in the organization. This was evidenced when the leaders in East London refused to allow him to give the reasons for his resignation to an ANC meeting, going so far as to have a man with a knife at the door of the hall. From that time on, whenever the local ANC leaders came face to face with Matoti they accused him of treachery and were generally hostile. Later his name appeared in the ANC leaflet and on walls,

6. Mdube/*Bongco*, pp. 363–64.

coupled with threats on his life. He was publicly charged with treason to the ANC and accused of giving evidence against it.

Attempts against his life were then mounted. One night, while in bed, he heard the window of his room break and, on getting up, saw a light outside. Thinking it might be the police, he went to investigate. His investigation was rudely interrupted when a gasoline bomb landed between his feet, setting fire to his legs. After giving the alarm, and despite the pain, Matoti set out after his assailants. In the course of the chase, in which he called on them to stop, he was able to get a glimpse of a man he recognized as the local volunteer-in-chief. Now incensed, Matoti decided to return the visit. He went to the home of the volunteer-in-chief and tried various ruses to induce him to leave the house, but the man was not to be drawn. Denied a personal settlement, Matoti went to the police, who promised him protection. But the volunteers were not to be outdone and planned a second attack. They were still determined to do away with him. The second attempt was, in the event, no more successful than the first. Shots were fired into Matoti's home and into that of his alleged girl friend, Mary Neer, but no one was hit.[7]

Another of those chosen for attack, Symington Dukade, was believed to have given the evidence on which eleven ANC men were convicted and sentenced to death at a trial in Umtata in the Eastern Cape. This made Dukade particularly obnoxious to the East London ANC and sharpened the members' determination to kill him. They possessed two pistols, which were in the safekeeping of a tailor called Mazisa. The guns were secured from him and were shared between the volunteer-in-chief, Washington Bongco, and a young volunteer named Tamsanqua Selani. As Selani knew where Dukade lived, it would have seemed a simple matter to seek him out and shoot him, but once again the confusion in lower-level ANC thinking is evident. For one thing, Selani was not told, and apparently had no idea himself, why Dukade was to be killed. This distinctly dampened his determination to do the deed. Bongco was taken to Dukade's house by Selani, but a search soon showed that their victim was not there. Selani, who had

7. *Daily Dispatch*, February 26, 1964; Matoti/Bongco, p. 18.

been edgy and apprehensive throughout the whole thing, was allowed to go home because of a sore leg. Bongco said he would accompany Selani, but they met a group of men who engaged Bongco in conversation. Selani then remembered that he had left a lamp burning at his home and excused himself.

The matter of Dukade, like that of Matoti, was not allowed to rest with one attempt. Bongco, as volunteer-in-chief, was committed to killing Dukade. Another effort was to be essayed, this time with the assistance of a different volunteer named Siduma Tanana. Once more the two revolvers were brought out, but Tanana, according to his later testimony, was very unhappy about the whole affair, not only because of humane consideration for Dukade but also because he had never fired a gun before. He later said that, having filled out his form as a volunteer, he felt obliged to obey. Bongco had another convincing argument: If Tanana did not shoot Dukade, he (Tanana) would be shot by Bongco. The point made, the two went to the bus stop where Dukade usually alighted on coming home from work. Tanana was ordered to shoot Dukade there, while Bongco watched from the shadows. It was quite dark, and, as luck would have it, Dukade came home in a taxi instead of on the bus. In a scene faintly reminiscent of an old Western, gunman and victim walked toward each other on the dusty street. Tanana, the reluctant assassin, let his victim walk past him, fired his pistol in the air, and ran away. Because of the gathering darkness, he was sure that Bongco could not have seen him miss deliberately, and so he reported to the place from which *Umkonto* was working, a photographer's known as Mafigo's Studio. To cover his dereliction of duty, Tanana professed that he was sorry that he had missed and asked Bongco, who had also been armed, whether he had killed Dukade. He was told that this had not been done because, at the wrong moment, Bongco had walked around the corner. Tanana returned his revolver to Bongco and, relieved, went home. Attempts to kill Dukade continued until, on August 12, 1962, he was shot and seriously wounded. He was still in the hospital in 1964 when Bongco was brought to trial.[8]

8. *Daily Dispatch*, February 26, 1964; Selani/*Bongco*, pp. 317–20; Tanana/*Bongco*, pp. 342–43.

These attacks, it will be evident, were on a relatively small scale. They were executed on a hit-and-miss basis and were not very effective. An attack on another man, Diza Ntonjeni, was on a much larger scale. The reason for the attack was that Ntonjeni was on the Advisory Board and thus an important man in the township. He was also the "ambassador" for one of the chiefs, which aroused the ire of the ANC as it indicated support for the government's policies. He had frequently been called a traitor to his face by the ANC leaders and was so described in their leaflets. ANC volunteers decided to kill him and to do it with gasoline bombs. As usual, the volunteers gathered in Mafigo's Studio and manufactured their bombs. The bombs were taken to some deserted ground and tested, after which the volunteers split into two groups, one of which headed for Ntonjeni's home. While they were on the way, the volunteers were caught in the headlights of an approaching car. Fearing that they would be identified later, the volunteers threw themselves flat, and all but two then ran away. The remaining two persevered in their mission. They threw two bombs at Ntonjeni's place, one of which fell short, while the other set fire to the house. Their work done, the volunteers ran home to report to Reginald Mdube, who was their volunteer-in-chief. The damage done by the bomb turned out to be slight, so another attack was planned.

In the second attack, eight men collected at Selani's house. (Selani had been involved in the first attempt to shoot Dukade.) They made another batch of gasoline bombs, which was rather a hazardous operation, given the conditions under which they were concocted. Selani was cooking his dinner over the open flame of a kerosene pressure cooker and could smell gasoline fumes distinctly as he cooked. In Selani's words:

I handed [over] a bottle of petrol and returned to the "Primus" stove where my food was cooking. While there I smelt the smell of petrol. I stood where my "Primus" stove was burning and saw Bongco with the bottle in his hands, he poured petrol in the bottles. He then asked for water. I gave him some. After that the bottles were tied down with string.

Once the corks were tied on, the bombs were ready for use; and the makers had met with no mishaps despite the chances they had taken. They were set to make their attacks.

Before leaving on their mission, one of the *Umkonto* men allegedly handed the guns to two of the volunteers, Tshawe and Monde. These two were mere pawns, otherwise unimportant, but one was nonetheless to be involved in a bizarre turn of the evening's events. The two had agreed to go with the party of bombers and to report back to Bongco at Selani's place after the mission was completed. At 10:00 P.M., however, Selani was awakened by one of the youths, who came to him in great distress. The precious pistol had been lost. Having seen what they thought was a policeman's flashlight, they had taken fright and run away; in their fear they had collided, with one dropping his pistol. Fearing the police, they had not stopped to pick up the gun but had run for cover. This was serious, and Bongco, who had been waiting for them at Selani's house, went with them to search for it. The gun was apparently recovered, but the revolvers were to land all the men in trouble later. As Bongco was told later: "The revolvers had been caught red-handed by the police, were found by the police, in the hands of Mark Mazisa's uncle." On his asking how this had happened, his informant said that "Mazisa and one Mdube had gone to test one revolver in a portion of Duncan Village and somebody chased them with a torch and they ran away and they were sure that they had evaded this somebody and went and placed the revolvers in the possession of Mazisa's uncle, but the police found them later there." [9]

In this tale of two guns, the story of Ntonjeni has slipped into the background. What had happened to the team that was to kill him? Tanana, the man who had spared Dukade and who participated in the second attack on Ntonjeni, first went to spy out the house to make sure that the windows were not covered with wire gauze, which would retard the bombing. As he feared being seen, he inspected the house from a distance, but could not make out whether or not the gauze was there. Tanana and his companions thereupon decided to come back in day-

9. Mashinyana/*Bongco*, p. 233; Tanana/*Bongco*, pp. 336–39.

light when they could better see what cover the windows had. Once again they carried arms. Their instructions were to shoot any policeman who tried to stop them and to shoot Ntonjeni should he try to leave his burning home. Ntonjeni was to have the unenviable alternatives of being either burnt to death or shot dead. Having decided to delay the attack by one night, the volunteers did not return to report to the volunteer-in-chief but instead retired to the home of one of their number to wait for daylight. In the morning the windows were inspected by the volunteers, who were still carrying bombs and revolvers concealed on their persons. Tanana, who by this time had had enough excitement, begged off the venture that night and returned the revolver to Mazisa's shop. The bomb attack launched that night, in which he did not participate, was unsuccessful.[10]

It would be a mistake to think that all attacks were this futile, though very many were. The attack on the home of Inkie Dombotie Hoyi, for instance, succeeded only too well, with tragic consequences. Hoyi was regarded as a traitor for much the same reason as was Ntonjeni; namely, that he was ambassador to a chief and had spoken in favor of Chief Kaiser Matanzima, the government's choice as prime minister of the Bantustan it was setting up in the Transkei. He had infuriated them further by writing, in an article, that in his view the Transkei would not be ready for self-government for another twenty-five years. As in the other cases, having made their decision as to a man's status, the ANC members made no secret of their intentions. At a meeting Hoyi had called favoring his own chief, Archie Sandile, two ANC people (who were also in *Umkonto*) called him a "sell-out" and a traitor. They told him that they did not want him as a representative of their tribe and that he was to be killed. He should go and live among the police, they said, for he virtually was one of them.

Despite pressures such as these Hoyi persisted in his determination to continue publicizing the government's plans, but he had asked for and received police protection. A constable was posted outside his door at night. In spite of this, on December 11, 1962, Hoyi's home was attacked through the front door, which he had left open for the police-

10. Tanana/*Bongco*, pp. 340–41.

man. A gasoline bomb was thrown into his room and, in the fire that followed, Hoyi's fourteen-year-old niece was burnt to death and his daughter severely injured. While Hoyi struggled to free the children, a shot was fired at him; and the bullet that was recovered corresponded with those fired from a gun in the possession of the ANC.[11]

Attacks on whites were rarer, perhaps because retribution was both swifter and stronger. Nonetheless, the death of Major Kjelvie at the hands of the volunteers showed that white policemen were by no means immune. There is also the story of Bongco's efforts to lure Sergeant Donald J. Card to a place where he could be killed. Sergeant Card was particularly feared, not only because of his detailed knowledge of the ANC but also because of his command of the language of the area, Xhosa, in which he was fluent. Bongco came to Card, professed a change of heart, and offered to help capture some saboteurs. He said that a few nights earlier a group of Africans has come together in the bush, where a few men from Johannesburg were training them. They planned a meeting for the following night, Bongco said, and he would show Card the place. Card must, however, come alone; if he came with others they would all know that it was Bongco who had informed, and they would kill him. Sergeant Card was not so easily trapped. He told Bongco in no uncertain terms that he knew what was afoot and that he had given Bongco's name to other police officers for instant arrest should anything happen to him. Card then arranged a rendezvous with Bongco, but, as he had expected, the appointment was not kept.[12]

Things were harder for African police for obvious reasons. They lived among the people, who could not help but view them as enemies. African police were far more accessible, both to attempts at assassination and to destruction of their property. Some of these attempts are listed in Appendix I. The surprising thing is not that these attacks took place but that there were, relatively speaking, so few of them. The reason may tie in with what was earlier said of revolutionary organization; that is, the local groups largely suited their own interests in interpreting directives and slogans. Attacks on police were dangerous to

---

11. *Daily Dispatch*, February 19, 1964; Mdube/Rvtr, pp. 54–55.
12. Card/Bongco, p. 517.

the local cell. The deaths of policemen would more certainly be avenged than those of informers, so the latter were more often singled out. In terms of revolutionary strategy, this is not bad reasoning. The police, denied information, would be helpless, so attacks on channels of information were at the same time less risky and more effective. The real problem was that as long as cells acted largely on their own, with minimal direction, attacks on such channels were not concerted. So although they constituted a threat to the intelligence-gathering efforts of the government, they were not on a scale large enough to seriously hinder or destroy the channels of information.

The attacks on individuals constitute only one part of the larger picture. In some cases they are not even among the most sensational perpetrated. They did not receive the publicity given the hanging of Vuysile Mini, a man who has played and will continue to play an important part in our story. Although Mini was accused of sabotage, of which he manifestly was guilty, he was actually executed for organizing the cold-blooded murder of one of his co-conspirators, Sipo Mange, who was shot down on January 12, 1963, because his associates feared that he was about to betray them to the police. The execution was represented as punishment for Mini's activities in the ANC or *Umkonto*, without reference to Mange's death. He was built up as a martyr to the cause; his name is still extolled from time to time in *African Communist* and *New African*. The case has not been discussed in detail, for it differs in few particulars from earlier cases.[13]

III

If the argument that lower echelons act independently with little relationship to their "headquarters" is not taken seriously, a problem of interpretation arises which could be resolved only with difficulty. The *Umkonto* leadership claimed their policy was to avoid loss of life, except in the case of informers and those who actively supported government policies. This claim seems genuine because it appears not

13. *Star*, April 12, 1964, February 23, 1965; *Eastern Province Herald*, February 12–13, 1964.

only in material that came to light after the organization was broken up but also in documents intended for outsiders. How can this be reconciled with violence against opponents and not merely against informers? Surely the sanctioning of these actions would be hard to square with the professed humanity of the leadership, particularly since denial of violent intent against persons was a recurring theme among ANC leaders, at all levels.

Leaders gave a number of answers when later questioned. In essence, their argument is that they could to some extent direct their members, but they could in no way control them. They could only argue that acts of which they disapproved were acts of individuals. Individuals had done things on their own initiative that were contrary to the policy of the organization. One of the leaders, Govan Mbeki, claimed to have investigated the acts of terrorism in the Eastern Cape. His researches proved them to have been contraventions of *Umkonto* orders. No record of action taken against the contraveners exists, and it is doubtful if anything could have been done even had action been found desirable. Mbeki could only say that, in its manifesto, *Umkonto* headquarters had made it quite clear that only the symbols of apartheid were to be attacked, and not individuals.[14] Even government property was to be left alone when it was in use. Once again, these instructions had been ignored when it suited individual cells or branches. A number of attacks on post offices, for instance, had taken place at times when they were crowded with people. Those who launched the attacks either did not understand their instructions or did not consider them binding. The leadership might have deplored such attacks, but there was nothing they could do about them.

When an effort *was* made to control acts which, on the face of things, seemed directly to contravene higher policy, it was done through the ineffectual bureaucratic bodies. Mbeki, for instance, asked the ad hoc committee in East London to investigate what was taking place. This served little purpose because the members of the ad hoc were themselves involved in these acts and were in effect judges in their own case. The committee simply told Mbeki that the members of

14. Mbeki/*Rvtr*, pp. 175–80.

Umkonto whom they had approached and questioned denied all knowledge and all responsibility.[15] It goes without saying that their denials were accepted without much scrutiny. Mbeki was not the only leader to advance these arguments, as emerges in the way Bongco's case was treated within *Umkonto*. Bongco was one of the worst contraveners, but Reginald Mdube, another leader, simply said that Bongco had exceeded his authority. Bongco had never been given permission to bomb private dwellings and to shoot individuals. These were contrary to the policy of both the ANC and *Umkonto*.[16]

In Natal, Curnick Ndhlovu maintains, the regional command had tried to keep actions within bounds, so that life would not be endangered. One man, indeed, was appointed with this as his sole duty. A young white man, Ronald Kasrils, Ndhlovu alleged, had the task of seeing to it that no targets other than those selected were bombed. As approved targets were often abandoned in favor of others, Kasrils would be reprimanded, Ndhlovu said, and then he in turn would reprimand the others. This was often necessary, for there were a number of members who would determinedly choose their own targets.[17]

Mtolo cites two examples in which an independent choice of target endangered life, contrary to decisions taken at the regional command. He speaks of a man whom they nicknamed "Gizenga" because he had denounced the moderate ANC policies and joined *Umkonto*. "At first we were very fond of this chap," writes Mtolo. "Later this love faded as we found he could not be disciplined." What is more, "Gizenga," like many Zulus, was a heavy drinker. A decision was taken to bomb the offices of the Nationalist Party in Natal when the building was unoccupied. The offices were on the top floor of the place where the Nationalist newspaper for Natal, *Die Nataller*, was printed. Mtolo prepared a bomb for "Gizenga," and when giving it to him could not help noticing that he was drunk. The following morning the news papers reported that the *Nataller* offices had been bombed, and that a woman and children walking past the building had been hurt by splinters. Inside the building someone had escaped death by a miracle.

15. Mbeki/*Rvtr*, pp. 115–16.
16. Mdube/*Rvtr*, pp. 21–22.
17. *Natal Witness*, February 14, 1964; *Natal Mercury*, February 14, 1964.

There was no mention of any attack on the Nationalist Party offices. The group waited for Ronald Kasrils to come and give them a full report, and they were told that "Gizenga" had bombed the *Nataller* because there were people in the Nationalist Party offices. Instead of returning with the bomb, he had decided to remove the timing device, light the bomb by hand, and, using it as a hand grenade, hurl it into the *Nataller* building.[18] Shortly after this, "Gizenga" placed three pipe bombs in beer halls which were being boycotted, with the result that several people were injured. After several such episodes, Mtolo says, he had to be sent overseas, both for his own safety and for theirs.

Attacks on government property were fully accepted in the ANC and *Umkonto* as a way of defying the government. Yet, in all the attacks made, there was a lack of discrimination, a lack of planned selection. Again, this typifies the organization in which selection has, in fact, to be left to the lower echelons within a broad policy. A saboteur, Abel Mthembu, described the method of selecting targets this way: "If there arrived an instruction, perhaps at short notice about any property of the Government that had to be destroyed, we must destroy it— blow it up. . . . The whole idea was, in the main, we had to cripple the Government." [19] The problem was, as before, how to interpret fairly broad orders so as to make them effective. In the event, what happened was that targets were selected and approved, and then others substituted at the whim of the individual saboteur or of a group. What this amounted to was that difficult targets tended to be ignored; the saboteurs selected those that could be more easily attacked with less risk to themselves. This often meant that targets which were economically significant were left alone, while relatively insignificant targets were bombed. Instead of acting as trained professionals, resolutely attacking vital installations, these were small men choosing small targets.

An example may, once again, tell more than pages of abstract theorizing. Such is the story of two would-be saboteurs, Bennett Mashinyana and Mark Mazisa, who were to blow up an electric sub-

18. Bruno Mtolo, *Umkonto we Sizwe: The Road to the Left* (Durban, 1966), pp. 55–56.
19. Mthembu/*Rvtr*, p. 16.

station in the township of East London. The story emerges in the cross-examination of Mashinyana; the counsel's questions are omitted and linking material is added in square brackets. Treated this way, it reads thus:

When we got to this place, our intention of course, [Mazisa] had asked me to take him to a place where he could pass water or urinate. . . . So we came to this place's fence and when we were urinated he suggested, we were conversing. The topic changed immediately once he saw that this was a sub-power station. He wanted to know from me what this place was, and I told him that it was a sub-power station, and then he said, "We could easily commit an act of sabotage in this place." By blowing it up with dynamite. . . . I agreed. I said it would be very easy for us to do it, because the place did not even have lights then, and it was near the location, and [Mazisa] in turn said all right. Now I asked him about the material, where were we to get the material? The dynamite, and he said no, do I not know of any person who is connected with dynamite, or somebody who works in a place where dynamite is used. So I told him, well, I would contact someone who knows another Bantu fellow by the name of Blues who works near dynamite. He [Blues] worked for the East London Divisional Council, the Roads Department. So I was taken to him and unfortunately, he was not in his sober senses when we met the first time, he was drunk, and we could not discuss anything constructive. So I left him off and I tried to make an appointment for him a later date and he did not fulfill it, until we met again with Mazisa, the following Saturday and . . . the following Thursday he said to me, I must expect a message. So I didn't ask him what type of message it was to be. So on a Saturday morning very early, at about 5 A.M. somebody . . . who was assistant to the Volunteer-in-Chief came. He told me that he had instructions that he must come and fetch from the Regional High Command. We went next to the golf course. So that was where I met with Mark Mazisa. Mark Mazisa told me that he had already spoken to Blues, and he had already voiced the issue to the Regional [contact], and the Regional [contact] has already promised that there is somebody who is expert in dynamite from Port Elizabeth who will be coming down to demonstrate to us how to use dynamite in this particular act of sabotage.[20]

The substation was not blown up after all, because both the "expert in dynamite" and Mazisa got into trouble with the police. Mazisa fled to Dar es Salaam, the city which was to prove a haven for South African political refugees and from where they would organize to continue their struggle.

The case just discussed makes clear the hit-and-miss way that much of the sabotage was organized. Oceanic Ngoza, who has appeared in these pages before, brings this point home. He personally did not instruct his volunteers which targets to destroy, he later said; as they went out in search of targets he would turn to them and say: "Let us part here, you go that way, I will go this way, and he will go that way." [21] Each of the volunteers then set off in a different direction to attack whatever likely looking government property he found. In some cases it was private rather than government property that was assailed, as a case involving Ngoza himself indicates.[22] After he and a friend of his had been shown how to make gasoline bombs, they went to the lumber yard where Ngoza had been employed in order to set it ablaze with the products of their newly acquired skills. Now it is difficult to imagine a better target for an arsonist than a lumber yard, where there was obviously a plenitude of inflammable material. But so inept were the efforts of Ngoza and his companion that only slight damage was done. The first man threw his bomb without lighting the wick, with the result that it failed to go off. Ngoza's bomb, on the other hand, burst into flame; but, as Ngoza put it, they were "disturbed" by the police and ran away. The fire was soon brought under control, and Ngoza and his friend determined to try once more. This time the target was to be the store of an African police sergeant who lived in Kwazakele Township near Port Elizabeth. They tried hard with their bombs, but the store would not catch fire. So instead they burned a truck belonging to

20. Mashinyana/Rvtr, pp. 23–25.
21. Ngoza/Magwayi, p. 44.
22. Ngoza/Magwayi, pp. 17, 39–43.

the sergeant. Ngoza also took part in the bombing of the Municipal Offices and the school board offices, as well as other minor government properties in New Brighton. Such minor targets made the most convenient and hence the most general targets, but petty sabotage of this sort was hardly likely to rock the South African ship of state or cause it to change course.

Later the idea of expanding sabotage in line with *Operation Mayebuye* took root, but even here there was little coordination of action. Before his arrest Vuysile Mini had ordered the preparation of maps of all police stations in the Eastern townships. The aim was to attack these at some predetermined point and seize their arms. Instructions to this effect had been sent through the ordinary mails by Mini and were considered by the regional committee. The maps were duly prepared, and Mini came down to inspect them. On this occasion he also told the committee of the meeting at Lobatsi and of the decisions taken there. (The conference at Lobatsi, which will be described later, served in lieu of the old annual conferences, which could no longer be held.) The conference resolution called for the extension of the range of sabotage, Mini told the committee, and arms were to be obtained as and when the police stations were attacked. He failed to say, however, when and how this was to be done. The maps thus remained unused and were in the end added to the voluminous documentation of the police, some of which has gone into the make-up of this book.[23]

IV

Something should be said, perhaps, about the efficacy of the different branches, for this varied greatly from area to area. The East London branches, for instance, seem to have been neither as determined nor as well organized as those in Port Elizabeth, and the national leadership was much concerned over this. Both Mini and Mbeki expressed displeasure at a meeting with the East London branches. They were displeased with the way East London "was doing

23. Mdube/*Bongco*, pp. 379, 385.

its work." They drew unfavorable attention to the insufficient recruitment, the slowness in forwarding subscriptions, and the slackness in
organizing people to become "Freedom Fighters." [24] They were also
derelict in educating the people about the "Freedom Struggle." The
people had to be told to "know and understand that the Government
of the country was actually our enemies, and that the Government's
laws were . . . a chain around our necks . . . because we were not
consulted about anything, even when new legislation introduced had
to do with us, we were not consulted about it. [The people] had to
be taught to defy the Government."

In sum, then, it comes down to the inability of the higher bodies to
control the lower ones. This failure, it has been argued, is inherent in
an organization working underground with a network of cells. These
cells seek autonomy and treat orders from above as no more than rough
guides to action. The notion that the ANC or *Umkonto* was a
bureaucratic structure has, it is hoped, been somewhat dispelled. No
leader could press on a metaphorical button and secure predetermined
results. Something may happen, but not necessarily what was expected.
The men, even if not dedicated, indoctrinated, and efficient revolutionaries, were working at great personal risk. Condemning their acts
might have deterred them, but it may also have crushed their morale.
Recruitment of desperate men, such as these, might have suffered. On
the other hand, failure to condemn acts which were, in the words of
the leaders, "contrary to policy" made it seem that policy was only
window dressing and that acts which endangered life were tacitly
approved, that anything done in the name of the cause would be
condoned if it succeeded. Success was the measure; failure alone was
condemned.

Defying the government required trained men, and though there
had been some effort to provide training for the "soldiers" of *Umkonto*,
the range of feasible achievement was limited. What was needed was
training not only in defense but in defiance, and this included both
secrecy in *Umkonto*'s own operations and in the means of attacking
government property. Defense involved the silencing of "squealers"

24. Mashinyana/Rvtr, p. 14

and the disciplining of ordinary Africans in the townships. Even such limited objectives were beyond the powers of *Umkonto*, which could hardly control its own members, let alone the public outside. Nevertheless, the very real achievement that *Umkonto* represents in a South African setting cannot be gainsaid, and this is particularly true of Port Elizabeth. About seventy acts of sabotage were committed in this area alone, which represents a great accomplishment from the ANC-*Umkonto* viewpoint. The efficiency of Port Elizabeth can be better understood if it is kept in mind that the total acts of sabotage in the country as a whole by 1964 numbered 203. But in the broader perspective, the kind of perspective envisioned by the top leadership of the ANC, the results were minuscule. Damage to government buildings was easily repaired, as was that to transport equipment and phone lines. The sabotage effort, which had cost so much courage and effort, barely scratched the impressive economic machinery of the country and had even less effect on the minds of the dominant whites. Yet, at the lower reaches, the struggle groups continued their work. They recruited the small numbers of men they could find for training overseas and kept alive their belief in freedom. It was this belief, ill-formulated in ideological terms, that gave *Umkonto* what thrust it had.

VII

Umkonto: Training and Recruitment

By THE MIDDLE OF 1961, the ANC leadership had abandoned the idea that passive resistance coupled with mass action would influence the government to change its policies or induce a change of heart in the white electorate. Nor was sabotage alone sufficient in the long run. Well-prepared guerrilla actions, taken together with a growing scale of sabotage, might both ignite the African will to resist and shake the resolution of the whites. To do this meant training men. A nucleus of guerrillas with the skill and the will to fight had to be mustered. The men had to be trained both in South Africa and abroad. One trained guerrilla coming back to South Africa, the leaders reasoned, could train another twenty, and so *Umkonto* could eventually become an overwhelming force. Guerrilla armies would grow organically.

The immediate problem was to get things started—to provide at least basic military and political training in South Africa, and then to supplement this with further training in other countries.[1] Using resources available abroad to maximum advantage and putting men to the best use when trained called for a master plan. *Operation Mayebuye* was such a plan.[2] The question as to whether *Operation Mayebuye* was

1. Sisulu/*Rvtr*, p. 268.
2. Sisulu/*Rvtr*, pp. 256–57, 280; Mbeki/*Rvtr*, pp. 158–65. It is interesting to note that Sisulu claimed that he did not know who drew up *Operation Mayebuye*

211

ever formally adopted, and to what extent it was to be implemented if it had been adopted, is still being argued. Joe Matthews, for instance, says that nobody took *Mayebuye* seriously. As Matthews allegedly was a Communist and also a banker for both *Umkonto* and the ANC (that is, he handled money from abroad), his view must be taken seriously. If, on the other hand, his involvement is taken into account, together with his having said this *after* the Rivonia raids, then it can also be interpreted as a playing down of failure. Bartholomew Hlapane, on the other hand, has argued that *Operation Mayebuye* was accepted by the Central Committee of the Communist Party, and, as this controlled *Umkonto* to a considerable extent, the plan was *Umkonto* policy. Hlapane, having been a member of the Central Committee and having said this at a trial where his evidence was subject to cross-examination, also deserves a hearing.[3] He had, however, come to hate the Communists and may have been prejudiced. If his word is taken, together with the actions of *Umkonto* leaders, it would seem that a version of *Mayebuye* was being applied, even if the plan was not executed in full measure.

It must be pointed out that the success of *Mayebuye* would have met the deepest wishes of far more Africans than were in *Umkonto*. As an organization, *Umkonto* had the tacit support and much of the sympathy, overt and covert, of many Africans in cities and towns. Had *Operation Mayebuye* not been stopped in midstep, there is no knowing what might have happened. It might well have jolted numbers of Africans out of their despondent apathy and into violent action. As this is not what happened, it is pointless to pursue the theme. Nevertheless, the feelings and emotions smoldering beneath the surface were known both to the government and to the National Liberation Movement (the name given the alliance of the Communist Party and the Congress Alliance).

As master plans go, *Operation Mayebuye* contained few surprises. It followed what has, by now, become orthodox in planning insurgency. For instance, the guerrillas were to rely mainly on the enemy

---

or where it was drawn up. Mbeki said it was drawn up by Arthur Goldreich of the Technical Committee.

3. *Star*, March 31, 1966.

for their supplies, once the action was joined. "But in order to make this possible an initial effective arming of the first group of guerrilla bands is essential. It is also vital to place in the field persons trained in the arts of war who will act as a nucleus of organizers and commanders of guerrilla operations." [4] With this end in view and in line with the *Mayebuye* plan, the National High Command set about building this nucleus.

Pressure now mounted for recruits. Bruno Mtolo, whose evidence on this is most detailed, speaks of regular visits of inspection by members of the National High Command to put pressure on the regional command to get more men. Recruits were wanted for the extension of the sabotage campaign, as well as for training overseas.[5] The first call from the National High Command was for eight recruits in 1962. Fairly strict (for Africans) educational requirements were laid down. Only men who were educated to Junior Certificate level (equivalent to American ninth-graders) or who were matriculated (had completed high school) were to be enrolled. This was a tall order, to say the least. A relatively educated African, at that time, had completed primary school or the first or second class of junior high school; people who held the prized Junior Certificate were rare indeed. Of a population of over ten million Africans, some 1,339,000 were in school, but only 2.12 per cent of these were in classes above what in America would be the seventh grade. On this basis there were approximately 28,000 at all high-school levels in 1960, the year for which these figures apply. Of these, not all were potential recruits. Some were women, and others had no interest in embarking on adventures. However, the pool was actually larger because of the fairly wide acceptable age range: men from sixteen to thirty years of age.

The Natal regional command could not meet its full quota but was able to find six men who met the qualifications. These men, Mtolo later learned, had been arrested at the Northern Rhodesian frontier.[6] The Natal command was again besieged with demands for recruits. Again the members applied themselves, and once more success at-

4. Read into the record at Sisulu/*Rvtr*, p. 268.
5. Bruno Mtolo, *Umkonto we Sizwe: The Road to the Left* (Durban, 1966), chap. 13.
6. *Ibid.*, p. 66.

tended their efforts. This time, however, the men they found, though unsuitable for dispatch abroad, were useful as saboteurs within the country. Still demands for men were pressed. At the beginning of 1963 George Qhabi visited Natal as a delegate from the National High Command. He had come, he said, to take stock of what Natal was doing. Had they received the request for an additional twenty men for training abroad? On being told that the main impediment was the educational requirement, Qhabi told them to ignore this in future, because interpreters were now available at the training centers. (This was essential, since many Africans spoke little or no English and the instructors at the training camps were unable to speak South African vernaculars.) Given the green light, members of the regional command began to search feverishly for the twenty men. They were able to induce fifteen to enroll, but on the appointed day no more than ten presented themselves. Leaving South Africa in April, 1963, the ten were arrested at the frontier, apparently because of poor arrangements for their transportation. This greatly worried the Natal command. Mtolo writes: "I could see that the position was bad, even for me, and all other members of the Regional Command. I personally had recruited three and should these people start talking, we would be collected by the police like day-old chicks from the incubator." [7]

The regional command survived this contretemps and attempted to continue recruitment of another eight men, as called for by Andrew Mhlangeni, another visitor from the High Command. Frightened by the capture of the other batches, the regional command was assured that this time the recruits would be safe. It was told that contacts had been organized where needed and precautions increased; the recruits were certain to get through. Although not greatly reassured, the Natal command tried to comply. It was once more able to find six men, one of whom had to leave the country anyway, being wanted by the police for the attempted murder of a watchman. The group was duly dispatched. Soon afterward the Natal command learned that, despite all the promised precautions, the new group had been arrested in what was then Northern Rhodesia. The men had been caught with their

7. *Ibid.*, p. 60.

papers out of order by the police in Northern Rhodesia and were handed over to the South African police. Despondency increased in the regional command. Mtolo writes:

It now became clear not only to me but to everyone that recruiting was a waste of time. The matter was causing unrest to the public and to the parents of these youngsters. Some parents were told that their sons were just going to further their studies because Bantu education was not good enough. They handed their sons over with joy. Now this had happened and how was it ever going to be explained to them? . . . Again we were not given any information from High Command, but learned everything from the newspapers.[8]

For instructions in the next stage of recruitment, Mtolo himself went to Rivonia in July, 1963. Here, at the National Headquarters, he met with Walter Sisulu and Govan Mbeki, who told him that Natal must organize some 200 volunteers in the towns and another 2,000 in the countryside, and of these the first group must be recruited by the end of October. Mbeki, in the course of their talks, stressed that the recruits called for were not the same as those needed when the ANC was still lawful. They were to be put into *Umkonto* and not into the ANC. Realizing how vast a request this was, Mtolo asked when the revolution was going to start and whether it was to be soon. This question provoked laughter from Mbeki, who told Mtolo that "some of the leaders in Natal were still sleeping in their homes," drawing attention to the number of leaders in the Eastern Cape and the Transvaal who now were fugitives, in hiding either at the secret headquarters or at other places maintained by *Umkonto*.

The demand for recruits was only part of the news Mtolo was to carry back to Durban. He was also to tell the people there how the Natal *Umkonto* was to be organized. The plan called for the division of Natal into seven regions, each with a full-time organizer paid a reasonable (by African standards) salary of about $28 per month. In addition, three regional subcommands were to be set up, bringing the

8. *Ibid.*, pp. 66–67.

total of such subcommands in Natal to four, if the one already functioning in Durban is included. Once this structure was erected, a *supreme commander* would be appointed for the whole, the appointment to be approved both by the regional high command and the ad hoc committee. These bodies could either approve or reject the appointment outright; if they did the latter, the appointment would be reconsidered. The functions of this official were to include visits of inspection to the regional subcommands in order to report on their activities to the National High Command and to make suitable recommendations. To enable him to do all these things, he was to get about $21 per month for traveling expenses. The names of suitable appointees were to be sent to the National High Command for approval.

Here once again the bureaucratic fallacy raises its head. Mtolo pointed out to the National High Command that the seven regions had been drawn by someone who did not know Natal well and, as a result, the organizers would continually be crossing one another's paths. Mbeki saw the logic of the argument and agreed that the actual division of Natal should be left to the regional command there. He insisted, however, that the whole of Natal be subdivided.

Other matters of a more technical nature were also arranged during this visit. Political education was taken up, and Mtolo was told that lectures had been prepared which would be put at the disposal of the Natal command. When he pointed out that they already had classes in Marxism and its applications to South Africa, he was laughed at once again. He was told that their lectures were suited only to townspeople; the problems of the countryside were different and called for a new approach. Organizers in the countryside could only succeed if they linked the demands of the peasantry with the aims of *Umkonto*. The peasants had to be shown the relevance of the "freedom struggle" to their daily lives and problems. The new lectures were to be put to use when ready and where possible combined with military training.

The techniques of handling recruitment and recruits were not ignored either. Mtolo was told that the fault had lain in sending recruits overland from South Africa. These routes, through the Protectorates or through Rhodesia, were now being abandoned as too dangerous. The High Command had arranged for the charter of aircraft to take the recruits from Francistown, in Bechuanaland, to Dar es Salaam, from which point they could be sent on. The minimum passenger load for a charter was twenty-eight men, and the different provinces would have to provide a sufficient number to make sure that seats on the aircraft were not wasted. Natal, as a result, was to send thirty men; and as the charter fee remained constant regardless of the actual number flying, the quota had to be maintained. The flow of recruits was now more important than ever.

The new directive on recruitment had some immediate results in Natal. One was the appointment of Solomon Mbanjwa as supreme commander; he was sent to Pietermaritzburg and to Bergville in order to set up the regional subcommands for which the National High Command had called. Names of regional organizers were put forward, and Mtolo was instructed to follow up on the work Mbanjwa had done to train the newly organized commands in the use of bombs and explosives. At the same time, the new commands were to be pressed to recruit more men.

From what can be learned of the *Umkonto* organization in Natal, it is difficult to tell how much of what was ordered by the High Command ever was achieved. Curnick Ndhlovu, who led the organization in Natal, claimed that four sections had been established in 1962: one at Durban, another at Kwa Mashu Township, a third at Clairwood, and the fourth at Hammarsdale. It is not clear if the 1963 directive was implemented at all, but it is doubtful that it was. Had it been, more would certainly have surfaced. Like so many bureaucratic visions, it seems to have remained a vision only. The matter is, however, still open to conjecture.

II

More needs to be said of the techniques used both to recruit and to send men to other countries. These methods were no better organized and standardized than was anything else in *Umkonto*. There was no particular pattern, rigidly adhered to, though again the leadership laid down general guidelines, which were varied to suit local conditions.

The ideal procedure, as envisioned, was for an agent to contact a prospective recruit and to make it clear to him that he would be going overseas for military training. After the initial contact had been established, the potential recruit was put into touch with the actual recruiting officer, a man such as Mbanjwa, who would interview him, determine his suitability, and, if he was found to be acceptable, arrange for his further transportation. This picture, as so much in *Umkonto*, was, to put it mildly, an idealized one. Recruits were frequently not informed of the purpose for which they were recruited, many being told that they were going to get scholarships overseas. And, with the pressure for recruits as great as it was, standards could not be too high. Almost anyone who expressed willingness to go usually was sent, as were people who either had made themselves troublesome or had come too prominently to the attention of the authorities.

Men joined *Umkonto* and agreed to go overseas for training for a number of reasons. The obvious grounds would seem to be a sense of oppression or of relative deprivation. Although this may have underlain many motives, it was not often the reason given. If a system is wholly resistant to protest and revolt and there is no evident alternative, what exists may be accepted even when men know that there may be better systems. Changing this attitude of apathy means shattering people's perceptions of political reality. This is by no means an easy thing, as witnessed by the experience of insurgents in the Algerian revolt, the most successful revolt on the African continent. Michael Clark, in a study of that rebellion, argues that the affair was the work of a small minority.[9] It never took the form of a mass uprising. The apathy of the Muslim population as a whole resisted the pressures of incessant propaganda, intimidation, and outright terror. Clark states that by the end of April, 1957, the rebels had killed 5,576 Muslims and wounded or abducted 5,480 more. It is unlikely that killing on this scale would have been necessary if the rebellion had had the spontaneous and unanimous support claimed for it by its instigators. In South Africa and in Algeria, the old political perceptions stood fast, although they eventually broke in the latter country. Those who responded to *Umkonto*'s call were,

9. *Algeria in Turmoil: A History of the Rebellion* (New York, 1959), p. 5.

therefore, not necessarily representative of all African youth. Nor were their reasons necessarily ideological. Mtolo gives some reasons for which young men went abroad for training: "The methods used in recruiting these young men were to tell them about the Influx Control Act, Job Reservation, and low wages. As soon as these things were explained to them, they wanted to fight." [10] The significance of this passage is inescapable.

But, Mtolo adds, many of the young men did not come for political reasons at all. The spirit of adventure motivated them; they wanted to see other countries, and this was an opportunity to do so. To this was added the incentive of status on their return. "The idea that they would be coming back as somebody important further encouraged them to go," writes Mtolo. "My experience showed that some would sacrifice good jobs, not primarily because of politics—they had never even heard of the ANC before—but simply for the experience." Once again the question of the extent to which political fanaticism influences men to revolt comes to the fore. How many are involved because of conviction, and how many participate for the "kicks"? This question cannot be easily answered. But if we turn from the general to the particular, a few answers may suggest themselves.

Mtolo has been used as a source for this book because in many ways he is a unique revolutionary, a man who has written about an unsuccessful revolution, in which he participated not as a major maker of decisions but as one of the cogs in the machine. In his book we see revolution from the ground up, and as this is the view of revolution under consideration here, his account and the accounts of others like him are stressed. Let us consider first the case of Mtolo himself. [11]

The night schools run by the Communist Party were Mtolo's first contact with politics. These schools were organized for Africans in the interwar years and served to make many Africans politically aware. The Communist Party was not, of course, the only body running such schools. [12] The great hunger for adult education was met, inadequately

---

10. Mtolo, *Umkonto we Sizwe*, p. 52.
11. Mtolo/Rvtr, pp. 2–10; *Umkonto we Sizwe*, chap. 3.
12. Edward Roux, *Time Longer Than Rope: A History of the Black Man's Struggle for Freedom in South Africa*, 2d ed. (Madison, Wis., 1964), pp. 342–48.

it is true, by a variety of religious and charitable bodies. But in this field, as in so many others, the Communists seem to have been the most persistent and tenacious. Mtolo, for instance, writes that he was "not politically minded" on entering the school, that the world did not seem too bad to him, and he thought of himself as getting along well. "Naturally I had clashes with some [whites]," he writes, "but they were not important. It never occurred to me that we had clashed just because I was Black and the other man White." This attitude changed very soon after Mtolo had attended the night school: "The anti-White feeling in me started to grow. . . . In my mind I was pleased that one day we would have to fight the Whites and take over the positions which they held. We would have motor cars, nice houses, and be the bosses." [13]

Mtolo left Durban after having participated unspectacularly in a strike; he went first to Cape Town and then to Johannesburg, where he arrived in 1948. There he got mixed up in an attempt to rob a train and received a four-year prison sentence. In prison Mtolo, whose intelligence is undeniable, was made a hospital orderly, and in this capacity met other prisoners who, for one reason or another, were sent to the prison hospital. Among those he met was P. H. Simelane, a prominent Congress leader, who influenced Mtolo greatly and led him to the ANC. On his release from prison, Mtolo returned to Durban and got work at a hospital there. He attended ANC meetings but, although he was convinced that theirs was the right way, took no active part in their enterprises. His inactivity stood the ANC in good stead, for during the State of Emergency Mtolo was not apprehended, although he was completely cut off from all political activity. He might have continued indefinitely in this way had he not learned from one of his many female conquests of Stephen Dhlamini, whom he had known before as a fellow-member of the ANC. Dhlamini lent him some Marxist books and, after finding out that Mtolo had been an inactive ANC member, urged him to join SACTU, as every member of the ANC who qualified for SACTU membership had to belong. Mtolo joined the Hospital Workers' Union and was told of classes which he

13. Mtolo, *Umkonto we Sizwe*, pp. 2–3.

was encouraged to attend regularly: "We had special lectures on trade unions which were based on political economy, which, I learnt later, is a basis for socialism, which is a road to Communism." The materialist interpretation of world history was also taught, from which Mtolo learned "that every change was violent and brought about by the people themselves, not by a supernatural being or somebody directing these forces from above." Trade union members could make such changes by participating in politics, he was taught, and "the workers' goal should be to overthrow the capitalist system and replace it with socialism which is the foundation of Communism." Mtolo eagerly read many books and pamphlets, bought or borrowed, all of which hammered home the same line. He did so well, he says, that he was once more approached by Dhlamini and asked how he liked the trade union movement. Mtolo answered that he preferred it to the ANC. Then Dhlamini asked him how he felt about the Communist Party. Because of what he had been taught, Mtolo decided to join and to help toward achieving its objectives. Secrecy was immediately enjoined on him. He was warned not to talk and not even to tell his current girl friend. He became one of a group of five and was instructed to attend Marxist classes every Sunday afternoon. At this time he also helped organize the Hospital Workers' Union in his free time and was made chairman of this miniscule SACTU union.

The initials SACTU run as a continuous thread through Mtolo's story, and indeed in this book. There is little doubt that SACTU members were a principal element in the planning and organization of the revolt. Mtolo, in his evidence at the Rivonia Trial, pointed to the eagerness of CP members to get Africans to join SACTU. The thrust of efforts by SACTU officers was less toward getting higher wages or benefits for members and more toward the need for Africans to seize power. Workers were to take over the government, take control of the country's wealth, and introduce the universal franchise. If these objectives were achieved, members were urged, the path to socialism and thence to communism would be open. SACTU thus served as a source of indoctrination, as a funnel to the CP, and as a source of recruits for *Umkonto*. Mtolo points this up by saying that all of the members of his own cell were both Party members and members of SACTU.

221

Functions overlapped, as was stressed earlier. For example, Billy Nair, an Indian, was not only secretary of a SACTU union in Durban but was also a member of Mtolo's sabotage group. His SACTU offices were used as a meeting place when sabotage was planned. Curnick Ndhlovu, the leader of *Umkonto* in Durban, was secretary of the small Railway Workers' Union. Mbanjwa was secretary of the Match Workers' Union. Eric Mtshali, one of the men on the regional command, was secretary of a SACTU branch in Pinetown, near Durban.

Therefore, to describe SACTU as one of the main Communist "transmission belts" is hardly to overstate the case. Mtolo claims that communism was gradually taught to those who joined SACTU, and by the time a man had become deeply embroiled in the affairs of the illegal party it was difficult to leave it in safety. By the time he had become disillusioned with the Communist Party, writes Mtolo, he was involved in so many criminal acts that there was no way out. "The reason is after being involved so far in sabotage and all these things, if I had backed out, I would have been killed . . . they would not have left me alone . . . they would have killed me." Even to express doubt was dangerous. "Once you showed any sign of being against them, you were considered a pimp," which meant that one was virtually taken as a traitor. The doubter might find himself in for much the same treatment as a man who actually sought to leave the Party.[14]

Mtolo's case was by no means unique. Other men were drawn into *Umkonto* and sometimes into the Communist Party through political classes, particularly if they looked promising. The case of Houghton Soci can serve as an illustration.[15] Soci, who was trained as a teacher, was thirty-one years old at the time of his recruitment, and was working for the Ford Motor Company in Port Elizabeth. As with Mtolo, political classes drew Soci into the hands of the underground. At the end of 1962, Soci was approached by another African who told him that as an educated man he should extend his knowledge of politics. Soci, his interest captured, duly joined a "study group." At the first meeting he attended, he was told that the purpose of the group was to "learn and teach politics in a secret method so that each and every

14. Mtolo/*Rvtr*, p. 217.
15. Soci/*Fazili*, Statement to Police, pp. 330–49.

one would in the future be in a position to teach others." It was also made clear that the members of this study group "should not be interested in knowing members of other study groups and that they should never discuss politics with people who pose as politicians because that will enable the infiltration of police informers in the ranks of the freedom struggle under the cloak of politicians." It was clear to anyone who attended that what was being done was illegal and tended to revolution. The call for secrecy was in any case not strange to men such as Soci, for discussion was becoming increasingly difficult for Africans. An African correspondent for a white paper, Harry Mashabela, put it in clear terms: "Politics [for Africans] is today a private business that must be discussed only with confidants. [Africans] have learned to talk about it only in whispers." [16] Thus secrecy did not in itself indicate anything necessarily subversive. However, the subject matter taken up made the nature of these meetings plain. In addition to discussion, members of the group were encouraged to read books purporting to be histories of South Africa, particularly in the area of black-white relations, which, not surprisingly, had a strong Marxist slant. It was at these meetings that the matter of going abroad for military training was raised, but no details were given. It was only after he had attended once or twice, Soci says, that he realized that he had joined the underground ANC.

Toward the end of 1964 Soci was visited by an ANC functionary who told him that the organization had decided to send him abroad for training. He was given no details, but he knew that it was for military training. He asked for permission to take his wife with him and, on this being granted, prepared to go to the town of Alice, where she lived; money for the fare was given him by the ANC, who also provided him with $14 pocket money. So equipped, Soci returned to his wife and told her that they were going away, without giving her the true reason. "I told my wife that I had got a teacher's post and that her presence was important in order to get a dwelling house at Somerset East [the place where the fictitious job was supposed to be]." But before leaving his home Soci heard that detectives had been there, and he and his wife left at once, together with the agent through whom the

16. *Star*, September 22, 1964.

contact with *Umkonto* had been made. Knowing that the police were after them, they tried to cover their tracks by leaving the train early, going to another town by bus, and walking to Grahamstown to take a train from there. All of them were arrested on the main road to Grahamstown, bringing their careers as freedom fighters to an end.

Another example of a man drawn into *Umkonto* through the SACTU funnel is Waycliffe Nyombo, who went all the way through indoctrination, sabotage, and guerrilla training abroad.[17] Nyombo, like both Mtolo and Soci, began as a member of SACTU. While in SACTU he was invited to attend secret classes, which were being held by flashlight in a garage in Athlone, a township near Cape Town. These classes covered much the same ground as do classes of this sort everywhere, and included such things as signaling, the repair and use of the internal combustion engine, first aid, and physical fitness. They were, in effect, a preliminary to training abroad. Mountain climbing, namely, the climbing of Table Mountain, Cape Town's famed beauty spot, was also done, less for aesthetic pleasure than as a field exercise. This schedule was followed for three months, following which Nyombo was invited to join another school to learn how to make bombs. He does not seem to have been too adept at this, for after one month there he confessed that he could not grasp how the bombs were made. Despite this setback, or perhaps because of it, Nyombo was once again approached, this time on June 6, 1963, and invited to go abroad for military training. Nyombo seems to have accepted this with pleasure and to have been sent abroad by means which will be discussed in Chapter VIII.

Two points of importance are evident here. The first is that Nyombo was not asked to join any organization other than *Umkonto*; that and his SACTU membership seem to have been sufficient. The second point is that the instruction was given by a white (believed to have been Dennis Goldberg) who had come from Johannesburg. As Goldberg, if it was Goldberg, could speak no African language, an African, Looksmart Ngudle, acted as interpreter. Both Goldberg and Ngudle will appear again in following paragraphs. More interesting

17. Nyombo/*Mbolompo*, pp. 641–45, 650–64.

now is the influence of white Communists, which seems to permeate the revolt. It could be said that, without them, the revolt would not have gotten off the ground.

III

If men were to be sent abroad, more was needed than just recruits. Military training would have to be financed in part by *Umkonto*, even if friendly countries were willing to meet some of the costs. Unsuitable people would have to be weeded out at an early stage, and a reduction of costs and of time spent abroad would have to be effected by providing at least some of the preliminary training in South Africa. The High Command of *Umkonto* was well aware of these things, as is evidenced by the holding of both political and practical classes. Preliminary training, as envisaged by the leadership of *Umkonto*, went beyond the classroom, extending to training camps conducted in secluded spots. How many such camps operated is unknown, but something can be said of at least one of them.

In 1962 a camp was planned near Mamre, in the Western Cape, which was intended to last three weeks. Due to start on the day after Christmas, it was to collect a number of young Africans and Coloureds and to provide them with basic guerrilla training. The organizer of this effort was Dennis Goldberg, who was assisted by Looksmart Ngudle. Goldberg, it should be added for the record, personally denied being a member of the Communist Party, though admitting that both his parents were members. If Goldberg is taken at his word, and there is no reason why he should not be, he nevertheless acted as if he were a member of the Party and was extremely sympathetic to its objects.

The camp as organized was to provide an ambitious program. Not only were lectures on politics and economics to be included, but also such things as the songs of the "freedom fighters" everywhere and lectures on guerrilla war based on Che Guevara's theories. Cuba seems to have been much on the organizers' minds, for one of the heroes presented as worthy of emulation was Fidel Castro, who had "freed" Cuba. Theory and songs were not the only subjects to be taught. More

225

mundane and less heady things were to be learnt as well. The use of field telephones, radio, and the mimeograph machine was included as part of the training. An internal combustion engine was taken to camp for lectures and demonstrations, for many of the men had little experience with motor vehicles. Training in first aid was to be given. Empty bottles were brought to demonstrate the making of gasoline bombs. In short, while those trained in the camp might not be the very models of modern guerrillas, they would have a fair grasp of some of the basic principles. For rather obvious reasons, the camp was sited in an obscure place, away from the road and in dense bush. The campers brought their own food, for suspicion might be aroused if food for fifteen to thirty persons were bought locally.

As the purpose of the camp could hardly be kept from the participants, it is not unlikely that the police got wind of it quite early. This must remain speculative at best. But once on the site, Goldberg called the group to order as the camp gear was being unloaded, telling them, according to witnesses, that the camp was to train them to fight the whites; that it was ordered by higher authorities; and that camps of this kind were being organized all over the country. With Ngudle as his interpreter, Goldberg told the assembled Africans that the camp was to be run on strictly military lines. He himself was to be addressed as "Comrade Commandant," and they were to stand at attention when they spoke to him. They were to elect a number of "Comrade Sergeants" from among their own ranks. The election of sergeants was not quite open. One group, for instance, selected a young African from their midst, but Goldberg insisted that they elect Looksmart Ngudle (although, as one witness put it, he had nothing about him to merit his name) and this was duly done. The "Comrade Sergeants" having been chosen, Goldberg told the men that they were to be taught the skills necessary for a soldier in a revolution and that the equipment brought to the camp was to be used to this end.

Once the camp had been set up, a regular routine was established. The campers started the day with physical exercises, for, they were told, "young guerrillas must be fit." Then they attended a series of lectures which differed from day to day. They were lectured on first aid and were told, among other things, that the wounded must be removed from the field so that they could not be captured and thus give information to the enemy. They were shown how to use a mimeograph machine to publicize successes and were told that they were to keep silent on failures. They were shown how to march and how to drill. At night they heard lectures based on Guevara's teachings, including one extolling Mandela, of whom, according to two of the witnesses, few had heard.

The camp could not realize its full program, however, for before long the police made an unwelcome appearance. On that day a young lawyer from Cape Town, alleged to be Albie Sachs, had come to the camp to deliver a lecture on economics. While he was there, the Secretary for Coloured Affairs, a government official responsible for the Mamre district, came to the camp. Dissatisfied with the explanation given of its purposes, that it was purportedly a "religious and recreational" camp, he sent for the police. The police, after a brief look at what was going on, went away for reinforcements. In the interval, the campers were told to burn all the notes they had taken in the classes and, if arrested, to give no more than their names and addresses. In the meantime, the two whites (Goldberg and Sachs) hid themselves and instructed a Coloured, Cyril Davids, to say that he was in charge of the camp. He was to persist in the story that this was a health and spiritual camp when questioned by the police. Davids was willing to tell the police this story, but they called him a liar to his face and ordered the camp disbanded. It had lasted for only three days.

The camp incident had a sequel for Davids. He was arrested some six months later under the ninety-day law, which permitted the arrest and holding of a suspect without charge for ninety days, after which his detention could be renewed indefinitely for ninety-day periods. The intention of the police obviously was to break down Davids' story and to do this in a way that could not be overturned in court. What they did, Davids later said, was to make it clear that they disbelieved his story, without suggesting what he should say to them. At first the interrogations were friendly, with the police trying to win his confidence. They urged him not to be stupid and take on his own shoulders the punishment really merited by others. But as he refused to yield, the tone of the investigations grew sharper. He was threatened with indefinite detention if he did not give evidence. Davids, who did not at first mind his imprisonment, began to miss his family as time wore on. He therefore decided to tell the truth about the camp. Other witnesses, in their turn, gave testimony, and it is on their testimony that the story of the camp has been presented.[18]

As their version of the camp and its objectives differs sharply from the version given by Goldberg, it is only fair to indicate what his was. Goldberg maintained that the camp had not been set up to train guerrillas but was a training camp for ANC leaders. This was urgently needed because so many of the older leaders were banned, exiled, or imprisoned. The aim was to take inexperienced men and teach them the principles of politics and political leadership. Goldberg argued, in his defense, that it was unlikely that he would have told the campers that the purpose of the camp was to make guerrillas of them, for he knew no more than six or eight of the men standing before him.[19] These arguments, which do seem weak on the face of things, were rejected *in toto* by the court at the Rivonia Trial. All the evidence points to the camp's having been set up for guerrilla training, and even the excuse that the men there were largely unknown to Goldberg does not hold much water. They had been selected by Looksmart Ngudle, who, as a skilled organizer for *Umkonto*, would hardly have been so stupid as to ask people on whom he could not rely. Ngudle himself later committed suicide rather than give evidence, which is indicative of his devotion to the cause.

As in all clandestine activity, the only evidence is that given by those who were caught or discovered. It is impossible at this stage to know whether the Mamre camp was unique or whether there were other camps like it. There is evidence that classes were held in many centers, including Cape Town, Durban, and Johannesburg, but very likely similar classes, for which there is no evidence, were held with like zeal in the Eastern Cape. The increasing discovery of classes by the police

18. Davids/R*vtr*, pp. B1–9, BB6–20; Mboxele/R*vtr*, D12–20, E3–16; Goldberg/R*vtr*, pp. 6–8, 12–16, 24–25, 84–85, 88, 110–12, 202–10, 250.
19. Goldberg/R*vtr*, p. 17.

and the growing pressure for recruits led to many being sent out of the country without preliminary training. The increased vigilance of the government thus meant that the standard of men sent abroad was necessarily lowered, but it is questionable if this mattered very much.

VIII

The "Freedom Fighters"

THE ULTIMATE OBJECTIVE of sending men abroad for advanced training in guerrilla warfare required a specialized kind of organization, an "underground railway," with stations in South Africa and in other countries along which men could be received and sent on their way. First they had to be transported to the frontiers of South Africa; then the frontiers had to be crossed and further transportation provided. All these procedures involved timetables, schedules, and coordination. Even then the problems of the trainer and trainee were not over, for the men had to be brought back again by some concealed route. Ranged against them was that arsenal of controls and repressive machinery that the government had built and perfected over the years. The population was registered and its movements restricted. There were networks of informers everywhere, even in the underground movement itself. The South African police cooperated with the police forces of adjacent territories and exchanged information with them. These factors had made the building of a guerrilla army impossible in South Africa itself and caused the leadership of *Umkonto* to consider the training of such an army abroad in the eventual hope of mounting a war of "national liberation."

Operation Maybuye shows that the use to which these men would be put conforms to orthodox insurgent theory:

230

Small secret guerrilla groups must be organized in areas where there is a good mass condition. Here we must expand the guerrilla troops into guerrilla units. We must select members who are absolutely reliable; that is, members who are ideologically reliable. By seizing arms from the enemy we will expand guerrilla groups into guerrilla units.[1]

The problem was to train the first guerrilla fighters. This meant money, a great deal of it. Such money was obtainable, as *Umkonto* leaders soon found out.

The initial and most obvious sources were African states, which naturally viewed the treatment of Africans in white-dominated South Africa with disgust. Having become independent, they were eager to help Africans elsewhere to achieve the same goal. Other sources were the Communist states of Eastern Europe, whose interest in Communist-dominated "national liberation fronts" was well established. To tap both sources two men were given missions abroad. Nelson Mandela was sent to the PAFMECSA Conference (Pan-African Freedom Movement of East, Central, and South Africa), while Arthur Goldreich, a white Communist, visited Eastern Europe. In addition, offices were established under ANC auspices in a number of sympathetic countries.

Among the features that capture the attention is the coincidence of dates: the decision to go over to violence was taken in June, 1961, and the first attacks were launched in December of that year, while the PAFMECSA Conference took place in February, 1962. Clearly, many in the African states must have thought that the time of liberation was at hand. In any event, the reception he was accorded exceeded even Mandela's expectations: "Wherever I went," he said, "I met sympathy for our cause and promises of help." [2] The whole of Africa seemed to him united against the South African government (and even outside Africa—in London, for instance—leading members of the Labour and Liberal parties expressed their sympathetic understanding of his aims and those of the ANC). Leaders of African states went further; they pledged their support. Ben Bella of Algeria even invited Mandela to

1. Quoted in Sisulu/*Rvtr*, p. 348.
2. Nelson Mandela, *No Easy Walk to Freedom*, ed. Ruth First (New York, 1965), p. 174.

Oudja, the headquarters of the Algerian Army of National Liberation. Sympathy, however heartening, would have meant little in and of itself. African states promised what were, for the chronically poor ANC, substantial sums of money. Now, with the establishment of *Umkonto*, funds began to flow. The Nigerian government of the time, for instance, promised the equivalent of about $28,000; that of Ethiopia, $14,000; Morocco, $8,000; and Liberia, $5,600. Other states promised lesser sums. This money, or as much as was collected, provided an indispensable basis for financing the broader operations of *Umkonto*. There were offers to provide military training as well. Ethiopia offered a base at Dabraseur, which was accepted, and an additional annual subvention of about $12,000 for training. Other bases were offered elsewhere. Even Mandela underwent military training in Algeria.[3] While there is no similar record for Goldreich, it would appear that he, in turn, was made many promises, for the inclusion of intervention by Communist states was built into the *Mayebuye* plan.[4]

Although Mandela had been well received and was promised assistance, there were flies in the African ointment. Racialism was, it seems, by no means a white prerogative. There was a black racialism as well as a white racialism. The African states, Mandela reported, were very anti-white. They objected in principle to the Congress Alliance with its multiracial congresses. They were equally sensitive to the Communist connections of the ANC and *Umkonto*. According to a diary entry of Mandela's made during his visit to the conference, which he headed "Political Climate in the PAFMECSA Area," the most striking feature of the area was the widespread hostility to anything at all redolent of black-white partnership. So strong was this feeling, Mandela recorded, that the African states refused to accept either white or Indian trainees for *Umkonto* and suggested that they be sent to Cuba. White and Indian Communists were obviously not exempt from racial antagonism in the new African states.[5] According to Bruno Mtolo, who speaks of a report to the Durban group by Mandela, those sent for training abroad were advised to conceal their

3. Mtolo/*Rvtr*, p. 78.
4. Sisulu/*Rvtr*, pp. 404–7.
5. Sisulu/*Rvtr*, pp. 115–17.

Communist connections. They were told of the sad fate of Eric Mtshali, who had boasted of being a Communist and as a result was now destitute in Dar es Salaam: "He had no food and no place to sleep," Mandela said. "He was just thrown away there." [6]

There was money now, but questions of its administration continued to vex the organizers. For, despite the money accruing to the ANC, organizers in the country complained that they were not being paid. The Durban group, with which Mtolo was associated, had been told that they would receive some $150 per month through Billy Nair, the treasurer in Natal. They were to put in a request to "Comrade" Curnick Ndhlovu, who in turn would approach Nair, who then would pass the request on to Johannesburg. Despite, or because of, this rather circuitous process, the money was frequently not forthcoming, and in the end the group sent Mtolo to Johannesburg to collect it. [7] It seemed that there was a pattern to the flow of funds, for whenever money was needed for train fares or to buy explosives it would be forthcoming, but when it came to paying organizers, there was nothing in the cash box. This was frustrating to the organizers, who had been promised salaries, but the situation did not, apparently, stop the flow of recruits.

Money was sent to Johannesburg from London, where the ANC office not only was responsible for fund-raising but also looked after propaganda. The very spread of the ANC and *Umkonto* in South Africa, Northern Rhodesia, and Tanganyika meant that the overseas representative doubtless had to do much traveling to hold the various threads together. He had, in addition, to visit African states and other countries sympathetic to the cause. As the man in charge of the London office, Oliver Tambo, put it: "Through these offices, the support and sympathy of governments and peoples for the freedom struggle of the South African people will be sought." Tambo was joined in 1963 by the veteran ANC leader and former general secretary of the Communist Party in its days of legality, Moses Kotane, and also by Duma Nokwe, who was a member of the Central Committee of the Party. As Tambo was not known to be a Communist, the

6. Mtolo/*Rvtr*, p. 77.
7. Mbeki/*Rvtr*, pp. 108–14; Bruno Mtolo, *Umkonto we Sizwe: The Road to the Left* (Durban, 1966), pp. 72–77.

233

Communist connection was strengthened with the addition of these two men. Together they established contact with a number of governments and organizations, as Tambo had predicted. These contacts and the material help afforded the ANC enabled the planning of *Operation Mayebuye* to be put on a realistic basis. The setting up of training sites was settled; the funds were obtained; and the sabotage campaign in South Africa continued.[8]

II

Reduced to its simplest terms, getting men out of the country came down to steps such as the following: First of all, men from all centers were collected in Johannesburg or in its satellite towns such as Germiston. From there they were taken to the townships and temporarily lodged in the homes of sympathizers; then they were taken to some place of common rendezvous where they were picked up in larger batches and taken to the South African–Bechuanaland frontier. The routes were varied with growing experience. The first few groups were taken from Bechuanaland to Plumtree, in Southern Rhodesia, and sent on from there, but this proved too dangerous. The most frequently used route was one in which trainees went by road to Zeerust and then crossed the frontier into Bechuanaland near Lobatsi.[9] They were then taken up through Bechuanaland to Northern Rhodesia (later to become Zambia), being ferried across the Zambezi River and met on the other side, in Kazungula, by members of the African party in Zambia, UNIP (United National Independence Party, the party of Kenneth Kaunda). Except for the first leg of the trip, between Johannesburg and Lobatsi, the Northern Rhodesia route also had to be abandoned; and air transport was the only feasible alternative. The cost of transporting recruits by air, and the fact that a minimum load was called for, intensified pressure for recruits.

How many men used these routes? This question cannot be answered. At least 300 trainees are known to have been sent out from

8. Sisulu/*Rvtr*, pp. 402–3.
9. Van Niekerk/*Gcabi*, p. 11.

South Africa; undoubtedly there were many more. The only firm evidence is how many were arrested on their return, or were apprehended in the Rhodesias. There were several reasons for the high arrest rate. The South African police had its spies everywhere in the Protectorates. The airfield from which flights took off for abroad was under the control of the agency that recruited Africans for work in the gold mines of South Africa. Although the company could not stop these flights, they were certainly made known to the police, even if the information did not come from the company.

If informing were not sufficient to cause disquiet to the High Command of *Umkonto*, the slackness, inefficiency, and loose talk of the cadres must have worried them. Indeed, the remarkable thing was not that so many of those leaving for or returning from abroad were arrested, but that any got through at all. In many cases the arrest of recruits was not the result of police efficiency alone, much as this contributed to their capture, but because of an almost criminal carelessness on the part of *Umkonto* men charged with receiving the recruits on their arrival in Johannesburg or its environs. No matter how carefully a revolutionary leadership may work out procedures, it is dependent on these procedures being carried out. Procedures can be rendered nugatory if they are carried out only partially or not at all. Individual cases may once again serve to illustrate the whole.

Gladstone Makamba and Freddie Tyulu had both joined *Umkonto* at about the same time in 1962.[10] The following year they were given a chance to go overseas, which both were willing and eager to do. Their journey began in February, 1963, when they left Port Elizabeth for Johannesburg on the first leg, with their final destination, they hoped, Dar es Salaam. At the railway station they were given their fare and advised to behave themselves and not to attract attention. If questioned, they were to say that they were going abroad to school. With them were some seven to ten others. They were met in Johannesburg and told to board another train for Krugersdorp, where once again an African, this time with a small car, met them. As the group could not all fit into the car, they were taken in batches to a town-

10. Makamba/*Gcabi*, pp. 3–18, 23–49; Tyulu/*Gcabi*, pp. 50–65, 67–96.

ship, the name of which remained unknown to them. There they were put in a private home and given food, and they conversed with a man who they thought was the owner. The next day they were picked up by a man in a Volkswagen Kombi, which also stopped at other houses to pick up temporary lodgers. The full van was then driven to the outskirts of the township, where it was met by two other Kombis and a car.

The little convoy then headed for the Bechuanaland frontier, arriving there at about 4:00 A.M.—the early hours of the morning. The convoy stopped near a clump of trees, which provided cover in the dark, and the men began to walk to the fence marking the border. Once over it, they were in Bechuanaland. But they were not yet safe. They were told to hide in some bushes near Lobatsi and to wait for a contact to come to them. Later someone came and spoke to the leader of their party, after which they were told to register with Immigration using false names. They were also told to keep their mission secret and, if asked, to say that they were students going abroad to complete their education. The business with Immigration in Lobatsi being quickly settled, they returned once more to their hiding places in the bushes. Although they had arrived on Monday, it was not until Wednesday evening that a truck came for them. Before they left, another man came to them and made a patriotic speech, telling them it was a pity that they should have to leave their homes in order to become soldiers, but it was necessary that they do so. They should remember that all the Africans in South Africa were depending on them, he added, and that this was the responsibility resting on their shoulders. Finally he wished them a pleasant journey and admonished them to behave themselves. Duly inspired, the recruits boarded the trucks heading for Northern Rhodesia and arrived at the frontier on Friday. It was now five days since they had crossed into Bechuanaland.

On the edge of the river they had to wait for a boat; once across, they walked to a Land Rover which they had been told would be there. In it were two UNIP members, who gave them about $14 each and then took them to Livingstone station, from where they were to take the train to Tanganyika. They had not been told one crucial fact: there was no direct rail link from Livingstone to Tanganyika. The ANC would, therefore, have had to provide trucks or buses to transport them. This was not done, it seems, and as a crowd of Africans waiting without apparent purpose on a railway station was bound to arouse police interest after a time, the men were in constant danger. The result was inevitable: after waiting at the station for half an hour or so, the recruits were arrested by the police and then returned to South Africa. They each received a sentence of two years in prison for leaving the country without a passport.

Should the impression have been created that the underground railway ran smoothly, and that sheer mischance led to the capture of the recruits, it would be misleading. The system of contacts did not work well; it put the recruits in jeopardy while they were still in South Africa. As a detailed example of inefficiency and poor planning, the problems facing Mtolo when he escorted a number of recruits are particularly enlightening.

On one occasion Mtolo was in charge of bringing a group of recruits from Durban to Germiston, near Johannesburg, from where they would presumably be transported for training abroad. This particular group seemed very promising, because it was composed of pickpockets, who were accustomed to a hard life. Now they were going to be soldiers of *Umkonto*. Mtolo was told that a contact would be waiting for them at Germiston; all he had to do was hand over the men and he could then return to Durban. Nothing could be simpler on the face of it. Mtolo did not know the recruits by sight and so, at his suggestion, one was introduced to him to act as the contact between him and the rest of the party. They were to travel separately, not meeting until their arrival at Germiston station. These precautions were necessary because a party of recruits with their escort had been arrested on a train a short time before. As an additional precaution, Mtolo was to take a taxi from Durban and board the train in Pietermaritzburg, where he would travel in the second class while the recruits traveled third class. This would allow Mtolo to get off the train first and so be ready to meet his contact with the group. Mustered in this way, it would be an easy matter to hand them over to the next escort.

Initially things seemed to go well. Mtolo had divided the young men into two groups while still in Natal, hoping to avoid the arrest of

237

all in case of trouble with the police. The first group was to take the night train to Germiston, and the second was to follow by the 4 P.M. train on the following day. The first batch arrived in Germiston safely; Mtolo recognized the contact from among the boys, and sent them all to the third-class waiting room while he sought the man who was to meet him and take over the recruits. This man was, it seems, Abel Mthembu, who was known to Mtolo. Mthembu, however, failed to appear at the appointed time. Mtolo hunted high and low at the station, but his search was in vain. Nobody appeared to take over the group. After waiting a time, Mtolo took a taxi to SACTU headquarters in Johannesburg in the hope of reaching the responsible ANC leaders. He found a man there who assured him that all would be well and advised him to return to Germiston station and wait. At the station Mtolo found his charges both worried and hungry. With what money he had, Mtolo bought each recruit a soft drink and a cookie. They continued their vigil. In the meantime, the other batch of recruits arrived. Mtolo, for the sake of security, now scattered his charges, but as time passed they clustered together in concern, increasing the danger of arrest. Though Mtolo could not hear what they were saying, he gathered that they were critical of the poor arrangements and were also afraid that he might leave them to fend for themselves in a strange city. The crowds at the station eventually began to thin out, leaving the recruits ominously exposed. Mtolo called them together. He advised them to say that they had come from Durban to work in the mines and, if they were asked for their papers, to say that the police had them at the mines. This precaution was just as well, for inevitably a policeman appeared and began asking questions; but, as their answers appeared to satisfy him, he went away.

At about 8 P.M. Mtolo saw a "dark looking, pimply faced chap" searching the platform. Mtolo realized from the way he eyed the youths that he was the contact to take over the recruits. This was not, of course, Mthembu. It was another man unknown to Mtolo. What he told Mtolo was of little comfort. There was no transport: all cars were being used for other purposes. Mtolo was told to buy rail tickets to Morafe Township, where he was to go to the contact's house. However, not all the recruits could be accommodated there; some would have to go to another "comrade's" home. In the course of explaining, the contact told Mtolo that he had only been instructed at 4 P.M. on that day to meet the group. This was insufficient time for proper preparations to be made. The contact said that he lived far from the station they were at and could not get there on time. Nor could he ask anyone else to come instead. At such short notice, the contact was poorly prepared to receive the hungry and tired recruits:

> The question of food arose as he had nothing in the house and it was too late to find an open shop. When I heard this I felt sick. It was worse when I thought of what could have happened if we [the regional command] had not decided that the group should be accompanied by someone from Durban. If we had taken Govan Mbeki's word that they would be met at the station in Germiston, it would have been a mess.[11]

Mtolo then went to Dube Township to check on what had happened. Arriving at the home of the original contact, Mthembu, he was, he says, disgusted to find the man in his pajamas acting as if everything were going according to plan. On hearing Mtolo's complaints, the man said that the recruits had been taken to Germiston on the wrong date, and that the time of arrival of the recruits had been planned for June 25, 1963. But the entry in Mtolo's diary, entered and checked after his conversation with Mbeki, gave the date as June 13. Either Mbeki had given the wrong instructions to Mtolo or the contact had made an error. In any event, this was now water under the bridge. The problem was what to do with the recruits. Mtolo pointed out that these men had eaten nothing since he had met them the night before, but the contact said that he had no money for food—they would have to see the treasurer of the ANC. He (the contact) would go down to the house in Morafe and everything would be well. At this point Mtolo told the contact in very plain language that he would not continue recruiting until he heard from the High Command that matters had been straightened out, and he returned to Durban a much disillusioned man.[12]

11. Mtolo, *Umkonto we Sizwe*, p. 86.
12. *Ibid.*, pp. 82–87.

Where had the error lain? An indication of the ineffectual operation of the recruiting system is seen in another case of the contact just spoken of. This man, Abel Mthembu, was given instructions to meet three groups of recruits and to take them to the *Umkonto* transport officer, Andrew Mhlangeni. Mthembu, according to his own evidence, went to the station to meet the first group on May 4, and, after waiting a long time, decided that the first group might have been combined with the second and that both could be met together. He therefore tried to meet the second group, which was due on May 11, and was once again unable to find it. The third batch was due on May 18, and now Mthembu hoped that all three groups might arrive together. He again went to the station and again drew a blank. This is no doubt surprising, but what is even more surprising is that Mthembu did not think the matter worth reporting to his superiors at the National High Command. The cross-examination of Mthembu brings out this astonishing matter:

Counsel:	After the first batch did not arrive, did you go and report their non-arrival to [Mbeki]?
Mthembu:	No, I did not.
Counsel:	And after the second batch didn't arrive, did you report their non-arrival?
Mthembu:	No, I did not.
Counsel:	And the third batch, did you report their non-arrival to him?
Mthembu:	No, I did not.
Counsel:	Although you realize that if these people are expected, arrangements have got to be made to receive them and to despatch them?—Why didn't you report their non-arrival?
Mthembu:	Why?
Counsel:	Why did you not report their non-arrival to Govan Mbeki if he gave you these instructions?
Mthembu:	Yes, I thought of that—that is, after the third occasion when they didn't arrive, I thought, well, in a few days I'll tell him then that these people didn't arrive.

Counsel: In a few days you'd tell them—why wait to tell them? Why wait a few days?

Mthembu: Because I didn't decide, I didn't think of going straight away.

Counsel: BUT WHY NOT? You were a member of this organization, you had a duty to carry out, if your evidence is true!

Mthembu: I told the truth, and I've already said that I didn't decide to go immediately and report it, after two or three days, I would have told them.[13]

Further comment would surely be superfluous.

The case described concerned recruits from Durban. Affairs did not go any better when the recruits came from other parts of the country. A witness in one trial spoke of being approached by one Zinakile Mkaba in Port Elizabeth and told that educated young men were needed for training in Algeria and that he should join. The witness was given about $28 for a train ticket to Germiston, where he was to be met in a way similar to that spoken of by Mtolo. No one met him at Germiston station, however, and after sleeping in the open for three days, he attempted to return home. He was arrested on the train for not paying his fare but was released on condition that he pay it in Port Elizabeth. Later on, the witness made another effort to go overseas but was arrested once again. Another witness at the same trial spoke of a similar experience. The Durban cases described, therefore, were not isolated instances.[14]

It is only fair to point out that the fault did not always lie with the *Umkonto* organizers; often the recruits themselves were to blame. A party of ten men from Port Elizabeth, for instance, were told to board a certain train and go to Germiston, where a man with a red beret would meet them. They missed the train and, after chasing it in two taxis, were picked up and arrested as they tried to reach it at another station. The men had only about $5 with them and, on questioning by the

13. Mthembu/*Rvtr*, p. 201.
14. *Eastern Province Herald*, February 19–20, 1964.

police, said that they were going on holiday, though they could give
no address to which they were headed.

III

Apart from ensuring that men turned up in the appointed places
and that they were met, there was the additional problem of arranging
transport out of the country. This called for a collection center and the
use of cars. It also meant extending the chain of contacts outside the
country.

One of the major collection centers was a two-story building, SK
House, belonging to an African herbalist named English Mashiloane.[15]
He had been a treasurer of an ANC branch, in George Goch Township,
while the ANC was legal, in the years 1955 to 1957. After that time he
had dropped out of the organization and apparently concentrated on
his prosperous business. In 1960, the year of the Emergency, he was
approached by Walter Sisulu and Elias Motsoaledi and asked if they
could use his home as a place to meet and to read. Mashiloane apparently saw no harm in this. He also had no objection when told
that people might come from time to time to hear about the laws by
which Africans were oppressed and so further their political education.
Mashiloane's home, an apartment above his shop, was used in this way
until 1962, when he was once more approached, this time to shelter
young men who were going abroad, he was told, to further their education. Groups of youngsters from Standard 6 (about seventh grade in
American terms) were being sent to Bechuanaland and Basutoland for
that purpose. Would he mind, he was asked, if these young men were
collected on his premises during the week so that they could leave as
a group on Friday nights? Obtaining assurances, as he later said, that
what was planned was not illegal, Mashiloane gave permission. It was
not until the second group was being collected and awaiting transportation that, Mashiloane says, he found out the real purpose for
which they were being sent abroad. One of the Xhosa youths told him

15. *Star*, December 18–19, 1963; *Rand Daily Mail*, December 19, 1963.

that all of them had enlisted as soldiers and that they were on their way to Ghana for training. Seriously concerned, as he says, Mashiloane reproached Motsoaledi, with whom he had concluded the original arrangement. Motsoaledi replied that, although it was a pity that the youth had given the game away, what he had said was true: some of the men had already returned as trained soldiers and "the war is already on." "Those people who are breaking buildings and electricity lines are fighting," Motsoaledi is alleged to have said. "This type of fight will continue till the real war starts." On being asked how the soldiers were to be armed, Motsoaledi answered that the real war would be waged in the cities, and there were plenty of weapons in the hands of whites that could easily be taken. "That is what these youngsters are going to learn, to take the weapons—and they will take them."

After about thirty youths had passed through his premises, Mashiloane objected once more, claiming that they interfered with his customers and were a general nuisance. Despite the pleadings of Andrew Mhlangeni, introduced to Mashiloane as the "boss," Mashiloane was adamant: other quarters would have to be found for the boys. Nonetheless, he agreed to allow the ANC to store dynamite on his premises and also to help *Umkonto* find further supplies. No doubt new collection points were arranged, and the private houses of "comrades" discussed earlier were utilized for this purpose.

From Mashiloane's SK House, or from other collection points, went a convoy of Volkswagen Kombis which belonged to an Indian, Essop Amod Suliman, who rented them to the ANC and *Umkonto*. Suliman and one of his drivers, Piet Adam Coetzee, gave evidence which the judge considered unreliable. Some of what they said was, however, corroborated by other witnesses and can be accepted on this basis.[16]

Suliman admitted to having transported some 360 recruits in about twelve convoys until the time he was arrested. In addition, he had carried the delegates to the Lobatsi Conference. The procedure under which the transport system operated was fairly standardized. Suliman asked a fee of about $75 for the rental of each Kombi with a driver, and he drove one of the vehicles himself. Suliman was notified when

16. Suliman/*Rvtr*, pp. 1–54 (handwritten pagination, 67–120); Coetzee/*Rvtr*, pp. 1–25 (handwritten pagination, pp. 122–47).

a convoy was needed, and he and his drivers would first go to a garage in Orlando Township and from there to the collection center, where they waited until their contact returned with about thirty Africans. The men were divided up among the different vehicles, their luggage was loaded, and the convoy was on its way. An excuse was invented to be used in case the Kombis were stopped by the police. They were to say that they were a football team on its way to play a match in Zeerust. On reaching the frontier the men would climb off the vans a short distance away, cross some fields, climb the fence marking the border, and walk to Lobatsi, while the vans with their luggage, described as travelers' samples, cleared the customs post. The van would then drive to Lobatsi, some distance ahead of the recruits.

This went on until Suliman was conveying the twelfth convoy, when they were all stopped and arrested. An overloaded Kombi broke down and, as Suliman turned back to help it, he found that it had vanished. As he again approached Zeerust, his van was stopped at the roadside by an ANC member, who warned him that the others had been stopped and everyone arrested. Suliman made a U-turn and headed back to Johannesburg but was arrested at Rustenburg en route. As he ruefully recalled in court, he had not been paid for that last trip.

In addition to the contacts inside South Africa who met—or failed to meet—recruits arriving in cities around Johannesburg, there were contacts in Bechuanaland and Basutoland whose task it was to facilitate the immigration of recruits and see that they were sent on their way. One such contact was William Senna, who not only helped others but also sent his own son away to be trained.[17] Living outside Zeerust at Gopane, some six or seven miles on the Bechuanaland side of the border, he had been a member of the ANC in its days of legality, since 1957, but did not rejoin after it was banned in 1960. He was approached by the ANC in 1964 and told that the government was refusing passports to people who wanted to go to Tanganyika to train as soldiers. This training was necessary so that they could come back and fight the government, an objective with which Senna had no quarrel. He therefore pledged himself to cooperate and subsequently

17. Senna/*Fazili*, pp. 191–211.

escorted at least ten people across the frontier, guiding them to where the border fence was screened by trees. He took no money, Senna said, but on one occasion was given about $14 and promised more later. The promise was not kept. As Senna needed money some time later, he approached the man from the ANC in Johannesburg, but was told that there was no money available. He nevertheless agreed to escort more people across the frontier. Arrangements were made for him to come back to Johannesburg and pick up a group, and it was on this occasion that he was arrested.

Senna's attitude, as he expressed it, was that he would have helped anyone to cross the border, although he was unaware of the ultimate destination of those he helped. He only knew that they were being taken for military training.

When a person is on the run, no matter where he runs to, whether it is out of the country or whether it is in the country, if you run to a man's house and should you [the fugitive] tell that person, "Look, I am frightened," and you give him a reason why you are frightened, and you ask him, "Give me shelter," you may be given shelter, and then when anybody comes to make enquiries about such a person, that person to whose home you have gone to, he will shield you from whoever is making these enquiries.[18]

In his view, and no doubt in the view of many other Africans, it was a duty even for those outside the organizations involved to shield those leaving the country. A common bond among the deprived obligated them to help those who worked against the government.

IV

The men who either failed to get out of South Africa or who were arrested soon after leaving the country represented only part of the manpower sent abroad. What happened to those who did get through? A number of men did reach training camps abroad and were trained as

18. Senna/Fazili, p. 209.

soldiers of *Umkonto*. One such case is that of Alfred Jantjies, who was trained in Ethiopia.[19] His story as a guerrilla begins with his joining the African Youth League (a disguised successor of the ANCYL) in Cape Town, his home. While in the Youth League, he was told by Looksmart Ngudle that "schools" were to be opened abroad and was asked if he wanted to go to one. Jantjies agreed. He and two others were given train tickets to Johannesburg, as well as black ties and armbands to enable their contact to recognize them. In spite of this they were not met at the station; therefore they fell back on the second set of instructions they had been given and went to the basement of a building in Commissioner Street, Johannesburg, where a white man told them what the arrangements were. They were then taken to the Marabi Hotel, which was being used as a collection point in Orlando Township, together with many other prospective *Umkonto* trainees, who, they noted with interest, seemed to come from all over the country: seven from Port Elizabeth, four from Durban, and five from Bloemfontein in the Orange Free State.

Their stay in the hotel proved to be a long one. They had to wait for three weeks before being taken to SK House by an *Umkonto* leader, Elias Motsoaledi. From there they were taken by the familiar route to the border and walked through the bush, to the accompaniment of the weeping of one very young and homesick lad. They first headed for Lobatsi and then for Palapye, another town in Bechuanaland, before going on to Francistown, where another ANC contact met them. In Francistown they were given about $84 each, for use in case they got separated, and arrangements were made for them to walk to the Limpopo River. There they were met by a truck and taken to the Bulawayo railway station, in Southern Rhodesia, where they took the train to Lusaka, in Northern Rhodesia. Then they walked to Tunduma, on the border, in Zambia, where the local UNIP representative arranged for them to be transported to Dar es Salaam. In Dar they found Oliver Tambo waiting to greet them; and, three weeks later, they were taken to Nairobi. Their papers were put in order for use in

19. Jantjies/*Rvtr*, C7–19; see also *Star*, December 20, 1963; *Rand Daily Mail*, December 21, 1963.

the African states, and they were given passports to Ethiopia. They duly arrived at the military cantonment at Dabraseur, in Ethiopia, where they were fitted out with uniforms and equipment.

Jantjies was told to change his name to Apiri, as his own was not African enough. He was taught such things as squad drill and the use of rifles, machine guns, hand grenades, and other weapons. He was also shown how to read maps, climb rope, perform first aid, swim, signal, and communicate by radio, as well as the arts of demolition, booby traps, and ambushing.

Their training over, Jantjies and his group were issued civilian clothing and taken back to Dar es Salaam, where the local ANC leaders told them that they had done very well. Each was instructed to use his knowledge to train fifteen others on returning to South Africa. At Bulawayo station they were detained by the police because a Kenya passport and some of the notes he had made in Ethiopia were found on Jantjies. He was sent back to South Africa under arrest and, together with eight others from the group, received a prison sentence.

Not all recruits were trained in Africa; some were sent to Cuba and others as far afield as Communist China.[20] Patrick Baphela, who trained in China and subsequently sported a mandarin-style mustache, was flown from Dar es Salaam to Moscow, where he studied trade unionism and was taught a little about the use of explosives. On returning to Dar he was met by Oliver Tambo and J. B. Marks, who asked him to go to Peking in January, 1964, where a certain Mr. Chen, president of the Nanking Military Academy, took him in hand. He was trained in the use of firearms, the manufacture and use of explosives, and the waging of guerrilla war. With all this training he returned just to fall into the police bag in Rhodesia as the others had done. Like the others, he was caught with incriminating documents on him—in his case, a book on explosives.

The cases considered above were of men who completed their training and managed to get back only as far as Rhodesia before being arrested. But there were men who made it all the way—men who,

20. *Rand Daily Mail*, March 25, 1965.

having been trained abroad, were able to come back to South Africa. Their cases are more infrequently recorded, probably because they did not get caught. Enough is known, though, to picture their subsequent careers.

John Metshane left South Africa in 1963, being, as he put it, "organized for a scholarship" outside the country.[21] Perhaps he was more successful than some of the others because he left on his own, without the assistance of the organization, and, in Bechuanaland, contacted people whom he knew personally that were connected with the ANC and who assisted him as far as Francistown. Once in Dar, Metshane met the leading ANC people and, after a wait of some four months, he and four others were sent on to China where they were given military and political training. On his return to South Africa, where he arrived safely in August, 1964, Metshane began meeting regularly with the members of the ANC and was paid an allowance of $75 monthly. He did nothing much to earn this allowance, though he drew it for some four months. His assignment then was to take four volunteers to Gopane; he was arrested with them at the frontier.

The ease with which different groups were arrested is highly suspicious, and it could well have been that there was an informer highly placed in *Umkonto* who was tipping off the police. This will be discussed in the conclusion, when some theories for which there is no evidence are entertained.

In addition to those taken out of the country for military training, others were taken whose continued presence in South Africa was a danger to *Umkonto* but who could yet be useful overseas. Elias Kunene was a case in point.[22] Arrested under the General Laws Amendment Act of 1962, the so-called Sabotage Act, in Durban on June 25, 1963, Kunene was held by the police and repeatedly questioned until September 21, 1963. Believing that others had already done so, he made a statement but refused to give evidence in court. Instead he advised the ANC of his actions, telling them that he could only main-

21. Metshane/*Fazili*, pp. 178–90.
22. Kunene/*Ngakane*, pp. 77–97.

tain this stance if he was helped out of the country. As Kunene had made a statement on his own admission, a meeting was called in February, 1964, at the church of the Reverend Mtlabata. This church, and many others like it, was regularly used for such purposes because the only way that Africans could hold political meetings was to disguise them as religious meetings. The case of Kunene and that of another man who had also made a statement were discussed, and it was decided to help them leave South Africa. Though Kunene knew that this step was necessary and desirable, he hesitated at its finality. He asked for two things if he went: first of all, to be allowed to settle in Swaziland; and, second, that the ANC give him money so that he could have his family follow him, for he had no money of his own. The meeting was inconclusive, and another meeting was called for the following Friday. Kunene had by then made up his mind to leave the country; however, he was told that he would be going not to Swaziland but to Basutoland because the ANC treasurer, Dr. Lethele, was there, and he had funds to assist the men. So Kunene decided to use Basutoland as a way station to Swaziland, stopping there long enough to be paid by the ANC.

Events moved swiftly. The ANC insisted that Kunene and other transportees leave the Friday night of the meeting, and Kunene, albeit reluctantly, agreed to this. They were to go from the church at 9:00 P.M. and were, he alleges, to meet Dr. Pascal Ngakane, son-in-law of President-General Luthuli, on the main South Coast Road at 11:30 P.M. They found an unattended car at the appointed spot and sat in it, waiting for the Reverend Mtlabata, who was following in his own car. This might have been a fatal error, for it turned out that the car did not belong to the conspirators. Fortunately for them, they were not discovered, for Mtlabata arrived and pointed out Dr. Ngakane's car to them. Each man was handed about $180 to assist him on his way. They then were joined by Dr. Ngakane and another man, and their journey began. They all arrived at Matatiele, some 15 miles from the border of Basutoland and South Africa, early the following morning.

On the way they gave a ride to an old man with a suitcase whom they found walking along the roadside. As the man seemed ill, Ngakane suggested it might help them get through if they said that they were taking a sick man home. They agreed to this, and continued on the winding road to the frontier. Dr. Ngakane had hoped that they would be lucky and find no police at the frontier post. If the post was manned, however, they might have to try to bribe the officer to let them through.

The post was manned, they found, and the frontier closed till 8:00 A.M. They tried to persuade the policeman in charge to open earlier, but he would not budge. Unwilling to increase their risks, they dropped the old man at the frontier and told him to say, if asked, that they would return at 8:00 A.M. They then drove to a part of the fence out of sight of the frontier post, which they climbed. Kunene had been told to contact Anderson Ganyile, an ANC leader in Basutoland, who would arrange the rest of their trip. Ngakane himself was to go back to the frontier post at 8:00 A.M. to maintain their cover, for the police would be suspicious if the car did not cross the border.

Safe for the time being, the men contacted Ganyile, who hired an aircraft to take them to Maseru, for which they paid out of the $180 given them by Mtlabata. At Maseru they at once contacted the administrators of ANC funds, Joe Matthews and Dr. Lethele. After a month there they had had enough of Basutoland. They decided to return to South Africa for they did not feel that the ANC had done enough for them. They did not want to settle in Basutoland and thought it better to go back and give themselves up to the police.

In Durban once more, they saw the Reverend Mtlabata, who persuaded them to go into hiding in the townships until after the trial at which Kunene was to have given evidence. The trial was over by May 10, 1964, and Kunene then went to the police. Brought to trial himself, he was asked how he felt about the ANC. His answer is instructive. He said that his sympathies were still with the ANC, though he had to give evidence against the organization in court. His position had not changed on what the ANC stood for, but he felt, as before, that things could not be changed by violent means. He was dissatisfied with the Communist connection of the ANC and with its influencing the organization in the direction of violence.

V

The discussion has so far centered on men who agreed to go overseas either for training or, as in the last case, to avoid the police. Not
everyone who was approached agreed to go. Edmund Tollie, for
instance, though close to the organization, was one who refused.[23] His
initial contact with *Umkonto*, like Mtolo's, was through a girl friend.
A man he had met at her home had found out that Tollie was very
fond of reading. As they shared this interest, they had a long discussion, in the course of which Tollie admitted that he, too, had been
a member of the ANC before it was banned. Now he was pressed to
rejoin. He declined, saying that he was now a member of another
organization supporting the government's moves to set up a Bantustan
in the Ciskei on much the same lines as the Transkei. He was told that,
in effect, this meant that his organization was supporting the government's apartheid policy, and he was urged to leave it. The contact
stressed that people in the underground were being sent abroad for
training and would return to train others. The army of freedom fighters
would grow strong enough to engage the government and then to
overthrow it and replace it with a system of "one man, one vote" so
that Africans could outvote whites every time. It was better, thus, to
join in with the freedom fighters. As a lure, Tollie was told much of
the way the underground ANC was organized, including details of the
M-Plan, and of the way in which people were sent from East London
to Johannesburg for military training. Indeed, the ANC seems to have
been very open with Tollie, who was an opponent, and this tells
much of its secrecy and security. He was, for instance, told of the
establishment of an illegal branch in Kingwilliamstown and was invited
to help set it up. Perhaps the reason Tollie was trusted was his tribal
affiliation with those he spoke to. This may have led them to think that
he would not betray them—that, having been in the ANC, he would
remain attached to its interests. By putting him on the defensive about

23. Tollie/*Fazili*, pp. 92–96, 107.

his pro-apartheid group and by involving him in illegal activity, they may have tried to gain a hold on him. Experienced men capable of leadership were becoming scarcer, and the risk may have been thought acceptable; this was perhaps reinforced by his detention, on a charge of public violence in 1960, during the State of Emergency. Tollie, however, remained uninterested in *Umkonto* and refused to rejoin the ANC.

The motivation for joining did not always come from the individual himself. Mtolo speaks of one sad case where a boy was sent abroad by his father because he "wanted all his kids to be freedom fighters. It turned out that he had his own personal grudge against Whites, especially against missionaries." The boy wanted to go because "he would be a big man in the African Government when he came back from overseas and moreover he would get free education in the same school as [white] boys." [24] The youngster, who had been recruited by his uncle, Solomon Mbanjwa, was singularly unfortunate. He was sent to Johannesburg with the group of pickpockets discussed earlier, and, as they were tougher, they could better endure the hardships during the time Mtolo was trying to arrange things for them in Germiston. The boy was mistreated by the man sent to look after them, who dealt with him in the same way as he had the pickpockets. The lad became ill and eventually was sent away. Mtolo was ignorant of what became of him but suspected that he had been caught and imprisoned with the others.

Although Mbanjwa claimed that he himself had never misled anyone who came to him to enlist in *Umkonto*, he admitted that there had been cases of this sort. The illusions that young Africans had are indeed fascinating. One young man, for instance, said that he had volunteered because he had been told that he could be taught to fly at a special school and would return after six months and earn a lot of money. "I thought it would be the same as the plane you see in the bioscope [movie] picture; we would travel along taking post [mail]." [25] Others were seduced by promises of other kinds of education abroad.

Something needs to be said not only of the training of freedom fighters, but also of its impact on those who had been lured abroad by

24. Mtolo, *Umkonto we Sizwe*, p. 87.
25. *Star*, December 13, 1963.

misleading promises. Disillusioned by their experiences, such men were eager to return to South Africa but found their way blocked by what they had done.

One of the most interesting of such reports has come from a former member of the ANC and the BCP (Basutoland Congress Party), Setsomi Gratitude Hoohla, a citizen of Lesotho (formerly Basutoland).[26] He speaks of more than eighty Africans having escaped from training camps in Tanzania, as indeed he himself claims to have done, who are now stranded in Nairobi, Kenya. Others who disagreed with the ANC leaders were beaten up or thrown into Tanzanian jails, Hoohla goes on; still others are believed to have been murdered and their bodies thrown into sanitation pits. He speaks of an assassination attempt on Duma Nokwe, which wounded Nokwe in the thigh, by one of the disgruntled soldiers. "The members are bitter and disillusioned because of the hardships they have had to endure over the last few years while leaders continue to live in luxury," he claims.

According to the story he told to press reporters, Hoohla had completed his Cambridge School Certificate and was approached by Joe Matthews, the ANC leader in Maseru, who offered him a scholarship to go abroad to study medicine. The group he was with were sent on to Lobatsi by train, where they were met by a certain Fish Kitching, known as a transport officer for *Umkonto*, who took away all the documents the men had, putting them completely in the hands of the ANC for further traveling arrangements. After a nine-month wait at Kazungula, on the Zambian border, they were taken by train to Mbeya, in Tanzania, about seventy miles away. "There," Mr. Hoohla says, "I spent two years waiting for the promised bursary." There were, he continues, eight others with him who had been recruited on similar grounds. Their living conditions were very hard: they were given only enough rations to exist, and each man received about 52 cents per week to buy cigarettes, toothpaste, and other personal articles. After some frustrating months, Hoohla and the other recruits realized what was afoot. The ANC and the Communists "were applying psychological pressure on us to abandon our ideas about further education,

26. *Sunday Times*, January 26, 1969.

and to accept training as guerrilla fighters instead." Three trained terrorists were put in a house not far from where the men were, and they lived in luxury with plenty of money, food, and alcohol. There was a strict rule, according to Hoohla, that untrained men could not enter the houses of the trained men or go into their camps. "In this way they hoped to break our morale, winning us over 'voluntarily' to undergo military training." In the meantime the men were cut off from their families and from the outside world, and letters sent to Joe Matthews or other ANC leaders remained unanswered. After two years, Hoohla was called to the ANC headquarters in Dar es Salaam and told that his scholarship was ready, but they did not tell him to which country he was to be sent. "I decided I was not going to be used as a tool for their purposes," Hoohla said. "I used the little money they gave me in Dar es Salaam to buy a bus ticket to Nairobi, where I arrived last September." There he found the other eighty men of whom he spoke. Most of them wanted to return to South Africa, as they felt they had been misled, but, being in trouble with the South African government, could not do so. "They are," Hoohla said, "people without a future."

Men joined *Umkonto* or agreed to go overseas because they believed in the promises of education, as Hoohla did, but it would be foolish to pretend that most of the recruits did not know the real reason. Hoohla's evidence, although reported in a South African newspaper, has the ring of truth. But such men cannot be in the majority. The reasons why many joined were made plain by two other men, who were arraigned at the sabotage trial in Natal. One of the accused, when asked why he had joined *Umkonto*, said it was because "the Government passes laws so that people with Black skins are made to suffer." [27] Africans were burdened, he said, with low wages, job discrimination, and the pass laws. Another of the accused, not inappropriately named Riot Mwanakazi, said that he joined because "our leader, Luthuli, was told to keep quiet and the African National Congress was banned in 1960. In 1961 when the three-day strike was planned, the police armed themselves and told the people to go to work. In 1962 the Congress of Democrats who had assisted us was banned. In 1962 the Sabotage Bill

27. *Natal Witness*, February 19, 1964.

was passed. This meant all meetings were banned." [28] Mwanakazi also said that when he came to Durban he was out of work and found difficulty in getting a work permit: "When I heard about *Umkonto* and that it was fighting the Government, I felt that this suited me." Many of the men who joined *Umkonto* must have felt much the same.

Hoohla's story was confirmed by the head of South Africa's security police, Brigadier P. J. Venter, who also spoke of division among the ANC leadership. He said that there was strife between the Nationalist African wing, led by Oliver Tambo, and the Communist wing, in which he included Kotane, Nokwe, Joe Matthews, J. B. Marks, Robert Resha, and Temba Mqotha. The Soviet Union was contributing some $2,800,000 per year alone, and there were other sums from other organizations, he said, but little of this trickled down to the freedom fighters. The matter did not end there, for Brigadier Venter also spoke of a consignment of seventy-two trained freedom fighters who, on arriving at Dar from Algeria, escaped. As a result, many men were being kept in cells till their time came to fight. The brigadier said that Joe Modise, in charge of military operations, had had a nervous breakdown. There are other reports of men who escaped to Kenya, ranging from seventy to more than three hundred. Another report speaks of four men stranded in Nairobi who were sending documents to countries which had supported the ANC, urging that no further financial aid be sent to the leadership because they used it mainly for their own benefit, living in luxury while the men in the camps suffered from poor health and bad conditions. It was also alleged that any who opposed the leadership were sent on ill-planned missions and that security forces were alerted to their arrival. Morale in the camps was said to be low, and it was claimed that fighting on tribal lines had broken out.[29]

The above cases have, it is hoped, shown the means by which men were persuaded or induced to leave their homes and to enlist in *Umkonto we Sizwe*, the military wing of the ANC and the Communist Party, and also something of the way men were removed who might have harmed the cause. The dispatch of these men involved a loosely

28. *Natal Mercury*, February 19, 1964.
29. Muriel Horrell, *A Survey of Race Relations in South Africa, 1968* (Johannesburg, 1969), pp. 10–11.

linked chain of recruiters, contacts, convoys of cars, and finances. Sometimes the chain was unbroken; often it was not. The men were sometimes members of the ANC; sometimes they were not. Success or failure rested largely with individuals; the organization itself could contribute little to this movement of men and money.

IX

The Conflict among the Cadres

Umkonto we Sizwe was the joint creation of the ANC and the Communist Party and was intended to receive its political direction from both of them. In fact, as Bartholomew Hlapane's evidence suggests, the Communist Party's influence was the greater, although the ANC considered itself the senior partner.[1] The basis for this belief was that the ANC gave the organization some of its brain and most of its muscle. The ANC controlled the flow of recruits, some leaders believed, giving it an outstanding voice in *Umkonto*'s councils. In fact, most of the ANC leaders involved in *Umkonto* were also in the Communist Party;[2] nevertheless the myth of ANC supremacy was sedulously fostered among the upper ranks of the leadership. ANC members could participate in *Umkonto*, according to Walter Sisulu, "in the sense that the matter is discussed and the ANC agrees to permit its members, including its sleeping members, to carry on the acts of sabotage."[3] According to this argument, if the ANC were suddenly to withdraw permission, the members of the ANC in *Umkonto* would presumably withdraw as well. So, because it could withdraw its members, and these

1. Hlapane/*Fischer*, pp. 218–19.
2. Hlapane evidence in trial of Mooroogiah Naidoo, *Natal Witness*, September 9, 1966. Hlapane said the leaderships were "indistinguishable."
3. Sisulu/*Rvtr*, p. 157.

were the bulk of men available, the ANC claimed it could control the work of sabotage. In truth, this was self-deception, if those propounding the claim believed it themselves. The ANC had long since lost all ability to act independently, and any attempt to repudiate an *Umkonto* action would simply have led to the fall of the leader acting in this manner. Nonetheless, it was believed that the ANC had retained its own identity and that the same was true of the Communist Party.

Several reasons were later advanced by ANC leaders as to why it had been necessary to keep the ANC and *Umkonto* separate. These varied from rank sophistry to pragmatic reasons of organization. Both kinds of argument are found in Mbeki's evidence in the Rivonia Trial. It seems sophism to argue, as Mbeki did, that because members had joined the ANC as a nonviolent organization, and as the decision to take to violence had been made after the ANC had gone underground, it was impossible to consult all the members and obtain their agreement on the change. As we have seen, the M-Plan was intended to provide the linkage with the leaders; and information did travel down the channels, as notification by chief stewards of different policy lines has shown. An example of the pragmatic argument is that variations such as age and health, to say nothing of sex, meant that the ANC could not be taken lock, stock, and barrel into the military wing.[4] Finally, Mbeki argued, the ANC had certain recognized symbols, such as salutes, songs, etc., which, if adopted by the sabotage group, might endanger ANC people who were not part of *Umkonto*.[5] The last point he made was that the ANC was a mass organization with a mass membership. A revolutionary group, on the other hand, needed not masses but small groups of trained and dedicated people. What is more, a mass organization was difficult to control; not all members could be relied on to take orders and to carry out acts of sabotage. This was the more true because of the heavy legal penalties for acts of sabotage, so that only a small number would be willing to take these risks. All these reasons put together explained why organizational separation was desirable.[6]

4. Mbeki/*Rvtr*, p. 33.
5. Mbeki/*Rvtr*, pp. 33–34; Hlapane/*Fischer*, p. 233.
6. Mbeki/*Rvtr*, p. 34.

Reality was something different. Keeping the organizations separate facilitated Communist control of *Umkonto*. The nature of Communist contacts is naturally difficult to trace exactly. As a result, much must be inferred. Sources have to be used that provide a partial picture at best and merely clues at other times. The picture that emerges is of leaders who were opposed to communism and unwilling to be compliant being retained in the ANC but kept out of *Umkonto*. Inasmuch as they had any prestige, that prestige would remain harnessed to the chariot of the National Liberation Movement, while they themselves were effectively neutralized. And with the progress of the violent struggle, such of the ordinary machinery of the ANC as remained operating could increasingly be ignored. Pushed to the sidelines in the liberatory struggle and reduced to an increasingly ineffectual role, the ANC could all the more be left out of account. Control of the underground, given the growing decrepitude of the ANC, meant control of *Umkonto*.

There had, as it happened, been quite a severe power struggle between those holding positions in the ANC alone and those who were in both *Umkonto* and the Communist Party. This struggle has been fully described by Bruno Mtolo in his evidence and in his book, and there is supporting material in the evidence of other witnesses. Mtolo saw only part of the picture, that is, what happened in Natal. Whether what happened there is similar to what happened elsewhere cannot be said with any certitude. There is, however, little reason to doubt that similar, if not identical, power struggles took place elsewhere. Only the outlines of this conflict can be presented here, and readers wanting more details are referred to the sources. What is presented here indicates how the two organizations operated and conflicted.

The leadership of *Umkonto* wanted to remain separate from the ANC, Mtolo writes, because "we could not let the dangerous underground movement be controlled by the leaders of a mass organization which included people who had different views from us as far as sabotage is concerned." [7] Officers of *Umkonto* feared that the devotion to the political struggle dominated ANC leaders to the extent that their

7. Bruno Mtolo, *Umkonto we Sizwe: The Road to the Left* (Durban, 1966), chap. 6.

knowledge of the violent struggle was in itself dangerous. The ANC leaders, on the other hand, demanded to know more about those in *Umkonto*, claiming that they, the ANC people, would be held responsible for the deeds committed by *Umkonto* although they themselves were neither members nor controllers of that organization. As far as the police were concerned, they argued, the ANC and *Umkonto* were one and the same. Therefore, if indeed *Umkonto* were under ANC control, they should know of its operations. There was a current of ill feeling between those in the ANC and those in *Umkonto*, Mtolo goes on to say, and as a result the view was that "if these people [the ANC leaders in Natal] could find out who the members of *Umkonto we Sizwe* were, we would be finished. They would not hesitate to sell us out." [8] *Umkonto* people in Natal, he says, feared and distrusted their counterparts in the ANC and were convinced that the latter were out to betray them to the police, possibly in return for immunity from prosecution. The ANC leaders, to those in *Umkonto*, were just another stumbling block. "All our men were handpicked for their political feelings and understanding," writes Mtolo, "whereas some of these ANC leaders only knew that they were fighting for freedom. What kind of freedom they did not know. All they knew was that Dr. Verwoerd should be thrown out and Chief Luthuli should take his place." [9] He goes on to make the position quite clear as to what political understanding consisted of:

We were working for the system of socialism based on Marx and Lenin. We did not want people with capitalistic ideas. The war that we were to fight was not a fight between Whites and Blacks—it was a war between the "haves" and the "have nots," a class struggle between capitalism and communism. We did not want people who, after winning the war, would start counter-revolutions when we started nationalizing the banks, mines, and industries. [10]

In discussing some of the reasons adduced for the separation of the ANC and *Umkonto* earlier in this chapter, the matter of ANC control

8. *Ibid.,* p. 26.
9. *Ibid.,* p. 28.
10. *Ibid.,* p. 26.

over its membership was raised. This matter must be gone into at somewhat greater length, for it was part of the broader question of control of *Umkonto* and relates to the clash of the cadres. In this area, theory and practice were never reconciled and continued as a running conflict.

The formal view of the relationship of the ANC to *Umkonto* was set out by Lionel Bernstein at the Rivonia Trial, and his argument, though generally similar to that of Sisulu, has some interesting differences. Bernstein argued that no constitutional provision subordinated *Umkonto* to the ANC. *Umkonto* was an autonomous organization and, as such, was free to act as its leaders wished without reference to any individual or any other body. But, Bernstein goes on to argue, if the leaders of *Umkonto* were to order actions of which the ANC leadership disapproved, such as the wholesale murder of whites, then the ANC leadership would advise its members to leave *Umkonto*. They would make this demand because wholesale murder was contrary to the declared policy of the ANC. The ANC being the older organization and as a result having command of stronger loyalties, Bernstein continued, there would be massive defections from *Umkonto*, which would make violent policies of this sort impossible to implement.[11] The argument of Mbeki, stated at greater length, was that *Umkonto* was formed specifically to commit acts of sabotage but was placed under the guidance of the Communist Party and the Congress Alliance. The Congress Alliance being led by the ANC, the latter would naturally be concerned if *Umkonto* pursued unacceptable policies. Being unable to order *Umkonto* to change course, it could only demand that its members desist from following such policies.

Clearly, Bernstein and Mbeki are somewhat at odds on the status of *Umkonto*, but even if this is set aside, there remains the fascinating question as to what would have happened had the ANC, in fact, asked its members to withdraw. Something akin to a minor civil war might well have been the result, with those desiring to stay in *Umkonto* attacking those who wanted to comply with the ANC call. The issue is academic, however, as no such call was made.

11. Bernstein/*Rvtr*, p. 154.

The above statements were made at the trials of the participants and no doubt reflect something of their situation, but the arguments cannot be rejected out of hand. Sufficient is known of the workings of the Communists and of the ANC to say that they were averse to unlimited violence and resorted to it with reluctance. Their thinking had been conditioned by the years in which they had sought a mass uprising, and they looked to this rather than to terrorism as a means to power. There were individuals of different mind, which is inevitable; but the policy was one of limiting force. The reason for separation of ANC and *Umkonto*, given that Communists apparently controlled the latter, was security. As long as the ANC committees were unaware of the membership of *Umkonto*, they could not betray them, as *Umkonto* people strongly suspected they would. And as long as they remained ignorant, they could not control ANC members in *Umkonto*. They only learned of acts of sabotage already performed, and this information was gleaned ex post facto and often from the press or other sources outside of *Umkonto*. *Umkonto* and the Communists had further advantages: If the ANC committees were not privy to *Umkonto* organizations, they could not channel any complaints they might have had. They could not know to whom in the High Command to put their grievances. As enquiry was prohibited, there was no apparent way of finding out who was responsible for one or another group. Finally, if *Umkonto* policy was not publicized, how could it be compared with that of the ANC? Information could be gathered only through rumor, indiscretion, or from the press. How was ANC control to be exerted? None of these questions was, or perhaps was intended to be, answered.

The stress on secrecy served to cement the independence of *Umkonto* from ANC control, once the principle of organizational separation was accepted. Ignorance and secrecy were seen as concomitant. As Mbeki said:

Security, more particularly with an organization like MK, is very important indeed. It's highly rated, so if one is going to be used to get anything, there is no reason why he should really know [more than is needed]. My position in Port Elizabeth was that I was a member of the National Executive Committee, and since I had nothing to do with MK [at that time], MK would keep its own secrets strictly to itself.[12]

Having established this trend to secrecy and autonomous working, how did the structures react to each other (for it is apparent from the Mtolo argument that they did in fact react to each other)? How, in other words, did the constituent bodies of the National Liberation Movement adjust their differences?

It is clearly difficult to describe adjudication of differences within a secret organization, but enough has emerged in evidence to allow some inferences to be drawn. One way of resolving differences, particularly when these had an ideological orientation, was to freeze out those who differed. The method was simple. If an ANC leader was hostile to Communist approaches, or was against violence, he was not expelled from the movement—a difficult matter in an underground organization—but was simply not kept informed. Exclusion from communication and information applied not only to the cadres but also to the top leadership. The isolation of Luthuli was the doing not only of the South African government, though it obviously was the principal agent, but also of the men in charge of *Umkonto*. This is not to say, of course, that Luthuli was at all times completely incommunicado. Visiting dignitaries from abroad often made his home in Stanger a point of pilgrimage. Members of the ANC did come to see him from time to time and, to a lesser extent, so did people from *Umkonto*. In the case of activists, however, it was more to tell him what was done or going to be done than to ask his permission or advice. Luthuli himself occasionally complained that he was not told what was going on.

As the violent struggle took shape and as the middle cadres tended to merge into the lower, questions of control and jurisdiction became more manageable. The prime example is the creation of a joint headquarters at "Lilliesleaf," the Rivonia farm of which we have read so much in these pages. By the time "Lilliesleaf" was in full swing, most

12. Mbeki/*Rvtr*, p. 369.

of the leadership had been reduced to the hard-core Communists. Others do not seem to have been taken there. Now that all were Party members, they could work together without friction. Those who disagreed with their approach were not there to make their views known. After all, the headquarters *was* secret. It was inaccessible to anyone likely to advance uncomfortable arguments. Indeed, toward the end, shortly before their capture by the police, the High Command and the NEC seem to have functioned largely as one. Combined in this way, the military wing, *Umkonto*, was synonymous with the ANC. On paper the ANC and the Communist Party could claim that neither controlled *Umkonto*, for on paper *Umkonto* took orders only from its own High Command. In fact, however, the Communist Party dominated, through its African members in both the ANC and *Umkonto* and from members of other races in *Umkonto*. There was no need for the Central Committee of the CP to issue orders as such. A decision of the Central Committee could simply be introduced by a Party member at meetings of the High Command. The number of Party members at such a meeting would ensure its passage. It would then be represented as a High Command decision without any formal nexus with the Communist Party being evident to outsiders.[13]

This happy arrangement worked less well for the Communists on the local levels. There was often much confusion, Walter Sisulu said, in the minds of members as to the nature of the meetings they were attending.[14] Was the meeting of the ANC, *Umkonto*, or the CP? It was difficult to know which organization was holding which meeting, and as a result meetings of different organizations often were duplicated. From what the ANC leaders said, the question may be resolved in this way: the ANC was to be the policy-making wing; that is, policies would issue in its name. The Communist Party, on the other hand, would decide "grand strategy"—the plans which coordinated all wings—and thus control overall policy. The "grand strategy" of this sort would be executed by *Umkonto*. Thus the Communist Party could dominate because it had people in each organization.

13. Hlapane, in *Natal Witness*, September 8, 1966.
14. Sisulu/*Rvtr*, p. 89.

II

The decision to turn to violence was well received, on the whole, in the cells. It did cause some heart-searching among the leaders, though this centered less on the principle of violence and more on the kind of violence. It was also a matter of which personalities were to lead the violent organization and how they and the organization were to be controlled. By 1961, as we have seen, most of those still active in the ANC—and this meant active underground—were quite willing to accept a measure of violence, if it was subject to some restraint. Indeed, even this was often absent when the decision for violence was announced in the cells, for, as one man put it, "It sometimes seemed that we were not successfully fighting for freedom" with nonviolence. Violence, they believed, could well bring freedom more quickly and surely. Among the leaders, violence was favored as long as it was directed against property. Their reasoning was that the capacity of the government to govern could be seriously impaired by strategic damage and that the white electorate could be stampeded into major concessions. The main intention was psychological. The ANC—and, hence, the CP—had been losing ground to PAC before the Emergency, and even afterward it seemed that PAC was the more dynamic organization. The challenge had to be met. As one ANC document put it, the "revolutionary African workers and intellectuals" would not accept Congress and fight for it, if they did not have confidence in its ability to "conquer the armed forces of Verwoerdism." This clearly meant that the ANC could no longer hold to the inadequate and ineffective methods of nonviolence. "The people must be one and persuaded to the understanding of the value and necessity of these new methods and their possibility of success." [15]

If violence was as broadly accepted as seems to have been the case, why should there have been any difficulty? The answer lies in the problems that remained to be resolved. Some of these problems are

15. Leaflet found by police at Rivonia and quoted in Sisulu/Rvtr, p. 151.

laid bare in the document quoted above. There it is argued that many Africans were still unaware of the change, of the fact that the old policy had been discarded. They were confused by the acts of violence. It was, in addition, difficult to persuade some people used to the old nonviolent line that violence was now to be preferred. This may appear self-contradictory. On the one hand, we have argued that violence was welcomed and, on the other, that it was not. The seeming contradiction is easily reconciled. The cadres were willing and able to engage in violence, but the support group was still reluctant. A few ambiguous statements on violence would win few converts, the leaflet argues; what was needed was a vigorous campaign to popularize the idea. The attempt at popularizing violence had the effect of increasing friction among the cadres in ways not anticipated.

When *Umkonto* opened its campaign friction developed between the regional command and the ANC leadership in Natal. As Bruno Mtolo's reasons for this conflict have already been set forth, they can be briefly restated and amplified. After the manifesto announcing the opening of the sabotage campaign was issued, the ANC leaders had two fears: first of all, they were afraid that they would be held responsible for the sabotage; second, they feared that *Umkonto* would supplant the ANC and that they would be supplanted along with it. They were afraid that, with the sabotage campaign publicly proclaimed, "the first people to be arrested would be the known members of the ANC." Somewhat uncharitably, Mtolo describes their reaction: "They were not only sacred of the new organization taking over the leadership, they were scared of their own skins." [16] The men engaging in sabotage were not too happy about the manifesto either, largely because it had been drawn up without their being informed or consulted. The saboteurs, Mtolo writes, were as surprised as anyone else. The ANC thus resented *Umkonto* as a twofold threat. *Umkonto* men in the cadres feared indiscreet announcements from the National High Command.

One of the most significant differences between *Umkonto* and the ANC, as has been pointed out earlier, is that the former was not

16. Mtolo, *Umkonto we Sizwe*, p. 23.

purely African. It included all races. The Natal regional command, in addition to Mtolo, consisted of three Africans, one Indian, and two whites at the time Mtolo was active. Of this group, Mtolo says, four were members of the Communist Party; and it is only of the two whites that he is unsure. Whatever their political allegiances may have been, however, they seemed to heartily approve of all that was done.[17] Those who were confirmed Communists, Mtolo continues, were only interested in the ANC as an instrument. They were willing to go along with it only as long as it toed the Party line. The only one still active in the ANC was "Captain" Curnick Ndhlovu, in his capacity as contact between the ANC regional committee and *Umkonto*. According to Mtolo, even Ndhlovu was "more of a Communist" than an adherent of the ANC.[18] Membership must, of course, be distinguished from activity. It may well have been that members of *Umkonto* did not sever their formal ties with the ANC—formally, they were members—but they no longer actively participated in it.

Had there been no conflict among the Communists, their control would have been firmer than it was, but to assume monolithic solidarity would be unrealistic, even in what claimed to be a highly disciplined group. There were sharp differences among the Communists on doctrine and on policy. There were men expelled as "revisionists" because they opposed either sabotage or guerrilla war or both. This happened not only where opposition was voiced on principle, but also where objections were technical, such as that the country was not ready.[19] In this connection, the case of a Durban lawyer, Rowley Arenstein, highlights the dilemma of many sincere and honest men. Arenstein, who was acquitted of contravening the Suppression of Communism Act, consistently affirmed that he had not changed his views on communism, that he was and remained a Communist. He had, he said, joined the Communist Party in 1938 and had organized the Durban and District branch in 1942. In 1947 he withdrew from active politics to concentrate on his law practice. Arenstein entered the Con-

17. Mtolo/Rvtr, pp. 19–20.
18. Mtolo, *Umkonto we Sizwe*, p. 23.
19. *Natal Mercury*, May 15, 18, 19, 20, 23, 1965; *Natal Witness*, May 21, 1965; *Star*, December 20, 1965.

gress of Democrats branch in Durban in 1952 but was banned in 1953. He nevertheless continued to act as legal counsel for members of the COD and to allow his home to be used for meetings. Arenstein was, in other words, a man with long-standing connections with the Communist Party—not a "Johnny-come-lately." When *Umkonto* was founded, there was some tension in the COD, for, to begin with, some members were not Communists (that is, of course, the aim of a front) and others were undecided on violence. There were those who opposed the new formation and those who were unable to make up their minds. Arenstein, according to witnesses, did his best to dissuade members from supporting *Umkonto* and at all times questioned the efficacy of sabotage in South Africa. In 1963 Arenstein apparently dissociated himself from the CP, according to another witness, claiming that the leadership of both the COD and the CP (which by then were virtually the same) were guilty of treachery. Arenstein, it is said, decided to form his own Marxist party and to contest elections in the Transkei, the government's Bantustan, where for the first time Africans could vote for their own legislative body.

Arenstein's case was not the only one. Mtolo claims that there were divisions between those who supported the Chinese and the Russian brands of communism, with the Natallers tending to the former and the Cape to the latter. These conflicting interpretations led to different perceptions of sabotage and of what should be done. There was, in other words, a series of cracks in the monolith that could easily widen into fissures.

The ANC had a record of breaking apart on policy differences. Issues of policy were intensely contested and had, on more than one occasion, led to competing bodies being formed out of the ANC. In the days of legality, the national conferences of the ANC had facilitated the engineering of a consensus of some kind. With the submergence of the organization, this was possible only with difficulty and on rare occasions. A conference was known to have been held at Lobatsi, in Bechuanaland (now Botswana), on October 28–29, 1962; and there is evidence of other conferences also held there. The conference in question drew together those ANC leaders still at large in South Africa and those carrying on the work of the organization abroad. It is interesting, not only for what was decided and discussed, for this is by no means clear, but also for the way it was organized and put together.[20] The conference also affected the organization and workings of the cadres.

As is so often the case in the story of the underground, much remains unexplained about the Lobatsi Conference. The inevitable secrecy, the fear of betrayal, and the fallibility of human memory have combined to obscure the picture. There is little solid evidence other than that of some admittedly unreliable witnesses and of the leaders of the underground ANC when on trial. Speaking for the latter at the Rivonia Trial, both Walter Sisulu and Govan Mbeki maintained that the Lobatsi Conference had been called because of the dangerous mood in the country due to the failure of an anti-pass campaign to materialize as planned, in June, 1962, details of which are lacking. The anger of the black populace made it imperative to think of something else. On the whole, this explanation seems unlikely. The aim of the ANC and *Umkonto* was to arouse African anger and to channel it in the appropriate directions. A conference of ANC leaders would hardly be called at such risk just to prevent disaffected Africans from venting their anger. On the contrary, a repetition of the Sharpeville incident might well have helped rather than hindered the cause. There obviously were bigger issues that had to be decided. From what can be gathered, the conference was called to settle the relationship of *Umkonto* to the ANC and to take up the matter of extending violence.

The evidence of the ANC leaders is not, of course, the only source on events at the Lobatsi Conference. Evidence has been given by two witnesses who were judged to be unreliable in court. Their testimony seems to hold together on certain particulars, however, and is offered with reservations. One, Peter Peyise, spoke of attending a branch meeting sometime in September, 1962, attended by Vuysile Mini. Mini told them of a meeting to be held in Johannesburg, and Peyise was elected to attend. He left Port Elizabeth in October and was met

20. The discussion of the Lobatsi Conference, as described here, is to be found in *World*, October 29, 1962; *Star*, October 29, 31, November 1, 1962; *New Age*, November 1, 1962; and also in the evidence of Mbeki/*Rvtr*, pp. 55–57; Peyise/*Rvtr*, pp. 202–21; Dondashe/*Rvtr*, pp. 85–90.

at the station by a man who, after making sure of Peyise's identity, took him to an unfamiliar building. There he was told to wait, for he would be picked up after sundown. Peyise was fetched in the evening and taken to an African hotel in the townships, where he rested before beginning his journey to a still unknown destination. It was not until a stranger with a car appeared that he learned his destination was Lobatsi.

The other witness, Norman Dondashe, tells a somewhat different story. Like Peyise, he first came to Johannesburg. There he was met and taken to the SACTU offices where he saw three other men, who traveled with him. As it was dark and he could not see where they were going, he asked his fellow-passengers about their destination. Laughingly, they told him it was Johannesburg. It was only after they had crossed the border that he was told they were in Bechuanaland. From a border town they were flown to Lobatsi, where Dondashe, like Peyise, recognized several of the major leaders of the ANC.

The Lobatsi Conference was closed to the public, for obvious reasons, and a serious effort was made to maintain secrecy. There were leaks, but what leaked out was sketchy and unsatisfactory. Among the information gleaned was that Oliver Tambo, the ANC representative in London, had flown to Lobatsi in a specially chartered German plane, which landed not at the official airfield but at some unknown and unspecified place. While in Lobatsi, Tambo's whereabouts were kept secret, a difficult matter in so small a place. The delegates who came to Lobatsi in vans and cars, as did Dondashe and Peyise, refused all interviews. As the World correspondent put it: "They told us to clear off from the places where they were staying in no uncertain terms." The government, on its side, took no chances. The police tried to infiltrate the meeting. At least four members of the Special Branch were identified and driven off by the ANC men standing guard.

A number of important topics were raised at Lobatsi: the crisis of the underground; the vexed question as to the use of money the ANC was receiving from abroad; the extension of the M-Plan; and the need for a more intense house-to-house campaign for funds and recruits. The formation of a United Front with the PAC was considered and also the means of establishing a better liaison between the ANC offices in Dar es Salaam, London, and elsewhere. A variety of stratagems were proposed to get around the ban on meetings; for instance, religious services might be held, with Congress propaganda used as sermons. The infiltration of "stooge bodies," to which Africans could elect members, such as Advisory Boards in the locations and Bantu Urban Councils, was proposed, as was the establishment of political organizations in the Protectorates. Little information could be obtained on what was said of the sabotage campaign.

The violent struggle was obviously a dominating theme, but what can be learned of the discussions is only from witnesses. It seems that the reluctant regional committees were told that *Umkonto* was very much the business of the ANC and that their quarrels with the sabotage group must be ended. They were to help in finding men for the sabotage group and for military training overseas, so that these men could "learn to fight and handle guns." The necessity for organization of the countryside was stressed, and the regional committees were instructed to increase their efforts. Both Dondashe and Peyise, whose testimony is being given, said that they heard of *Umkonto* properly for the first time at the Lobatsi Conference, when Mini told them that there was such an organization and that it was secret, although he did not tell them what *Umkonto* was to do.

Though the Lobatsi deliberations were secret, the resolutions adopted there were widely publicized. They were set forth in a mimeographed leaflet with the following lengthy and cumbersome title: "The People Accept the Challenge of the Nationalists: Our Political Line of Action." [21] The conference was significant, it said, because it represented all regions of the ANC, because of its militancy, and because youth were represented for the first time since the last meeting in 1960. The aim was to promote mass political action, to raise and reinforce the spirit of revolt among the people, and to "liquidate" the whole "status quo" through seizure of political power. The targets were to be the Nationalist government and the "instruments of oppression." White supremacy was to be "destroyed wherever it was found." The leaflet continued:

21. In *Hoover Collection*, reel 7.

In the changed South African conditions we have the mass political wing of the struggle, spearheaded by the ANC, on the one hand, and by the specialized military wing, represented by *Umkonto we Sizwe*, on the other. *Our emphasis still remains on political action.* The political wing will ever remain the necessary and integral part of the fight. Political agitation is the only way of creating the atmosphere in which military action can most effectively operate. *Umkonto* cannot survive in a sterile political climate. Our primary objective is the conquest of political power, and in doing so African unity is indisposable [*sic*].

There was a clear need to conciliate the politicals, and the aim of the Lobatsi Conference, that of reconciling *Umkonto* and the ANC, emerges in these lines. The italics used in referring to the political struggle are in the original document.

The pamphlet shows that, first of all, the glowing ghost of the "mass uprising" still stalked. Second, it represented something of a victory for the political as opposed to the violent struggle. The need for the political wing to create the "climate" of victory is indicative. It shows that the basic conflict in the National Liberation Movement was still not settled. Only the dangers of division were recognized.

The military wing, according to the leaflet, was to be guided by the same principles as the political wing; it would only act after "scientific analysis of the objective conditions," and would so act "not only during the elementary phase of sabotage, but also during the advanced stage of guerrilla warfare." The campaign was divided into three stages. The first, passive resistance on a mass scale, was over. The second phase, now in progress, involved attacks on property without loss of life. The third phase was to be guerrilla war with no holds barred. But if these policies were to be implemented, the ANC could no longer directly control *Umkonto*. To take effective action *Umkonto* would have to bypass the ANC. Thus, despite the superficial victory for the political forces that Lobatsi represented, the real victors were *Umkonto* and its leaders. The fact was that, according to the resolutions, the political wing served the military and not the other way around. It had become no more than an auxiliary, supplying recruits and propaganda support. Lobatsi, whatever lip service it gave the ANC, freed *Umkonto* from the last vestiges of control by anybody other than the National High Command and indirectly by the Communist Party. The politicals had won no more than a paper victory.

III

The pressures between the ANC and *Umkonto* had, it seems, become so acute that, apparently early in 1962, "Captain" Curnick Ndhlovu was sent to Johannesburg to obtain a ruling from the NEC as to the extent to which the ANC in Durban could intervene in *Umkonto*. The answer Ndhlovu brought back to Durban, according to Mtolo, was that under no circumstances was he to give in to the ANC regional committee. Instructions would come to him exclusively from the National High Command of *Umkonto*, and the regional committee of the ANC was to communicate with the regional command of *Umkonto* only through Ndhlovu himself. The regional command was thus confirmed in its autonomy. It had always seen the ANC in the region as a stumbling block, and this was now removed. The ANC leaders, in its eyes, were only willing to sit tight and do nothing, while *Umkonto* "took the bull by the horns and started organizing people." The ANC was infiltrated by members of *Umkonto*, who organized their members into groups of four men each and inserted them into branches in the different townships. This took place, it is self-evident, without the branches in question knowing of it. Much the same can be said of the recruiting of men for service overseas, which also took place without the branches being fully aware of what was going on.

SACTU was one of the most useful of instruments in all this. The trade union organization, though much mutilated by banning, deportation, and removal of its leaders, and increasingly harassed by the authorities, was not yet illegal. The mere fact that it could operate, however limited its operations, meant that it could still provide a cover for other things. Mtolo's description seems particularly applicable here and is quoted at some length:

We of the S.A.C.T.U. were educating all our members in our committee meetings and preparing them for whatever might happen. We were having open meetings and secret meetings to tell the people about the change from non-violence to violence, and they were also told about the existence of Umkonto we Sizwe, its objects and its relationship with A.N.C. We did this in such a way that we did not expose ourselves as members, but they were shown that we were fully supported by the military wing of the A.N.C., which was temporarily operating underground.

They were also told that it was time that they should know their true leaders who were prepared to fight to the bitter end, and had to realize that the leaders who were against the Umkonto we Sizwe were leading them nowhere.[22]

There was indeed pressure, both from the Youth League, insofar as this still functioned, and from the Women's League for the leadership of the African struggle to pass from the ANC to SACTU, as the more realistic and vigorous body. It is only fair to say that the implication of SACTU and its use as an ANC front were denied by Govan Mbeki. Speaking at a later trial, in which he was a defense witness, Mbeki gave three reasons why the ANC would not use SACTU as a front. He argued, first of all, that at the time of the Lobatsi Conference the ANC numbered some 125,000 members, so why should they get their "baby," SACTU, to do their work. (This figure is open to very much doubt. The numbers cited correspond with the estimate for ANC membership when the organization was still legal.) He argued that, at that time, the underground cell system was "working perfectly" so the ANC need not risk "contaminating" a legal organization, such as SACTU, by involving it in illegal work. It was vital, he argued, for SACTU to remain legal.[23] Mbeki's argument may hold for the ANC, for one can argue that SACTU was not an ANC front but a CP front, which served not the ANC but the CP and *Umkonto*. There is also much to be said for Mbeki's argument that, although the memberships of the ANC and SACTU overlapped, the ANC people in SACTU were there as "workers." None of this would invalidate the thesis put

22. Mtolo, *Umkonto we Sizwe*, p. 25.
23. *Eastern Province Herald*, June 23, 1965.

forward here that SACTU was not under the control of or a front for the ANC.

This was the position when Ndhlovu returned from Johannesburg to Durban with the instructions that bestowed virtually complete autonomy on *Umkonto*. A decision was taken shortly after his return for a joint meeting of the regional command and the regional committee of the ANC. Here, it was hoped, mutual differences could be thrashed out. To maintain secrecy, SACTU was to provide a cover for the meeting, and the point to be discussed was how to gain access to the countryside. It seems that the ANC had such access through its branches, whereas *Umkonto* had not yet been able to establish it. Now *Umkonto* wanted contacts with the "peasants, chiefs, and indunas" in order to propagate its ideas, to involve the tribes in the sabotage movement, and to obtain recruits for use either at home or for training elsewhere. If the plan was to be made effective, given the absence of *Umkonto* contacts among the "peasants," it meant cooperation with the ANC. The latter agreed to a joint meeting and then largely did not appear on the appointed day. This left *Umkonto* up in the air. It seems definite that the ANC was not prepared to sacrifice its hold, in any case not very great, on the peasantry for the sake of the "liberation struggle."

The conflict between the rival cadres of ANC and *Umkonto* remained undiminished. It was in a sense intensified by the fact that most of the activity that was going on was *Umkonto* activity. Efforts at effecting some repairs were mounted from time to time. One was that of Govan Mbeki, who visited Natal and helped found the ad hoc committee, which became a kind of provincial committee and was apparently intended to coordinate the work of both the ANC and *Umkonto*. However, it was staffed mainly with people either in *Umkonto* or very sympathetic to it and, therefore, did little to placate the ANC. The fact that it was under Solomon Mbanjwa, who was mentioned earlier as a member of *Umkonto*, SACTU, and the Communist Party in addition to the ANC, makes this very clear. There had been, as was earlier suggested, a sorting out of organizations. The ANC was largely left to the men with no clear Communist connections, and it became increasingly ineffective. Among the ineffective bodies was the regional committee, whose only contact with the regional command was Ndhlovu, believed to be a Communist. Ndhlovu was also the contact with the Ad Hoc. Control of *Umkonto* more and more fell under the Communist Party, which also controlled SACTU and the other Congress Alliance fronts. The ANC was isolated and left to carry out the increasingly fatuous political struggle, while the armed struggle, which was increasingly important and envisioned as being even more so, was the province of the other organizations.

The ANC was not abandoned altogether. The Communist Party and its activists, though drawn increasingly to *Umkonto*, were unwilling to surrender control of the mass organization altogether. Some men who either were Party members or were extremely sympathetic to the Party were left at the head of the ANC and expressly forbidden to join *Umkonto*. The case of Walter Sisulu is one in point. According to the evidence of Bartholomew Hlapane, Sisulu was present at a conference of the Communist Party in November, 1962 (he is unsure of the month), which Hlapane attended. Now, if Hlapane's evidence is correct, it is highly unlikely that Sisulu would have been there if he was not a Party member.[24] Indeed, until the Fischer Trial Sisulu had always been advanced as the non-Communist most involved in the underground. A similar example is that of Raymond Mhlaba. Giving evidence at the Rivonia Trial, where he was one of the accused, he said: "It had been decided that for purposes of maintaining the African National Congress to run its affairs properly, that certain members will be instructed to confine their activities purely in the African National Congress."[25] This provision did not prevent the highest leadership, on the national level, from being involved in the planning of *Operation Mayebuye*, and no doubt was not intended to be so interpreted. The intention seems to have been to ensure that the ANC did not escape CP influence entirely by switching all Communist leaders into the ranks of MK. It would hardly have suited the Communists to lose their leading position in the oldest African organization. There was already pressure among the cadres for the national leadership to take a more independent stand, but the presence of Party members in

24. Hlapane/*Fischer*, p. 218.
25. Mhlaba/*Rvtr*, p. 11.

the NEC, coupled with the prestige that this carried, would prevent this from coming about. It would ensure that, whatever the sentiment lower in the organization, control of the ANC would remain in the "right" hands.

A further reason is to be found in the dependence of the ANC on sympathy and contributions from abroad. It could have been most damaging to the ANC were its Communist connection to be made clear. Many well-meaning people, with natural sympathy for the plight of the African, might turn away from the ANC if its Communist affiliations became obvious. Operating *Umkonto* through the less well-known (abroad) SACTU and through the CP avoided this obstacle. The ANC continued with its personality split to the end.

X

Communism and *Umkonto:* The Interweaving of Relationships

Neither the ANC nor the Communist Party in South Africa has ever denied their intimate relationship or failed to affirm their organizational independence. Memberships in both were permitted, as Albert Luthuli wrote in his autobiography:

> There are Communists in the South African resistance, and I cooperate with them—though how many have any connection at all with Moscow I do not know. The Congress stand is this: our primary concern is liberation, and we are not going to be sidetracked by ideological clashes and witch hunts. Nobody in Congress may use the organization to further any aims but those of Congress. When I cooperate with Communists in Congress affairs I am not cooperating with Communism. We leave our differing political theories on one side until the day of liberation, and in the meantime we are cooperating in a defined area, in the cause of liberation. Even in the days when the Communist Party was in its infancy, Congress did not debar them.[1]

Nelson Mandela, speaking from the dock at the Rivonia Trial, was even more specific:

1. *Let My People Go: An Autobiography* (Johannesburg, 1962), p. 154.

278

It is perhaps difficult for White South Africans, with an in-grained prejudice against communism, to understand why experienced African politicians so readily accept communists as their friends. But to us the reason is obvious. Theoretical differences amongst those fighting against oppression is a luxury we cannot afford at this stage. What is more, for many decades communists were the only political group in South Africa who were prepared to treat Africans as human beings and their equals; who were prepared to eat with us; talk with us, live with us, and work with the Africans for the attainment of political rights and a stake in society. Because of this, there are many Africans who, today, tend to equate freedom with communism.[2]

There obviously were many Africans who felt as Mandela did, and the question can be asked whether they were primarily African Nationalists or Communists—which interests would they, in a pinch, put first? This question cannot be answered with any certainty, and little attempt will be made to do so here because of paucity of evidence. The case of Bartholomew Hlapane will be discussed later in this chapter, and his reasons for leaving the Communist Party and for giving evidence against it will be set forth. How representative these are is left to the reader to decide.

The whole question of evidence is, indeed, a vexing and confusing one. Before 1960 the Communist Party was eager to conceal its connection with the ANC and the Congress Alliance. After 1960 *Umkonto* increasingly held center stage. After the Rivonia and Fischer trials, in 1964 and 1965, the interest of the Party seems to have returned to the ANC. The evidence for this, and for many other things that are to be said, is in part inferential. An anonymous author in *Africa Report* has pointed up the dilemma: "Most of the identification of Communist influence depends on knowledge of individuals, their past histories and travels, and on the circumstances that created their organizations, rather than on identification of a palpably left-wing statement or policy." [3] So, although the aim is to avoid inference as much as possible,

2. *No Easy Walk to Freedom*, ed. Ruth First (New York, 1965), p. 181.
3. *Africa Report*, VI (March, 1961), 5.

it cannot be avoided entirely. Where analysis is introduced, it is the author's; and it is introduced in the knowledge that other interpretations are possible.

II

Despite the overlapping memberships, there is some ground for accepting the idea that the ANC and *Umkonto* remained separate. Piet Beyleveld, for instance, described the jealousy with which each guarded its autonomy and the resentment that would have been felt had the Communist Party attempted to interfere with the ANC.[4] Bartholomew Hlapane, on the other hand, consistently gave evidence to the effect that the executives of the different organizations were virtually identical.[5] It would seem, therefore, that Communist strength in the ANC, before *Umkonto* was founded, was in the form of an inverted pyramid —great at the top and narrow at the bottom. An assessment was published in *African Communist* of the third quarter, 1969. Although it is not clear to which period this refers, it can well be to 1964–65, the period under consideration:

Whatever the achievements, however, the mounting tempo and stress of the struggle had pitilessly revealed weaknesses in the structures, emphases and style of work of the movement which urgently called for correction. Political activity and information was lacking, especially at grass-roots level; and virtual collapse of the old Alliance machinery had left a gap which resulted in a failure to integrate all revolutionaries in the work of the movement; a dangerous chasm was opening up between the leadership and the rank-and-file which provided soil for various divisive tendencies foreign to the spirit of the ANC and its traditional allies.

The "gap" and the "divisive tendencies" have already been described in preceding chapters, as was the failure in organization. More can

4. *Natal Witness*, November 11, 1966.
5. *Ibid.*, September 2, 1966; *Star*, March 31, 1966.

be said of the forces pushing leadership and rank and file apart, as well as of counterforces pulling the opposite way.

Among the lesser lights in the ANC, suspicion of Communists and of their motives remained to the end. The suspicion was particularly directed against non-African Communists, who were distrusted because, to Africans, they seemed to be acting against the manifest interests of their own racial groups. Why should a white man, who had all the benefits of white society (benefits an African might desire for himself), be willing to throw them all away for the African cause? Why should whites, or Indians for that matter, turn against their own people for the Africans' sakes? Surely there was an ulterior motive, reasoned many Africans, and what could this motive be but to further exploit Africans? There was heightened dislike for Indians, who were seen not only as exploiters of Africans but as people who, while despising Africans, enjoyed only marginally higher status. Coloureds, of whom there were a number in the Communist Party, were no "nation" at all—they were people who tried to ape the whites and who, though at least partly African in descent, regarded Africans with scorn. Given all these factors, many Africans argued, were not professions of friendship and offers of collaboration merely the means to make the African a tool to political ends which were of no interest to him?

What then of the Africans enrolled in the Communist Party? For obvious reasons they were less distrusted than whites, but there was much skepticism as to where they stood. They were sometimes seen as tools of the whites, who were using them to maintain white supremacy under the guise of a new political system. African nationalists saw them as men who had "sold out" to whites, even if not to the whites in power. They had not, what is more, the aura that whites, despite all enmity, still have for Africans in South Africa. These suspicions rested with the lower ranks even after the Pan-Africanists had split off from the old ANC. The men at the bottom of the ladder had therefore little personal experience of white Communists. The Communist Party itself was organized along racial lines, a necessity imposed on it in part by the exigencies of underground operation. Only the Central and District Committees were multiracial. The cells were segregated ethnically, and separate Area Committees operated for whites,

281

Indians, Coloureds, and Africans.[6] The Africans' lack of personal contact with whites meant that they did not quicken with the glow which, one author wrote, comes to some Africans when they associate with whites on equal terms.[7] However, the willingness of Communists of other races to associate with Africans as equals was not without effect. It won the Party many converts who, in turn, set up cadres among Africans lower on the status ladder. However, the Party as a whole, whatever the standing of individuals, never overcame the barriers of distrust.

It would be unfair to imply that it was the pleasure of experiencing social equality even briefly that motivated the Africans who joined the Communist Party. Some became convinced that the doctrines of Marx and Lenin explained the otherwise inexplicable. It seemed to them that Communist doctrines not only offered a solution to the ills besetting South Africa but also explained white attitudes. Marxism comforted them, for it implied that the African's status and the low regard the whites had for him were not due to defects in himself but to defects in the social system. In other words, there was nothing inherent in him that assigned the African to the lowest reaches of the society but rather an inevitable and historically determined set of relationships. The doctrine also offered a way out and a promise for the future, so that those convinced of Communist doctrines were ready to serve the cause to the limit of their abilities.

It may well be asked how many men convinced of Communist doctrines were in the ranks of *Umkonto*. If by this question one means those convinced *and* well versed in Marxism-Leninism, the answer must be that their numbers were small. The Communist Party, which sought its members among the more politicized of the different racial groups, primarily among the members of the Congress Alliance,

6. See, for instance, Gerard Ludi and Blaar Grobbelaar, *The Amazing Mr. Fischer* (Cape Town, 1966), p. 30. The self-righteousness of these authors is repellent and their political views are bizarre to non-South Africans. Nevertheless, where they stick to facts and to Ludi's courtroom evidence, they are accurate.

7. Article by Nimrod Mkele, a market researcher and psychologist, in the *Star*, November 16, 1961. Mkele says that the most cherished friendships that an African can make are with whites, for he thus acquires status attributes in a society where such association is not only frowned on but actively discouraged.

held study classes as a means of recruitment. People were invited to attend but were not told that they were at a Communist meeting. Those who responded to the doctrines were taken into the party.[8] A number responded, but what most Africans seized on were some slogans, a few catch phrases, and the belief that, even if they did not fully understand it, communism provided an answer to their ills.

The Communist Party had other ways of attracting Africans, particularly younger men. Before it became illegal, it did provide some education and sometimes a job and food as well. A recommendation from an employed Party member might mean a secure job with a good salary and plenty of time to do Party work with an employer who was either a member or a fellow-traveler. Once the Party was illegal, it employed a small number of paid, permanent African functionaries— Hlapane, for instance, received R70 (about $98) per month. In addition, SACTU could give jobs to a limited number of "trade union organizers" who could proselytize for *Umkonto* among the workers.

Yet, when all is accounted for, the promise of social and economic equality was doubtless the biggest draw, for Africans felt exploited in South Africa, and with good reason. The promise that communism would end exploitation of man by man must have had great emotional appeal. To many, particularly to those with Communist friends, it must have seemed, as Mandela said, that they were the only ones dedicated to African interests. The Communist Party, in turn, saw that it could gain strength from its close relationship with those who could be mobilized by the "creative application of the universally valid science of Marxism-Leninism to the conditions of South Africa."

III

Fascinating as it would be to explore the history of the Communist Party in South Africa, it is beyond the scope of this book to do so in any depth. The Party had a tortuous career, sometimes tolerated and sometimes repressed by officialdom, which at best regarded it with

8. *Cape Times*, March 31, 1966.

suspicious distaste. Within, doctrinal and factional disputes ensured that the Party line was not always the shortest distance between two points. Africans had not always been of major concern to the Party. The contrary is true. At its founding and for some time after, the Party concentrated on winning the white worker. Only when it became clear that the white worker was not to be won did the Party switch its attention to the African. The International Socialist League, the precursor of the Communist Party in South Africa, was founded in 1915. Two years later, in 1917, it groped toward friendly relations with the African National Congress and, at the same time, tried to establish African trade unions; among them, interestingly enough, was a General Workers' Union. It also tried to establish an organization, which it named the Industrial Workers of Africa, modeled on the American Industrial Workers of the World (IWW). But, for all this seeming activity on the African's behalf, the League concentrated on the white worker, whom it saw as militant and good material for a revolutionary force.

This remained the dominant trend of thought even after the Communist Party of South Africa was founded on July 29, 1921, and joined the Third International. Concentration on the white worker, rather than on the African, was climaxed in the General Strike of 1922, which, though neither led nor organized by the Party, won its full support. This strike was hardly in the Africans' interests; indeed, they were among the victims. The strike was directed partly against the undercutting of white wages by mine owners, some of whom were replacing whites with cheaper black labor. The slogan of the striking workers was: "Workers of the World, Fight and Unite for a White South Africa!" [9]

What caused the Party to change its mind after the 1922 strike? The Communists' own interpretation was expressed in a very interesting article, written under the pseudonym of A. Zanzolo, in *African Com-*

9. For a more detailed treatment of communism in South Africa and its relationship to African resistance, see Edward Roux, *Time Longer Than Rope: A History of the Black Man's Struggle for Freedom in South Africa* (Madison, Wis., 1964), p. 148. See also Sheridan W. Johns, "Marxism-Leninism in a Multi-Racial Environment: Origins and Early History of the Communist Party of South Africa, 1914–1932" (Ph.D. diss., Harvard University, 1965).

munist.[10] Zanzolo explains the changes in the usual Marxian dialectic triad. The first period, from 1917 to 1922, was the *thesis* stage of the Party's development. At this time, he says, the Party saw South Africa at the stage of capitalist development, with one-quarter of the people enjoying democratic rights and with the majority still out of the labor market. "In these conditions it was thought that the working class of the White group would seize power and then proceed to free the oppressed nations. The slant of party work continued to be largely among the European workers." (European, in the South African context and in South African usage, means white.) This belief foundered in 1922. The strike aroused the fears of the ruling class and led them to make "vast concessions to the White workers to make them part and parcel of the ruling group."

By Marxist logic, the thesis is followed by its opposite, the *antithesis*, and this, Zanzolo argues, happened in South Africa. The Communist Party now swung away from the white worker and concentrated on the African worker. It was now the "development of the African liberation movement" that was to be the Party's goal. In 1928 the Communist International, sitting at its Congress in Moscow, raised the South African issue and resolved that it would be best to develop the Party with emphasis on Africans. The future belonged to the African, the reasoning ran, and winning the African for communism meant winning South Africa for communism. Africans should be encouraged to work toward a "Native Republic" which would be ruled by them. (Native, in this context, does not mean anyone born in South Africa, but is confined exclusively to Africans in popular parlance.) [11]

This change was not well received by white Party members. The South African delegation to the International strenuously opposed the resolution, but to no avail, for it was adopted. The South African delegation, which included many well-known Negrophiles, argued that the greater number of Africans were not yet ready to enter the Party and were insufficiently trained to take the leading positions, as demanded by Moscow. "The party saw the struggle as a colonial one," writes

10. A. Zanzolo [pseud.], "The Theory of the South African Revolution," *African Communist*, no. 12 (March, 1963), 17–22.
11. Roux, *Time Longer Than Rope*, p. 256.

Zanzolo, "with Africans of all classes fighting for self-determination and aiming at the establishment of a bourgeois democratic republic. . . . Work among workers of other sections declined, and almost exclusive attention was paid to mobilizing Africans." The decision taken in Moscow, without real knowledge of South African realities, was almost fatal for communism in the country. The International did not, for instance, realize that conditions for disciplining and tempering members entering in large numbers just did not exist. Much of this new membership consisted of Africans from the smaller, semirural townships. Few members were gained from among the African intelligentsia. The Party preferred this in a way, as it could mold such men more easily; but as several hundred joined in a short time, the machinery of the Party was severely strained.[12] And if this were not enough in itself, a left-oriented group, extreme and doctrinaire, gained control of the Central Committee just at this time, and began a Stalin-like purge of the Party. Those who were in disagreement with this left-oriented faction were expelled, with the result that the Party was stripped of some of its most able and energetic leaders, including its founder, W. H. (Bill) Andrews. By the time the line twisted in a new direction, much of the damage had been done and not all of it was redeemable. The Party was in sorry array, devoid of either able leadership or constructive ideas.

Although on the whole this policy had harmed the Party, the time was not wholly wasted. These were, after all, the years in which the Communist Party cemented its hold on African politics. Among many of little competence, some Africans who joined were of superior ability and intelligence, and these men were later to serve the Party well. African membership rose steadily, while white membership declined as members resigned, were expelled, or reduced to despondent silence. A measure of the growing influence of the Communist Party among Africans is seen in the jump in African membership, which, in 1929, had risen to some 3,000. There was an African majority in the Party, and there were twenty accredited African delegates to the 1929 conference, as opposed to half that number of whites. In addition to actual African

12. *Ibid.*, pp. 214–15.

members, the Party had gained much favor among Africans in general by its attack on the unpopular pass laws, against which it had organized a large-scale campaign in 1930. It was on December 16 of that year that the campaign reached its climax, with Africans burning their passes. The campaign was marked by serious rioting and by stern police action. In Durban, for instance, a prominent African Communist leader, Johannes Nkosi, was killed by police gunfire and became the first in the pantheon of African Communists to die by official action.[13]

In spite of such events, these were times of frustration and dissension among Communists. Another pseudonymous author, A. Lerumo, writes of the "chaos, confusion and despondency" that "reigned in its ranks" at that time.[14] Because of the serious decline in morale, the Central Committee was moved from Johannesburg to Cape Town on January 1, 1939. Although Johannesburg was the principal center of Party strength, it was also the scene of factional conflict centering around rival personalities. The move to Cape Town, together with an enlarged Central Committee, would, it was hoped, enable a fresh start to be made. But the troubles of the Party were not yet at an end. Obedient as always to the dictates of the International, the Party was obliged to declare the Second World War "capitalist and imperialist" and, therefore, of no interest to workers. This was an agonizing position for the Jews in the Party, of whom there were quite a number. But things were easier once Germany invaded the Soviet Union, and the war at once became a crusade against fascism. Communists, who had been unsympathetic to the war effort, now went to the other extreme and pressed for its ever more energetic prosecution. After all, with the invasion of the Soviet Union the "essential character" of the war had changed, and now the "defeat of Nazi Germany," previously viewed with indifference, became a matter "in the vital interests of all humanity." The changed line, coupled with reflected glory from Soviet victories, gave the Party a new lease on life. Many intellectuals turned to what seemed to them a bastion of anti-nazism, and the lukewarm neutralism the Party had earlier espoused was forgotten in the new

13. A. Lerumo [pseud.], "After 40 Years an Important Anniversary for Africa," *African Communist*, no. 7 (September, 1961), 73.
14. *Ibid.*, pp. 62–82.

fervor. This fervor lasted through the war, but with victory it began to erode. The Soviet Union was increasingly intransigent. Its expansionist designs were manifest to all who would see. Its position became harder and harder for clear-sighted men and women to hold. In addition, with the end of the war, life in South Africa increasingly returned to normality and caused some of those who had joined the Party in its heroic wartime phase to leave its ranks. Still, what remained was a hard core who had joined the Party in its lean years, to whom had been added a new generation, some with war experience, who were to bolster the Party in the years of struggle ahead. This new generation, many of whom were students, made this, in Abram Fischer's words, the "golden age" of the Party at the universities.

The third and highest stage of the Party's history was the *synthesis,* which, following Zanzolo's reasoning, came in the postwar years, growing out of seeds implanted in the war. It is best described in Zanzolo's own words:

In the new program of the South African Communist Party the synthesis is complete. The main features of our society are described in detail. It is shown how South Africa is a country with a highly developed modern economy in which monopoly capitalism has reached its final stage—imperialism. That South Africa at one level operates as a bourgeois democratic republic in its final stage of imperialism in which it exports capital and seeks to control other territories. That in fact fascism is now a factor in our country. At another level—that of the majority of the people—South African reality projects itself as a country with a colonial people fighting for national liberation and freedom. That at this level the struggle of the African people becomes one with the great anti-colonial revolution in Asia, Africa and Latin America. It is the integration of the two aspects in a single economic complex within the bounds of a single country that the program characterizes as a *Special Type of Colonialism.* The program illustrates once more the fact that no pure societies exist in the world which fit exactly some previously defined social formation. It is the duty of the social scientist to find the dominant feature of the society and thus to characterize it. The Africans constitute by far the vast majority of the people in the country; they are the main labor power and therefore the liberation of the African people is the main content of the national democratic revolution. Because of the highly developed nature of South African capitalism and its exclusive control by a bourgeoisie drawn from a particular racial group, the national freedom of the African and other oppressed people involves the destruction of monopoly in the country. In the absence of a national bourgeoisie among the Africans and the great numerical strength and experience of the working class the national democratic revolution has a far-reaching and radical program which will usher in a state of national democracy. Under South African conditions the national democratic revolution has great prospects of proceeding at once to socialist solutions.[15]

The Party thus, according to its own perceptions of its role, fights "the monopoly capitalists and landlords who are the servitors and allies of American, British, and foreign imperialism." The revolution against them is, according to this account, headed by the working class in alliance with the national liberation movements of the Africans and other "oppressed peoples." The list of the oppressed naturally does not include the oppressed of the Communist countries, who never are mentioned in Zanzolo's account. It is the oppressed peoples, together with the Communists, and in alliance with "democratic elements" of similar stamp, who are to effect this "liberation." But these groups in the country are not alone, for on their side are "the international working class and all democratic forces the world over," ensuring, according to Zanzolo, "the speedy victory of the revolution," which was "now definitely on the agenda in South Africa."

Zanzolo, writing in an official Communist publication, was obviously expressing the views of the Party. Indeed, these ideas conform entirely with the new notion of "people's democracies" which in recent years has replaced the formerly crude conceptions of class conflict in the developing world. The "people's democracy," as it now is seen, is that of a "popular front" against imperialism. Imperialism, as Francis J. Kase has shown in his recent study, is a catchall term under which is

15. Zanzolo, "Theory of the South African Revolution," p. 22.

lumped "everyone who is opposed to the communist's interests and desires." [16]

Although the idea of a popular front of "democratic forces" is relatively new, the desire to capture the ANC goes back quite far in Communist Party history. The cultivation of the ANC by the International Socialist League has already been mentioned. Efforts did not, however, end with the League's conversion into the Communist Party. True, it was mainly the white workers who were courted from 1921 to 1928, but African workers were never entirely forgotten, even though they may have been neglected. Even in the twenties the party made a deliberate effort to cultivate ANC leaders. An example is that of James Gumede, then president of the ANC, who, after acting as a delegate to the 1927 conference of the League Against Imperialism in Brussels, was invited to the Soviet Union and returned an enthusiastic Communist. In numerous meetings all over South Africa he did much to popularize communism. His downfall came when the chiefs, opposing a system that in its own country overthrew traditional rule, were able to muster support against him. Nonetheless, the trouble and expense put forth by the Soviet Party indicates the importance attached to the ANC at that time.[17]

Communist efforts extended beyond cultivation of the existing leadership to the training of future leaders. Promising people were sought out and sent to night schools in South Africa. Those who showed particular promise and commitment were sent for further training to the Soviet Union. Writing of these changes in *African Communist*, Lerumo tells us something of the way in which this was done:

> Serious attention was given to organizing trade union activities, night schools and other educational activities amongst the African workers, and as a result many of the best elements of the African working class were attracted into the ranks of the Party. Those who joined the Party at this time included men such as Albert Nzula, the first African to become general secretary of the Party, Gana Maka-

---

16. *People's Democracy: A Contribution to the Communist Theory of State and Revolution* (Leyden, 1968), p. 28.
17. Roux, *Time Longer Than Rope*, p. 211.

beni, well-known and respected in the African trade union movement for many years, E. T. Mofutsanyana, later Editor of *Inkulu-
leko*, Johannes Nkosi, African hero and martyr who was murdered
by the police, J. B. Marks, subsequently President of the African
Mine Workers' Union, the Transvaal Council of Non-European
Trade Unions and the African National Congress (Transvaal), and
Moses M. Kotane, General Secretary of the Party from 1939 to
1950.[18]

Edward Roux also points to the influence of education as provided by
the CP. But he cautions that the best recruits to the Party were those
who had not been "spoilt" by an apprenticeship in the ANC. "The
best of all were rank-and-file Bantu members, often semiliterate, who
received their education through the party and had never been in any
other organization." [19] It was men such as these who could later be infiltrated into the ANC, particularly after the CP was banned in 1950.[20]
The evidence seems quite convincing that by the mid-fifties the
Communists had become the preponderant influence within the ANC.
The ANC was operated like many of the other "fronts" which will
presently be discussed, in the sense that relatively innocuous figures
apparently led the organization, while all real decision-making powers
were in the hands of Communists. Membership in the Party was often
well concealed, however, as emerged from the evidence of one witness
in the Fischer Trial, Bartholomew Hlapane. This trial, for those unfamiliar with it, was held in 1964, and the defendants were among the
major leaders of the illegal Communist Party in South Africa, at whose
head was a brilliant lawyer, Abram Fischer. Hlapane's evidence was
not challenged in cross-examination at the Fischer Trial, for Fischer
confessed soon after it. Hlapane gave substantially similar evidence
in other cases, however, notably those of Fred Carneson and of Dr.
Naidoo, where it emerged relatively unshaken. It is unarguable that
Hlapane knew what he was talking about. Among those who attended
meetings of the various CP committees were Walter Sisulu and Govan

18. Lerumo, "An Important Anniversary for Africa," p. 65.
19. Roux, *Time Longer Than Rope*, p. 215.
20. Hlapane evidence, *Star*, March 31, 1966.

Mbeki.[21] What makes this evidence interesting is that both Mbeki and Sisulu had been presented to the world as non-Communists. Mbeki confessed to Communist Party membership at the Rivonia Trial. Sisulu denied it then, and his denial was widely accepted among those sympathetic to the African cause in South Africa. Hlapane's evidence makes it clear, however, that Sisulu was not only a Party member but in its highest councils. Indeed, the provision that membership in any "front" such as SACTU must be accompanied by ANC membership makes matters clearer.

The relationship of the Communist Party, the ANC, and the Party's fronts can be roughly fitted into four phases. (1) The first phase is that during which the Party operated openly. It was then a lawful if suspect political organization. This period lasted from the time of the Party's formation in 1921 to 1950.

(2) Once the Party was banned and its continuance made illegal, the second stage commenced, where the membership dispersed into a number of fronts. These were the multiracial South African Congress of Trade Unions (SACTU); the Congress of Democrats (for whites only); the South African Coloured People's Organization (for those of mixed descent only), later renamed the Coloured People's Congress; and the South African Indian Congress—all being bound together in what was collectively termed the Congress Alliance. The fronts and the ANC were meshed by interlocking memberships. Thus Africans were urged to join SACTU and the ANC, as well as to hold their Party membership. They were to gain prominent positions in the ANC and thus to assist in maintaining it on a course congruent with the wishes of the Party leadership. Jordan Ngubane describes the relationship of Party and fronts thus:

The inner nonracial core of real Communists, with headquarters in Johannesburg, was in direct communication with the [Communist

21. Present at the secret Party conference (November [?], 1962) were Fred Carneson, Lionel Bernstein, Hilda Bernstein, Joe Slovo, Ruth Slovo, Mike Harmel, Moses Kotane, Bob Hepple, Walter Sisulu, Dan Glume (Tloome?), Duma Nokwe, Govan Mbeki, Mark Shope, Joe Matthews, Billy Nair, M. P. Naicker, Stephen Zamini (Dhlamini?), and elected to the Central Committee were Harmel, J. Slovo, L. Bernstein, Marks, Kotane, Nokwe, and Hlapane himself. Hlapane/*Fischer*, pp. 215–17.

Party] of the Soviet Union, partly through agents in Lourenco Marques, London, and more recently Dar-es-Salaam. The members of the core joined a number of "national" organizations of Africans, Indians, Coloureds, and Whites, which in turn, belonged to a bigger alliance called the Congress [Alliance].[22]

As long as the fronts were not banned, both the Party and individuals known to be or to have been Communists played down Communist influence and stressed the independence of the fronts. This proved difficult, even at the best of times, for international events frequently forced the hand of front leaderships. The stand of the components of the Congress Alliance in the cases of Hungary and Israel in October, 1956, made their partisanship and associations only too evident. The pretense that these were autonomous organizations with opinions of their own could have deceived only the most naive and gullible.

Where men of good will still hesitated, it seems to have been largely because of opposition to the policies of the South African government, policies repugnant to most intelligent people, who feared that if the Communist connections of the ANC were known others might be prejudiced against the African cause and more sympathetic to that of the whites. The Communists, both in the illegal Party and the fronts, were not slow to capitalize on sentiments such as these. They continued to disclaim control and tried to keep their public statements free from that heavy-handed pedantry usually so much a part of their writing and speaking. This needs to be stressed once more, as many men and women of good will seem reluctant to believe the extent of Communist influence on the African opposition in South Africa. They are strengthened in this view by the policy of the government in labeling as Communists all radicals opposing them. This, many argue, has made the label "Communist" meaningless. It is doubtless true that some people without Communist connections appeared on the government's lists. In some cases these were secret Party members for years, which was generally unknown. The most obvious of these cases

22. Jordan K. Ngubane, *An African Explains Apartheid* (New York, 1963), p. 183.

is that of Piet Beyleveld, mentioned earlier. Beyleveld, it will be recalled, was the "show" non-Communist in the Congress of Democrats despite his high rank in the secret Party. Whenever members of the Congress of Democrats and of other fronts in the Alliance were asked who on the COD Executive was not a Communist, they would point to Beyleveld. Those not made purblind by partisanship or sympathy had suspected Beyleveld's Communist connection for some time. His admission, at the Fischer Trial, to having been a Party member since 1956 was less surprising than it might otherwise have been.[23] There had, however, been no proof, and no one was prepared to assume the public burden of fastening the Communist label on him, except, of course, the government. The same holds true in other cases. Even today the author is reluctant to name names, unless the individuals have admitted Communist Party membership or it has been demonstrated in a court.

(3) The third phase began with the reemergence of the Party after 1960, the year in which a number of the fronts were banned. The Party had been secretly reconstituted in the 1950s but had, in the second phase, denied all association with the fronts and the ANC. This policy ceased to pay once the fronts could no longer operate legally and provide platforms for public addresses. The Communist Party now made known its existence as an illegal organization and entered into a closer association with the ANC. The fronts of the Congress Alliance were dropped as they were banned, and the Alliance became, in effect, the National Liberation Movement (NLM), which, while nominally claiming the fronts as members, consisted in fact only of the Party and the ANC. Remaining outside the NLM officially, but actually supporting and reinforcing it, was SACTU. It is the third phase that has been treated in this book.

(4) The fourth phase is now in progress and consists largely of guerrilla activity directed from abroad. This was begun in 1965, as far as can be ascertained, and is beyond the scope of the present work.

23. Beyleveld joined the Party in 1956 and was elevated to the Branch Committee in 1961, and then through the District Committee to the Central Committee in 1963. He was detained in 1964.

IV

An actual example of the progression of one man in the Communist Party may help put much of the more theoretical matter in perspective. It may also serve to explain something of the Party's activities in the underground revolt. It is fortunate that the evidence of Hlapane exists to provide such an outline.

Hlapane had joined the ANC in 1952 and had, he claimed, been recruited to the Communist Party in 1955 by Joe Slovo, a lawyer and a leader of the Party. He had been placed in a cell in Soweto Township, in which he served as an ordinary member until 1959, when he was placed in the Area Committee. He was transferred to the District Committee in 1961, given special duties, and paid what was for an African the handsome salary of $96 a month, given a traveling allowance, and allowed the use of a car.[24] Once on the District Committee, Hlapane attended all its meetings, where, according to him, a member of the Central Committee was always present to act as a kind of contact. In his case, he alleges, this man was Joe Slovo. *Umkonto* was, it hardly need be said, frequently discussed at the District Committee meetings, where it was referred to as the military wing of the ANC and of the Party. Matters concerning this military wing were important, for the District Committee would have to pass down instructions to the lower levels of the Party. Only the High Command of *Umkonto* could give orders to *Umkonto*, confirms Hlapane, and the High Command did not have direct contact with the District Committee. Thus any instructions for the High Command would come from the Central Committee, presumably passing through the District's contact.

Hlapane was promoted to the Central Committee toward the end of 1962 either by Alexander Hepple or by Joe Slovo (he claimed that he could not remember which), and was taken to a secret conference by Duma Nokwe in October or November of that year. This con-

---

24. The material that follows is a summary of Hlapane's evidence which appears in the Fischer Trial on pp. 209–37. See also *Cape Times*, March 3, 1966.

ference was difficult for the South African Communist Party to organize under prevailing conditions, but the urgency of the pending decisions made the risk worth taking. The delegates had to be drawn together in secrecy, and Hlapane speaks of being taken to a house in a Volkswagen Kombi—a vehicle popular with the ANC—the windows of which were covered with sailcloth. The conference apparently had a twofold purpose: one, to ratify a new Party program; the other, to consider broadening the conflict. The new program was duly approved, but no decision was taken on the conflict. Hlapane is vague on the point, but it seems that many felt that the Central Committee should prepare the plan for broadening the conflict, which needed the approval of the High Command of *Umkonto*. A new Central Committee was also elected at this conference, which, according to Hlapane, included Joe Slovo, J. B. Marks, Moses Kotane, Duma Nokwe, and Hlapane himself. Raymond Mhlaba was later coopted, together with some others.

The ball was now thrown to the Central Committee, who shortly afterward—sometime in December, 1962, or January, 1963—met at "Lilliesleaf," the organization's secret headquarters in Rivonia. The purpose of this meeting was to set up the various Party committees—the secretariat, the district committees, committees for propaganda, and so forth. It was then decided, again according to Hlapane, that Slovo was to be the representative of the Central Committee at the *Umkonto* High Command. He was to draft the plan, previously referred to, showing how the second phase, the move from sabotage to guerrilla warfare, was to be introduced and made effective. Slovo was also to be responsible both for recruitment to *Umkonto* and for reporting *Umkonto* actions to the Central Committee.

In his capacity as a member of the Central Committee, Hlapane participated in discussions of *Operation Mayebuye*. He speaks of a decision made during April or May, 1963, to send two people abroad to discuss it. Marks and Slovo, says Hlapane, were selected for this task, and both left the country at the end of May, 1963.

Among the other things that Hlapane claims to have discovered was that the farm and the other properties used by *Umkonto* had been paid for by the Communists and belonged to the Party. This clearly took money, and Abram Fischer was in charge of obtaining the funds to finance *Umkonto*. This he did through a contact in London, England. Some of these funds were allegedly coming from the coffers of Defense and Aid, an organization in London which apparently collected money for the legal expenses of those arrested and for the support of their families. Other money came from Moscow and Peking. In addition to these funds, smaller amounts came from monthly subscriptions assessed against all Party members according to their financial position.

Hlapane was arrested in 1963 and was kept confined for some 172 days. On his release he was not at once allowed to rejoin the Party but was kept in "quarantine" until it was certain that he was not under police surveillance. At the same time he was questioned by officers of the Party. A two-hour interrogation by a woman member took place soon after his release. She particularly wanted to know the kinds of questions the police had put to Hlapane, whether he had made a statement or not, and any other information that might be helpful to others interrogated by the police.

The Party interrogation took place during Christmas week, but it was not until the following April that the Party was fully satisfied and allowed Hlapane to attend an Area Committee meeting. As the Area Committee was lower than the Central or District Committees, Hlapane knew that he was being tested. By May, 1964, confidence in Hlapane was sufficiently restored for him to be invited to another Central Committee meeting, and he was again coopted, although his functions were changed. It now was Hlapane's job to receive monies for the sabotage organization. These he paid out to another African, Wilton Mkwayi, who was, Hlapane believed, carrying on the work of the High Command of *Umkonto*. From a later trial it emerged that, in addition to Mkwayi, four men, two whites and two Indians, were actually conducting the affairs of the moribund movement. This, of course, was unknown to Hlapane. Hlapane paid over some $1,880 a month to Mkwayi, and in addition handed over some $840 to Tiny Nokwe, wife of Congress leader Duma Nokwe. An additional $560 was given to a certain Mike Dingaka. For his work Hlapane received a monthly salary of $244 and was given about $840 as part payment for a car to be used for Party work. The money was paid to Hlapane by an Indian known to him as "Mac" for about three months, after which "Mac" was arrested. His contact arrested, Hlapane was now linked directly with Abram Fischer, who was acting as treasurer for the Communist Party, receiving some $5,000 from Fischer in all.

Hlapane became, in effect, a contact between Fischer on the one end and Mkwayi on the other. Mkwayi, who had received his training in China, gave reports of attacks on post offices in the townships of Pimville, Dube, and Jabavu, and of other incidents which Hlapane could not remember at the trial. In his reports, Mkwayi continually complained of the difficulty of obtaining dynamite, and when Hlapane reported this to Fischer, the latter urged that work not requiring explosives be substituted. He suggested breaking down telegraph poles, cutting wires, and rendering railway signals inoperable. Despite the fact that the Party seemed to command quite large sums, in other words, it was reduced to quite small-scale sabotage.

The ideological dimension of Hlapane's evidence is also interesting. He was not able to tell, for instance, whether there was any difference between the ANC and the Communist Party. It was the rule that all Party members *had* to join the appropriate front, and they could not *only* be members of the Party. He speaks of ANC matters being discussed at a Communist Party meeting before they were approved of by the former, but says that, as the ANC knew that the Communists were the party that had established socialism, it did not mind. The confusion in Hlapane's mind is evidenced when he says that the only exception to the cross-organization memberships was in the case of *Umkonto*. He argues that members of *Umkonto* were not permitted to belong to any other front or to the Party or the ANC. The reason he adduces is that they could get the ANC or the CP "in trouble" if they were captured. The two organizations were, however, "in trouble" already, since they were illegal and those who tried to continue them in any form were subject to heavy penalties. What Hlapane may have meant was that the men arrested might betray others. The important point that Hlapane makes, which must be stressed, is that the prime source of instructions for *Umkonto* was the Communist Party.

The method of working for African support through an existing and recognized African organization, the ANC, allowed the Party itself to remain small, while the apparently independent, but actually captive, ANC could be made to grow and grow. The most able people in the ANC could be recruited to the Party, and this in turn would enable it to further cement its control. The theoretical knowledge the Party possessed, the "science" of Marxism-Leninism, which assured inevitable victory, gave them confidence, as did their discipline, flexibility of tactics, and authoritative voice. These were used to gain and maintain influence in the ANC—to gain access to the organization, to infiltrate it, and to make sure that those who infiltrated remained loyal to the Party.

This picture of the Party should not obscure one important fact: the appeal that communism would seem to have for Africans in South Africa was actually quite limited. This is true even if the Party's vaunted goal of "vanguard of the masses" is kept in mind. What were the reasons? Some suggestions made earlier in this chapter may suggest answers, but these can only be partial. It was certainly true that some were put off by the close association of different racial groups, which was seen as exploitation of the African under a new guise. Others again were suspicious of the mirroring of racial separatism in the Party itself. Others, again, may not have believed in the credibility of Communist goals. Then there was the resistance of African traditionalists and of African nationalists, both of whom saw communism as a threat, though for different reasons. Nor can the massive propaganda campaign which the South African government conducted over the radio be entirely discounted. Radio South Africa, broadcasting in nine African languages, reached a far larger audience than did the ANC when it was illegal.

The government, in addition to propaganda, had made Party membership subject to very heavy sanctions, which few would risk unless they were already converted. Doubtless many other factors of a similar nature were involved. The fact is that, apart from the war years, the Party seldom had more than one or two thousand members and often not as many as that. It drew its strength from several sources, among them the ablest and most courageous of African leaders, but the masses they sought to win often remained both apathetic and hostile. The ANC continued to command general loyalty until its connection with and control by the Communist Party could no longer be concealed, and then a major schism almost destroyed it. Subsequently, as an illegal organization, it tried sabotage. Part of this story has already been related; now that the Communist connection has been made plain, the rest can be told.

Conclusion

THE TERMS "INSURGENCY" AND "REVOLT" have been used interchange-
ably throughout. Such free use of terms is possible because so many
different writers have put their own interpretations on them that there
is no standard meaning. In Chapter I, insurgency was described as an
attempt to overthrow a political system by bringing disorder to an unbearable level. Once the existing system has collapsed, it can be re-
built to the insurgents' own design. Disorder, in turn, means making
the predictable working of institutions impossible by generating shocks
in the system. If the level of disorder can be maintained, the supporters
of the existing system will eventually press for concessions to the insurgents. As the insurgents are committed to the restructuring of the
society, each concession only leads to demands for further concessions;
so concession is self-defeating to the government. Pressure for concession can be increased, nonetheless, if a large number of people
can be led to believe that the government is not in a position to protect them from the insurgents.

This view, so baldly stated, may not be palatable to those who
would argue that, in its terms, it makes all demand for change tantamount to insurgency. This is not so. The main factor is whether the
disorder is aimed at destruction or at reform. There is obviously a
gray area between the two, but, in the main, the difference should be

301

clear. Nor is any moral judgment implied. It might be argued on moral grounds that some systems should be overthrown. Questions such as these are outside the scope of this book and are left to social ethicists. The fundamental question to be put here is: why do insurgencies fail to go beyond their initial stages?

First we must deal with the fact that revolutionary situations are fairly unique. Robert C. Tucker, for instance, argues that the revolutionary situation, as Lenin used the term, is extremely rare in social history and particularly so in modern societies: "Lenin saw revolution as an elemental movement involving millions, occurring at a time of 'particular upsurge' when masses of aggrieved humanity were driven by unusually harsh adversity into an insurrectionary mood that could find outlet in action owing to a partially incapacitating crisis at the top of society and government." [1] Tucker goes on to say that such crises have occurred only as the result of unusual circumstances in developed polities, and that this has always involved an element of the fortuitous.

Revolutionary situations are scarce, it can be argued, because two forces act against a successful uprising, even where numbers of oppressed are apparently available. The first of these is the routinization of power; the second is the extent to which the threat of potential revolt is perceived. Two recent works shed light on these themes and are pertinent to the problem of urban revolt in South Africa: *Prozesse der Machtbildung*, by Heinrich Popitz, and an article by Joseph Lopreato, "Authority Relations and Class Conflict." [2]

Popitz has set himself the old question: what enables minorities to govern majorities? To discover the answer, he turns not to historical examples, with their obvious difficulties of analysis, but to three simple cases in which *all legitimation for the power structure was lacking at the outset*. His examples are a group of passengers on a ship who were

1. *The Marxian Revolutionary Idea* (New York, 1969), pp. 154-55.
2. These comments on Popitz' work are derived from the review, by Hans Peter Dreitzel, of *Prozesse der Machtbildung*, Reihe "Recht und Staat," no. 362-63 (Tübingen, 1968), in *Social Research*, XXXVI (Spring, 1969), 158-63. The actual work by Popitz was not available to the author. See also Joseph Lopreato, "Authority Relations and Class Conflict," *Social Forces*, XLVII, no. 1 (September, 1968), 70-79.

able to monopolize the only scarce resource, deck chairs, without challenge; four prisoners of war who built a camp stove, which enabled them to bring the entire camp under their authority; and the building of a power elite, complete with "police forces," at a probationary school for boys, based on control of the two pieces of bread each boy received in the morning. This brief statement does not do justice to the care with which Popitz chose his examples, or to the subtlety of his arguments. There would be little point in recapitulating the examples themselves. Readers who are interested can either read the original work or, as it is not available in translation, the review article by Hans Peter Dreitzel in *Social Research*. Only the main principles enunciated in Popitz' model will be outlined.

The majority, like the minority, is distinctive, and yet the numbers of the majority seem to carry little weight. If the relative strengths of minority and majority are compared, two things stand out starkly: (1) the superior chances of the privileged to organize quickly and effectively; and (2) their ability to legitimize their privileges before the unprivileged can develop a counter-ideology.

The privileged can organize more effectively because they have a clear common interest to defend. What is more, this interest is maintained by exchanges among privileged individuals. Individual and common interests are, therefore, congruent. The case of the unprivileged is more complicated. Unquestionably, it is in their interest to challenge the privileged, but to do so means thinking yet another step ahead: what will happen if we should succeed? The individual, called on to take risks, has no certainty that he personally will benefit by the change. The problem of distribution—of who will get what, when, where, and how—remains unresolved. Agreement on what is wrong is no guarantor of agreement on what would be right. The privileged, on the other hand, have solved the problem of distribution. If asked what new order would be better, they can simply answer "none." Thus, while the problem of distribution forces the unprivileged to concentrate on the next step but one, the step that would follow successful revolt, the privileged can concentrate on the next step alone. They can offer selected members of the unprivileged advantages of immediate effect

—premiums for loyalty and service, as well as opportunities for personal advancement. These advantages, and their own drawbacks, can be countered by the unprivileged, but the impulse to organize has to be *far stronger* than that of the privileged if they are even to attain equality of force. Mere resolution alone is not enough. Great willingness on the part of the individual to submerge himself to the common purpose and a plan for distributive justice that is generally acceptable are needed to bring the unprivileged to the *niveau* of the minority.

The minority rule not only because of vertical legitimation of the kind suggested by Max Weber, but also because of a horizontal legitimation among the elite. The elite, in other words, legitimize themselves. They are in power not only because they have solved the problem of distribution to their satisfaction, but also because they agree on the order which makes organization possible. This legitimation of the elite rests on their belief that the existing order is just, and on the spill-over effect of this belief on subjects. There is, in other words, a *basic legitimacy of the established order*. Once a certain ordering of things exists, even the unprivileged have something at stake: "It is only rarely true that they have nothing to lose but their chains." [3] If there is order and not mere arbitrariness even in exploitation, and if order is enforced by effective threats of violence, the unprivileged may well come to believe that what they are receiving from the political system is better than nothing at all—and nothing at all may be the result of revolt.

The relevance of the Popitz model is at once apparent in the South African case. Popitz writes: "The main problem for the rulers is at the beginning to avoid carefully anything which could affront the apathetic, individualistic majority, and at the same time to reduce this potentially dangerous group by appointing some of its members to the service class and stigmatizing others as outcasts." [4] The creation of a client elite of Africans, by coopting them through the system of "separate development" which offers them (relatively) well-paid jobs, is an example of the kind that Popitz no doubt had in mind. The presence of

3. Dreitzel, p. 162.
4. *Ibid.*, p. 161.

13,044 Africans in the South African police forces, together with 16,755 whites, is another case of this kind.[5] Much the same could be said of the arrival of the white settlers at the Cape, with historically conditioned organizational techniques that were superior to those of indigenous peoples, who were divided into warring tribes. It also brought about, both for whites and, to a lesser extent perhaps, for blacks, the notion of a general white superiority.

Lopreato's study ties in well with Popitz' findings. Lopreato sought to test empirically Dahrendorf's proposition that conflict between two "aggregates," in any association, rests on whether they are in superordinate or subordinate positions. Those in positions of authority will seek to maintain the status quo, argues Dahrendorf, while those without authority will seek to change it. Lopreato's findings would seem to indicate that more intense status conflict takes place within the authoritative group than between that group and those excluded from authority.[6] Such conflicts, extrapolating Lopreato's findings, if protracted, can spark the kind of "incapacitating crisis" of which Lenin wrote.

From Popitz, one can say that a given social and political system has inherent strength just because it is there and because it is working. From Lopreato, we can posit a tendency for conflict to arise among the group in authority which may be conducive to the kinds of crises that make revolution possible. Whether or not such a crisis takes place depends, it would seem, on whether the fissiparous pressures among the privileged can be contained in the face of a common interest or a common threat. This depends, in turn, on the perceptions of the interest or threat among the privileged. If they see the threat to their interests as real and imminent, the tendency to unite may be stronger than the tendency to faction. What of the ruled? Can they revolt successfully? Popitz is skeptical as far as overturning an established power is concerned. The possibility of change rests on overcoming the "organization gap" between the integrated minority, providing that it remains integrated, and the disintegrated or even mutually hostile majority

5. See Muriel Horrell, comp., *A Survey of Race Relations in South Africa, 1968* (Johannesburg, 1969), p. 109. The figures are those of 1968.
6. Lopreato, "Authority Relations and Class Conflict," p. 78.

groups.[7] The question remaining unanswered is the *form* of organization that would enable the unprivileged to bridge the organization gap. What is the best vehicle with which to resist and through which to learn the arts of resistance? This question, though related to the others, stands partly on its own.

The crisis of authority Lopreato has investigated exists not only among the elite of the privileged, but also among the counterelite, the elite of the unprivileged. One need only look at the internecine strife in the ANC for living examples. The challenges to the leadership of that body, from the Africanists on the right and from the Youth League on the left, coming at different times (see the Introduction), generated intense tensions. Tension was heightened from outside by the government, for it was in a position to "deauthorize" any leader by exposing the emptiness of his threats or promises.[8] By showing that an African leader was powerless to influence the course of events, it could, in effect, stir up challenges to his authority. Thus, in the first clash, the young men derided their elders, saying that they were "hoary with age and ashen grey with the snubs of [Nationalist ministers]." [9] Later, the Pan-Africanists accused the former Youth Leaguers, now at the helm of Congress, of being "Eastern functionaries" who had "sold out" the ANC to "Whites and Indians." [10]

The response of an older leadership intent on maintaining power is to routinize authority to the greatest possible extent, thus ensuring that the revolutionary movement will be organized on bureaucratic lines. Indeed, the difficulty of control is enhanced, as Leo Kuper points out, by the elevated status the leadership of the African majority enjoys among its own people, compared with its low status among whites, who, on the whole, discriminate not among Africans of different classes but against Africans as a whole.[11]

7. Dreitzel, p. 163.

8. Lewis Feuer, *The Conflict of Generations: The Character and Significance of Student Movements* (New York, 1969), pp. 150–54, 184.

9. *Inkundla ya Bantu*, December 10, 1949.

10. See Edward Feit, *South Africa: The Dynamics of the African National Congress* (London, 1962), pp. 15–18.

11. Leo Kuper, *An African Bourgeoisie: Race, Class, and Politics in South Africa* (New Haven, Conn., 1965), pp. 398–400.

The problem of control is intensified by the need for a revolutionary organization to produce results. In order to gain a following, a revolutionary organization has to make many promises; and these promises must soon be realized. If a leadership fails to achieve the results promised, its status is open to challenge. Campaigns launched with fanfare must at least partially achieve their objective. Where a government meets challenges with success and parries threatening political actions with counter actions, the revolutionary leadership is either deserted or displaced. Even if the leaders and their cadres survive, and these will shrink with failure, the support group will become harder and harder to mobilize with each succeeding campaign. Failure and factionalism feed on each other in a revolutionary organization. The more often the movement fails, the less likely it is to succeed in the future unless it is extraordinarily fortunate. The insurgent leaders under pressure will seek to retain control by imposing a bureaucratic pattern on the revolutionary organization, the protection of their own status being rationalized as protection of the revolution itself.

Lenin, in his *What Is to Be Done?*, conceived just such a pattern of party organization and met objections that such a party might easily be decapitated with the answer that it was easier for a dozen intelligent people to escape than "a hundred imbeciles." [12] The decapitation of *Umkonto* with the Rivonia raid and the subsequent arrest of the leading white Communists would seem to give lie to Lenin's idea. Although urban cells can succeed for a time through ingenuity or with the backing of a support group, their situation is at best precarious. It is difficult to carry on insurgent activity and at the same time to go about the business of living a relatively normal life.[13] The administrative and military system is, in any case, more closely coordinated and concentrated in urban areas than it is anywhere else, and attacks can easily be concentrated on one or another point. The life of the cells is, therefore, inclined to be short.

It is insufficient to attribute the tendency to bureaucratism entirely to the leaders, though theirs is the main initiative. The logic of the

12. *What Is to Be Done?* (New York, 1929), p. 116.
13. Roland Gaucher, *The Terrorists: From Tsarist Russia to the OAS* (London, 1965), p. 304.

revolutionary situation forces this on them in part. In his book on urban guerrillas, Martin Oppenheimer shows that, as revolution is a kind of war, revolutionary organization must have some military attributes. Yet the very attributes that are essentially antibureaucratic—quick decisions, rapid execution of orders, and minimization of lengthy discussion and debate—are essential to successful insurgency. He denies that the organization can be loose and without a clear-cut chain of command, although it is difficult to see how the necessary kinds of decisions, and their execution, could be achieved by bureaucratic command structures. Indeed, as has emerged from this study, these chains of command, whenever employed, worked badly; and in the end the initiative of individuals or of small groups accomplished whatever could be accomplished. More importantly, Oppenheimer raises the point that the need for secrecy and the fear of informers poison the atmosphere among the revolutionaries, who can never fully trust one another. As the police must be prevented from discovering the whole organization if any part is uncovered, a fractionalized form of organization is all the revolutionaries can permit themselves. As a result, those who feel comfortable in an atmosphere of this kind are hardly the kind to further a just and humane society.[14] It is to the credit of the members of the African underground that they did not fit well into this atmosphere, but this did facilitate the ease with which the police penetrated and eventually broke down the ANC and *Umkonto*.

The cadres on their side seek to escape bureaucratic control and to conduct operations on their own, partly because operating through "channels" is tantamount to not operating at all. The procedure is too cumbrous when quick action is called for in response to quick decisions, and in any case if too much is demanded it could not be implemented. Lenin was normally an ardent bureaucratizer; retaining control of his organization was an obsession with him. But even he called for an end to bureaucratism in the Russian revolution of 1905:

> Judging by the documents, the whole thing threatens to degenerate into office routine. All these schemes, all these plans of organization

14. Martin Oppenheimer, *The Urban Guerrilla* (Chicago, 1969), p. 69.

of the Combat Committee create the impression of red tape. . . . Schemes and disputes and discussions about the functions of the Combat Committee and its rights are of the least value in a matter like this. What is needed is furious energy, and again energy. . . . Otherwise . . . you will be too late and will be left with "learned" memoranda, plans, charts, schemes and magnificent recipes, but without an organization, without a living cause. . . . Form fighting squads *at once* everywhere. . . . Let groups be at once organized of three, ten, thirty, etc., persons. Let them arm themselves at once as best as they can, be it with a revolver, a knife, a rag soaked in kerosene for starting fires, etc. Let these detachments at once select leaders, and as far as possible *contact* the Combat Committee of the St. Petersburg Committee. *Do not demand any formalities*, and for heaven's sake, forget all these schemes, and send all functions, rights, and privileges to the devil. Do not make membership in the [party] an absolute condition—that would be an absurd demand for an armed uprising. Do not refuse to contact any group, even if it consists only of three persons; make it the sole condition that it should be reliable as far as police spying is concerned. . . . The principal thing in a matter like this is *the initiative of the mass of small groups*. They will do everything. Without them your entire Combat Committee is nothing.[15]

Later in the same month (October, 1905), he again inveighed against this same tendency:

It is, of course, desirable for combat groups to unite their activities. . . . Under no circumstances, however, should this be carried to the extreme of inventing complex plans and general schemes, or of postponing practical work for the sake of pedantic concoctions, etc. . . . All delays, disputes, procrastination and indecision spell ruin to the cause of the uprising.[16]

Why bureaucratic organization is not very useful in waging revolution has been discussed earlier. It was suggested that the reason may lie in that bureaucratic structures, being founded on predictable action, are

15. *Collected Works*, IX (Moscow, 1962), 344–45.
16. *Ibid.*, pp. 423–24.

unsuited to producing continuously unpredictable actions—the foundation of successful insurgency. Bureaucratic organizations tend to concentrate on readily achievable goals, on what does not require much innovation, and on what can be reduced to routine. Their ranked structures are, what is more, relatively easy to penetrate. The rise of Roman Malinowski to the Central Committee of the Bolsheviks in the early 1900s and of Gerard Ludi in the Communist Party of South Africa shows that this is not as difficult a task as would appear, though there is risk for the agent. The effectiveness of a revolutionary organization depends not on its complexity, which often exists only on paper, but on its ability to strike unanticipated blows. These blows must either cause great damage or, if the damage is small, have great symbolic impact. Not only must the actions be unanticipated by the opponent, but the results of the action must be anticipated by the leaders. They must rally and avoid antagonizing the actual and potential support group. To cite an example, the East London riots of 1952 certainly were sensational. They did not, however, rally Africans behind the African National Congress. The reverse was true, for people left in large numbers.

Besides a natural desire to retain authority by making it routine, the bureaucratic tendency can also be ascribed to the view leaderships have of the future. Leaderships whose view of the future is based largely on abstract principles will be more likely to adopt bureaucratic forms. The reason for this is, perhaps, the influence present events are perceived to have on the future. An intense conflict with groups whom it may be necessary to reconcile tomorrow would be harmful; hence, present actions must be predicated on the desired future shape of the society. If, on the other hand, a regime is oriented to maintaining the present, the status quo, it can act with greater freedom and less circumspection. The ANC, in other words, committed to the idea of a multiracial socialist society, was reluctant to take steps which, by their violence, might endanger the dream. The government, on the other hand, envisioning continued repression of the Africans, could act efficiently against them. The ANC had to think of the next step but one; the government, of the next step only. This had, perhaps, influenced the ANC in its emphasis on nonviolent campaigns, its reluctance to turn to violence, and then its insistence that violence, when employed, was not to endanger life. The hotheads who were to realize the insurrectionary acts were not necessarily imbued with the same goals. Hence, bureaucratic command and structure tended to break apart.

The Communist Party, because of its character and the discipline to which its members were subject, went through a less public conflict. The struggle between those pressing for violence and those who wished to maintain non-violence was more muted. The latter, those favoring non-violence, or rather limited violence, seem to have won out initially. Nevertheless, those of the Party active in *Umkonto* leaned more and more to violence. The stages of this process are set out by Lerumo. When the Party was declared illegal in 1950, its cadres were in a quandary. Since the Party had been lawful both before and during the war, security precautions had been allowed to lapse. As A. Lerumo writes, "Practically every member was known to the public—and hence to the police—and large numbers of new members had joined who were unequipped, mentally and practically, to face the rigors and dangers of underground work." More significantly, Lerumo points out that "legalistic illusions" had gripped the Party leaders, influencing them to rely on permitted ways of working, on fighting repression through the courts and "neglecting revolutionary vigilance and determination." Faced with all these difficulties, the decision to dissolve the Party was taken, which, Lerumo says, should not be seen in isolation "but as the culmination of a series of legalistic errors." [17] The Party was no more effective underground, except for those who joined *Umkonto* and who either trained the sabotage teams or who participated directly in sabotage.

"In all cases," Gaucher states, "terrorism betrays weakness." It "is the arm of a small minority [of the majority] that has scanty resources, and in fact wages a poor man's war. In spite of the terrorists' exploits and however great their courage and ingenuity, the chances are that their groups will eventually be wiped out, unless political, economic, or diplomatic circumstances enable them to play on a world stage and

17. A. Lerumo [pseud.], "After 40 Years an Important Anniversary for Africa," *African Communist*, no. 7 (September, 1961), 77–78.

pass on to other forms of combat." [18] Terrorism was forced on the ANC, its leaders claimed, by the intransigence of the government. It was used because there was nothing else to do, because "the forces of the disaffected were so weak that they had no choice." [19] It was at the same time an attempt to reauthorize the ANC and with it the Communist Party. The authority of the ANC had been deflated among Africans, as one nonviolent campaign after another failed. Far from leading to alleviation of oppressive laws, the campaigns led to their intensification and the closing of the few loopholes open to Africans. By turning to violence, the leaders of the ANC may have hoped to reestablish the ANC as the leading African political organization, in response to the challenge of the Pan-Africanist Congress and its militant wing POQO. This did not happen. The ANC failed in its campaign of militancy, though the last word had not been said or the last action taken in 1964. Why was this? Why did the ANC fail in waging the "poor man's war"?

African revolutionaries, in the first place, were reluctant to engage in civil war. As Nelson Mandela said:

> We viewed the situation with alarm. Civil war could mean the destruction of what the ANC stood for; with civil war, racial peace would be more difficult than ever to achieve. . . . It has taken more than fifty years for the scars of the South African War to disappear. How much longer would it take to eradicate the scars of an inter-racial civil war, which could not be fought without a great loss of life on both sides.[20]

The ANC, in addition, did not really do much to "deauthorize" the white group—to challenge their authority and to tear it down. Such "deauthorization" might have been accomplished by the systematic humiliation of whites, or by attacking white values per se. As an instance of what is meant, the Congo comes to mind. The attacks on and humiliation of whites there were accomplished (however un-

18. Gaucher, *The Terrorists*, p. 303.
19. *Ibid.*
20. *No Easy Walk to Freedom*, ed. Ruth First (New York, 1965), p. 170. The African War referred to is the Boer War, which ended in 1902.

consciously) to destroy white authority in the most effective way, by demonstration. The ANC was against such attacks or demonstrations and, given their partnership with white Communists, this is fully understandable. Less understandable is their continuous appeal to the government, as the source of authority, to grant them their wishes. It was the government to whom they looked for cessions of rights and for the calling of "national conventions."

Fear of violence may have had other roots. Here Gaucher poses the significant questions. When the revolutionists, whose means cannot match the government's, try to answer terror with terror—or, in this case, attack with attack—will they frighten the government or merely provoke it to anger, engendering counterviolence, increased repression, and finally the collapse of the terrorist group? [21] Considerations such as these conditioned *Umkonto* action at all levels.

Another explanation can be suggested in the case of the white leadership of the Communist Party. Many were men and women of superior intellectual attainment. Yet they made one error after another, many quite foolish and obvious. They bought the house "Travallyn" as a secret munitions factory—and then did not maintain payments on it. As a result, when the owner and his son inspected the premises, they found a hoard of documents and other suspicious articles and called the police.[22] Another such contretemps is the arrival, in a car crammed with documents, of the supposed "tenant" of "Lilliesleaf," the Rivonia headquarters, just as a police raid was in full swing. Why were errors such as these made? There can obviously be no final answers. One that can be suggested is an unconscious "will to fail." The white Communists were, on the one hand, dedicated to the Party and to the notion of racial equality. The risks they took and the sacrifices they made attest to this. On the other hand, they were whites and doubtless felt a strong and unconscious identification with their own people. The clash of loyalties and beliefs could be reconciled by acting out the roles of fighters for African liberation, while seeing to it that this struggle always came to nought. Let it be once again stressed that

21. Gaucher, *The Terrorists*, p. 299.
22. H. H. W. de Villiers, *Rivonia: Operation Mayebuye* (Johannesburg, 1964), p. 9.

this is a purely theoretical proposition and is advanced only as a suggested possible explanation.[23] There is a hint of this in an APDUSA (African People's Democratic Union of South Africa) publication. APDUSA was admittedly hostile to the ANC, but there is some perception in the excerpt below that merits attention:

> The kernel of our criticism is that the Whites who constituted the leadership of the Communist Party were liberals to the core. They lived with liberals, moved about in liberal circles and acquired their habits and attitudes of thought. In short these so-called communists had their roots embedded in the White liberal world, with all that that connotes in the South African milieu, that home of fanatical racism where Blacks and Whites are divided into two worlds bridged only by a lily-livered condescending liberalism. We have always said: "The Communist Party of South Africa is the only Communist Party in the world that never had a single communist as a member." We must however add that there was one exception, the late S. P. Bunting who broke completely with the White world in the early thirties. For this he paid with his life. He was hounded out of the Communist Party of South Africa and died a pauper deserted by his fellow travellers.[24]

The publication from which this is drawn stresses that it does not oppose the Communist Party for having a white leadership but for professing a radicalism that it really does not feel.

There is another explanation that can be briefly considered, once again without proof. It is quite common for Communists to deliver members of the Party who either have become known or who are of doubtful loyalty into the hands of the police. Cases have been known where the old leadership, often with its own consent, has been "captured" by the police through clues supplied by the Party. The arrested, when caught, are weighed down with evidence of guilt. Capture of such a leadership serves to put the authorities off guard

23. For an example of the psychology of conflicting beliefs and their reconciliation in an individual, see Leon Festinger, A *Theory of Cognitive Dissonance* (Stanford, 1957).

24. "The Conspiracy Against the O.A.U. and Nationalist Movements," *We Build a Nation*, Vol. XI, no. 10 (March–April, 1967).

while a new, unknown leadership takes over. The blatant errors committed at the time of the Rivonia arrests might, therefore, be a case of this sort. The leaders captured at Rivonia were all known to the police, and their mobility and usefulness were restricted. Their capture might have been designed, therefore, to take the pressure off others who could function more effectively. This is, of course, pure conjecture.

Another suspicious point can be raised with the same caveats. It can not, however, be raised without some background information on the men involved and the incidents of which they were part.

On July 12, 1963, Arthur Goldreich, Harold Wolpe, A. Jassat, and Mosie Moolla escaped from a police cell in Johannesburg. Of these, Goldreich and Wolpe were considered the prime catches of the Rivonia raid. Goldreich was the lessee of "Lilliesleaf"—the site of the *Umkonto* High Command. He was allegedly the author of *Operation Mayebuye*, and some fifteen documents in what was purported to be his handwriting were found in his car and on the farm. It was also alleged that lengths of aluminum piping, of the sort used to make pipe bombs, were found in his car. He had, according to evidence of servants, been seen helping the various members of the High Command in their tasks. Harold Wolpe, it was alleged, had manipulated the trust funds of the law firm in which he was a junior partner to receive and disburse monies from abroad on behalf of *Umkonto*. The Indians were lesser fry, except that Moolla had been secretary of the Transvaal Indian Youth Congress.[25]

Their escape seems to have been effected with remarkable ease considering their importance as prisoners. A nineteen-year-old warder was offered a bribe, the greater part of which would be paid to him afterwards by a third party. Being in financial trouble, according to later evidence, he accepted. The prisoners obtained his keys in a faked attack and tied him up to lend support to the story that he had been knocked out by Goldreich. When the warder was brought to trial, his demeanor was hardly that of a man charged with serious dereliction of duty and betrayal of his people's trust. It was, if anything, quite jaunty and relaxed.[26] Now it is inconceivable that the police would have "blown

25. De Villiers, *Rivonia*, chap. 2.
26. *World*, September 23–24, 1963.

the cover" of Gerard Ludi (a young police undercover agent who penetrated the Communist Party) without having another man, or men, concealed within the ANC–CP–*Umkonto* network. It is feasible that one man among the four was such an agent, and that the entire escape was engineered between this man and the police. If this is an accurate reconstruction, the warder was in on the game, which would account for his attitude at his trial—the attitude of a man who was *not* about to serve a prison sentence. Again, it must be stressed that this is speculation, though the circumstances seem strange, to say the least.

What can be said of the revolutionary leadership? The leaders of the ANC or the CP were essentially cautious men, conservative in their planning and disinclined to rash action. If there was pressure for violence, it could come only from below. Yet, despite a sentiment for violence among the lower ranks, few were really fanatical. This emerges in the evidence given by those involved in sabotage, part of which has been mentioned earlier. Leaders and followers mirrored each other faithfully. The followers may have wanted somewhat more violence than their leaders, but neither seems to have wanted too much. Saboteurs, in any case, apparently sought to tackle projects involving the least risk of capture. The really suicidal urge, found in the Russian revolutionary movements, seems to have been absent.

II

What impact does insurgency have on the ruling groups? Do they become more or less cohesive under such pressure? In the South African case, as Newell Stultz has written in a recent article, the effect of the African threat has been to cement the otherwise divided elements of white society. He points out that the South African government needs less to create than to protect, and that the latter is a much easier task. He also states that the material success of the regime, particularly in the field of economics, has not weakened ideological support for it.

In the context of domestic and international threats against white South Africa, security is not a terminal condition that, once achieved, can be forgotten. Security is, rather, an ongoing need. The enemy . . . can be thwarted but not defeated . . . most South African whites, despite their comforts, view the future with apprehension and uncertainty. Few are vulnerable to growing complacency or cynicism regarding the security-oriented values of the regime.[27]

A survey conducted for the newspaper *Natal Mercury* by Market Research Africa bears out this defense-mindedness.[28] Of the sample, 60 per cent said that they saw terrorists as a "real threat," and about 30 per cent said that they saw them as "some threat." Only about 6 per cent felt that they were "no threat at all," and 4 per cent stated that they did not know. (The percentages have been rounded out here for convenience.) It is significant that a far higher proportion of Afrikaners saw terrorists as a threat than did English-speakers, the figures being 70 per cent and 48 per cent, respectively. Significantly, people in the country felt the terrorists as more of a threat, which is logical, as peasant revolts are more persistent and dangerous.[29] In any event, no slackening of white vigilance and white cohesion seems likely under these conditions, no matter what internal grievances different white groups may have against one another.[30]

Why did the ANC and *Umkonto* have so little success in mobilizing Africans? Why did their target population not feel itself threatened? The argument derived from Popitz has already been set forth above. It can be extended in the light of the South African situation. Although there is a growing number of permanent African town-dwellers in South Africa, much of the population of the towns is temporarily recruited from the countryside. Many Africans are only partly men of the cities and towns. This, it can be argued, is true even in cases where no permanent return to the countryside is foreseen. Such an attitude is, of course, encouraged by the government, which segregates Africans

27. Newell M. Stultz, "The Politics of Security: South Africa Under Verwoerd," *Journal of Modern African Studies*, VII, no. 1 (April, 1969), 19.
28. *Natal Mercury*, January 27, 1969.
29. See, for instance, Oppenheimer, *The Urban Guerrilla*, chap. 2.
30. See Stultz, "The Politics of Security"; and Edwin S. Munger, "New White Politics in South Africa," in *Southern Africa and the United States*, ed. William A. Hance et al. (New York, 1968), pp. 33–84.

tribally even in the townships, and by the traditional African authorities, whose interests it serves. As Oppenheimer argues, peasants are fundamentally conservative and even reactionary as long as life is at all livable.[31] They tend to see their culture as being of one fabric, and no part can be changed without changing it all. They are distrustful of reformers and suspicious of those who promise them amelioration. As a result, revolutions are quite difficult to foment in South Africa despite the manifest and real grievances of most Africans. The stability of South African society and the slow change for the better in economic terms, even for Africans, have reinforced this conservatism, as has the power of the police. The failure of the illegal ANC to grow from its initial cells indicates this.

To the conservatism of the target population must be added the difficulty of doing serious damage with small groups of saboteurs. While it is possible for saboteurs of great determination to sometimes damage, or even destroy, some fundamental structures, sabotage is mostly directed to targets readily reached. As the South African government guarded the major installations well, the damage that could be done was, on the whole, minor and not likely to either shake the white population or bring the economy crashing down around its ears. In an industrialized society, minor damage can be readily repaired, and its effects are only marginally felt. A normal or stable social order, Oppenheimer writes, must be significantly disrupted before masses of people will engage in collective behavior, particularly a social movement.[32] Such disruption was not evident in South Africa.

The destruction of the insurgent organization required a high degree of control, not only of Africans but also of the white population. In addition, information had to be gained on Communists in the country and on leaders of the ANC, where these did not in any way overlap. As Gaucher puts it, the "bedrock on which any police system is founded is its records." [33] The South African police had been building its records on communism since the strike of 1922. Describing the record room of the "Grays," the building that houses the Special Branch, the *Rand*

31. Oppenheimer, *The Urban Guerrilla*, p. 47.
32. *Ibid.*, p. 23.
33. Gaucher, *The Terrorists*, p. 35.

Daily Mail reported on September 9, 1964, that "in a strongroom are hundreds of files of known and unknown Communists—many detailed biographies of subversion and intrigue. There are files on the living and the dead and top secret reports on many people, some probably unaware of the police interest in them and their activities."

This information, to which more is continually added, is supplemented by the information given both by informers and by former members of subversive organizations who decided to confess and avoid heavy prison sentences. Not much is known of the methods by which such information is obtained. Accused persons and prisoners have from time to time complained of police maltreatment, and, where these acts have been proved, the officers in question were brought to court and in most cases punished. Generally, it would seem that the Special Branch relied on more subtle, psychological methods of interrogation. The main aim was to isolate the prisoner by putting him in solitary confinement and then to subject him to infrequent interrogations. The effect of ninety days' detention, which could be renewed indefinitely, was sometimes shattering. Gaucher puts the case of the detained vividly:

> Arrest, prison, and deportation were hard trials which either strengthened or weakened a man's character. He was alone. His ties with the outside world had been either severed or stretched to the breaking point. He was in the power of the enemy; he could taste the bitterness of defeat. If the company of fellow prisoners offered an opportunity to renew common interests and to continue the fight, it also led to bitter quarrels in which souls were laid bare and in which corruption could begin. The police knew all this. They knew that time worked in their favor, that threats were sometimes effective, that the hope of freedom was tempting and the fear of death a trump up their sleeves.[34]

This also emerges in the evidence of Sylvia Neame in the Fischer Trial. She said that she had been detained under the ninety-day law and was released after forty-five days. She was held incommunicado with only a Bible to read. She went on to state,

34. *Ibid.*, p. 38.

I was held in a cell six paces by four paces, with an hour out a day. Except for weekly interrogations which lasted from one to two hours, I had no other contact whatever during my period of detention. Food was brought by wardresses who refused to talk at all. During these periods of prolonged solitude I was completely battered emotionally. I developed an intense feeling of being cut off. I no longer belonged. . . . When I was released after forty-five days I could not adjust myself to a strange environment of people, faces, and places. I mistrusted everybody, recoiled from all human contact.[35]

On the other hand, Cyril Davids, the man who told of the Mamre camp, adjusted to the ninety-day detention somewhat better. He said that he did not mind the first three months too much, but the second promised him was just too much. He was bored by the inactivity, and began to feel that even a long jail sentence would be better.[36] He also said that the interrogators would begin courteously but would get "sore" when he refused to answer their questions. They would often inform prisoners that it was useless to deny what the police already knew, and would confront them with evidence that indicated others had talked. They would often hint that the prisoner's own comrades had already volunteered the required information. Cut off from others, the prisoner would frequently confess, and his confession in turn would be used against others. In this way a formidable body of evidence, and indeed information, would be built.

The gathering of information on the ANC, the CP, and later *Umkonto* was made easier by the fact that the former two had operated legally for a long time, and everyone connected with them had become known to the police. The ANC did not begin its life as an insurgent organization but as one attempting to open a dialogue with the government of the time. After that, it operated by attempting to exert nonviolent but extralegal pressure. There was then, and later, little opportunity to check the credentials and bona fides of members seeking to join. It was, therefore, an easy matter for the police to penetrate it

35. *Star*, March 1, 1965.
36. Davids/R*vtr*, pp. BB3–4; *Star*, December 19, 1963.

and to seed it with their own agents. Given the power of the government to ban people, to prevent them from taking part in politics, and to rusticate them to remote parts of the country, members of the police could even rise to high rank in the ANC. The turn to secrecy did not much hinder the police, for the leaders of the ANC and *Umkonto* still could not tell who really was with them, and this still further lessened the effectiveness of the Spear of the Nation—*Umkonto we Sizwe*. The result was that, assured of information, it took the police little more than a year to crack the underground and to arrest its leaders at their headquarters.

III

When revolutionary theorists discuss the dynamics of failure, they usually think of failure in terms of the failure of the government. However, revolutionary situations in which leadership can bring about the downfall of an established government are rare. The dynamic can then be said to work in the opposite direction: once an insurgency begins to fail, it goes from failure to failure. The very pattern of the insurgency is determined by the forces aligned against it. The cell structure, hard to control and harder to organize, is forced on the insurgents by police vigilance. The cellular structure has advantages, true, or it would not be so widely used. It prevents the extirpation of the organization in one sweep, as the cells must be routed out a few at a time. But it also means that only a series of small-scale actions can be achieved, unless the cells are unusually favored by fortune. This in turn means that the level of disorder that can be generated is small, and the system remains largely unshaken. Pockets of trouble may develop, as happened in Port Elizabeth in 1962, but if the government is determined on suppression *à l'outrance* these can be quickly snuffed out. It is, in other words, extremely difficult to concert the actions of many cells through a national headquarters, if it is possible at all. The central headquarters may issue orders, but these orders will be carried out, if they are carried out, by the cells largely as they please. The ability to create disorder thus tends to be continually hampered.

That the aim was to maximize disorder in South Africa was generally understood by the leaders of *Umkonto*. Even their first manifesto drew attention to the vulnerability of South Africa's communication net. What they overlooked was that the need of the government was not so much to prevent *all* disorder as to prevent only *serious* disorder. Once sabotage became a threat, laws were passed declaring certain strategic installations "protected areas," and a countrywide survey was made of all installations—public and private—that qualified for this description. The installations selected included gasoline storage depots, power stations, dams, and other places important to the economy of the country. These were subjected to strict security regulations, and only authorized personnel were allowed to enter them. The regulations imposed were, in fact, as strict as those imposed during a war. Any unauthorized person found on the premises was subject to imprisonment of up to fifteen years, and owners of such places who did not provide the requisite protection, at their own cost, might find the state installing the protective devices and billing them.[37]

Steps such as these further limited the effectiveness of *Umkonto* and made it impossible for the insurgents to do enough to restructure reality for either blacks or whites. They were not able to make the government seem incapable of maintaining order; on the contrary, the obvious capability of the government to do just that served to weaken the insurgents. Even the sabotage did not have the anticipated effect; for it was never fully reported in the press, partly because of censorship, often self-imposed, and partly because the attacks themselves often were not important enough to be newsworthy. The bigger things got reported, but bigger things were not often achieved. This author, who was living in the country at the time, can say that most whites were hardly aware that there was a sabotage campaign going on and would have been greatly surprised had they realized that over 200 acts of sabotage had been performed. Even if allowance is made for the more spectacular of their actions, in no sense can *Umkonto* be described as an unexampled success. Its actions did little to hearten Africans, to dishearten whites, or to sway the government from its course.

37. *Star*, February 3, 1964.

Umkonto, like so many other organizations of revolt, was significant less for what it did or did not do than for what, unchecked, it might have become. What it might be was the vision of *Operation Mayebuye* and, earlier, of the M-Plan. This did not come about, for reasons which have been enumerated and discussed. The organization failed to capture a substantial support group; the closest it came was in Port Elizabeth, but even there support was not sustained. The organization failed to grow substantially there as elsewhere. The ANC had come back to life in 1960 through the spontaneous efforts of men who were not arrested and who were determined to see the ANC continue. An attempt was made to organize the movement along the lines of the M-Plan, which was to link cells, branches, regions, and the national headquarters. There was little difficulty in setting up the cells, and membership remained constant on the whole. The turn to violence was then taken by degrees; first, the cells were told that violence in defense of their meetings was authorized; and a year later *Umkonto* was established. In this time the middle bodies, the regional committees, tended to fade away. Their members began to operate in the cells, and the cells were directly united, in effect, with the central body. The regional committees met hardly at all and were not very effectual when they did meet. In *Umkonto* the regional committee—in effect, the regional command—became synonymous with the membership. Contact with the national headquarters was maintained though orders were frequently not carried out, or were carried out as the cells wished. The actual officers involved were the contact and the volunteer-in-chief, who became the most important men in the organization. As a result, the national headquarters gave orders directly to the cells, and the cells carried them out as they could or as they pleased. The organization was loose; it could not have been otherwise.

Yet, what was achieved was remarkable, given the resources massed against the ANC, the CP, and *Umkonto*, even when allowance is made for their overseas help. Pulling the organization together after the Emergency of 1960, setting up the cells, organizing the underground railway, and arranging the commission of acts of sabotage was, from the viewpoint of the sabotage groups, no mean feat. They were, however, ranged against determined opponents who had the skill and the

323

force at their disposal to render all these efforts of the insurgents nugatory.

What has worked well for the South African administrative forces in suppressing the insurgents might not work as well for others. First of all, in South Africa, the enemy was clearly identifiable by the color of his skin. The allies of Africans could also be easily isolated, because few whites made a practice of associating with Africans, and those who did were often radicals. This situation was in a sense unique. The enemy not only was easily identifiable, but the "political class" drawn from the elite who wished to lead the enemy could also be easily identified. Other countries under insurgent attack might not have so easy an identification problem. In addition, the South African government was able both to capitalize on and to harness the errors of its opponents. It harnessed them as a means of maintaining white rule, as Newell Stultz pointed out in the article cited earlier. It capitalized on them by learning from them. Thus the government was able to pass laws and to close security loopholes that were found to exist.

This is, however, no more than a partial explanation. It is certainly true that efficient administration, especially an effective police force, backed by legislators, is a *sine qua non* in the suppression of insurgency. But one must look beyond this to understand the strength of the forces of white South Africa. The South African government was able to act against the incipient insurgency because, whatever other issues divided white South Africa, there was one issue on which they were all united: white rule. This has enabled the government to build a defensive system, restricting the freedom of whites as well as blacks (though not proportionately), and still to maintain economic progress. The spill-over of this progress, which is improving the lot of Africans in the towns, has dampened revolutionary ardor. South Africa has, in the process of defense, become a police state. All freedom is restricted, and the lines between what can lawfully be done and what cannot be done are drawn increasingly tighter. What cannot be done is growing and what can be done is shrinking. Is the strain of defense worth the economic benefit? White South Africans have made their choice. Only time can tell if the choice was the right one.

Appendix I

Record of Acts of Sabotage

Serial No.	Object and Place of Commission of Act	Date	Time	Description of Act
1.	Public post box, central, Cape Town	8/9–10/61	Night	Burning cigarette, to which live matches were attached, placed in post box.
2.	Public post box, central, Cape Town	8/9–10/61	Night	Burning cigarette, to which live matches were attached, placed in post box.
3.	Public post box, central, Cape Town	8/9–10/61	Night	Burning cigarette, to which live matches were attached, placed in post box.
4.	Main line telephone cables near Springs	10/2–8/61	11.00 P.M.	2 cables sawn off with hacksaw against pole—4 wires cut. Cost of repairs: R299.37
5.	Telephone cables between Johannesburg and Krugersdorp	10/7–8/61	Night	Telephone cables cut off underground. Cost of repairs: R20

Taken from the record introduced in the Supreme Court of South Africa (Transvaal Provincial Division) as Annexure A to indictment. The difficulties of deciphering the poor typing of the court records may have resulted in some minor errors.

Serial No.	Object and Place of Commission of Act	Date	Time	Description of Act
6.	Telephone wires a mile outside Alberton on the road to Heidelberg	10/8/61	Night	20 telephone wires cut. Cost of repairs: R183.27
7.	Pylon at Jukskei-river, Lombardy East, Johannesburg	10/8/61	9.15 P.M.	2 outside legs of corner tower sawn off —tower toppled over. Cost of repairs: R8,000
8.	Telephone cable, Meredale, Johannesburg	10/8–9/61	Night	Telephone cable sawn off against pole. Cost of repairs: R4
9.	Telephone cable in inspection pit between Leeukop and Johannesburg	10/9/61	Night	Dynamite placed in inspection hole and cables shot off. Cost of repairs: R50
10.	Telephone wires about 25 miles from Port Elizabeth on the road to Grahamstown	10/12/61	12.30 A.M.	7 pairs of wires between two poles cut.
11.	Telephone cable near Dept. of Bantu Administration Offices at Pietermaritzburg	10/26–27/61	Night	Telephone cable severed with an axe.
12.	Wooden electric light poles, corner of van der Linde and Smith Sts., Bedfordview	11/16–17/61	Night	2 poles sawn off. Cost of repairs: R40
13.	Municipal Bantu Administration Offices, Ordnance Rd., Durban	12/15/61	9.15 P.M.	Explosion, plastic holder with blue-grey powder packed against office door.
14.	Electric substation, Framesly, Port Elizabeth	12/16/61	9.15 P.M.	Chemical bomb exploded, damaging electric substation. Cost of repairs: R100

Serial No.	Object and Place of Commission of Act	Date	Time	Description of Act
15.	Electric sub-station, Brick-makerskloof, Port Elizabeth	12/16/61	9.15 P.M.	Chemical bomb ex-ploded, damaging substation. Cost of repairs: R50
16.	Bantu Labour Of-fice, New Brighton, Port Elizabeth	12/16/61	9.15 P.M.	Chemical bomb ex-ploded. Cost of repairs: R15
17.	Bantu Adminis-tration Offices, New Brighton, Port Elizabeth	12/16/61	9.15 P.M.	Chemical bomb ex-ploded. Cost of repairs: R200
18.	Bantu School Board Offices, New Brighton, Port Elizabeth	12/16/61	9.15 P.M.	Chemical bomb ex-ploded. Cost of repairs: R10
19.	Municipal Bantu Control Office, Dube, Johan-nesburg	12/16/61	9.20 P.M.	Chemical bomb ex-ploded. One Afri-can male killed and another injured.
20.	Central Rd. Post Office, Fords-burg, Johannes-burg	12/16/61	10.12 P.M.	Homemade bomb ex-ploded, shattering doors and damag-ing windows. Cost of repairs: R375
21.	Office of the Por-tuguese Cura-tor, Market St., Johannesburg	12/16–17/61	Night	Incendiary bomb thrown into post box of office.
22.	Phirima Post Of-fice, Orlando West, Johan-nesburg	12/16–17/61	Night	Chemical bomb placed inside.
23.	Peri Urban Dis-trict Office, Kliptown	12/16–17/61	Night	Dynamite explosion. Cost of repairs: R16
24.	Bantu Affairs Of-fices, Carr St., Fordsburg, Johannesburg	12/17/61	2.15 A.M.	Chemical bomb ex-ploded, damaging doors and walls. Cost of repairs: R383
25.	Bantu Adminis-tration Offices, Market St., Ferreirastown, Johannesburg	12/17/61	2.20 A.M.	Chemical bomb ex-ploded, damaging doors and windows. Cost of repairs: R415
26.	Bantu Affairs Commis-sioner's Office, Engcobo	12/17/61	9.00 P.M.	Petrol poured over floor from a red plastic container.

Serial No.	Object and Place of Commission of Act	Date	Time	Description of Act
27.	Rissik St. Post Office Bldg., Johannesburg	12/17/61	Night	Chemical bomb placed inside.
28.	Superintendent's Office, Zone 3, Meadowlands	12/18/61	Night	Dynamite explosion.
29.	Two electric pylons, Lombardy East, near Edenvale Hospital	12/20/61	10.50 P.M.	2 legs of each of 2 electric pylons damaged by dynamite explosion. Homemade electric starters used.
30.	City Hall, Cape Town	1/8/62	11.45 P.M.	2 petrol bombs placed in storeroom beneath stage. Cost of repairs: R45
31.	Private storeroom near New Brighton, Port Elizabeth	1/16–17/62	Night	Homemade bomb placed against door of storeroom. Explosion damaged door and walls. Cost of repairs: R3
32.	Transformer station on premises of Roads Dept. near New Brighton, Port Elizabeth	1/24/62	9.30 P.M.	Roofing torn apart by explosion of chemical bomb. Cost of repairs: R6
33.	Caledon Post Office, Cape Town	2/3–4/62	Night	Burning cigarette, together with live matches, placed in post box. Cost of repairs: R3
34.	Telephone booth in Donkin St., Port Elizabeth	2/7/62	8.00 P.M.	Chemical bomb placed in booth. Door torn apart and roofing cracked by explosion. Cost of repairs: R50
35.	Rissik St. Post Office Bldg., Johannesburg	2/7–19/62	—	Chemical bomb placed inside drawer of desk of Commissioner.
36.	Telephone wires, Kwazakele Location, Port Elizabeth	3/10/62	9.00 P.M.	30 telephone wires cut. Cost of repairs: R200

Serial No.	Object and Place of Commission of Act	Date	Time	Description of Act
37.	Railway telephone wires, New Brighton, Port Elizabeth	3/10/62	Night	19 telephone wires cut. Cost of repairs: R100
38.	Riots—Langa Location, Cape Town	3/10/62	11.00 P.M.	Police vehicle bombarded with petrol bombs, overturned and set alight. One Bantu constable killed and others wounded. Cost of repairs: R912
39.	Roeland St. Gaol, Cape Town	4/15/62	10.00 P.M.	Homemade bomb placed against gaol door. Perpetrator caught in the act.
40.	Bantu Commissioner's Office, Evaton	7/7–8/62	Night	Homemade time bomb placed under hand basin in office. Bomb found before explosion.
41.	African dwelling, 404 Mtyeku St., Duncan Village, East London	7/15/62	Night	Petrol bomb thrown through window.
42.	Post box, Mill St., Cape Town	7/20/62	11.00 P.M.	Burning cigarette and live matches placed in post box. Cost of repairs: R1
43.	Post box, corner of Darling and Adderley Sts., Cape Town	7/20/62	11.30 P.M.	Burning cigarette, together with live matches, placed in post box. Cost of repairs: R6
44.	Wilberforce Post Office, Evaton, Vereeniging	8/12/62	Midnight	Dynamite placed in Post Office. All windows shattered, holes ripped in floor and ceiling. Cost of repairs: R500
45.	Electric pylon approximately 2 miles from Putfontein Police Station, Benoni District	8/26/62	1.00 A.M.	Loaded blasting cartridges, 12–15 ins. underground, placed at outer legs of corner tower with electric starter (watch type). One blast exploded. Cost of repairs: R5000

APPENDIX I

Serial No.	Object and Place of Commission of Act	Date	Time	Description of Act
46.	Office of Bantu Resettlement Board, Orlando East, Johannesburg	9/2–3/62	—	Dynamite explosion, damaging window and wall. Cost of repairs: R90
47.	Dwelling of African Sergeant, New Brighton, Port Elizabeth	9/18/62	9.45 P.M.	Incendiary bomb thrown into dwelling. Cost of repairs: R16
48.	Beer hall, Kwazakele Location, Port Elizabeth	9/19/62	2.00– 3.00 A.M.	Paraffin thrown against door and set alight. Cost of repairs: R1
49.	Beer hall, New Brighton, Port Elizabeth	9/20/62	8.00 P.M.	Paraffin poured against door and set alight. Cost of repairs: R1
50.	Bantu Single Quarters, S.A.P., New Brighton, Port Elizabeth	9/22/62	10.40 P.M.	A bottle bomb thrown into single quarters. Cost of repairs: R5
51.	Bantu Administration Offices, Duncan Village, East London	9/23/62	4.30 P.M.	Inflammable bottle bomb left in offices. Cost of repairs: R20
52.	Bethelsdorp, Port Elizabeth	9/23/62	8.30 P.M.	Stone crushers' explosive arsenal forced open and percussion caps stolen. 2 telephone wires cut. Cost of repairs: R17
53.	Telephone wires, Kwazakele Location, Port Elizabeth	9/23/62	9.30 P.M.	4 telephone wires cut. Cost of repairs: R10
54.	Factory at Korsten	9/24/62	1.00 A.M.	Incendiary bomb thrown through window. Cost of repairs: R1
55.	Wool store at New Brighton	9/24/62	1.50 A.M.	Window broken, petrol poured on floor and wool and then set alight. Cost of repairs: R4097

Serial No.	Object and Place of Commission of Act	Date	Time	Description of Act
56.	African shop, New Brighton, Port Elizabeth	9/24/62	8.45 P.M.	Petrol poured against walls and set alight. Cost of repairs: R400
57.	Bantu School Board Offices, Port Elizabeth	9/24/62	12.00 P.M.	Incendiary bomb used.
58.	Dwelling of delegate of Chief Matanzima, Langa, Cape Town	9/25/62	10.10 P.M.	Incendiary bomb thrown through window. Cost of repairs: R60
59.	African dwelling, New Brighton, Port Elizabeth	9/25/62	Midnight	Incendiary bomb used. Cost of repairs: R1
60.	African dwelling, member of Advisory Board, New Brighton, Port Elizabeth	9/25/62	Midnight	Incendiary bomb used. Cost of repairs: R1
61.	Dwelling of African Sergeant Gazo, New Brighton, Port Elizabeth	9/25/62	12.00 P.M.	Bottle bomb used. Cost of repairs: R1.50
62.	Railways, Port Elizabeth	9/25–26/62	Night	38 telephone wires cut. Cost of repairs: R444
63.	The firm of "Boxes & Shooks," Port Elizabeth	9/28/62	7.45 P.M.	Benzine-soaked sack placed next to wooden pole and set alight.
64.	Radio mast of S.A.R. & H., Coronationville, Johannesburg	9/29/62	10.15 P.M.	Dynamite explosion. Cost of repairs: R9.99
65.	Telephone wires, New Brighton, Port Elizabeth	9/30/62	Night	18 railway telephone wires cut. Cost of repairs: R200
66.	Dwelling of B/Sergeant, Stand 1504, Kwazakele, Port Elizabeth	10/1/62	11.30 P.M.	2 incendiary bombs used.
67.	Private dwelling of Bantu Regional Representative, Port Elizabeth	10/2/62	9.00 P.M.	Incendiary bomb and stones thrown through window. Cost of repairs: R9

Serial No.	Object and Place of Commission of Act	Date	Time	Description of Act
68.	Dwelling of B/Constable Nkwakwa, New Brighton, Port Elizabeth	10/6/62	9.30 P.M.	4 petrol bombs used. Cost of repairs: R10
69.	Power pylons, Noordgesig, Johannesburg	10/7/62	1.40 A.M.	Concrete base damaged by dynamite explosion. Cost of repairs: R411
70.	Petrol depot, S.A.S.O.L., Langlaagte, Johannesburg	10/7/62	2.00 A.M.	Chemical bomb exploded, damaging outside of tank. Cost of repairs: R40
71.	Electric pylon, Lyndhurst-Bramley (Alexandra), Johannesburg	10/7/62	9.30 P.M.	Concrete base of electric pylon damaged by dynamite explosion. Cost of repairs: R100
72.	Electric power line poles, Municipal Power Station, Orlando, Johannesburg	10/7/62	Night	Dynamite explosion, destroying base of poles. Cost of repairs: R20
73.	Railway line, New Brighton, Port Elizabeth	10/11/62	Night	Sleeper placed across rails.
74.	Railway signal cables near Georgedale, Durban	10/14/62	9.15 P.M.	Railway signal cables cut in 3 places. Cost of repairs: R10
75.	Security Police Office, Madeline Bldg., Durban	10/14/62	9.30 P.M.	Incendiary bomb. One-gallon tin containing inflammable substance placed against office door. The detonator exploded, but not the tin.
76.	Railway carriage, Phoenix Station, Durban	10/14/62	9.30 P.M.	Incendiary bomb placed in carriage of passenger train. One-gallon tin containing inflammable substance and detonator. Detonator exploded, but substance in tin was not set alight.

Serial No.	Object and Place of Commission of Act	Date	Time	Description of Act
77.	Bantu Administration Offices, Kwa Mashu Township, Durban	10/14/62	10.00 P.M.	Incendiary bomb placed against door and exploded.
78.	Storeroom of Administrative Bldg., Nyanga Location, Cape Town	10/14/62	11.30 P.M.	Incendiary bomb thrown through window of storeroom. Cost of repairs: R150
79.	Bantu Affairs Offices, Stanger St., Durban	10/14–15/62	Night	Incendiary bomb placed against door.
80.	Location Authority Office, Kwa Mashu Township, Durban	10/14–15/62	Night	Incendiary bomb placed against door.
81.	Langa Post Office, Cape Town	10/15/62	1.15 A.M.	Incendiary bomb thrown through window. Cost of repairs: R30
82.	Subpower plant, railway bridge, Braamfontein, Johannesburg	10/15/62	10.15 P.M.	Drum placed against transformer, with explosive on top. Explosion damaged pipes. Oil leaked and a fire started. Cost of repairs: R40966
83.	Post Office, Suider Paarl	10/15/62	Night	Attempt to throw petrol bombs through window.
84.	"V" Bldgs., Hamilton St., Pretoria	10/19/62	8.30 P.M.	Dynamite thrown through office window of the Minister of Lands, Economy and Marketing. Minister's office and adjoining office gutted. Cost of repairs: R1000
85.	European dwelling, 3 Gold St., Sidwell, Port Elizabeth	10/21/62	7.30 P.M.	Paraffin bottle bomb thrown through window.
86.	Telephone wires near Kwazakele, Port Elizabeth	10/21–22/62	Night	7 telephone wires cut. Cost of repairs: R20

Serial No.	Object and Place of Commission of Act	Date	Time	Description of Act
87.	Telephone wires connecting Port Elizabeth and Veeplaas	10/28– 29/62	Night	2 telephone wires cut. Cost of repairs: R3
88.	Telephone wires in New Brighton Location, Port Elizabeth	10/28– 29/62	Night	24 telephone wires cut. Cost of repairs: R49
89.	Pylon near Sarina Railway Station, Pinetown, Durban	11/1/62	9.45 P.M.	Pylon damaged by explosion of dynamite which was connected to props with putty. 3 props badly damaged. Cost of repairs: R495
90.	Pylon near Clearemont Location, New Germany, Durban	11/1/62	10.25 P.M.	Pylon damaged by explosion of dynamite, which was connected to props with putty.
91.	Pylon near Montclair Quarry, Durban	11/1/62	10.45 P.M.	Pylon damaged and overturned by explosion of dynamite, which was connected to props with putty.
92.	Telephone wires between Kleinskool and Missionvale, approximately 8 miles from Port Elizabeth	11/2–3/62	Night	2 telephone wires cut. Cost of repairs: R10
93.	Railway station, Perseverance, Port Elizabeth	11/6/62	9.04 P.M.	Lock of points sawn off and thrown over. Cost of repairs: R1
94.	Telephone wires on main line, Kwazakele, and New Brighton Location, Port Elizabeth	11/6/62	11.15 P.M.	22 telephone wires cut. Cost of repairs: R218
95.	Centlivres Railway Station between Uitenhage and Klipplaat	11/8/62	Night	23 bolts loosened from railway lines.

Serial No.	Object and Place of Commission of Act	Date	Time	Description of Act
96.	Telephone cable near Langa Location, Cape Town	11/11/62	Night	Telephone cable sawn through about 6 ft. above the ground. Cost of repairs: R66
97.	Telephone cables, Nyanga Location, Cape Town	11/12/62	Night	Telephone cables chopped. Cost of repairs: R50
98.	Telephone wires, New Brighton, Port Elizabeth	11/12– 13/62	Night	12 telephone wires cut. Cost of repairs: R36
99.	Wooden telephone poles, Dubula St., New Brighton, Port Elizabeth	11/14– 15/62	Night	Wooden telephone poles sawn off. Cost of repairs: R14
100.	Telephone cable, Oak Ave., Gardens, Cape Town	11/15– 16/62	Night	Telephone cable sawn off 3 ft. above the ground. Cost of repairs: R8
101.	Dwelling of V. Tonyeni, Meki St. 770, Duncan Village, East London	11/17/62	11.45 P.M.	Petrol bomb thrown through window. Curtains and part of settee destroyed by fire. Cost of repairs: R60
102.	Home of D. Dyani, Duncan Village, East London	11/18/62	12.05 A.M.	Incendiary bomb used.
103.	Telephone pole in "A" Ave., New Brighton, Port Elizabeth	11/18– 19/62	Night	Telephone pole sawn off. Cost of repairs: R15
104.	Railway bridge mast, Cliffdale, Durban, on railway property	11/19/62	7.30 P.M.	Dynamite explosion destroyed one leg of mast.
105.	Vasco High School, Goodwood, Cape Town	11/27/62	1.30 A.M.	2 classrooms destroyed by fire and 2 others badly damaged. Cost of repairs: R20000
106.	Vasco Preparatory School, Cape Town	11/27/62	1.30 A.M.	Paraffin poured against door and set alight. Cost of repairs: R5

APPENDIX I

Serial No.	Object and Place of Commission of Act	Date	Time	Description of Act
107.	Pylon on farm in Petit, Police District Benoni, 3½ miles from police station	11/28/62	4.40 A.M.	2 outside legs of corner tower above concrete tower blown off with dynamite (electric starter—watch type—used). Tower toppled over and damaged power line adjoining it.
108.	Telephone cable in Goodwood St., Goodwood, Cape Town	11/28/62	10.15 A.M.	Telephone cable partially sawn off. Cost of repairs: R10
109.	Telephone cable in Aubrey Rd., Salt River, Cape Town	11/28/62	Night	Telephone cable sawn off. Cost of repairs: R28
110.	Signal boxes at Wipsey Bridge near Maraisburg, Johannesburg	11/29/62	8.55 P.M.	Explosion of dynamite placed in railway signal boxes. Electric wires destroyed. Cost of repairs: R856.17
111.	Signal boxes at Canada Station, Johannesburg	11/29/62	8.55 P.M.	Signal coupling transformer box damaged by explosion. Cost of repairs: R883
112.	African dwelling at Pongolo St., Uitenhage Location	11/30/62	12.15 A.M.	A bottle bomb thrown through bedroom window.
113.	African dwelling and shop, 2, 18th Ave., Uitenhage Location	11/30/62	12.15 A.M.	Bottle bombs of benzine thrown through lounge window of house and window of shop.
114.	African dwelling, 6 Nobakada St., Uitenhage Location	11/30/62	12.15 A.M.	2 bottle bombs of benzine thrown through window.
115.	Concrete stand of pylon at Diepkloof, Orlando, Johannesburg	11/30/62 to 12/5/62	Night	Dynamite explosion.

Serial No.	Object and Place of Commission of Act	Date	Time	Description of Act
116.	Telephone booth, corner Water St. and Menin Ave., Newlands, Cape Town	12/3/62	9.30 P.M.	Homemade bomb in tin placed in telephone booth and exploded. Booth destroyed.
117.	Municipal Workshops, New Brighton	12/3/62	10.00 P.M.	Incendiary bomb thrown through window.
118.	Telephone wires, Matomela St., Kwazakele Location, Port Elizabeth	12/3/62	10.15 P.M.	30 main line telephone wires to the north were cut. Cost of repairs: R42
119.	Telephone cable, Landsdowne Rd., Phillippi, Cape Town	12/3/62	Night	Telephone cable sawn off. Cost of repairs: R50
120.	Electric transmission pole at Umlaas Bridge near Louis Botha Airport, Durban	12/5/62	8.30 P.M.	Dynamite explosion, damaging pole. Cost of repairs: R100
121.	Telephone cable, Shapel St., Cape Town	12/7–8/62	Night	Telephone cable cut off. Cost of repairs: R23
122.	Office of Indian A. S. Kajee, 26 Alice St., Durban	12/9/62	7.30 P.M.	Dynamite and safety fuse placed against door. Explosion damaged front door and inside door. Cost of repairs: R100
123.	Railway bridge mast near Hammersdale Station on main Durban–Pietermaritzburg line	12/9/62	10.20 P.M.	Dynamite explosion damaged mast. Cost of repairs: R1271.92
124.	New uninhabited dwelling in Indian Township, Laudium	12/10/62	9.00 P.M.	Inside and outside walls and corrugated iron roof badly damaged by dynamite explosion. Cost of repairs: R1300

Serial No.	Object and Place of Commission of Act	Date	Time	Description of Act
125.	Port Elizabeth	12/10–11/62	Night	3 telephone wires along railway lines cut. Cost of repairs: R6
126.	African dwelling —F.1460 Kwa Mashu Township, Durban	12/12/62	10.00 P.M.	Bomb, made with piece of hosepipe, thrown through window.
127.	African dwelling —E.307, Kwa Mashu Township, Durban	12/12/62	10.00 P.M.	Homemade bomb placed against window.
128.	African dwelling —G.914, Kwa Mashu Township, Durban	12/12/62	10.00 P.M.	Homemade bomb placed in front of door.
129.	African dwelling —774 Kwina St., Duncan Village, East London	12/15/62	11.30 P.M.	Incendiary bomb thrown through bedroom window. Considerable damage to clothing and bedding. 2 young Bantu girls badly burnt.
130.	Government vehicles at Cape Town Castle	12/18/62	2.40 A.M.	Incendiary bomb thrown amidst parked vehicles.
131.	Dwelling of D. Goldberg, Claremont, Cape Town	12/19/62	12.30 A.M.	Bomb, made with a piece of pipe, exploded in garden.
132.	Telephone wires near Coega, Port Elizabeth	12/22/62	10.15 P.M.	2 telephone wires cut. Cost of repairs: R5
133.	Main Post Office, West St., Durban	12/23/62	9.30 P.M.	Homemade bomb placed in air-mail post box.
134.	Railway cable on the Esplanade, next to bay on main line from docks to Weats Station, Durban	12/23/62	10.00 P.M.	Time bomb made with a water pipe fixed to cable.
135.	Railway line between Umgababa and Karridene—23 miles from Durban	1/8/63	10.10 P.M.	Main railway line damaged by dynamite explosion. Cost of repairs: R76.30

Serial No.	Object and Place of Commission of Act	Date	Time	Description of Act
136.	Telephone wires between Coega and Adelaide—12 miles from Port Elizabeth	1/9/63	10.30 P.M.	6 telephone wires cut off and removed. Cost of repairs: R30
137.	Bata Shoe Factory, corner Pine and Grey Sts., Durban	1/11/63	10.10 P.M.	Homemade bomb thrown into letter box. Cost of repairs: R10
138.	Garage of Bantu Administration Offices, Boipatong Location, Vanderbijlpark	1/11–12/63	3.15 P.M.	Explosion of dynamite placed in a bucket between 2 vehicles.
139.	Telephone inspection pit, South Coast Rd., Mobeni, Industrial Zone, Durban	1/15/63	10.00 P.M.	Dynamite blew off one cable and broke lid. Cost of repairs: R260
140.	Telephone wires in New Brighton Location	1/16–17/63	Night	21 telephone wires damaged and 2 wooden telephone poles sawn off. Cost of repairs: R50
141.	Kirkwood, Addo Rd., Port Elizabeth	1/16–17/63	Night	7 telephone wires cut. Cost of repairs: R20
142.	Vicinity of power station, Swartkops	1/16–17/63	Night	9 telephone wires cut. Cost of repairs: R50
143.	Sondagsrivier Irrigation Store, Addo	1/16–17/63	Night	Paraffin thrown on floor of store and set alight.
144.	Petrol supply tank, Table Bay Harbour, Cape Town	1/17/63	9.40 P.M.	One of the petrol pipes unscrewed so that petrol flowed out. Rope saturated with petrol and set alight.
145.	Telephone wires at Coega, Port Elizabeth	1/17–18/63	Night	2 telephone wires cut. Cost of repairs: R5

Serial No.	Object and Place of Commission of Act	Date	Time	Description of Act
146.	Office of *Die Nataller*, 305 Umbilo Rd., Durban	1/18/63	9.15 P.M.	Front walls, windows, and office furniture badly damaged by an explosion. A European male passing by in the street sustained injuries as a result of the explosion. Cost of repairs: R1000
147.	Bantu Room at McCord Zulu Hospital, Durban	1/18/63	11.00 P.M.	Homemade bomb placed in room.
148.	Old Jewish Synagogue, Paul Kruger St., Pretoria	1/24/63	2.00 A.M.	Bucket containing 12 sticks of dynamite and a tin of raw linseed oil found in building.
149.	Signal box S.A.R. & H. between Dube and Phomalong Stations, Johannesburg	1/31/63	12.45 A.M.	Dynamite placed in signal box.
150.	Telephone poles at Avoca, north of Durban	1/31/63	Night	3 telephone poles sawn off. Cost of repairs: R50
151.	Telephone booth, corner Queen Victoria and Thomas Sts., Cape Town	2/2/63	7.50 P.M.	Homemade bomb placed in booth. Cost of repairs: R20
152.	Wooden telephone pole, Dubula St., New Brighton Location, Port Elizabeth	2/9/63	3.30 A.M.	Pole sawn off. Falling pole broke 2 wires. Cost of repairs: R20
153.	Telephone booth, corner Victoria and Thomas Sts., Cape Town	2/9/63	9.00 P.M.	Homemade bomb in tin. Explosion badly damaged the telephone and broke the door of the booth. Cost of repairs: R30

Serial No.	Object and Place of Commission of Act	Date	Time	Description of Act
154.	Municipal beer hall, Bell St., Durban	2/10/63	1.15 P.M.	Bomb made with a piece of water piping placed under a table. The explosion injured 3 Bantu males.
155.	African dwelling, New Brighton, Port Elizabeth	2/10/63	10.00 P.M.	Incendiary bomb thrown through window. Cost of repairs: R10
156.	Railway line, Landsdowne Station, Cape Province	2/10/63	11.49 P.M.	Sheet of iron placed on railway lines.
157.	Provincial Hospital, Uitenhage	2/11–12/63	Night	2 telephone wires cut. Cost of repairs: R5
158.	Telephone wires outside Uitenhage Location	2/11–12/63	Night	2 telephone wires cut. Cost of repairs: R5
159.	Innesdal Post Office, Pretoria	2/12/63	3.00 A.M.	5 sticks of dynamite and 2 detonators thrown through window.
160.	Telephone wires, Bestersrus, near Ladysmith	2/13/63	Night	Telephone wires cut.
161.	Telephone wires outside Grahamstown Location	2/14–15/63	Night	20 telephone wires cut. Cost of repairs: R10
162.	African dwelling, 707 Meki St., Duncan Village Location, East London	2/14–15/63	Night	2 petrol bombs thrown at the home of V. Tonyeni. One burst against the wall and the other fell about 30 ft. from the house.
163.	Railway line at Pinelands Station, Pinelands	2/16/63	Early morning.	2 sheets of iron and 25-in. bolt placed on railway line.
164.	Telephone cable, corner Settlers and Modderdam Rds., Athlone, Cape Town	2/18/63	Night	Telephone cable sawn off about 6 ft. above the ground. Cost of repairs: R20

Serial No.	Object and Place of Commission of Act	Date	Time	Description of Act
165.	Telephone cable near Heideveld Railway Station, Cape Town	2/18/63	Night	Telephone cable sawn off 6 ft. above the ground. Cost of repairs: R20
166.	African school, Langabuya Location, Paarl	2/18/63	Night	Fire set to hard-board wall of school. Cost of repairs: R20
167.	Derailment between Alberton and Vereeniging	2/23/63	9.00 P.M.	Rails loosened.
168.	Post Office inspection pit, near Leeukop, Johannesburg	2/26–27/63	Night	Dynamite explosion caused damage to cable. Cost of repairs: R80
169.	Telephone cables, Rifle Range Rd., Booysens, Johannesburg	2/26/63 to 3/1/63	4.00 P.M.	30–35 sticks of dynamite affixed to lead covering of cable.
170.	Wooden poles carrying power line between Alice and Kingwilliamstown, about a mile outside Alice	3/2/63	2.00 A.M.	2 poles sawn off, causing line to fall and resulting in a short circuit.
171.	African school, Langabuya Location, Paarl	3/3/63	Night	Fire set to hard-board wall of school. Cost of repairs: R4
172.	Telephone cables, Nyanga East	3/3/63	8.00 P.M.	2 telephone cables sawn off at Post Office and also at a cement factory.
173.	Telephone cable, Landsdowne Rd., Phillipi	3/3–4/63	Night	Telephone cable sawn off against pole.
174.	Signal box, corner End and Noord Sts., Johannesburg	3/8/63	Night	Safety fuse, gelignite, and 2 percussion caps.
175.	Bantu Affairs Commissioner's Office, Cato Street, Durban	3/10/63	6.30 P.M.	Dynamite bomb placed against corner of temporary structure. Explosion damaged asbestos wall and windows. Cost of repairs: R53.82

Serial No.	Object and Place of Commission of Act	Date	Time	Description of Act
176.	Railway line under Victoria St. bridge, Durban	3/21/63	1.05 A.M.	Part of rail ripped away by dynamite explosion.
177.	Telephone cable across Nyanga Station, Cape Town	3/21/63	Night	Cable sawn off 5½ ft. above the ground. Cost of repairs: R135
178.	Telephone cable about 200 yds. from Langa Police Station, Cape Town	3/21–22/63	Night	Cable sawn off about 3 ft. above the ground. Cost of repairs: R30
179.	Telephone cable, Klipfontein Rd., near Whitfields Dairy, Cape Town	3/21–22/63	Night	Cable sawn off 2 ft. above the ground. Cost of repairs: R30
180.	Bantu Administration Bldg., Bezuidenhout St., Ferreirastown, Johannesburg	3/22/63	10.20 P.M.	Dynamite explosion caused damage to floor and windows. Cost of repairs: R103
181.	Passenger train between Verulam and Durban [?] Stations, Durban	4/7/63	7.30 P.M.	2 bottles containing inflammable substance thrown on 1st and 4th carriages of moving train carrying European and non-European passengers.
182.	Dwelling of B/ Constable L. Fanylo, Dube Location, Johannesburg	4/10/63	—	Bottle containing petrol and oil thrown through window.
183.	Fordsburg Post Office, Johannesburg	4/12/63	6.45 A.M.	18 sticks of dynamite connected with 2 pieces of fuse, each with a detonator connected, were placed in a shoe box. One detonator and 4 sticks of dynamite exploded.

343

APPENDIX I

Serial No.	Object and Place of Commission of Act	Date	Time	Description of Act
184.	Empty building and signal box of S.A.R. & H., Riverlea, Johannesburg	4/17/63	12.30 P.M.	Empty building blown up with dynamite. Cost of repairs: R1000
185.	Bales of cotton on board ship from Port Elizabeth to Liverpool	4/19–21/63	—	Matches placed between bales. Bundles of 5 matches each were found in 5 bales. Only the match heads appeared.
186.	Inspection pit of Post Office, corner of First Ave. and Second St., Lower Houghton, Johannesburg	11/1/62 to 4/25/63	—	Telephone cable sawn off. About 900 wires. Cost of repairs: R50
187.	African beer hall, Langa Location	6/14–17/63	Night	2 bottles containing oil, wrapped in brown paper, were set alight and thrown on thatched roof of beer hall.
188.	Bottle store in course of erection, Langa	6/17–18/63	—	5 bottles containing diesel oil, wrapped in old pieces of cloth, strewn around the building. 3 burnt.
189.	Railway signal box, ½ mile from Duffs Rd. Railway Station, Kwa Mashu Township, Durban	6/21/63	1.50 A.M.	Railway signal box damaged by dynamite explosion. Cost of repairs: R207.37

Serial No.	Object and Place of Commission of Act	Date	Time	Description of Act
190.	S.A. railway trailer parked on corner of Lilian and Avenue Rds., Fordsburg, Johannesburg	6/26/63	9.00 P.M.	Fuel, presumably paraffin, turpentine, or brake fluid, was strewn over trailer. A 4-gal. tin containing the same fuel was placed between the rear wheels and set alight. 4 tires, 2 canvas covers, and body of trailer damaged. Cost of repairs: R500
191.	Beer hall in Langa Location	6/30/63	5.30 A.M.	2 wine bottles, containing petrol mixed with some unknown substance, thrown on asbestos roof of beer hall.
192.	Home of B/Constable No. 129003 J. Makgoale, 738 Dube Location, Johannesburg	7/3/63	3.00 A.M.	Petrol thrown under front door and set alight. Fire started on back verandah.
193.	Underground power cables, Bridgetown, Athlone	7/6/63	—	Power cables damaged with some sharp instrument.

Appendix II

Selected Biographies

Luthuli, Albert John

President-general of the ANC from 1952. Born in Groutville, Natal, nephew of the reigning chief of the Abasemakholweni (Zulu) tribe. Mission educated, was a teacher till petitioned by fellow tribesmen to assume the chieftainship. Acted as chief for seventeen years, until deposed by the government for refusing to resign from the ANC in 1952. Was arrested and was an accused in the Treason Trial of 1956, but released a year later, for it was evident to the government that even then his powers were more nominal than real. Banished to his village in May, 1959, he remained there till his death in 1969. Awarded the Nobel Peace Prize in 1961.

Mandela, Nelson Rolihlahla

Born 1918, son of Chief Henry Mandela. Showed early interest in history of African people. Obtained law degree from Fort Hare University College and began practicing law in 1942. Entered into partnership with Oliver Tambo in 1952, as first African law firm in country. Joined ANC in 1944. Founder of ANCYL and its national president, 1951–52. Volunteer-in-chief for whole country in 1952, during Defiance Campaign. Banned from December, 1952. Accused in Treason Trial of 1956–61, and acquitted with all other defendants. Member of illegal ANC from 1960. Attended PAFMECSA Conference in 1962, and traveled seeking funds and bases for *Umkonto*. Arrested on return to South Africa and sentenced to five years' imprisonment for inciting strike and leaving country without passport. In jail when other leaders of *Umkonto* arrested, July 11, 1963.

Mbeki, Govan

Born in the Transkei, July 8, 1910. Parents were highly religious people in comfortable circumstances. Won a bursary to Fort Hare University College. Obtained a bachelor's degree in arts, 1956. Interest in politics led to his success in organizing the underground ANC. Arrested at Rivonia, July 11, 1963.

Mhlaba, Raymond

One of the mystery men of Rivonia, together with Mhlangeni and Motsoaledi. Virtually unknown in country before the Rivonia Trial. Was forty-four years of age at the time of his arrest at Rivonia. Born at Fort Beaufort in the Cape Province, and educated by missionaries. Showed early interest in African politics then, and later when a laundry worker in Port Elizabeth. Joined the ANC and the Communist Party and became prominent on the Cape Executive of the ANC.

Mhlangeni, Andrew

Thirty-eight years of age at the time of his trial. Son of a poor washerwoman, he was one of twelve children; losing his father at the age of twelve, he took up work as a golf caddie. Was self-educated to Junior Certificate level (equivalent of American 10th grade). Also worked as a bus driver. Joined the ANC in 1954 and became a branch secretary in 1956. Denied his role in Umkonto but seems to have been transport officer.

Motsoaledi, Elias

Grew up in Sekukuniland, Eastern Transvaal, one of a family of ten trying to subsist on four acres of land. Worked first as a domestic servant in Johannesburg, and later in a boot factory, when he joined SACTU. Joined the ANC in 1948 and was banned in 1954. Later joined the illegal Communist Party. Served on Technical Committee of Umkonto and on the Johannesburg High Command in 1962. Arrested at Rivonia.

Nokwe, Philemon Pearce Duma

Secretary-general of the ANC. Born 1927 in Evaton, Transvaal. Was educated at Evaton, where Oliver Tambo was one of his teachers. Awarded a Bachelor of Science degree by Fort Hare University College in 1949 and an Education Diploma in 1950. Was a teacher in 1951. Active in the Defiance Campaign in 1952–53, and dismissed from his teaching post as a result. In 1953 attended the World Youth Festival in Bucharest, and then returned to South Africa to study law. In 1956 became the first African advocate of the Supreme Court, but was refused permission to occupy chambers in the building in which most of the other advocates were situated. Banned in 1954 and again in 1959. Was an accused in the Treason Trial of 1956, and acquitted with the rest of the accused. Detained in 1960 during the State of Emergency. Left the country with J. B. Marks and was active in the ANC overseas.

Sisulu, Walter Max

Born 1912 in the Transkei to poor but tribally important Xhosa family. Forced to leave school at age of fifteen; death of uncle made it necessary for him to support family. Worked in a number of enterprises and educated himself at home. Joined ANC in 1940, helped found Youth League, and became its treasurer. Helped oust moderate leadership of Dr. Xuma and pressed for more militant course. One of the principal organizers of Defiance Campaign of 1952. In 1953 traveled to China and Russia. Banned from ANC by the government in 1955 and had to sever all official connection with it. On his return played crucial role in organizing Congress of the People. Originally a militant anti-white, later was ready to work with white progressives. Sisulu did *not* join *Umkonto*, on advice of ANC, but kept in touch with the organization and attended some of its meetings. In June, 1963, came to Rivonia apparently as secretary-general of the illegal ANC, the role he had held when the organization was still legal. He was arrested there.

Tambo, Oliver Reginald

Deputy president-general of the ANC until the death of Luthuli, and its chief representative abroad. Born 1917 in Bizana, Eastern Cape. Obtained a Bachelor of Science degree in 1941 at Fort Hare University College and an Education Diploma in 1943. Taught both Duma Nokwe and Joe Matthews. In 1948 began studying law, and established a partnership with Nelson Mandela. Was a founder of the ANCYL, becoming successively its national secretary and national vice-president. Member of the NEC of the ANC, 1955–58, when he was elected deputy president-general. Banned in 1954, was one of the defendants at the Treason Trial in 1956, and was released a year later. In 1959 was again banned for five years. A week after Sharpeville and two days before the State of Emergency, left the country at the request of the NEC to represent the ANC abroad.

FOLLOWERS

Makeke, Sipo

Born ca. 1937. Was fifteen when first involved with ANC. Educated to Standard IX level (about 10th grade). Had been a member of POQO first and then joined ANC.

Mashinyana, Bennett

Born 1929 (?); educated to Junior Certificate level (about 10th grade). Worked for an attorney. Considered himself detribalized, though he grew up in East London, a Xhosa area. Joined ANC as a very young man.

349

Mbanjwa, Solomon

Born 1930 (?); joined ANC in 1956 in Durban. Became volunteer-in-chief, and later branch secretary in 1959. Elected to Provincial Executive ANCYL in 1959. Was at the same time full-time SACTU organizer and active in ANC. Resigned from ANC in 1960 and rejoined underground ANC in 1962.

Mtolo, Bruno Sipiwe

Born at Ephateni, near Richmond, Natal, June 30, 1927. Father worked for railways in Durban; family lived on land. Educated to Standard IV (5th grade), and then went to work, first in a military camp, then in the mines, and then as a hospital orderly. Attended night school in Johannesburg but could not advance, despite fluency in English. Arrested for train robbery in 1950, and not released until 1954. Joined ANC in 1957, but inactive. Joined SACTU and later Communist Party. Active in *Umkonto* in Durban.

Biographical material on African leaders and followers is both limited and scarce. For the national leadership the sources were Ronald Segal, *Political Africa* (London, 1961), and H. H. W. de Villiers, *Rivonia: Operation Mayebuye* (Johannesburg, 1964). The court records of the Rivonia Trial were also used. For the lesser fry the source for Mtolo was his book, and the sources for the others cited were the court cases. This is by no means a complete collection of biographies, nor are the biographies complete in themselves.

Selected Bibliography

A. Microfilm Collections

From Microfile Ltd., Johannesburg:
"Treason Trial"—Regina vs Farid Adams and 29 Others (Documents).
"Rivonia Trial"
"Sundry Trials" } See Index to Court Cases (p. xvii).
"Abram Fischer"
From Hoover Institution, Stanford, California:
South Africa: A Collection of Miscellaneous Documents.

B. Newspapers and Periodicals from South Africa

Africa South (Cape Town)
African Communist (London)
Cape Argus (Cape Town)
Cape Times (Cape Town)
Contact (Cape Town)
Counter-Attack (Johannesburg)
Daily Dispatch (East London)
Daily News (Durban)
Drum (Johannesburg)
Eastern Province Herald (Port Elizabeth)
Evening Post (Port Elizabeth)
Fighting Talk: A Journal for Democrats in Southern Africa (Johannesburg)
Friend (Bloemfontein)
Golden City Post (Johannesburg)
Inkundla ya Bantu (Pietermaritzburg)

SELECTED BIBLIOGRAPHY

Natal Daily News (Durban)
Natal Mercury (Durban)
Natal Witness (Pietermaritzburg)
New African (London)
New Age (Cape Town)
Pretoria News (Pretoria)
Rand Daily Mail (Johannesburg)
Spark (Cape Town)
Star (Johannesburg)
Sunday Express (Johannesburg)
Sunday Times (Johannesburg)
Sunday Tribune (Durban)
World (formerly *Bantu World*—Johannesburg)
Zonk (Johannesburg)

C. OTHER SOURCES

Bienen, Henry. *Violence and Social Change*. Chicago: University of Chicago Press, 1968.
Brokensha, Miles, and Knowles, Robert. *The Fourth of July Raids*. Cape Town: Simondium, 1965.
Cantril, Hadley. *The Pattern of Human Concerns*. New Brunswick, N. J.: Rutgers University Press, 1965.
Clark, Michael K. *Algeria in Turmoil*. New York: Grosset & Dunlap, 1960.
"The Communist Party in South Africa." *Africa Report*, VI (March, 1961), 5–6, 15.
De Ridder, C. J. *The Personality of the Urban African in South Africa: A Thematic Apperception Test Study*. London: Routledge, 1961.
De Villiers, H. H. W. *Rivonia: Operation Mayebuye*. Johannesburg: Afrikaanse Pers-Boekhandel, 1964.
Dreitzel, Hans Peter. Review of *Prozesse der Machtbildung*, by Heinrich Popitz. *Social Research*, XXXVI (Spring, 1969), 158–63.
Ellul, Jacques. *Propaganda: The Formation of Men's Attitudes*. New York: Alfred A. Knopf, 1965.
Feit, Edward. *African Opposition in South Africa: The Failure of Passive Resistance*. Stanford: Hoover Institution, 1968.
————. *South Africa: The Dynamics of the African National Congress*. London: Oxford University Press, 1962.
Feuer, Lewis. *Conflict of Generations: The Character and Significance of Student Movements*. New York: Basic Books, 1969.
Galula, David. *Counterinsurgency Warfare: Theory and Practice*. New York: Praeger, 1964.
Gann, Lewis H. "Liberal Interpretations of South African History: A Review Article." *Rhodes-Livingstone Journal*, XXV (March, 1959), 40–58.
Gaucher, Roland. *The Terrorists: From Tsarist Russia to the OAS*. London: Secker and Warburg, 1965.

352

Goffman, Erving. *Behavior in Public Places: Notes on the Social Organiza-
tion of Gatherings*. New York: Free Press, 1963.
———. *Encounters: Two Studies in the Sociology of Interaction*. Indianap-
olis, Ind.: Bobbs-Merrill, 1961.
———. *Interaction Ritual: Essays on Face-to-Face Behavior*. Chicago:
Aldine, 1967.
Guevara, Che. *Reminiscences of the Cuban Revolutionary War*. Trans-
lated by Bobbye Ortiz. New York: Grove Press, 1968.
Gurr, Ted. "Psychological Factors in Civil Violence." *World Politics*, XX
(January, 1968), 245–78.
———. *Why Men Rebel*. Princeton, N. J.: Princeton University Press,
1970.
Hopkinson, Tom. *In the Fiery Continent*. New York: Doubleday, 1963.
Horrell, Muriel, comp. *Legislation and Race Relations: Revised Edition,
1966*. Johannesburg: South African Institute of Race Relations, 1967.
———, comp. "The 'Pass Laws': A Fact Paper." Johannesburg: South
African Institute of Race Relations, 1960. Mimeographed.
———, comp. *A Survey of Race Relations in South Africa, 1950–1969*.
Johannesburg: South African Institute of Race Relations. Annually.
Huntington, Samuel P. *Political Order in Changing Societies*. New Haven,
Conn.: Yale University Press, 1968.
Johns, Sheridan W. "The Birth of Non-White Trade Unionism in South
Africa." *Race*, IX (October, 1967), 173–92.
———. "Marxism-Leninism in a Multi-Racial Environment: Origins and
Early History of the Communist Party of South Africa, 1914–1932"
Ph.D. dissertation, Harvard University, 1965.
Kase, Francis J. *People's Democracy: A Contribution to the Communist
Theory of State and Revolution*. Leyden: Sijthoff, 1968.
Kuper, Leo. *An African Bourgeoisie: Race, Class, and Politics in South
Africa*. New Haven, Conn.: Yale University Press, 1965.
———. "The Political Situation of Non-Whites in South Africa." In
Southern Africa and the United States, edited by William A. Hance
et al. New York: Columbia University Press, 1968.
Lenin, Vladimir Ilyich. *Collected Works*. Vol. IX. 1905. Edited by George
Hanna. Translated by Abraham Fineberg and Julius Katzer. Moscow:
Foreign Languages Publishing House, 1962.
Lewin, Julius. *Politics and Law in South Africa* (London: Merlin Press,
1963). See esp. "The Rise of African Nationalism."
Longmore, Laura. *The Dispossessed: A Study of the Sex Life of Bantu
Women in and around Johannesburg*. London: Jonathan Cape, 1959.
Lopreato, Joseph. "Authority Relations and Class Conflict." *Social Forces*,
XLVII (September, 1968), 70–79.
Luthuli, Albert John. *Let My People Go: An Autobiography*. Johannesburg:
Collins, 1962.
Mandela, Nelson. *No Easy Walk to Freedom*. Edited by Ruth First. New
York: Basic Books, 1965.

Mayer, Philip. *Townsmen or Tribesmen: Urbanization in a Divided Society.* London: Oxford University Press, 1961.

Mitchell, William C. *Sociological Analysis and Politics: The Theories of Talcott Parsons.* New York: Prentice-Hall, 1967.

Mtolo, Bruno. *Umkonto we Sizwe: The Road to the Left.* Durban: Drakensberg Press, 1966.

Munger, Edwin S. *African Field Reports: 1952–1961.* Cape Town: Struik, 1961.

————. "New White Politics in South Africa." In *Southern Africa and the United States,* edited by William A. Hance et al. New York: Columbia University Press, 1968.

Neame, L. E. *The History of Apartheid: The Story of the Colour War in South Africa.* London: Pall Mall Press, 1962.

Ngubane, Jordan K. *An African Explains Apartheid.* New York: Praeger, 1963.

Nokwe, Duma. "The Great Smear: Communism and Congress in South Africa." *Africa South in Exile,* V (October–December, 1961), 5–14.

Oppenheimer, Martin. *The Urban Guerrilla.* Chicago: Quadrangle, 1969.

Pauw, B. A. *The Second Generation: A Study of the Family among Urbanized Bantu in East London.* London: Oxford University Press, 1963.

Pike, Douglas. *Vietcong: The Organization and Techniques of the National Liberation Front of South Vietnam.* Cambridge, Mass.: M.I.T. Press, 1966.

Pye, Lucian W. *Guerrilla Communism in Malaya: Its Social and Political Meanings.* Princeton, N. J.: Princeton University Press, 1956.

Rapoport, David. "A Comparative Theory of Military and Political Types." In *Changing Patterns of Military Politics,* edited by Samuel P. Huntington. New York: Free Press, 1962.

————. "The Political Dimensions of Military Usurpation." *Political Science Quarterly,* LXXXIII (December, 1968), 551–72.

Reader, D. H. *The Black Man's Portion.* London: Oxford University Press, 1961.

Rigg, Robert C. "A Military Appraisal of the Threat to U. S. Cities." *U. S. News and World Report,* January 15, 1968.

Roazen, Paul. *Freud: Political and Social Thought.* New York: Alfred A. Knopf, 1968.

Rodda, Peter. "The Africanists Cut Loose." *Africa South,* III (July–September, 1959), 23–27.

Roux, Edward. *Time Longer Than Rope: A History of the Black Man's Struggle for Freedom in South Africa.* 2d ed. Madison, Wis.: University of Wisconsin Press, 1964.

Sampson, Anthony. *The Treason Cage: The Opposition on Trial in South Africa.* London: Heinemann, 1958.

Seale, Patrick, and McConville, Maureen. *Red Flag, Black Flag: French Revolution 1968.* New York: Putnam, 1968.

Selznick, Philip. *The Organizational Weapon: A Study of Bolshevik Strategy and Tactics.* New York: Free Press, 1960.

354

Stone, Lawrence. "Theories of Revolution." *World Politics*, XVIII (January, 1966), 159–77.

Stultz, Newell M. "The Politics of Security: South Africa under Verwoerd." *Journal of Modern African Studies*, VII (April, 1969), 3–20.

Swanson, Maynard W. "Champion of Durban: An African Politician and the ICU." Mimeographed, nd.

Taber, Robert. *The War of the Flea: A Study of Guerrilla Warfare in Theory and Practice*. New York: Lyle Stuart, 1965.

Thompson, Robert. *Defeating Communist Insurgency: The Lessons of Malaya and Vietnam*. New York: Praeger, 1966.

Trinquier, Roger. *Modern Warfare: A French View of Counterinsurgency*. New York: Praeger, 1964.

Tucker, Robert C. "The Deradicalization of Marxist Movements." *American Political Science Review*, LXI (June, 1967), 343–58.

———. *The Marxian Revolutionary Idea*. New York: W. W. Norton, 1969.

Van den Berghe, Pierre L. "Race Attitudes in Durban, South Africa." In *Africa: Social Problems of Change and Conflict*, edited by Pierre van den Berghe. San Francisco: Chandler, 1965.

Walshe, A. P. *The African National Congress of South Africa: Aspects of Ideology and Organization between 1912 and 1951*. Los Angeles: University of California Press, forthcoming.

Wilson, Ira G., and Wilson, Marthann. *Information, Computers, and System Design*. New York: John Wiley, 1965.

Index